I0224314

Fire on the Sea
An Allegorical Tale

"It took some moments for Will to comprehend properly what was going on. Moments as long as the men dragging away their stumbling prisoner and vanishing into the curling mists. As long as it took to listen for the muffled footfalls along the flagged path which led to the far tower. Right up until he heard the odd metallic clang of the tower's iron door echo through the fog like a muted bell. A bell of death, he realized then. The prisoner had been sentenced to die in the cruelest way – in isolation and by starvation.

The man was a criminal of the most threatening kind, but even so, was this legal? Will turned his back on the tower and closed the door. There was a chill in the house which went deeper than winter ice. He stoked the fire and lay more sod then wearily he returned to his bed. But he couldn't sleep. He was afraid that if he did he would dream of a man dying slowly and miserably in a cold, dark tower."

Thus begins the compelling story of a quest for freedom from tyranny – the tyranny of a dark world obsessed with rule and control, a world so deluded by its own lies that its citizens accept their capitivity as normal and unavoidable. But not all citizens – there are those who will rebel, taking their lives in the own hands and claiming their freedom, by turning their faces from darkness………

Zend-Kao Wa Mai

First published in Australia in 1998 by
Light Pulsations Ionic Healing Pty. Ltd.

Cover photo and design: LightPulsations.com

ISBN: 0996744150
Previous ISBN: 095848943

Fire on the Sea

Table of Contents

Foreword

This is a book which will challenge your attitudes and open your heart and mind, increasing your desire to be free and one with the Light of all.

As the author, Zend – Kao Wa Mai has stated, "Fire on the Sea" was written as fiction but, more succinctly, it is a Spiritual Adventure. However once you become involved with its characters you will share an affinity between them and your own life. The more you deepen your daily attunement with the warmth of the love which is the total expression of One Light, the greater will be your experience of the oneness with the life changes of others.

The characters in this book represent those indefinable inner experiences you live with and which at times create stress and suffering to your consciousness, but at other times joy and enlightenment. This work is a moving spiritual experience universally shared by everyone.

When Rose, Carl, and myself received the first Transmissions of Zadore, they changed the focus and direction of our lives forever. What I did not realize properly at first was the impact which "One Light" would have on its readers. It was only after receiving a flood of letters from seekers around the world who constantly recounted the instant opening of their hearts and minds to the truth and light of their being, as well as their understanding of the nature and intent of those forces which hold humanity in darkness and bondage, that I did. But, more wonderfully, the opening of this Light continues.

"Fire on the Sea" is a living testimony to one such opening. It is the life experience of its author and as you flow through this book your life and being will be brought into alignment with the essence of your total consciousness. It calls forth that intensity for life which only the serious seeker can sustain.

Through the leading characters, Marek and Faran, you too will discover that the journey back to freedom and light is the common thread which bonds all humanity. You will witness the constant to and fro movement between those forces which attempt to hold us in bondage and fear, for as you move closer to your Light you will remember who you are, and in so doing will weaken the forces which hold us as slaves to their Illusion.

This is a book which is not only about personal freedom, but also the freedom of our beautiful planet, which, as you know, is also a Light Being. As the children open to their Light, so too does it. The conclusion of this adventure leads us to experience the beauty of "Fire on the Sea" in all its intensity, and the expansion of the Light of the Earth. My heart warmed to the command of Ozira – "Rise and heal the World! For you are the Light of the World!"

There is only one journey for all humanity and it includes not only all the children of the Earth but also the animals, burds, fish, insects and plant life, for they are all the consciousness of the Planet.

Like me, you too will warm to the beauty and upliftment of the story and share the trials and tribulations experienced by Zend – Kao Wa Mai. As an opening into personal Light it is a book of the Earth and part of our collective rememberrance of our Light.

Light Pulsations has delivered another inspiring book, one which I am sure will not only enlighten the minds of its readers but also open them to the beauty of their being and transform their lives.

Jon Whistler
September 1998.

PART 1

Chapter 1

Two tall round towers stood on the height of a lonely plateau, wreathed in the fog of a winter evening. They were separated by some distance, two beacons of darkness in a vast solitude signalling to one another across a broiling sea of grey, and as the fog surged and drifted, they swam in and out of view, at times appearing far apart then seeming to wash closer, like the masts of two great, invisible ships.

Beneath one of the towers was a little stone dwelling crouched in the turf. Hidden in the mist and dwarfed by the tower, it seemed almost to be drowned by the soft watercolor splashes of winter, so as to appear devoid of life. Yet that was only an illusion, for in the spring and summer there would be a garden around the cottage filled with flowers and two children would play there.

Standing further up on the height, the other tower was starker and more isolated, having no other building beneath it. Nothing played under it or above it except an occasional circling of crows. It had a crueller aspect and its blank face was broken only by a single low iron door and just above that, a circumference of window slits each no wider than a man's two hands.

Will Crafter, Caretaker of the Towers, stood by his cottage door and watched as the fog gradually thinned in a rising wind, writhing as it dispersed and growing pearly and alive in the moonlight. Now, with midnight gone and the wind up, it would mean a clear night and a sharp, though not frosty, morning. Will shivered as the breeze discovered his bare neck. He stared out and upward at the far tower. It seemed ghostly and luminous in the shifting air, a haunted thing. After what had happened that very midnight he did not think he would ever want to go near it again.

"Which is just as well," he said to himself. "I have my orders." Yet, in himself, he was not easy with the thought and his belly groaned with a sort of agony of guilt that would not give him any peace.

For the first time since coming to live and work at the Towers, the isolation of the place began to bother Will. There was no telephone at present. Two days before, a big storm had brought down many of the lines all over the north, and, as usual, the repair crews were much slower in getting to the high country than they were to the cities and the settlements of the lowland areas. The highlanders were poorly served by government, as if they hardly counted at all, and they were always last in line for everything.

The children were asleep and Will hoped they had not woken. Just before midnight the strangers arrived at the house, without much sound or fuss, for the fog had dulled the noises of their approaching vehicles. A half dozen or so of them, and they roused Will and frightened him at first with their cold, unkind faces and sharp words. They had come with orders from his employer and theirs, they told him, which he must obey without question.

"Caretaker," they said. "His Lordship, the Baron will be making use of the far tower for a certain number of days, and from this time on, until you are told otherwise, you will not approach the place nor allow anyone near it."

A strange demand, Will thought, because it was his job not only to care for the two towers but to show them off to the public too. Both towers were a piece of the ancient heritage of Telaia and were of interest to tourists and visitors to the region. He had been employed chiefly to care for them on behalf of the people of Telaia but also because of his knowledge of local history which made him a good guide. He knew that the towers did not belong to his employer, for that grandiose man's personal use, any more than they belonged to him, a simple caretaker.

"Sir," he said to the one who seemed to be in charge. "I don't know that I can do that. My job is to inspect the Towers regularly and see that nothing is amiss."

The one to whom he spoke, a dark gnomish man with a sneering upper lip, leaned up towards him provocatively. "Of course you can say that, if you want to take the chance that you won't be dismissed. But the Baron has a good reason for needing the tower; he doesn't need to make explanations to the likes of you."

That's not true, Will thought. The Baron doesn't own the Towers, even though he's in charge of them as the head of Telaia's bureaucratic machine. In spite of being employed by bureaucracy himself, Will didn't like it much and liked even less the self important behavior of men like the Baron who used their high position for personal advantage. Will said, "Sir, the Towers are my charge. I think I ought to know what goes on in them."

The dark man shrugged hunched shoulders. "Okay. But you may wish you hadn't said that when I tell you." He tossed his head at the group of men behind him who shuffled about uneasily. Will had not noticed, the fog being thick until then, that one of the men was not very upright and that he was wrapped up and hooded so that nothing of his face was visible. Another movement from the group and Will saw the glint of manacles beneath the bent man's folds.

"A criminal," the gnome said. "A traitor and a threat to every man, woman and child on Telaia. Too dangerous for a normal prison. Our orders are to lock him up here until something more can be decided."

Will Crafter sagged. A traitor, a dangerous criminal in his tower! "Are you the guards?"

Laughing, the little dark man turned away, then turned again and stretched out his hand. "The keys to the far tower, Caretaker! They will be returned to you when this is all over. We shall come after seven days, for a look-see."

It took some moments for Will to comprehend properly what was going on. Moments as long as the men dragging away their stumbling prisoner and vanishing into the curling mists. As long as it took to listen for the muffled footfalls along the flagged path which led to the far tower. Right up until he heard the odd metallic clang of the tower's iron door echo through the fog like a muted bell. A bell of death, he realized then. The prisoner had been sentenced to die in the cruellest way, in isolation and by starvation.

The man was a criminal of the most threatening kind, but even so, was this legal? Will turned his back on the tower and closed the door. There was a chill in the house which went deeper than winter ice. He stoked the fire and lay more sod then wearily he returned to his bed. But he couldn't sleep. He was afraid that if he did he would dream of a man dying slowly and miserably in a cold, dark tower.

"What was it, Dad, last night? Some men came to the door. What did they want?"

The Caretaker gazed at his daughter and sighed. So the girl had heard after all, and she was curious, as was natural enough. He regarded her fresh flower face with tenderness and protectiveness. How could he tell her of the tower and its wicked inhabitant? But the worst of it … how could he tell her that?

He had to. He did not want her wandering by the tower or his young son either. "Faran," he said. "The far tower is out of bounds for a while. Those men last night came from the Baron and brought with them a criminal whom they locked up in the tower. It's a bad man that they've locked in there and you and Young Will shouldn't go near."

Faran's eyes opened wide. "A criminal? What sort of criminal?"

Will would have preferred no discussion at all, but the curiosity of this intelligent fourteen year old girl was not to be allayed or dismissed. For too many years now Faran had been his mainstay in life – his right hand and his best friend. She had cared for her baby half-brother from as early an age as seven when the little chap's mother had left them, and Will reckoned her wise and reliable beyond her years.

"A traitor and a danger to many, they said. That's why they locked him up out here, away from the world, I guess."

"And left you to stand guard over such a bad man?" Faran's color was high. She said indignantly "But Dad, you're a gentle soul. You're not cut out to be a jailer!"

"No, I am not," Will said forlornly. "And they don't expect it. I'm not to go near the tower either." His heart seemed to drop into his belly as he said the words. He could not bear that she would understand and see the part he was expected to play in such a sordid business.

And of course there was no release for him. Faran stared at him, and stared interminably as her mouth dropped open, wider and wider. "Oh, Daddy, NO!"

The house was dark with the winter day, but not so dark as Will's heavy heart. He was afraid to go outside save for a brief dash to the goat's stable or the chicken coop or to the lavatory, and then he scuttled quickly around the side wall while he fought the temptation of his eyes to rivet themselves on the far tower.

The Towers had been Will's life for nearly fifteen years and he enjoyed showing them off to anyone interested. He knew their official history as well as he knew his own and he loved the myths and legends and fantasies which had been woven around them over time as much as the visitors who came there did. But now, for Will, the far tower had become a magnet of revulsion; he hated it.

For two days his home had seemed like a tomb. Faran barely spoke to him and he was miserable without her sunny discourse. She was not angry with him, though. Rather, she shared the same depression of spirits as he was experiencing, although he doubted if she shared his sense of guilt. The atmosphere of shame permeated the house so thoroughly that even Young Will was downcast without knowing why. They had not told him about the prisoner – Will didn't want to – however, he worried over what he ought to say in explanation of the tower's being out of bounds. Then fate, it seemed, took a hand, for Young Will developed a cough and a slight fever, so it was into bed for him.

Night was the worst time of all. Because Will had no enthusiasm for any distraction, all he could do was sit by the fire and listen to the silence. On one hand he was glad of the cold night air which necessitated that the windows facing the far tower be heavily draped and shuttered, especially now that the moon waxed full. As if by the merciless purity of its bright face it was determined to illuminate the sins of men, the moon scoured the landscape like a heartless charlady, pointing out every detail of stone and hillock, and the tower too, with its chilling light.

But on the other hand nothing could stop him from thinking how cold it must be in the tower. The warmth of his own fire was almost a pain to him because of it.

Faran had just come from Young Will. "He's asleep now, but he's still restless. Maybe I should stay with him tonight," she said to her father.

Will sighed and shook his head. "No, I'll do that. You go to bed. I can't have you getting sick too." "But Daddy, you don't look very well yourself. Are you feeling poorly?"

Was he? It wasn't a cold or fever that ailed him, not anything bodily. Yet he was sick, if guilt and bad conscience were illness too.

Faran's bedroom was the attic chamber. It was small, but she liked its cosy intimacy, the sloping walls, the dormer window with its high view of the wide, empty plateau. She loved most, though, the wild openness of the land below, the freedom of it, and to watch the changing lights and colors of the days and the seasons which made magic that flux between morning and midnight and the solstices of summer and winter.

She had also liked the Towers once. But now, as her father did, she hated the far tower, at least.

She could see it from her window quite plainly and it glinted in the moonlight, coldly.

"No, I don't really hate the tower," she said to herself, shaking her head. "I just hate what this thing is doing to Daddy. It's going to make him ill, I just know it is. And I hate how it makes me feel too."

Something pale and ethereal fluttered past her window: an owl searching for its dinner. It was so quiet that she could hear her own breathing and the world outside seemed more like a screen upon her mind than a fact. It was then she conceived a desire, formed as much by curiosity as out of the need to understand her own feelings. No matter what it might mean, no matter how shocking it may be, she wanted to see for herself the criminal in the tower. "I'll go at dawn, before Dad wakes," she decided.

Faran wrapped up quickly in warm woolens, and in one nervous minute she was downstairs and running the length of the stone path to the far tower. She did not look back to see if her father might be watching, she was certain he would not. Even if, by chance, he'd woken early, he would not look out. Faran knew without him saying so why he had shuttered all the front windows; it was not just to keep out the cold.

The scant openings in the tower which served as its windows began at a spot way above Faran's head. She cursed softly – she hadn't realized that, never having had a reason to want to see through them before. A pile of framed-up lumber off to one side which Will had been preparing to use in the making of forms for a new bit of path served her as a temporary scaffold which she built as quickly as her frozen fingers would allow. When she gripped at the tower wall to haul herself up to the window, her fingernails scraped on the rough stones and two nails broke.

"Hell!" The makeshift scaffold was indeed temporary; it rocked dangerously as she shifted her weight for a better foothold. "This had better be worth it," she said boldly, but, in truth, she didn't feel bold or brave or even certain that she was doing the right thing.

Dawn had begun to turn the dark morning ashen, then softly lit with pale rose. Faran's hands were red with cold but her knuckles were white as she gripped the window edge. She peered down into the tower and groaned in disappointment. Another thing she hadn't thought of! It was still too early for enough light to enter the tower yet. How long would she

6

have to wait? Would she even have time before her father woke and realized she was gone?

Half frozen, she clung to the knobbly edge of the sill. Her resolve was weakening as she thought of her father. Not of any anger he might express that she had disobeyed him, but of the pain he would surely feel at her willingness to explore his shame. She was sensitive to her father's plight; she had always felt his pains as her own. When Young Will's mother – her stepmother – had run off with a much younger and more prosperous man, Faran had felt her father's loneliness and sorrow as if it had been her own. She had only been a little girl at the time.

The scaffold wobbled. Faran gritted her teeth and aimed to stand very, very still. The first sunlight began to thread its way into the top crevice of the windows on the opposite side of the tower. Since the windows were long and vertical rather than horizontal and squat, the sun entered them as channelled streams of light, and the tower floor began gradually to materialize out of darkness, in a pattern of stripes or bars.

The longer and more precarious and risky the wait, the more Faran would see. Now she had gone this far she might as well chance it, she decided.

And after a seemingly endless while she had her reward. Small and alone in the emptiness of the tower's interior, a bundled figure crouched on the only platform available, a single bench of ancient planks. It hugged itself against the wall, as if it was possible for stone to give heat or comfort. At first the figure was dark and undefined, then, as the sun rose higher, it was more visible. A hooded figure wrapped well and close beside it a large pitcher, obviously of water. To Faran, now, such imprisonment seemed all the more cruel, for while a man might starve without food, provided with water, his suffering would be prolonged.

The scaffold rocked and Faran's stomach lurched with it. She felt horrified and sick at the same time, though not from fear of falling but from an outrage which came to her naturally, without thought or judgement. This was not merely imprisonment she was observing, this was torture! What kind of monster deserved this? What kind of evil was this locked up in her father's tower?

As if in response to her curiosity, or perhaps the growing light, the figure stretched a little. Faran saw the manacled arms and legs unroll from their tight coil. What shocked her most was the paleness of the man's hands, all she could actually see of him as yet apart from his coverings. But his hands, how fair they were! And on one hand, the left,

7

on the middle finger, was a ring of gold, with a jewel in it larger and more dazzling than any she had ever seen!

A yearning, inexplicable but unstoppable, rose in Faran's heart. Oh, let me see more of you, she thought. And as if to oblige his invisible audience, the man then threw off the covering from his head and reached for the pitcher, to drink. He had thick dark hair, which, whilst wavy, was tangled and untidy, but his face was lit by sun bright, drifting motes, as if gold dust had been sprinkled upon it.

Faran nearly cried aloud. The scaffold teetered, close to collapse, and in her startled state she lost control. Her fingers lost their purchase on the stone sill and the whole unstable structure tumbled.

Faran didn't wait to fall with it but launched herself away. She hit the ground and rolled into the wet turf, drowning in surprise and dew. She was not so much hurt as in shock, and with that shock went horror and dismay and a great need to run to her father right away.

Chapter Two

Will Crafter woke slowly then remembered he was not in his own bed. The boy had been restless all night, keeping him awake and anxious, and only a few hours before morning had both of them finally fallen asleep.

He rested his hand lightly on Young Will's forehead. The child seemed more peaceful, he thought. The house was so quiet and he could not smell the early morning scents he expected. By now, if he hadn't done it himself, Faran would have lit the stove and begun the breakfast. But the house was still and dead.

He climbed the stairs to her room and found it empty. For fear of waking Young Will he didn't call out but trudged sullenly downstairs. Where was the girl?

At the back door he almost crashed into her as she ran in from the path. She was dishevelled and breathless, her woolens were sodden and there was a scrape along her chin. But she scarcely noticed either that or his astonishment. She grabbed at his hand, tugging at him.

"Dad!"

Between heavy breaths Faran shot out words Will did not want to hear. "Dad, the prisoner, you have to see."

Will pulled himself away angrily. "What have you been doing? At that tower? I forbade you!"

Her face was not that of a guilty child or of a contrite one either, and was totally without defiance. He did not understand the look of her face, but her eyes begged him and tears were starting to well up in them.

"Dad." She said the word softly, and breathed in a long sigh. A tear spread slowly over her cheek. Will dropped onto the settle by the door. "Child, why did you go there, why?"

She seemed unconscious of the tears as she stood there. "I had to, I don't know why. I needed to."

How could he answer that when his own guilt had pressed on him the same need? And yet, so far, he had avoided facing it. Will shook his head.

"But Daddy, you must go there too. You have to know."

"Know what? That a man is starving to death while I obey orders?" Only now did he understand how thoroughly he hated himself for his inaction.

Faran knelt and with the uncompromising gaze of the innocent she looked into his eyes. "Yes. He will die if you do obey. Daddy, I don't think he's a bad man at all, and I know you are not. We can't let him starve. Daddy, he's young. I thought he would be terrible to look at, you know, almost like some kind of monster. But he's not; he's only a young man. He seems harmless."

"Then why is he locked away?"

"I don't know. He was so quiet, so calm. I-I don't understand."

Will did not understand either. "Two days without food, or more that we don't know about; he may just be weak. But he might not be harmless. You can't always tell by how a man looks. But he's a young man, you said?"

"Yes. A lot younger than you, Daddy. Not very old at all."

Will sighed. "I don't know what will happen when they come back and find him still alive. But you're right, I can't let another man starve, and do nothing, no matter what he's guilty of." He shrugged. "Come on then, child, you'd best get changed, you're soaked to the skin. I can't have you catching cold the same as your brother."

"Is Young Will any better this morning?"

"Maybe a bit. But it's that cough of his that bothers me, and the fever, it comes and goes. If he doesn't pick up soon I'll have to be thinking of what to do."

Together, Will and Faran prepared a breakfast of porridge, new bread and tea, not for themselves but for the prisoner. Young Will had taken

10

medicine for his cough and had drifted back to sleep. "Stay here and look after the boy," Will said.

But Faran wouldn't hear of it. "I'm coming too, Dad. Please, let me. I want to know if I'm right about that man."

"You could be in for a big let down," Will said. "He may not be what you think and I don't want my girl hearing things she ought not to."

"I don't care, Dad. What's worse, knowing the truth or what we've been putting up with for the last two days?"

Will couldn't disagree. "All right, but don't expect too much. You have no idea what this prisoner is like, apart from the look of him, and that may well be a deception."

At the tower door Will stopped and frowned. Something had just occurred to him. He gazed up at the window slits, above the line of his head also. "Just how did you manage to see this prisoner anyway?"

Faran grimaced and looked away. The answer was not going to please her father, she knew. "That wood you have around the back, I made a sort of … ladder-thing, on the other side."

"You what?"

He strode around to the far side of the tower and came back, fuming. "You could have hurt yourself, broken something! Then where would we be, no doctor for miles around, and Young Will ailing as well!"

"I'm sorry, Dad, I really am," said Faran in a small ashamed voice. This time she truly did look contrite.

Will took a great iron key from his coat pocket and pushed it into the antique lock. "Hm. What's done is done, I suppose, and no harm, except if this be a mistake, of course. Those men who put the poor wretch inside thought they were taking the only key. They don't know that both towers have the same locks. Yet it's a little stiff in here, this one." He coaxed and twisted the key until it grated open the lock.

A little trembling butterfly of fear fluttered in Faran's stomach as the door swung heavily open.

Why, she did not know, but this moment seemed to have some import beyond the discovery of a prisoner. It was a moment she would remember all her life and, later on, with gratitude; but for now the moment was only exciting and a bit scary.

For Will, he was also afraid, but more because he worried about the consequences that would follow. Even now he was planning his excuses, and if they were not good enough, his way of escape. The men who had done this were not kind men, and Will had his family to think of.

11

The early morning light swept in with a draught, and the prisoner glanced up in surprise, shielding his dazzled eyes with his hands. Will Crafter suffered the same shocks his daughter had. The man was young, certainly not older than twenty five, and through the unshaven scruffiness of his incarceration, a personable young man with no cast of the criminal upon his features. But then, while a girl like Faran might be easily swayed by these things, in Will's experience, nice looks and youth did not guarantee either innocence or virtue. Then Will's stare fixed itself on the young man's hand, upon the ring of bright, rich gold glinting above the harsher, greyer, colder sheen of manacles.

A silence followed as all three adjusted to the shock of the moment, Will and Faran in their own separate worlds of speculation and apprehension, and the prisoner merely accustoming a vision dimmed by two days in mostly darkness. Then it was Will who spoke, sounding harder and more abrupt than he felt but conscious that for the time being he must be seen to be in control. After all, he didn't know the mind of this man, how hostile he might be, and there was Faran to protect.

"I am the Caretaker of this tower and I have orders not to bother with you."

The young man did not reply but his gaze shifted to Faran hiding partly behind her father, to the steaming pots in the basket that she held.

"Why you're here or what you've done, I don't know," Will continued, "But I do know that it's not in me to let a man starve to death."

Hope lit the young man's eyes. He coughed as if his throat was dry. "That's what I've been put here for though, simply that." His voice was hoarse and slightly rough, but it was also mild and seeming without anger or hostility. And it was a cultured voice.

Will listened with dread to the polished accents of the ruling classes. A political prisoner, he guessed; the worst kind for Will Crafter and his children at least. Mentally he began working harder on his half formed plans of escape. "No reason is good enough for me. Don't tell me anymore," he said. "Faran." He motioned for the basket but Faran brought it forward herself and set it down by the pitcher on the bench. When she opened the lid of the porridge pot the young man could hardly contain his desperation.

In mild embarrassment they watched him eat, awkwardly because of the manacles, for a solid five minutes before he paused and looked up at them. "I'm sorry for my manners, but it's been a while," he said, and continued. He stopped only when Faran bent to stir and pour the hot

12

sweet tea. Their eyes met for a moment and lightly the young man touched her hand. "Thank you."

Will swooped. "Okay. We'll leave you to the bread and the rest of the tea. You can help yourself, I'm sure. Come along, Faran, there's Young Will to be thinking about, we have to get back."

The prisoner said nothing more; nevertheless, even as he beat his swift retreat, Will could feel how his back was burning with the heat of the young man's watching eyes as they followed him out the door.

Will had to practically drag his daughter back to the house and all the way home she argued with him.

"We shouldn't have gone just like that! Why didn't you ask him anything, Dad? Why did you say you didn't want to know?"

"He was too busy eating, you saw that. Besides I don't want to know, not a thing." "Why not?"

"You don't understand." "Then tell me so I shall!"

They reached the back door of the house. Will shook his head helplessly. He had always respected his daughter's intelligence, but he was well aware of how easily a girl who was almost a budding young woman could become a victim of her heart, and he had seen the soft sympathetic look in Faran's eyes that was more than interest or concern. So now he must lie along with the truth, just a little. Or rather it must be a sin of omission this time. "You heard how he spoke; you could see what he was."

Dumbly Faran stared at him. "No, I don't know what you mean. What about the way he spoke? He hardly said a word."

Of course. How stupid Will felt! He shook his head once more. He had forgotten, Faran had never been near the cities of Telaia, much less been exposed to the idea of class in society. She had heard many varying accents from the tourists who visited the Towers and assumed all of them equal, if different. And none of that rich, ruling class ever bothered to visit the Towers. In notions of class Faran was an innocent, a beautiful simpleton of Nature who knew not prejudice or shame, and that had been the way Will preferred it.

So as best he could, Will explained. "That man is there maybe because someone in power wants him out of the way. I mention his speech because he speaks with the accents of the people in charge of Telaia."

"He's a lord, like the Baron?"

13

"I don't know about that, but he's certainly one of that class." "Then the Lord you work for must be trying to get rid of him." "That could be so."

"And I was right, he isn't bad, he's just in someone's way – your boss's way."

There were times, few enough but occasional, when Will wished his daughter's simplicity extended to her brain. "I think that might be true, although we don't know what he may have done. He could have done something."

"Nothing," Faran said vehemently. She sat down on the seat by the door. "At least nothing bad, I'll bet. But Daddy, it could be bad for you, couldn't it? What shall we do?"

"I'll have to think. The Baron's men will be back here in five days, they said. Right now, though, my main concern is Young Will. I hate to think we might have to pack up and travel with a sick boy on our hands."

Young Will was eight. Ordinarily he was a bright, energetic, chatty child who was not satisfied unless he knew everything that was going on around him. Which was why Faran was worried now. He was awake when they came inside and knew they had been somewhere and that breakfast was not even begun, and yet he seemed totally disinterested. He was listless and away from them somehow and Faran felt the fever in him, like a tide of heat which refused to abate.

"I don't think he's getting any better," she told her father. "In fact I think he's worse."

"Then we will have to get a doctor here," Will said. "I won't risk Young Will's health another minute. The closest one is in Troi, and without a phone I'll have to go there. I don't want to leave you here alone, especially with that man in the tower, but I can't see there's any choice now."

Will hated to go, to leave Faran with the heaviness of a sick child and the prisoner; but his son's life meant more to him than he could say. With orders to Faran to make as little contact with the prisoner as possible, he set off right away. He had to walk the long cold way – a full day's travel – because they had no car, and the pony, which had been their only form of transport, had died last winter and they could not afford another on caretaker's wages. As Will travelled, every step he took felt heavy with fear. The nagging sense that his daughter might be swayed by her heart and would disobey him lay over his back like a burden which only

14

slowed him down when he ought to have been travelling faster.

Faran spent the rest of the morning in her brother's room, sponging him down and feeding him with cool drinks, and talking quietly to him so that at least he might not wander deeper into the fever. And, at intervals, staring restlessly from the window. Her attention outside was divided, between the road her father had travelled down – how much more empty and desolate it seemed now that he had gone – and the tower, which pulled at her like a magnet, irresistibly. She could not stop thinking of the young man and wished her father had not been so strict about visits. Even if Will wanted to stay in ignorance, she did not. "Well I shall have to go there in any case," she told herself. "I still have to keep feeding him, and I'm going to take him some blankets; it must be freezing in there."

As soon as Young Will seemed to be sleeping more soundly, Faran loaded herself with two sheep fleece rugs and a pail of food. Vegetable soup with a broth of dried meat, bread and more tea: a veritable feast for a starving man. On the way to the tower she caught an image of herself in a dew- pond by the path, and in spite of everything she giggled. She looked like an explorer's bearer in far- flung lands; she'd seen pictures of them in a book. Little thin men with stick legs and backs bent under bundles bigger than themselves, while the lord and master marched grandly ahead. Suddenly she was shocked and the giggles rapidly subsided. Never before in all her life had she thought that men might serve other men unwillingly. Now she was learning otherwise. Living in the wild open freedom of this land, she had always thought of herself, and her father, as free.

She was sombre when she reached the tower. She set down her burden and turned the key slowly, feeling sad and a little afraid.

"Hello," she said when the prisoner looked up. "I brought some things." The young man squinted into the light. "You've come by yourself?"

"Yes. Daddy had to go to Troi to fetch the doctor." She was not supposed to tell the prisoner that; Will had warned her against telling him anything.

"Someone is ill? Your mother? Why not telephone?"

"My little brother. There's only Dad and me and him. And the phone lines are down." Faran bit her lip. The second mistake. She shouldn't have said she was alone and without outside contact. She dodged out the

15

door, returning with the bundle. "Blankets and more food."

That was stating the obvious, but it served to cover the confusion she felt. Worse though was the blush that came when the young man smiled and said thank you in a way that made it sound like the most beautiful word in the world.

Being manacled, he could not arrange the blankets properly himself so Faran helped. She opened the food pail for him too and cleared away the morning things. He ate hungrily again and when he was satisfied he thanked her once more. He also apologized for the state he was in, for the smell of the place and that he was so unwashed. Which could not be helped in the circumstances.

And which made Faran blush all the more and promise a bucket and a bowl of water and soap and a towel as soon as she had taken back the basket and the pail.

"You're very kind," he said.

She ran all the way to the house. Young Will was still asleep. She bathed his hot face gently so as not to wake him then raced back up the path to the tower. In her haste she had not even locked the tower door, but the young man could go nowhere because his manacles were bolted by a long chain to a ring on the wall. She knew her father would not be pleased though, if he knew.

The bucket had been heavy and the water in it hot when Faran had started for the tower. Arriving, the bucket was three quarters full and the water had cooled noticeably. "The path is a bit rough and the water kept sloshing out," she explained. She omitted to mention how she had hurried.

The young man did not seem to mind a wash in cool water. Better than nothing, Faran supposed. He also seemed unconcerned by her presence as he worked around the manacles and stripped down of everything but his trousers in front of her. His clothes hung like limp, heavy laundry on the chain between his hands as, carefully and laboriously, he washed his body. There was something very natural and unposed about him, and, strangely, it was not as though his predicament appeared to trouble him all that greatly. Faran watched, covertly, admiring what she saw, embarrassed by her feelings and thinking it would be easier for him if she could help. But she was too shy to offer and very conscious of her father's ire, should he ever find out about any of this. Well, she would just have to make sure that he did not.

The young man's muscles twitched in the cold and goose-bumps appeared on his smooth, fair skin.

Where the manacles had rubbed, his wrists were bruised and raw, but he only smiled a little when Faran expressed concern. "I'm all right," he said. "I'll keep the water and do the rest when you've gone." He grinned at Faran's reddening face. "You've been very good to me, I shan't ever forget it."

His cheerfulness was so out of place that Faran could endure her ignorance no longer. "Why are you here?"

The young man shrugged damp shoulders. "That's not easy to explain. It's a matter of politics, you might say, of me being what someone else doesn't want."

"Dad thinks you're in the way of someone." "More out of step; the wrong flavor."

Faran didn't understand. "But you're not a criminal? I mean, you haven't done anything wrong?" "Nothing criminal, no. But I'm definitely wrong for the powers that be."

"Can I know your name?" Faran asked.

The young man finished towelling and replaced his shirt. "Yes, if you want. It's Marek." "My father's name is Will Crafter, and I'm—"

"Faran." "You know?"

"I heard your father say it."

Faran blushed. Fancy, he had paid such attention! "It's a pretty name," Marek said.

Faran blushed again. She wasn't used to compliments from strangers, but she took it for what she felt it to be, a simple and honest courtesy which she wanted to return. "Yours is nice too. It sounds sort of foreign, and I've never heard it before."

"It is. My mother named me after her grandfather. He wasn't from Telaia."

"Oh." Faran didn't ask what country. She was more interested in knowing the rest of his name instead. "But your name's not just Marek?"

"No. But that's good enough for now. Something tells me your father wouldn't be too happy about your knowing even this."

"My father says that if you are a political prisoner then what we've done could be dangerous for us."

Marek replaced his coat and pulled one of the blankets of fleece around his shoulders. He sighed and frowned and appeared to sink into thought, so that Faran had to wait for the answer. Finally, he said: "I'd like to talk to your father about that. I won't say any more now. When he

17

gets back, tell him to come and see me."

For the first time Faran saw and sensed the lordliness in the prisoner. Here was a man accustomed to giving orders and having them obeyed. Prisoner he may be, but for the moment the tower might have been his castle, his stronghold. But Faran didn't mind the lordliness much; she wanted to help this man; she liked him and wanted to save him, and that was all that mattered. Besides, she had begun to remember Young Will. She could not neglect him.

"I shall. Daddy won't be here until tomorrow. I have to go now, my brother needs me; he's not well."

The lane between the dark buildings was a hollow of well-trodden stone which dipped in the center and rose at the sides. A thousand years of pedestrians had worn the lane into a furrow long before the present buildings were even thought of. It was so poorly lit that Will had to feel his way with his feet. During rain the lane would become a gutter and people would have to walk along the outside edges if they wanted to keep dry. Troi was a very old settlement, more of a village than a town, but a doctor was resident, usually. Someone he passed on the road had told Will that he thought the doctor had gone out of town for a day or two, but in case the doctor had returned, and since he was almost there, Will decided to press on to Troi.

It was nearing midnight when Will reached the village. Troi was asleep except for one public house, The Cockerel, and Will opened its front door gratefully. Yet that was also empty apart from the landlord who still cleared away the dregs of a festive evening. Taking Will for a persistent reveller returning for one more drink, the landlord was not pleased to see him at first.

"Ah, you're a traveller," the landlord said when he understood. "If you're wanting a room for the night, I'm afraid we're full up."

"What I want is the doctor. I've travelled all day, on foot, to find him. Can you point me to his house?"

"Doctor's not here. He went down to Cruen last week and I don't think he's come back yet."

Cruen was another three days journey for Will. Even if there had been a bus leaving Troi in the morning, it was no use to Will because he didn't have the fare. "Do you know when he's due to return?"

The landlord shook his head. "His wife might. Shall I direct you?

Can't say she'll be pleased though, you turning up on her doorstep this time of night."

The doctor's house was one of an identical set of four poised on the end of the lane overlooking a black hole of darkness which Will knew to be a stone quarry in the day. That was how Troi had been built, raised up out of its own bedrock, time and time again, as old stones crumbled and newly cut ones replaced them. The town carried within every pebble and rock the history of its ancient line, and Will knew also that a certain amount of moral and spiritual darkness still permeated the fabric of these ancient hill places. A doctor was a novelty here, and why he lived here Will didn't know.

Perhaps he had come to escape a past, or merely the same press of cities and illusory culture that Will himself so disliked. Whatever the reason, it was sure that he would only scrape a living in Troi and roundabout. People here preferred the old ways when it came to healing and were more likely to call in a herb-woman or herb-man for their ills.

Will was not prejudiced either way. He had seen some wonderful cures by herb doctors and such in his time, but he knew that the one or two close around Troi were scarcely more than witches or shamans, and he didn't like or trust that kind of thing himself.

At the door of the doctor's house he knocked. And knocked. Until finally an elderly woman opened the door a crack and peered out grumpily. But when he explained she softened and asked him in, full of sympathy and regret. Will sighed; he would find no joy here in Troi, the doctor was gone to help in an epidemic in Cruen and his wife did not know how long he would be gone.

"I've seen you before. You're the man in charge of the Towers, aren't you? We went there once, on a trip. It was very interesting; you were a good guide. I'm sorry your son is ill but there's little I can do myself," she said.

Will must have looked so forlorn and so very weary that she offered him some supper and a bed in her spare room for the night. He accepted gratefully, although his good fortune in finding such unexpected kindness in Troi was allayed by disappointment and fear. He should never have left the Towers on a wasted errand such as this, should never have left his children alone.

Chapter Three

As Will Crafter lay under the doctor's roof in Troi, the prisoner in the tower stretched out on the bench under the roof of his prison. For the first time in days Marek was warm, although not exactly comfortable on the hard wood. However his belly didn't growl from hunger and he was able to think rather than dream restlessly.

When they brought him to the tower he was drugged and did not know where he was. Even when he came to on the next morning he had a devil of a time working out where they had put him, until he calmed his fears and fancies and listened to the world outside. None of the din and racket of city noises came to his ears: no roaring of engines; no grinding of wheels or hooting of horns; not even the sounds of other men. Instead, a natural silence spoke for itself in the moaning whisper of the wind as it played through holes in stone, in the fuller pitched wail of the wind skittering over wide open spaces. He heard the high keening of a bird of prey and, at night, an owl hoot and the scratching of small creatures just beyond the wall. By day he observed the ancient stones around him and stared upward into a gloom which seemed to be unending. But an open stairway began from his flagged floor, growing out from the wall as it spiraled on and up into nothingness above, so he guessed that he was in a tower of sorts and that tower was somewhere far from home or civilization.

Home. He realized he didn't have one in this world any more. But that had been his choice from the beginning, when he had first comprehended the truth about himself and about everything. His choice. And it was ironic that those who had sent him here, in the delusion that a tower and starvation would either subdue him or destroy him, also brought him closer to ultimate freedom.

His adversaries played this game with him, for they were sure they knew which way it would go. Yes, they had him figured, that is according to their own mind set of beliefs. But he would not give them what they expected.

Yet he had no idea of how he was going to get out of the tower without some kind of deception and therefore appearing to revert to his adversaries" control. The Caretaker and his daughter had been a surprise and had become, by way of their own compassion, part of the dilemma.

That made it necessary to do some straight talking with Will Crafter, for the Caretaker's protection chiefly, and his children's. But just a little straight talking, not too much. The less these honest, loving people knew the safer for them.

As long as the father would believe him, though. The daughter, he knew, was already convinced of his innocence, for she knew and felt with her whole being rather than just by intellect or fear. What a lovely child she was! She gave him hope and the confidence he sought for in his quest. That there should be more like her in his life now. He would have enjoyed a longer talk with her and to feel the comfort her presence gave. It was strange: though she was a child, yet there was about her a strength which reassured him. How odd, to feel so comforted by a child!

The darkness seemed lighted by these last thoughts, even though the physical darkness was so complete now the moon rose in the morning hours, that it was almost palpable, a blanket of black velvet to add to the fleeces given him by Faran. He clung to thought of her, to the light she shone unconsciously and without effort, and he gathered that light into his own and played it into the darkness around him. It was his shield.

With the morning, Faran came bearing the familiar porridge, bread and tea and, to Marek's joy, a bowl of sweet stewed fruit. All that would have made it perfect then would be to breakfast outside in the brisk fresh air, in sunshine.

The girl looked strained, as if she hadn't slept much. Well, neither had he and the hard boards accounted for most of that. But what had kept her from her rest?

"Young Will isn't doing very well," Faran told him. "I wish Daddy would hurry home. I'm afraid." "Fear won't help your brother," Marek said gently. "Tell me, what are his symptoms? How long has he been sick? Is he eating, drinking? Does he have fever? Or chills? Is he vomiting?" "Are you a doctor?" she asked, wide eyed.

"Not as such, no, but I have some skills in healing. It's something I've been drawn to do." "Could you help him if I brought him here?"

"I would try."

Hand over her mouth, Faran looked at him hopefully. "If only you weren't all chained like this, you could come to the house."

"No." Marek handed her the basket of empty pots. "Your father wouldn't like it. He doesn't know enough of me or my situation to trust me."

"But I trust you. I believe in you."

Sympathetic, Marek smiled. "Yes, and I appreciate your trust. But your father is the key, he's in charge. Bring the little boy here, or will it be too hard to do?"

Faran thought about it. "I I don't know yet. He's big for his age. I'll just have to try."

The atmosphere in Young Will's room was heavy with desperation, and Faran realized it was all hers. Young Will himself was far away, in a land where he recognized no one, where there was no coherence. The bed was a tangled mess of sheets and lumped blankets. They had fought all night long, he and she. Faran to keep him cool and herself sane, Young Will to frustrate her at every turn. He was very ill; Faran had never seen such illness before and she did not know what to do any more.

It was a risk to take him out of the house, into the cold winter air, but she was desperate, and that called for drastic measures. "Willie." She strove to call him out of his comatose state, but got no reply. She managed to roll him to the edge of the bed, but it was as she had feared a huge difficulty to lift him further. If only she was not so small herself, if she were stronger, and he was not such a big boy. The comatose are such dead weights, so uncooperative. Even if she got him to the door, and she might just do it, dragging him all the way, getting him down the stairs and up the long steep path to the tower would be impossible.

In frustration she sat by the bed and cried a while, thinking also of Marek. Why could she not bring him here? Why? Why?

But tears were useless things; they made her wearier than ever. In wiping them away, she caught sight of her reflection in the mirror opposite. An oval, slightly pointed face under an untidy sweep of hair that Will described as corn silk, although Faran had never seen corn growing in a field. Blue eyes too big for their setting, lashes all wet and sticking together, puffiness underneath, a nose red from crying. Not a pretty sight. A puffed up, miniature face above inadequate, narrow shoulders. Yes, she was small and still locked in the thinness of childhood; not much had developed yet. Even fully grown she was never going to be a large woman, she told herself. She was lithe and wiry though, but it was not enough for Young Will's weight. He took after his father, and would be tall and strongly built when he was a man. If he got to be a man.

Immediately, mentally, she slapped herself to end such foolish

22

thoughts. Marek had said that fear would not help her brother, and he was right.

Which made her think of Marek again. A vision of him seemed to appear in the mirror, layered above hers. How old was he? In spite of his obvious youth something about him was aged and experienced, or ageless, perhaps. So he appeared, even though his face was unlined and his physique was as vigorous looking and as well defined as any young working man's. Although he was not rough and hairy or heavily muscled, but was refined and fairly slender, he was not soft. He could not be soft, to endure the deprivations of the tower with so little complaint. He was not as tall as her father either, nor as big, but with a quality of sureness that made him appear more definite, more authoritative. That, she guessed, may have been the result of his upbringing, whatever that upbringing was or meant. Faran had no real conception of the worlds her father had seen, so if he said Marek was a Lord then she must believe him. But even that lordliness was unreal to her, and she had only glimpsed it in Marek in a vague way.

He possessed another quality too, which intrigued her more. He was both beautiful and strange to observe, she thought. He was a mystery. Young men came to the Towers on occasion, with touring parties or on the way to somewhere else. Yet she had seen no one like Marek, none with that veiled quality married somehow with openness. She could not understand what this meant; it was an unformed notion as yet. Veiled, because there was much more to him than he revealed. Open, because his eyes were direct and honest. However they were strange, those eyes of his, for she had the impression that they had changed color since she saw him the first time. Was it so? Had they not been brownish or hazel then? Or was she mistaken? Because they were a definite green now.

Poised at the edge of the bed, Young Will groaned and for a brief moment, opened his eyes and focused them on her. "Faran, I'm hot, I hurt all over," he murmured. Faran helped him sip at some water, and then she washed his face. Her heart started to beat harder. Here was the chance she needed. "Do you think?" she began, but he had already slipped away again and she couldn't wake him.

Faran hurried to her father's tool shed. Inside the shed was organized chaos, meaning that Will knew where everything was but that Faran or anyone else would have to search for what they wanted. Faran did that now, rifling through drawers and shelves filled with metal and string, bits of wire, sanding blocks, blunted and rusted knives, sharp shiny ones, a cast iron shoe last almost as old and as well used as the towers.

Fidgeting impatiently in curls of wood shavings, she hunted through the rows of tools, some ancient, a very few nearly new. What she sought for was the right tool, or tools, for she was determined now that Marek would come to the house. She had ceased to worry about her father's orders; Young Will's life that was more important.

The manacles around Marek's wrists and ankles were not keyed. Instead, their separate parts were locked together by a long bolt which took two hands and two tools to undo. This ensured that even if a prisoner had got hold of the right tools, he couldn't manage to undo the chains around his wrists by himself. And Marek was also shackled to the wall, so that unless he got the manacles off his wrists first, he could never get free.

Faran was looking for something to do the job, one tool to hold the bolt and another to turn the thing that held it locked in place. She had a picture in her mind of what she wanted; she'd seen the very things here on the shelf above the workbench; but nowhere were the tools to match the picture. Her father must have taken them with him then; they were definitely gone.

Tears started prickling in Faran's eyes. Surely not! Will had taken the tools! As if he might suspect something just like this! Well, she had known he was serious about his orders to stay away from the prisoner. But that serious?

So, he did not trust her. And she had proven him right. It seemed to Faran then as if she and her father had betrayed each other and some feeling inside her fell away, forever lost. She hardened against the pain of loss. What did she care, now?

She lifted her smarting eyes to the grimy little window behind the bench. From here you could just see the top of the far tower, rising above the cottage roof. How grey and grim and harsh and cruel it looked against the freedom of the sky, the sky that nothing ruled or imprisoned. A wheel of birds punctured the sky above the tower with the dark slashes of their flapping wings. They circled the tower once and then were gone.

If Marek was a bird he could fly away. Perhaps, given wings, she would even fly away herself.

Once Young Will's mother had run off with her lover and Will had gotten over his initial despair, life at the Towers had settled down into some sort of serenity with not a lot to hamper growing children or to tell them that they were not free. But they weren't free; no one was free. Will

24

Crafter was not free, Marek was a prisoner, Young Will was caught in serious illness. And she? Well, she had been trying to do something to help, but it was just one frustration after another and all she had was a skinny child's body which was too weak to do what she wanted.

It was gone eleven o'clock and she had managed not a single useful act this morning. Marek would wonder what had happened and Young Will probably needed her. First she would see to him then she would have to tell Marek she had failed.

"Try not to worry," Marek advised. "Your father should be home by tonight and he's bringing a doctor, isn't he?"

To hide the shame she did not want to reveal, Faran hung her head. "Yes, but you haven't seen Young Will. I wish I could have—"

"No. It wouldn't be right." Marek read her thoughts as easily as if she were transparent to him.

Bringing the sick child to the tower was impossible, so her next step was to try to free himself somehow. He could not allow it.

"I couldn't find the right tools for the manacles, but maybe, if I brought a hammer and chisel, you could hack the ring out of the wall," she suggested.

"No. Your father will be angry with you."

Faran was about to say something more when they heard footsteps on the path outside. The tower door was wide open, letting in the little bit of warmth which the feeble winter sun could provide. And through the doorway, with the sunbeams, strode Will Crafter; he was furious.

"What did I tell you, Faran? Good Heavens, girl, what were you thinking of?"

Away from the tower, Will harangued his daughter, over and over. And not once did he pause to listen to anything she might say. Not until she burst into tears. Then he was silent, as through her tears, Faran told him.

He could have whipped himself; he was so sorry and ashamed. After all it was he who had left the girl with such a burden of worry and decision. His only excuse for his bad temper was tiredness and his own emotions. He'd been up and on the road since well before dawn and

25

although his journey had been made speedier because the kindly doctor's wife gave him the lend of a pony and cart, that hadn't helped with the fear. Still, the woman promised to send her husband along to the Towers as soon as he got home.

He was even more ashamed when he saw Young Will. "What are you telling me?" he asked Faran again. "That this Marek says he is a healer? What sort?" He found it difficult to believe, but looking upon Young Will's blank, fiery face he was inclined to want to believe in miracles just now.

"I don't really know," Faran said. She had finally recovered her own equanimity, although Will could see that she was still upset by his anger. "I never got that far in finding out. I wanted to let Marek out of those chains, so he could come here."

"Do you think, once off the leash, he would have?" Will said, regretting his words immediately.

Faran gave him such a look of scorn that it hurt him to the quick. "He would have come. But he wouldn't let me do it."

Faced with that, there was nothing else left but surrender, and his son's health, of course. Will gathered up the little boy in his arms. "Let's take Young Will to the tower then. Let's see if this prisoner is as good as his word."

Chapter Four

Faran unlocked the tower door and Will Crafter carried his son from daylight into gloom. The prisoner stood at once and made a space on the bench for the child to lay on.

"Faran says you told her you are a healer. Can you help my boy?" Will asked. Marek nodded. "I'll do my best."

Young Will was swathed from head to foot in a blanket. Will and Faran stood and watched as Marek uncovered the child's head, neck and shoulders. At the first touch of cool air Young Will shivered and his body jerked in spasms of reaction. Marek ran a searching hand along the length of the boy's neck then down to the armpit. He repeated the procedure on the other side.

Will leaned over them, nervously. He itched to do something himself. He hated feeling so helpless. "Anything you need, I'll get. What are you looking for?"

Marek did not speak or glance up but silenced Will with an up-raised gesture of his hand and a shake of his head. It was as if he was placing the anxious father at a mental distance, where his presence would not disturb him. Faran saw a strange intensity on Marek's face, a look of concentration so deep that it was almost trance. He had laid both hands on the boy now, one on the top of Young Will's head and the other on his chest. Faran reached out and drew her father away, and he went as meekly as a lamb. She felt his clammy palm and squeezed it gently, for reassurance, and to show her forgiveness and her love.

What was Marek doing? She could not see his eyes but felt they were closed. Like the rhythm of a slow heartbeat his body rocked ever so slightly. Watching, Faran found herself moving with the same deep pulse, although it was not her body which swayed back and forth but her mind. The pulse seemed to beat its way from Marek to her brain, down to her hand and through it into her father's. It was like being swept away on the waves of a flowing river, or in the sea, the delight of which she had experienced only once in her life.

Was there a white light around Marek? And around Young Will too? Marek's hands, were they glowing as they held the child? The gold ring on his finger was a bright nimbus around an emerald star that shot forth blaze after blaze. Everything had the semblance of a dream, with the

27

shifting sense of reality that a dream creates. But it was more real than any dream, more real than even the stones around them, or the sun that lit the doorway of the tower.

Marek raised his head and looked at Will and Faran. He smoothed Young Will's hair from his damp forehead. A sweat had broken out on the boy's skin – a good sign; his eyes fluttered open and he smiled, not knowing where he was or who the stranger was, but seeming content. That smile said everything. "Keep him well wrapped on the way back. He needs food and good water and rest now," Marek said.

Will did not hesitate. He scooped up the boy and hurried outside. He said nothing to Faran about locking the door; he did not even glance back when she lingered on the step. She lingered because she had to say what her father, in his emotion and intensity, had failed to, and because, once more, she needed to see the light in Marek's eyes. She stepped forward a little, back into the tower's shadow, where the eyes of the healer burned, two deep green fires lighting the darkness.

"Thank you."

In his bed, the little boy slept sweetly. His cheek was cool and his sleeping face was peaceful and untroubled. He had eaten a meal of soup and a slice of bread and had asked about the strange man in the tower. "A friend," Will said, "Now go to sleep."

"Dad, we can't leave Marek like that now, not after what he's done for us," Faran said.

With a tender hand Will caressed his son's fair head. "True. There's none I could explain this to, though. I can't even explain it to myself. What I'll say when they come and find their prisoner gone, I don't know."

"But you'll free him?" "Yes."

Taking the long upward path to the tower, Will tried to think of the lies and excuses he'd need to convince his employer's men. But nothing would come, nothing that would satisfy even himself, if the boot was on the other foot. He was a poor liar and he knew it. What was left to him then but to take his children and run? And hope they didn't bother to track him down. He had two full days to escape, the same as the prisoner.

28

Maybe they could collaborate on a plan.

He confessed this to Marek as he wound out the bolts of the young man's manacles.

Marek massaged wrists bruised by the chafing of iron. "Just get me out into the sun," he said. "Then I'll tell you some things that you need to know, and I beg you to believe me, just as you believe and know your son is healthy again."

Will had no problem with that. Right now he was ripe for acceptance of anything that would help. "Ah, I wasn't sure that I'd see the sun again." Outside, Marek stretched his arms wide and let the sunlight fall onto his face. He breathed deeply and stood still as his eyes roamed the hills and skimmed with the breezes across a waving sea of pale, grey-green grasses. Freedom. He could have been a gull with silver wings, dipping over the ocean. He turned to the tower, and to Will. "The old people who built these towers loved the high places much better than the low, and I can understand why. The air is so clear up here."

"There used to be a whole settlement spreading over these hills," Will informed him. "The Towers are all that's left. No one really knows what purpose they were built for but their history is interesting."

Marek turned his back on the tower again. "I don't care much for history. It's history that locked me up in that pile of stones." He lifted his face to the sun once more. "And it's history that imprisons us all. We have to turn our backs on it, if what we want is truly to be free."

Will did not know what Marek meant. To him the young man looked like a king idly surveying his domain. This impression and all that had gone before made Will feel suddenly deferential. But he also needed a solution to his problem. "What is it you wanted to tell me, Sir?"

"Don't call me that," Marek said. "I'm not a part of that world any more. Forget that you ever thought it."

Will nodded. "If you say so."

Marek smiled, but to Will it seemed a grim kind of smile, a sad one, perhaps. "Firstly, I thank you for setting me free." The young man then crossed to the stair of the tower and putting his hand against the open door, he fingered the key in the lock thoughtfully. "The manacles, they're still on the chain.

That's good. Would you be so kind as to bolt them together again as they were and leave them on the bench?"

A strange request that Will did not understand. But, why not?

While Will re-bolted the manacles, Marek leaned on the door jamb and watched. He said, "I'm not a criminal and I never was."

"I know that now. No criminal could do what you did for my boy."

"Thanks. Your daughter trusted me from the start. She's a very special girl. She has a big heart."

Will glanced at the healer, unsure. "A gentle but vulnerable one. She's easily moved by suffering or need."

"That's not what I'd call a fault of character exactly." Marek smiled absently. "You have nothing to fear from having dealt with me, Caretaker, if you do what I suggest. There are several things you should know. I was put here illegally – no law of the land would countenance it – so my escape will be kept quiet, just as my incarceration was."

"But won't they be angry, those who put you here? And take it out on me and mine?"

"Not if you do what I say. A small deception, unfortunate because you're clearly an honest man, but necessary, and the manacles are a part of it," Marek said. He stepped down into the tower to gather up his cloak and the fleeces Faran had brought. "Clear all away but what was here when I came. Nothing but that pitcher, I think. Then you shall lock up."

Mystified, Will did as he was ordered, picking up a bucket and Faran's basket left there earlier and forgotten in all the excitement. But he could not comprehend the meaning of it all. Outside again, he ground the iron door to a close and locked it, pocketing the huge key. The key weighed him down with a burden heavier than he had ever borne before and the feeling that this was the last time in his life he would come willingly near this tower.

As they walked the length of the path to the cottage, Marek said, "Before we reach your house I'll tell you what I can. Some things I'll leave out; it's better for you if you don't know too much. You'll have to tell a lie to protect yourself, though. But rest assured the lie will be accepted, as long as you keep it simple. All you must say when asked is that as ordered you have been nowhere near the tower. You must feign ignorance of me, and keep your children quiet, especially the boy, who might give you away accidentally. Your daughter is wise. If you explain, she'll understand."

Understand? How would Faran understand when it was beyond him? Will stopped in his tracks, shaking his head. "But I don't see how I will be believed. That a man can simply vanish—"

"A man you know nothing about, remember. A man you only glimpsed once, when he was taken to the tower. A man whose face you didn't even see. That man disappeared and you didn't even know he was gone."

"Yes, but—"

Marek shifted the weight of fleeces to his other arm and took Will firmly by the shoulder. "Mister Crafter, you are an intelligent man, but there are some things in this world which may not be part of your experience."

Will nodded. Such a thing had happened that very day, so he was not inclined to disagree. And somehow, at this moment in time, he felt like a child in the presence of someone half his age. It was all very strange.

Marek continued, "You must trust me. I know very well the mind of the one who sent me to the tower. He put me here to either destroy me or bring me to my knees. Neither has happened. But if he believes I've escaped by my own efforts, then you are safe from any retribution."

"You're sure of this man's reaction? You know him that well?"

Marek sighed, not sadly, but as if he had already long ago accepted some unpleasant fact of life. "Yes, Mister Crafter. That man is my brother."

Will could not help himself, he stared.

Marek looked philosophical, shrugging. "A family conflict not easily resolved. Don't trouble yourself about it."

Will knew that families in high places often did not behave like the norm. But a brother! "Then the Lord I work for is—"

"My brother Silene, yes."

"Great Heavens," Will said. "I didn't know he was such a bad man, until now."

Marek said, "I should leave this place immediately. The less you see of me, the quicker it will be for you to put me from your mind and the easier your story when the time comes."

Will did not think he could forget such a man all that quickly or easily. Besides, it would be growing dark in an hour or two and too late to be setting out across the high country in the wintertime. He scraped his boots on the step and opened the front door of his house. He held the door open for the healer. "I wouldn't advise tackling the moors at night. Frost's coming down, it's going to be bitter, and you're not familiar with the roads."

As Will always did, Marek had to duck his head under the low lintel

31

to go inside. "I hadn't intended to take the roads. Safer that way, you understand?"

Will followed. "Yes, I understand. More reason to wait until morning then. The moors are spotted with bogs and holes. You could step into one in the dark and never be seen again."

Marek grimaced. "I take your point. Thanks for the advice; I didn't think of that. Okay, one night, and then I'm away."

As they came in, Faran was waiting. Her eyes were overly bright as she gazed at Marek, but she appeared lost for words. Will noticed that she had brushed her hair till it shone like golden silk, and she had changed into her one and only good dress. Thought Will then, Yes, one night and he's away, that's for certain.

"How is your brother?" Marek asked.

Faran seemed shyer now with the young man in her house. She smiled at him though. "He's doing fine. He woke up again so I gave him a bath and changed his bed sheets. He's more comfortable now. He even asked when he could get up."

"Not for a day or two," Marek advised. "Please, sit down." Will offered a chair.

"Thanks." Marek sat. "This is much more comfortable than hard planks."

"And so shall your rest be this night," said Will. "Faran, please make up my bed with new sheets for Marek. I'll go in with the boy."

Faran's face flushed slightly and Will had the impression she was annoyed with him for sending her away to work. But her reply came willingly enough and she smiled again at Marek as she said it. "Yes, Daddy."

Will sat down to face his guest. "A good bed, a hot bath and some solid meals inside you, not necessarily in that order, and you'll be fit for the demands of the road. I'll see that your clothes are washed and they can dry overnight by the stove. You can borrow some of mine in the meantime.

They'll be a might big, but no matter. I've some spare shaving things too you can have, if you wish." "Mr Crafter, you are a real gentleman. Thank you," Marek said.

"Can't say I can give you much more, though," Will continued. "Except some food for along the way. I'm short on finances, as you may have guessed. Caretaking doesn't pay well, but it's the life I've preferred, up till now that is."

Marek stared down at his boots which, while they were new and of the best quality, were scuffed from his having been dragged about when drugged and unconscious. "Mr Crafter, I'm sorry about all this. I've made life difficult for you."

"Not purposely."

"No, that's true. Nevertheless it is unfortunate. But I have money on me still, enough until I can earn some. I will be all right."

Will was astonished, "They didn't take your money?"

Part of the game, Marek thought. Throw me into a tower, starve me, but leave me with enough resources to get by on, if and when I escape. Enough to get me back home; except that I'm not going back, not ever. Marek did not share Silene's enthusiasm for games.

In answer to Will he only shook his head. The Caretaker would have to remain as puzzled by that as he was by most everything else that had happened. It could not be helped. "Indeed, I have enough to pay for what I've already cost you," he explained.

"No." Will was adamant. "What you did for my child makes us even, absolutely even."

Chapter Five

In her room at the top of the cottage Faran could not sleep, so she lit the lamp and turned it down on low and its soft orange glow played vague wavering shadows against the wall. The shadows matched her mood, which was sombre but ill defined. To see Marek free was a joy, yet to know that he would be gone in the morning made her sad. However he must leave, for his sake and theirs, but where would he go and what was going to become of him? Would he be safe? Would she ever see him again?

Feeling so restless made her want impossible things, so she chose the dark again lest the image in her bedroom mirror should destroy the fantasies which constantly arose in her mind. She knew that, to her father, she was still a little girl, and how could Marek not see her in the same way? She did not want to think of her child-like body because every image of it was a contradiction of what went on inside it. Inside herself she was not a child, had never been one, not from the earliest years. Always she'd had a sense of self that was vast, huge; maybe even eternal. It seemed a self that had no relation to the little girl picture. So what did it mean?

Then Marek had come and something new was born inside. The first feelings of a love which was not like the love she felt for Will or her brother, or the distant, disembodied love for the mother she had never really known. Those new feelings were the first touch of womanliness, of the woman's heart that desired its other self, in the embodiment of the male, that special friend and companion of soul which her true woman's instinct had always knew existed. She didn't fully realize this yet, it was so sudden, but she felt how much it hurt to think of Marek apart from herself.

But even if Marek stayed he would still see only the child in her, and to know that would be just as painful to bear. He would go, as he must, since his life depended on it, and she would bear that for his sake. Worse than anything would be to see him in danger again.

To Faran, Marek had ceased to be strange any more. He was only beautiful to her now, and desirable. Except that his eyes still puzzled her. She was sure that, at first, they had appeared to be brown. Then, quite undeniably, they had changed to green. And now, at dinner, she had

chanced to glance into them, shyly, because her new feelings were making her self conscious, and she would
swear that the green had shifted to a bluer hue. Yet how could such eyes be a true thing? Or was she only imagining it?

She gazed out through her window onto the darkened world. Yet the stars burned brightly in the sky and the frost below picked up a glimmer from their light, reflecting it back so that the darkness itself seemed to shine. The morning would be cold for Marek, setting out. After dinner he had asked a favor of Will that he might have the oldest of Will's two thick quilted jackets, his own coat being inadequate for a journey across the wintry moors. Well, it wasn't so much a favor, since he had offered to pay well for it, but when Will refused to accept money Marek had gotten him to agree to an exchange.

Inadequate for the climate as it was, Marek's coat was beautifully made and impossibly fine, as were the rest of his clothes, and Faran understood that Will would never wear such expensive goods. But she had plans for it. She would ask Will for it and if he thought she only wanted it for the gorgeousness of the fabric, to make something for herself out of it, well that was okay. But she'd do nothing of the sort. It was the closest she could get to keeping Marek with her, and she would never change one thread or alter one line of that beautiful coat. She had a special place picked out for it, the fragrant box where she kept all her treasures. There it would stay, folded in wreaths of lavender and sweet thyme, and when she needed to she would take it out, or merely run her hand across its softness, and think of him.

Morning came too quickly for Faran. Before she knew it she stood with her father by the front door to say goodbye. Now that the moment had arrived there seemed to be little anyone could say. At least Faran could not say what she felt and she didn't know what the others were feeling.

Clean and brushed, Marek's dark wavy hair had the gloss of a raven's wing. Now properly bathed and shaved, and standing taller than he had seemed in the tower, Marek looked like what he was, a gentleman and thus beyond them, although Will's bulky quilted jacket disguised the fact somewhat when Marek buttoned it up. The jacket pleased him, he said. It would make him less noticeable by covering up his other clothes, since he was on foot and would have to pass through civilization eventually. But no humble covering could disguise the lordly bearing, Will observed. A man used to command and privilege all his life did not walk or behave like a man born to serve others. People would notice, especially the hill people who came across high born strangers only too rarely. Will just hoped that Marek would be far enough away before his wicked brother set out to look for him.

"Well, goodbye, and thank you." Marek extended a hand.

Will returned the handshake, noticing that the weals and bruises around the healer's wrists were fading so quickly that they had almost disappeared. "Fare you well, and good luck," he said.

"I don't think luck comes into it. Better I'm careful," Marek said. He turned his eyes to Faran and smiled. "Farewell," he said softly.

Faran nodded, forcing back tears; she could not speak in case the words made her cry. But was that a look of tenderness in Marek's eyes for her? His smile lit his face and passed from him to her, and his eyes, yes, now they were a maddening blue, as blue as the skies above. He reached a hand to her, not to shake hers but to touch her lightly on the forearm. "Take care of your dad, and Young Will," he said. "And, most of all, take care of yourself."

"I will." Faran found a voice at last but her eyes were fixed not on Marek's face but on the jewel of his gold ring as it lay against her arm. If it had been an emerald not so long ago, now it was a sapphire burning blue to exactly match his eyes!

He was gone.

Will turned back to the house. "You know, I'm grateful to that young man more than I can say. I'm impressed by him. But, Faran, I'm truly glad he's gone."

Her father's words did not seem to be asking for a reply, and as for Faran, she did not feel inclined to give one.

Two days later the Towers had visitors again but this time the little gnomish man was not in charge.

He was there though, at the head of a troop of surly faces, and fawning on the one who was. The gnome was a message carrier only – a cur who brought bones to its master on demand. He ran up to the cottage, to Will, who had seen them coming and had already hurried Faran upstairs with Young Will before he opened the door.

Will was nervous but so far he was managing to keep his cool. Over the stunted form of the gnome he observed the man to whom the troop obviously deferred. It was certainly a great man, if a silk suit and a haughty demeanor were anything to go by, but just who it was he didn't know.

He soon found out. With the pompous tones of the servant of the very important, the little man informed him. "His Lordship, the Baron, is here. He won't speak to you unless it is necessary. We will approach the far tower but you will stay here. Is that clear?"

Will nodded. Perfectly clear and perfectly acceptable, as far as he was concerned.

But when they had left he shut the door and stood behind it, trying to slow his breathing; he thought he was going to hyperventilate.

The Baron here? Great Heavens, how was he going to pull off this lie?" He thought of his children, upstairs. For once in his life he had to lie and do it well; he had no choice.

By the time the troop returned, he had steadied his nerves and armed himself with an air of stupid, country bumpkin innocence. Nothing more than a great lord like the Baron De Ravana would expect from a lackey who was also a high country yokel, he guessed. He had warned Faran, had told her Marek's story on the day he left, so she understood to keep Young Will quiet and out of the way. But what she had thought of the story he hadn't been able to tell, for afterward she was only silent.

The gnome ordered him out of the house and he went, trying to make himself seem as cur-like as the man he followed. He remembered though his insistence of the night they had brought Marek, that he must know what went on in his tower. So he must go that far again at least, playing the part of the boorish Caretaker devoted to duty, but obedient and stupid with it. It was new to him, this playacting; he hoped he could pull it off successfully.

He was brought to the great man before whom he made himself bow with sufficient servility. "You are Carver, the Caretaker?" the Baron asked.

Will made himself upright again. "Crafter, Your Lordship."

So this was Silene De Ravana, the lord whose power reached its tentacles into most of life in Telaia. This was Will's employer, Marek's brother and a bad man.

The Baron stared at Will. His face had the same sort of well balanced proportions as Marek's; indeed, the two men were strikingly similar in looks. But the Baron was a good ten to fifteen years older than his brother, and time and possibly other things had hardened those looks into a mask which was much less personable. A mask etched by cold lines which would rarely bend or soften into a smile. A mask that showed haughty disapproval as its most natural expression.

"Carver, you know that a criminal was put into the tower as a sentence for the foulest crimes?" "Yes, Sir," Will replied, ignoring the mistake of his name which he guessed was deliberate. A put down of lordly proportions, the sort of thing which entertained great men, he supposed. "And you did not see that prisoner at all?"

"No, Sir, yes, Sir. That is a glimpse, when they brought him. It was very dark that night and foggy. It—"

"Yes, yes! But you did not see the prisoner's face at any time?" the Baron asked impatiently. "No, Sir."

"Then you cannot tell me what he looks like?"

Will gaped, hoping that his expression was stupid enough to convince the Baron. "No, Sir, I never saw him. It was dark and—"

His Lordship, Silene rolled his eyes, and behind him someone sniggered. "And since that night, Carver, what have you seen?"

Will dropped his jaw wider. "Seen? Sir?" "Of the prisoner!" the Baron snapped.

"I haven't seen nothing, Sir. I was told not to go near the tower and I always obey orders. I care for the Towers, and that's my job, but if you tell me not to go there, I don't. Why, did the prisoner say I was there?" Will replied. He couldn't resist that last line, although there was some danger in uttering it.

"Watch your manners! His Lordship asks the questions, not you!" barked out the gnome from just behind his master.

The Baron barely turned his head. "Thank you, Klider. Now be quiet!" His eyes returned swiftly to Will, and they narrowed. "Carver, the prisoner has escaped. What do you say to that?"

Will trembled visibly, as if in stupid awe. But the fact was that a tremble or two was not so difficult when you were really afraid. "Sir, how? I mean, he couldn't have! I mean—"

"So you claim ignorance? Or innocence?"

"Which?" said Will with, he hoped, maddening idiocy. As long as he hadn't gone too far with the act so that the Baron might actually suspect some irony. "Yes, Sir!"

More sniggering continued itself amongst the ranks of men behind, but the Baron frowned and glanced back angrily. Klider muttered something, and silence ensued.

"Both, I'll warrant, and chiefly the first," the Baron said, however he stared intently at Will for an uncomfortably long time. Then, dismissively, he turned away to address the gnome, Klider, "Just to be sure of this man's story you will search the other tower, the outbuildings and the house. Split the men up into groups and do it quickly; I don't want to waste any more time in this dreary place than I have to."

Hearing this, Will almost fainted. Of course no one would find anything outside, but in the house was Marek's coat; Faran had it. And if they were to find that, what then?

From her high window Faran watched the scene below. Young Will was with her, playing on the floor rug with one of his toys. He knew nothing of the importance of what was happening outside and after a brief look below had lost interest. He was used to seeing his daddy speaking with groups of strangers; Will did that when he took tourists through the Towers.

Faran saw the group break up and the men spread out, some heading for the nearby tower and some towards the house and back garden. She saw her father standing helplessly to one side. Very briefly, he glanced up. Even from this far she could read the fear on his face. Instantly she understood.

Quickly she turned to Young Will. "Let's play a game," she said. "Some people are coming inside and they're very silly people. Let's trick them."

"Why?" Young Will asked.

"Because they're not nice people either, that's why, and if we don't trick them they might be bad to Daddy."

Without delay Faran stripped her bed of its bottom sheet. She threw open her box of treasures and took Marek's coat and lay it on the bed, replacing the sheet on top. "Quick, get on the bed," she told her brother. "You're going to pretend you are sick."

Young Will obeyed. "I was sick before. Why do I have to be again?"

Faran tossed the blankets on top of him and tucked him in. "To trick the bad men. You have to pretend. You have to lay there and look as sick as you can and say not a single word. Can you do that?"

Young Will nodded. "Are the bad men going to hurt Daddy?"

"Only if we don't trick them properly. Remember, don't say a word and look really, really sick."

39

Heavy footsteps, sounding as if they were in a big hurry, shook the stairs, and two rough looking men burst into the room. One man began searching Faran's wardrobe, banging the door open hard enough to almost throw it off the hinges. The other man stared around and at the children. There was nothing much in the room big enough for a prisoner to hide under except the bed. He stared at Young Will then at Faran.

"What's he in bed for?"

Faran kept her face solemn. "He's sick."

"Look under the bed," said the man at the wardrobe.

"The doctor said he's highly infectious," Faran said and, appropriately, Will coughed and, wearily, closed his eyes.

The other man backed away slightly. "Under the bed," the wardrobe man repeated. He was obviously the one in charge.

"Let me." Faran went to the bed and lifted the hanging blanket aside. From his safe distance the man bent and peered. "Nothing under there."

The man giving the orders then began searching all the drawers. Faran wondered what he hoped to find. A very small escapee perhaps? He stopped when he came to her treasure chest. It was now locked. "What's in this?"

Gazing up at him with big, wide open eyes, Faran said, "That's my glory box, for when I get married."

The man sniggered. "Open it."

She took her key and opened the chest. Fragrances of lavender and thyme wafted into the room. "Okay. Let's go," the man said to the other.

Faran waited until the house was quiet before she went near the window. It seemed an age before she heard the sounds of vehicles on the move up the road, then she looked out. Her father was beating his retreat up the path whilst trying to appear calm and unhurried.

"Can I get up now?" Young Will asked.

"Of course." Faran hugged him. "You were the best, Willie. You were the greatest! Just wait till I tell Dad!"

"I was so afraid when they went to search the house," Will confessed. "I almost lost it when the Baron gave the order."

Faran gasped "That was Marek's brother?"

Will watched as his daughter smoothed wrinkles from Marek's coat. He saw how carefully she folded it and tucked it away, leafing the sweet smelling herbs through the folds. He knew then why she had really asked to have it, but he was beyond caring at the moment. "Yes. Come to gloat, I imagine.

But it was odd; he didn't seem all that upset at finding his prisoner had bolted. Marek said some strange things to me when we were coming to the house. I didn't understand him and I don't understand his brother either. They're a peculiar lot, those high families, nothing like us at all. I guess that's why I'll never work this out. We're better off not having anything more to do with them. I'm glad we won't be."

Faran did not dare look up. "What do you mean, Dad?"

"I had to play a bit of a game with His Lordship," Will explained. "I told him I couldn't be a caretaker any more because my little boy got too sick in this cold climate. Your trick fitted in quite well because the men who'd been in your room said there was no one but two children in the house and one of them was sick."

Faran was unsure. "Did he believe you? He didn't think you wanted to leave because of everything else, did he?"

"I hope not. I don't think so. I'm afraid I played the idiot too well, I almost convinced myself. Silene said I could leave at any time. He didn't offer to pay me what I'm owed for my long service though,nbut I don't care. I just want out of here."

The wild hopes that still held fast to Faran's heart seemed suddenly swept away, beyond all saving.

If they left the Towers how would Marek ever find her again, or she him? She could not face her father lest he see the pain she was feeling. She stared blindly into her box then, bitterly, she closed the lid. "Where are we going then, Dad? Where will we live after this?"

"Well, I've been thinking about that ever since this terrible business began. You know my sister lives down south. She was often after me to come and join her there. I'll get work of some kind, I'm sure. It's a long way from here but a change will do us all good. We have to forget about what happened here and get on with our lives. Such lives as those others live are not for us to be involved with."

Chapter Six

For seven days and nights Marek roamed the lonely hills. Three of those nights were spent half frozen in shelter worse than any tower, but he had supplies from Will's store and a small, old fashioned flint spark maker that was better than matches because it did not run out. He made a good fire from old dead wood and dried bracken and counted himself fortunate. At least he wasn't a prisoner, and a little frost meant nothing to a free man.

Will had given him a compass and a map, hand drawn but filled with the caretaker's detailed knowledge of the high country. Will had been born and bred up here, he said. He knew every village and every ruin of the past. The villages were all one day's walk apart, built to suit times when feet were the most common form of travel. That would have been okay for Marek, had he been taking the roads, but overland, skirting bogs and the dangers of a few old mine workings and having to climb one or two rocky outcrops, occasionally made the journey longer and he had to sleep out in the open. The rest of the time he managed to make the villages just upon nightfall and since every settlement sported a public house or hotel, and it was the off season, he was able to buy a bed and a meal.

He was glad he was not as soft as he had been a couple of years earlier. Then he was twenty three and it was the terrible time when his mother had died. Her death had come as a great shock to his system. He felt the loss acutely, for she'd always been such a special person in his life, the only one who loved him in a loveless world, the only one he had loved, and it had shaken him out of a complacency that was leading him deeper into dangerous waters. The kind of world he and families like his inhabited assumed certain things about life. Things like privilege and power and the right to use them without conscience, they classed as belonging to themselves by some sort of divine decree.

Only his mother had not given tacit approval to these beliefs, although she was never allowed to voice objections. Her innate distaste for such things and her frustration in being silenced led her to try to save himself, her youngest child, the only child of her older years. The other children had gone all too easily into the corrupted world; it was too late to save them. Then, when Marek was twelve years old, his brother, Silene, had

42

swooped on him like a bird of prey, trying to break her influence and draw Marek into the net he had prepared. Why Silene would want to bother with a boy half his age, Marek didn't understand then. But he understood now. How successfully Silene captured him and, as he grew, wanting the exciting, manly things which a big, important brother could provide, seemed a victory for the Dark. Marek sometimes thought he had broken his mother's heart, however she never let on that she was hurt by his childish betrayal, and she never gave up on him, always welcoming him with love whenever he came back to her.

But with her death he was instantly taken back to that world of heart and light she had striven to keep before his gaze. And to be able to deal with the struggle of feelings and contradictions, he had to escape. Her death was a good excuse to run and even Silene had countenanced a "holiday". Visiting the home of an old school friend by the sea, Marek recovered his equilibrium, and discovered a vision. At that time something of importance happened which changed everything and taught him what health and happiness were. In the two years since, he'd grown fitter and stronger than he ever was before and he would never go back to Silene.

But he didn't want to think any more about that for the time being. After seven days and thanks to Will's excellent map, he'd come to the margin of the high country and was standing on the very edge of the escarpment, gazing at the view below. It was almost like being in a cloud land above the earthly world, out of time and space, in a place where the two worlds regarded each other but never met.

Except that he was looking forward to being warm again he almost did not want to go down. He could see the length of the whole plain, even to the bright, far off glint of the sea. The lowlands were spotted with so many towns that he would easily make his way between them and find work when his money ran out. What work he could do would be very different to what he had been trained for, which was only to control and order and deceive. Young Will's illness had taught him something more about himself. As he had been told one day in the sunshine by the sea, but at the time had not fully understood, he was a healer.

Descending to the lowlands meant that Marek would now have to use the road. He wasn't keen on that but he pulled the quilted coat around him and vowed to speak to no one and to not stop until he had reached the first town. From this height he could already see where he was headed. The plain looked like a child's printed bed quilt, a coverlet of green with lumps and bumps and little valleys decorated with embroidery patches of red brick and chimney stacks and swathes of dark forest and farms.

In the high country he'd made his journeying more valuable by collecting the various herbs and flowers that he knew were commonly used in natural medicine and stuffing them into his bag of supplies. Just over two years ago he was absolutely ignorant of anything to do with healing of any kind, although it had always interested him. But what he'd learned that springtime by the sea had pushed him into a study of botanicals, medicinal and otherwise. Of course he didn't know as much as a lifetime could teach, but he was learning. When Silene discovered his interest, as Silene invariably did, he pooh-poohed the idea. "What do you want to bother with that for? People don't need that old fashioned nonsense any more, when there's a drug for every ill. That is, unless you've found a way of making some big cash out of it."

And Marek gave answer before he thought, saying to Silene that helping others interested him more than making big fortunes, and that answer was the beginning of the slide from grace which had dropped him into his present trouble. Silene never asked an idle question, he always had a reason.

And the part about the cash, that was irrelevant but significant. Silene liked money as well as anyone and he always had plenty without having to worry about where it came from. But money was only a side interest; it was merely the energy to buy more control. By mentioning it he had just been seeking Marek out, to understand Marek's mind of the moment. And he didn't like what he heard.

After making the slip up over the cash, Marek realized that he'd been blinded to his brother's deviousness simply because eleven years of companionship with Silene had made him less vigilant than he ought to be in regard to the man. Or asleep; yes, asleep was closer to the truth. At twenty three he had only just begun to truly wake up, so a slip up was inevitable, if unwise.

He should have been more careful, Marek told himself, because Silene's anger at watching the little brother, whom he'd championed and trained patiently for so long, turn his back on everything he thought important and valuable, was fierce. However it was hardly reason enough to send an errant, younger brother to a tower. That required another, much stronger reason.

Marek saw very few people or traffic on the road to the first town.

That was because not many journeyed to or from the high country in the winter. He had the leisure then to make a few unobserved excursions aside into fields where wild weeds grew amongst the crops. He added to his store such plants as he knew to be useful. In a way, though, he understood that for him, as a healer, the plants would be not so much necessary as they would be window dressing. It was not substances which healed; the healing lay in the energies of the body itself and in the focus of the healer. Substances assisted, and he would use them for that and to draw all attention away from his part in the healing process. What he had managed to do for Young Will he could never be seen to do again. After all, a man on the run did not go looking for fame and attention exactly.

Arriving at the town in late afternoon, the first thing Marek did was to seek out a secondhand clothes store where he exchanged his clothes for the everyday kit of a working man. Except for the good boots, which he kept for the sake of his feet. Between him and the shopkeeper it was a bargain on both sides. The shop owner got to keep goods far better than he swapped for, and Marek got instant anonymity for free. He felt happier, knowing that now he would be less noticeable on the road. Even if Silene traced him this far, the sitings would most likely stop here as he blended in with the crowd.

Two things were a problem, though: the ring, which had been too tight to get off for several years now, and his eyes. To solve the ring problem he went to another store and keeping his left hand out of sight, bought gloves. His eyes were more difficult, they were unique and would probably get him into trouble one day. Yet people were generally very careless in their observations of others. Ask anyone the color of the eyes of someone they'd just met and they wouldn't have a clue.

Marek found temporary lodging in a dingy little inn way off the main street. It looked like a place where sailors might hang out and there was a bright hued, screeching bird in the front bar, the kind of bird which came from exotic lands. However they were too far inland for sailors. Marek intended to reach the sea coast in three or four days, where he could lose himself in a maze of busy ports and no one would know which way he had gone. Only Silene would know how he fared. Well, at least that he was alive. Just as he would have known instantly, without even being there, if Marek had died in the tower.

In a scruffy room which smelled of rising damp and cheap booze and was not much bigger than a large cupboard, Marek tossed off his jacket and flopped onto the bed. The bed springs squealed in protest and sagged and the mattress produced a new lump every time he moved. But he was too tired to care. He pulled off boots and gloves, the gloves were hot in this stuffy hole. He stared down at his ring. Traitor, he thought. Damn you! For the hundredth time he struggled to get it off, with no luck. In recent weeks he had tried everything short of amputating his finger, he wanted it off nearly that much. It was ironic that, had he starved to death and become a skeleton abandoned on a tower floor, the damn thing might well have fallen off, eventually.

It was the ring which linked him to Silene, and betrayed him constantly. Silene wore one the same and by this he could read how Marek was, just as now, if he'd wanted to, Marek could focus on the jewel at the center and on Silene, and know whether he was ill or well, or whatever. But he had no desire to focus his consciousness on Silene, no desire at all.

The link the brothers shared, and which Marek was determined to destroy, was more than familial. The link was Brotherhood. A Brotherhood of Mastery, and Silene its Grand Master. His power was far reaching and much more than merely temporal and it was not a power he would let go of willingly. It was power he would fight for until it was either lost to him or he had won.

Marek gave up his battle with the ring. Rest seemed the most important thing now. He let himself relax, into the hollows and lumps of the bed, and in seconds he was asleep.

Somebody was singing, not a song of words, but with high, sweet sounds which rippled the air then dove into mellow heartfelt notes, bringing tears to the eyes because it was so beautiful. The light was peculiar around him; it was crystalline and filled with rainbows. It seemed that every object, including himself, shone from within. Each thing of air, earth, sea and fire shone with its own special rainbow rays. He looked at himself shining a pure white light which dazzled him because it was so bright.

He was not dreaming; he was remembering.

Somewhere in the middle of the night he came awake, not fully, but into that state halfway between sleep and waking where the mind is fluid and conscious but unbound from the strictures of reason and objectivity. His bed was a boat and he rocked above shallow green water. He could hear the cries of sea birds and smell the salt and taste it on his tongue.

It was real. 'Reality is relative," Marielle said with a mischievous laugh. "You are your own reality."

She had hair so white that it outshone the quartzite glint of the sand. It waved out from her head as the wind lifted it. She liked to wear seashells in her hair and sometimes a piece of pink fringed seaweed. Marek could not work out how she managed to keep them there without their falling out.

Her skin was a coppery brown, like the ochred earth. She was not from Telaia. "My home is far away. It's an island in the middle of the greenest, bluest, deepest of oceans. Not like the shallow waters here which are always churning against the land, always grey, always in trouble. One day you will go to my island, my dear," she told Marek. "My people shall welcome you, for they shall know who you are."

"Are you alive? Does it hurt?" she had said, finding him half drowned and washed up like flotsam on the sand.

From above the elbow nearly to his wrist, Marek's right arm was blown up like a balloon and bluer than a jellyfish sting. "The storm blew me in and my boat got holed by the reef," he explained. "I managed to swim ashore, but not here, up there." He gestured weakly with his good arm to a headland some distance away. "I was okay until I got ashore, then I had to go and slip on the damn rocks."

She helped him up and dusted the sand off his clothes, as if to make him tidy, at least. "It's the green weed, makes treacherous going when it's wet. You took quite a tumble. But you got this far."

"I was making for the trees. I passed out."

Marielle inspected him. "There's a gash and a bump on the side of your head. You must have been out a while, your clothes are nearly dry."

He hadn't realized. His arm hurt so much he hadn't noticed his head.

Marek's friend, Hal, had told him that the islands off this part of Telaia's coast were all uninhabited and uninhabitable. "No fresh water," he explained. But Marielle said she lived here. She led him back into the trees, helping him because moving with the pain in his arm was making him dizzy. He was too dazed to notice how he got in through her front door and was inside before he had the presence of mind to look around.

They were in a cave, not a house. The walls were lit by several low-burning lanterns perched on rock cut ledges at eye height which Marielle turned up so that Marek saw the personal touches here and there which made the cave a home. Marielle had a few pieces of rough furniture, a table, a bed, shelves covered with rocks and unpolished crystals, dried ferns and the skeletons of small sea creatures. The problem of fresh water was solved when she led him further, through a fissure as wide as a door, into another, deeper cavern. Here he discovered strange, blood red walls illumined by several small chimneys coming from outside, and a pool of clear, drinkable water, although it was stained by the same redness as the walls. "A spring of chalybeate," Marielle explained. "It travels from somewhere on the island's little mountaintop and gathers here. I've never known it to run out although sometimes it drops a bit."

She bathed his arm in the chill water and tended his head. Beside the spring, on a stone table, were more crystals and some closed ceramic jars. She showed him the pastes inside the jars. "Herbs. My special preparations," she said. Later on she would show him how they were made. Right now she palpated his aching arm with careful, searching fingers, seeking out the damage, then she spread it with one of the pastes and wrapped it in soft cloth. Marek cradled the arm against his chest, he could not move it and even her gentle touch had made him want to scream. "I'd say that you've cracked your elbow, the bone just above, but not all the way through. There's no distortion, nothing sticking out; it will be okay," Marielle told him as she made a sling which she tied firmly so that the arm would stay hanging in the correct position. "You need rest. Are you hungry? Young men usually are," she said.

He didn't need to eat but he had to lie down. Marielle's bed was small and cramped and his arm ached abominably. Because of the pain he did not think he could sleep, but Marielle knelt by him and with the familiarity of a grandmother, brushed her hand across his forehead. Almost immediately he felt drowsy. "Sleep, Marek, sleep," she said softly. "You are safe here; you are almost home."

As Marek drowsed, his dulling brain struggled with a vague thought. What did she mean ... almost home? He was sure he had not told her his name either, so how did she know it?

Chapter Seven

The town of Kallana was at least three hours walk away, a hazy vision on another hill. The road ahead was long and wide, the sea coast still distant and beckoning. Marek had a purpose in seeking the sea; he wanted to find Marielle again.

Orchards filled the valley, but at this time of year they were bare and stick like. Following the wide avenue of the road, Marek seemed to pass through a world of trees like broken hands with thin, reaching fingers. There was a silence here, and an emptiness. Yet visible off the roadway, behind the woven screen of gray-brown sticks, were the huge orchard sheds and the dwellings of the farm workers, and a faint hum of voices and machinery came to him like the far off drone of bees.

He was hungry and hadn't eaten for many hours. It was a long way to Kallana and food. He wondered how he would be received if he tried to buy a little fruit at one of the orchard sheds. Well, he thought, I'm not going to get anything in this world by just wondering.

He chose the next gate he came to and walked gingerly up the length of the drive. He wasn't used to asking things from strangers, not that he was begging anything for free. However, with the upbringing of his kind he had never been taught to ask, only to expect and to demand. These days on the road had been a lesson to him that what some took for granted most others had to work hard for. It was a novel conception to realize that now he was a part of the laboring majority.

There was something wrong in this place though, some sort of commotion Marek could hear but not see. Somewhere behind or inside one of the sheds, he thought. He followed the sounds and turned a corner.

At the wide open doorway of a shed crammed with large vats, a group of agitated men and women crowded around a woman with a baby in her arms. Although no one was actually doing anything, the whole scene gave the impression of frantic activity having just occurred, and the energies of all concerned were so anxious and aroused that the air fairly trembled with upset.

They were all so concentrated on the woman and child that nobody noticed a stranger's arrival. "What's happened here?" Marek asked the nearest man.

The man gave him a blank stare. "The baby fell into a vat. He must have crawled up onto the stirring step just after his mother set him down. But nobody saw and when she couldn't find him we looked everywhere before we thought of the vat. Who would have thought the little chap could get up there?"

Marek peered over the shoulder of a woman in front who was crying softly to herself. The distraught mother also sobbed. She was on her knees, cradling the baby. The skin of the half naked child was tinted all wrong. Some of it was stain from the juice in the vat but the rest evidenced a distinct lack of oxygen.

"Poor little devil, he's drowned," said the man.

That baby isn't lost, Marek thought. The energies enclosing mother and child were confused and stirred by the mother's emotions, but the child's light was still present and struggling against contraction and the oppression of the mother's fear. Fear, the greatest enemy, how easily it controlled the human mind. Marek was not immune to it himself either, not yet.

He had to act. This was no time for disguise or playing with herbs and potions. Marek pushed forward through the crowd. "Let me help," he said, kneeling by the mother. "There might be something I can do."

The mother looked up at him, dumbly, yet she clung to the child, refusing to let go. Persistent, Marek prised her hands away, finger by finger. "I can help you," he whispered. The crowd had ceased its murmuring and no one moved to interfere. They were as much in shock as the mother and a newcomer's sudden appearance had yet to impact on their stunned brains.

With the baby's head cradled in his gloved left hand, Marek pulled off his other glove with his teeth. He let the head roll back and covered the baby's nose and mouth with his own mouth and breathed gently. He massaged the tiny chest and held his hand over the heart, concentrating the light there. Again he breathed, massaged and breathed, while he focused the light. He was oblivious now to anything else; even thought of the mother or the others had vanished along with his surroundings. He focused from a vast distance which was, at the same time, immediate and utterly present. It was being both vast and centered all together, and being that Light which was One Thing and Every Thing.

The little heart jumped; the baby's light cleared and held. Marek felt a rise and fall under his hand. He smoothed a purple-stained fringe of hair from the baby's forehead and the child opened it's eyes. It stared for a moment, trying to focus, then seeing that Marek was not it's mother, screwed up it's face and bawled loudly.

The baby's father had been summoned from where he had been working in another, distant orchard.

He arrived to find the crisis over and a complete stranger downing tea and fruitcake in his kitchen, while the center of the crisis, the child, was blissfully asleep.

Without wanting to or trying, Marek overheard the parents" conversation in the next room. The mother was still tearful, but all of a wonder to tell her husband what had happened. The father, though, was merely grateful, yet for a few moments there was tension in the air as he sounded off at his wife for having lost sight of the baby in the first place. It was interesting how differently people reacted to their fear, Marek thought. For some, the reaction was to dissolve into helplessness; for others, a shift to anger and attack. He wondered how he would react if exposed to some terrifying fear. When Silene trapped him and drugged him and locked him up in the tower, his fear had first manifested as the despair of abandonment, and then, afterward, as doubts of survival. Only after that had he stood aside from the fear and begun to think clearly. But never once had the fear made him want to give in. The urge to turn away from Silene and all he represented was a million times greater than any fear.

The father returned to his work and the young, chastened mother returned to the kitchen, to Marek. She gazed at him with such grateful, worshipping eyes that he was embarrassed. "This is good cake," he said awkwardly.

Her name was Anna and she cared absolutely nothing about cake. Instead she was interested in him. "I can see you are a gentleman, despite your clothes," she said. "Though I've not had much to do with gentlemen, I can see that."

Marek did not answer. So much for disguises, he thought. What now then?

"You're an educated man. Would I be prying to ask why you are wandering like a gypsy?"

You would be, Marek thought. Yet he answered as honestly as he could. "I'm not wandering. I'm headed for the coast, to see someone."

"But on foot?"

"I like it this way. I want my life to be something different from before."

"Oh," she answered, perhaps not really understanding. "Where did you learn to do what you did for my son?"

"From an old woman, a healer. She taught me about plants too: how to use them." "Like that medicine you made for my boy?"

"Yes. It's not really a medicine, just a restorative to make sure he's free from any after effects." The young mother smiled. "Twice a day, right?"

"For a couple of days, yes. But he's strong, your son. I know he'll be just fine."

She began to clear away the tea things, stacking the cups and plates in the sink and throwing a cotton apron on over her dress. "Are you still hungry? Would you like something more?"

"Well, I wouldn't say no to a piece of fruit," Marek said. "It's actually what I came here for, to see if I could buy some."

She turned to him, flushing. "Buy? No need for you to pay for anything here. There's a big bowl of fruit in the other room. Take as much you want." She laughed. "If there's one thing we're not short of, it's fruit."

He heard her splashing in the washing up water as he took two apples and a pear. As he came back into the kitchen she tossed him a towel. "You're welcome to anything we have here. I can see that you're tired and dusty. There's a bathroom two doors down the hall if you wish to use it."

Later, Anna entertained Marek with the baby, now awake and seemingly no worse for wear. "He's a real little rascal. Always into everything. I get exhausted sometimes just trying to keep up. How long will he stay this awful color, do you think?"

It was only the stain of the fruit, so Marek made a guess. "A couple of bathes ought to do it."

Anna humped the baby on her hip and took Marek to a little side room filled with pictures of many kinds. She seemed very much to want to share herself with him. "It's my passion, besides Baby Jo," she explained. "I've always loved to paint and draw although I haven't had much time since he came along."

Marek was astonished by the vista of talent he saw before him. "They're extremely good. They're beautiful. What does your husband think of them?"

Her face reddened with pleasure. She said, "Oh, he likes them. He thinks they're okay."

While the baby crawled about the floor and tried to climb up Marek's legs and anything else perpendicular, Anna asked him more about healing. She wanted to know whether he intended to make a profession out of it, how long he had been practising, would he come back this way again? "There are a lot of people around here who would love to have you stay. The country folk don't like the city doctors at all and the doctors won't come here anyway because they don't think they'll make a lot of money. We like the old ways best, we always have. We like healers, not drug merchants who only care about their purses."

"I'd like to do it full time," Marek said. "But for the moment I have to keep on the move. And I've no way to advertise myself, short of carrying a great big sign."

He had meant the last for a joke but she took him seriously. "You could carry a sign, I mean." At his bemused face she elaborated, explaining, "The old herb-healers in Kallana, and elsewhere, I guess, all have a symbol painted above the doors of their offices. The medical doctors hate them and their signs and have tried so many times to put them out of business and to prevent them showing an advertisement, but they never succeed. You could have that symbol on your kit bag, then wherever you go people would see it and know. If you like I'll paint it for you, it's the least I can do to say thank you."

Marek was touched by her thoughtfulness. It seemed to him that beginning with his spell in the tower the world was showing him another, kinder face. Faran, Will and now, Anna, were part of that world he had entered not recently but two years ago, however they added another dimension.

Marielle had opened his understanding, stimulating the desire to change, to turn away from what he had been involved in. And helping him find in himself the courage to do it. So she was his catalyst, his opening to awareness. Through her he had seen where he wanted to go, if not exactly how to get there. There were, after all, some things he must discover for himself as he lived and moved through the world.

Beauty and love and light were here in this world, if you wanted them enough to look for them.

From his high perch, Silene was always contemptuous of the rest of humanity, saying that they were nothing more than stupid, obedient animals. Silene believed that few men were his equals, very few, and there was only one he had considered to be on a par with him in power and ability. The rest were nothing to Silene, and except that they were useful to him, he would gladly cast their consciousness into the abyss. Sure, he was human himself, or something resembling it, but so long ago that time meant almost nothing, he had sold his humanity for something else. Marek saw now how blind Silene really was, and how blind he himself had been once. But then how could anyone so blinded recognize beauty, love and light when his own consciousness was immersed so completely in ugliness, hate and darkness?

"You are your own reality," Marielle told him. Thus Marek's reality changed as his understanding and his point of view did. When he had said goodbye to Marielle on the island, she kissed him, then touched him lightly on the forehead, saying, "The magic is in there, in you, my dear." She waved her hand across the line of the horizon. "And the magic is out there, in the others who will resonate with you. Go and unleash the magic. Go and be the magician you are. Make your magic in the world, because the world needs it very badly."

Well, he had uncovered a little of that magic already. Faran, Will, Anna: they raised in his thoughts such possibilities...

Chapter Eight

The sail dipped, sagged, then snapped to attention as the wind picked up the boat and tore with it into the tight little harbor of the island. In winter the eastern shores of Telaia were harried by storms and the seaports often closed down for days at a time. Marek had taken a big risk in making for the island, and for several hair raising moments he thought he would arrive there in the same condition as two years ago. But this time he made it in one piece, and hopeful. Would Marielle still be here?

At first, coming to the coast in wild weather, he suffered only disappointment, believing that now he would never see her. To find a boat to take him to the island was impossible since no one was willing to hire out anything that might not come back. And besides, Marek didn't wish to spend money needlessly. The sign made by Anna had brought him some work, enough to restock his dwindling wallet, but a worry he could not seem to put his finger on continued to pester, to keep the money where it was.

Marek had already given up the plan when suddenly he remembered Hal. Or, more particularly, Hal's parents' fleet of small sailing dinghies. They had half a dozen kept in boat sheds at the beach on their estate, and in winter they were not there, because they always chased the sun and wintered in the South.

He had never thought of himself as a thief before, even though, like Silene, he had stolen much, had appropriated much to himself during the selfish living of many lives. It was this life as Marek, though, which counted, and Marek did not want to be a thief. So he had every intention of returning the boat, without damage and undetected.

The beach did not welcome him. It was wild and lonely, scooped out by the wind and waves and empty even of the screeching gulls. Marek fought his way through white foam and tied the boat to the silvered relic of a huge tree lodged deep and high in dry sand. The island looked as if it had been stripped of life. Some of its trees were down, the rest blown ragged, and the ground was wet and matted with soggy leaves, and spongy underfoot.

Marek pushed through undergrowth which seemed to weep. He knew the place so well he could have navigated in his sleep, but time and wind had made a few changes and he was forced to work his way around a tangle of fallen trunks and branches to gain entrance to the cave. By this very fact he knew in that instant that the place was deserted.

It was disappointing. No, it was worse. The place, with Marielle's presence enlivening it, had remained in his imagination as a center, a place to which he could still attach some thought of belonging to someone or something, and return to in spirit. And now it was empty. Not since he'd woken to the cold, dark walls of the tower and knew himself to be a prisoner, had he felt as lost as he did now. He shouldn't have, he told himself. After all, what did he expect? That Marielle would wait around indefinitely for him to turn up? She'd wanted to return to her home, was planning it even as they met, so of course she had. Come to think of it he had never even asked her why she was on this island in the first place.

Which explained the measure of his self obsession in those days. And his current expectation, did it not show that he was not yet free? He was still capable of believing the illusion that the world revolved around his own concerns but he desired no self recrimination. Putting the self through trials of criticism and reproach was the sort of thing which would have Silene chortling with satisfaction, if he knew. Self reproach meant self doubt, and that meant the constant return to fear. And fear was Silene's greatest and most effective tool in his management of the human race.

With some sort of trepidation, Marek stepped in through the cave mouth. He didn't know why but he felt hollow inside, like an empty vessel waiting to be filled. Yet all that could fill him now must be remembrance, for the place was bare, swept clean of Marielle or any inhabitant.

Marek left the small, outer cave, pressing through the fissure to the larger one behind. The inner cave greeted him with its strange blood red luminosity and the odd, reflective shimmer of its pool. And it too was empty.

He sat for a while by the pool, staring into the red chalybeate water, without thought. He was startled awake by a sound of dull drumming. Rain. He returned to the outer cave and peered outside. Another storm on the way, maybe a big one.

He ran through the rain all the way to the beach where he pulled the boat higher onto the sand and secured it well. Then he got thoroughly drenched collecting wood for a fire and dragging it back to the cave. At least he had shelter, warmth and the food he'd had the foresight to carry with him. But he was now effectively marooned.

The wind and rain played their duet of wild music all afternoon and on into the night. When Marek was not coaxing the fire along and watching his wet clothes steam like cooling hotcakes, or finding something in his cache of food to cook and eat, he was staring into the pool, at the golden lights of the fire which tinted the red water with fierce orange suns. When he was not staring into the pool, his gaze was following the curling smoke as it found the chimneys in the cave roof. When he was not watching the smoke rise, he was thinking. When he was not thinking, he was sleeping, fitfully. And all about him, sharing every activity like a silent companion, was the image of another time. Lonely and empty as this cave was, yet it was alive with memory.

A twinge in his elbow where it pressed against the hard ground made him remember the day that Marielle found him. The elbow ached occasionally even now, when the air turned damp and cold. It had troubled him sorely in the tower until Faran's gift of the fleeces had made him warmer. However, with Marielle's care the break had healed so quickly that he was amazed. When he awoke that first time in Marielle's narrow bed, after an incredible sleep of twelve hours, he found his arm so free of pain that he could scarce believe it.

He was interested right away in the powers and potions of the strange woman, but she held off his questions for three whole days before she would speak plainly. Instead she began to talk to him and draw him out of his shell, and by her comments and counsels, it was to Marek as if she knew the intimacies of his life from start to present.

She had a merry face, with bright brown eyes which appeared ready to crinkle into a laugh at every opportunity. Yet she knew that she was dealing with a desperate soul and was appropriately solemn and stern, although her gaze at Marek always held a smile which was compassionate and loving. This puzzled Marek at first, for he did not know why a stranger should love him; however, before the first day was out her smile seemed the most natural thing in the world.

"What makes you so unhappy?" Marielle asked.

How did she know he was unhappy? Marek hadn't realized it showed. "My mother just died."

Marielle bent her white head in assent. "I know you miss her. You

57

relied a lot on her." She glanced up and fixed his gaze with such a look that he could not turn away. "And now you must rely upon yourself; there is no other way. You are your only hope, young man. So, tell me, what makes you so unhappy?"

Marek flushed. He felt like a fly caught in the web of a kindly spider. He chewed his thumb and tried to avoid her eyes, but she said firmly, "Don't look away. Look at me and tell me."

"I don't know," he said. "For as long as I can remember I've never been really happy. I only know what unhappiness feels like."

"So what does it feel like?" Marielle asked.

He was about to be broken down into little pieces by this woman and he was helpless to stop it, he realized. He wished he had his boat back whole and seaworthy so that he might escape. How could he tell anyone his deepest miseries? They were his entire life; he had spent twenty-three years perfecting them. He was ashamed.

Shuddering, Marek gave in. "It feels like being lost, like being in a prison, like someone has roped me to the ground and I can't break free."

"Yes?"

Must he say more? She would not let him run away and there was nowhere to run to, so he must. "It feels like darkness … pressure … something hard and heavy holding me down. I can't be what I want to be; it prevents me!" Marek began breathing quickly. He was conscious of his heart beating hard under the press of his broken arm, of damp, sticky palms and a sweat starting across his forehead. "It's knowing that I'm all wrong as I am; it's doing things I don't like; it's feeling disgusted with myself." He was on a roll now, unstoppable. "Doing things with my brother, Silene. Things I hate … that make me feel sick. It's … it's Silene, he's been controlling me since I was a kid, he makes me so unhappy!"

"Hold it there!" Marielle silenced him, placing a hand over his. Her hand was much smaller than his yet when she gripped his he could feel the unyielding strength in her fingers. "This is not about your brother. What he does is his own business. We're not here to discuss him. And it's not him that makes you unhappy, and you know it. Forget him."

"But he's part of it," Marek insisted. "He twists my life, he hurt my mother, he makes me so angry—"

"No." Marielle tightened her grip. "Look at me. Your unhappiness and your anger are not because of him. You chose the things which cause them yourself. They are nothing to do with him, they never have been. You can't deny that."

Could he deny it? Did he even want to? His head felt so heavy and he realized that was because a whole fountain of tears was about to burst itself from his eyes. He didn't want to cry. He tried to pull his hand away so that he could shield his face and maybe stop the tears, but Marielle wouldn't loosen her grip. He struggled against collapse, but it only made things worse.

"Let it go," Marielle said. "Let go, child. Let yourself be."

And he let go. Tears were much more than release, they washed him clean, they purified. Not just the miseries of one short life but the accumulated dross: the sickness, the pain, the guilt and despair of many lives lost in selfishness and greed, in the lust for power and fame, in colossal deceit. Marek had always known that he could master the world and that many of his former lives had been devoted to ruling and controlling the obedient and stupid beasts, as Silene disparagingly called other men. It was why Silene had wanted him so much, for he recognized power and mastery when he saw it, even in a twelve year old boy. A power and mastery as great as his own, and, he hoped, as corrupt.

Yes, tears released him; tears remade him. The burdens of centuries which had held him down, like chains, were built of the tears of a grief which had been always denied and never expressed. They had hardened like ice into a weight so heavy and cold that he had thought he would never get out from under. Then along came Marielle and melted them. She put her arms around him when the tears were ebbing. "My dear, you have nothing to reproach yourself with, you have done only as other men have done. And I say, what's done is done and let there be an end to it."

"But why did it take so long? Why didn't I turn away long ago, since I hated everything I was doing so much?"

"Why?" Marielle held his hand gently. "Power is all too easy, too seductive and although it moves only through illusion, yet it gives everything an ego desires in this world. It becomes a drug, a habit hard to break. To turn away means to abandon this illusory world, totally, and to remake another, truer world in yourself, as was meant to be. But you had already turned away before you ever came to this island, otherwise you would not have sought me."

"Did I seek you? I thought I just happened here, in the storm," Marek said, in wonder.

Marielle smiled. "Does the sun shine? Or the wind blow? Is water wet?" She laughed. "You were always wanting to remember home, so you came to me. As I said, you wanted your freedom long ago and you understood that it was attainable. This life as Marek is the flower, the blossom of knowledge and a long held desire, and the fruit follows quickly once the flower is unfolded."

A springtime sun warmed bare flesh, it did not burn. Its heat felt good on Marek's shoulders and back. The sun energized him; it brought him alive again.

He watched as Marielle stood in the wash of a breaking wave. She did a little dance, twisting her body in opposition to her feet and as the wave ran backwards from the sand her feet were lost in two wet hollows. She bent and caught something up in her hand. She showed him. "Clam. Clams make a good, tasty meal. We'll get a batch."

"An easy way to fish," Marek said. "Why do you twist about like that?"

"To dig them up. You feel them with your feet and the twisting helps the water wash them out. Have a go."

He tried, with no luck at first. Marielle, however, seemed to know where they were somehow because she never missed. After another wave had swept the sand, leaving it smooth and glistening, she pointed out a tiny hole and an air bubble, and at last Marek was successful.

"You have to know what you're looking for, otherwise you just drift and fool around and get wet all for nothing. And to know what you want you have to observe what is. You have to look and pay attention. See and hear and feel," Marielle said.

Marek knew she was not talking only of clams and fishing. "Will you teach me about healing?" he asked.

Marielle counted the clams. "A dozen and a half, no more. Good. We should never take more than we need." She straightened. "There's nothing I can teach you about healing; you're already a healer, you just haven't remembered that yet. But I will show you what I know and how to make medicines. And maybe I will remind you of a few things."

60

Marielle's few things turned out to be a revelation of the whole secret of his existence. And she was right when she said that all he needed was reminding, for everything that was revealed he had always known somewhere deep inside himself. It was as if Marielle had discovered a lost key, a key to the gateway of his true nature, and handed it to him, to open that gateway for himself.

She called him a magician.

Which was what he was. And which was what had drawn Silene to him, for he knew it too.

Magician was not a fashionable word in modern Telaia. It was an archaic title which popular belief relegated scornfully to an ancient, more fanciful time, when the Towers had been but newly built. But the modern sleepers of Telaia, they did not know that nothing ever changes in the illusory world of mankind. Ensorcelled they were in olden times, ensorcelled they were now. Beguiled, entrapped and manipulated by the hands of magicians as they had always been, their minds held in darkness, their spirits imprisoned by illusory fears. And Silene was the Master Magician, although there were others, darker and unknown to the world that were more powerful still.

"I don't want to be that any more," Marek said to Marielle.

"And, understanding and feeling as you do now, you shall not," Marielle replied. "But the knowledge and the skills you carry are still there; they only need to be redirected. It's where you turn your face to that matters, my dear, and for all of us it is the same. We all have skills, so how do we use them? Either we serve the illusory world with them or we turn our faces to our Light and do what we originally chose to do. There are no half measures in this; it is all or nothing; it is complete or not at all."

"You are a magician," she said. "And you have another name – your true, essence name. One day that name shall come to you and when it does there will be no stopping you in your purpose. Nothing will prevent you then from doing what you have to. But beware then the hatred and vengeance of your brother, for he will try with all his wiles to bring you down."

Chapter Nine

It rained all night, drumming steadily on the earth outside the cave, so that all other sounds disappeared into a thundering ring of blackness excluding everything but thought. And in harmony with the rain, Marek's thoughts soon became rhythmic, forming themselves in an orderly, dimming fashion, like ever slowing heartbeats, until he lost them altogether and forgetting even the discomfort of the hard ground, expanded into a wider consciousness that was something like the rain itself – constant, limitless, impersonal.

Then shortly before the dawn the rain cleared and the stars came out and although inside the cave, Marek saw them, as one by one they appeared like little kindled fires. He saw them through the rent veil of consciousness, though earth and stone were between his body and the sky. He had been chasing a great blue white light across a waking dream and now he held that light in his hands. He had fire in his hands that did not burn, had snatched a great star out of the sky and held it. He did not pause to think what it meant; he had no use for thoughts now. He let come what would come.

The star leapt away and drew him with it, into a field of stars, and the field spiralled into a star filled center as thick as soap suds crowding down a drain. Facing that swirl of turbulent light, Marek felt the same hollowness inside that he'd felt earlier when entering the cave. It was the emptiness of waiting to be filled with new discovery. It was the thrill of knowing that discovery lay beyond and that it required entry through nothing less than a core of fire.

Set on a swirling course through chaos, he poured like a little bubble into a world of other endless bubbles. A most profound and absolute peace lay over this different dimension and he wondered for a moment where he was. Then he understood. Limitless and eternal was this world, in fact it was no world, but was all worlds. He had entered the Mind of the Source of All, and was one with It.

In every shining bubble was a universe, and he saw into his own as if that universe had become like the star that he could hold in the palm of his hand. Connecting all the bubble universes was a membranous veil like a film of clear, transparent water. When anything happened in one of the universes, the film shimmered, passing rainbow waves across its length and breadth. In that way every bubble was in resonance and the Mind of the All was instant and everywhere.

Marek wondered at it all. For a brief second a thought intruded from the past and he asked of this Mind where Its center lay. Then immediately the answer came: What center? There is no center in limitlessness. Of course, for so long had he been conditioned to think of a potentate God – a Godhead – a single point of power, that he had not understood. His old idea of God, Silene's God, the God or gods whom so many believed in, was an unreality creating a false idea of separation and hierarchy. It was a fabrication and it held no meaning here. For, that God, those Gods of separation, were the Gods of the Fathers, and the devils and demons they appeared to oppose were cut also from the same fabric. All in the illusory world who believed in their Great Deception had only to come here, and the lie would be overturned forever.

At dawn, Marek rose up and stretching the stiffness from his muscles stepped out into the light. A clear, rain washed sunrise greeted him, pale gold and apple green, tinted with a blush of rose above a limpid, rolling sea. It was the most beautiful sunrise he had ever seen and it matched his mood entirely.

He stood facing the growing light, watching as it blossomed brighter, whiter, more brilliant and alive with each second. Everything came into focus with its increase. Each thing of earth, air and water, sharpened into view with the light upon it. The birds had returned, wheeling and crying over the blue, dipping silvery into the sea for fish. A pod of dolphins skittered across the waves, stirring up the fish for the birds. And in the sky the great fire blazed and, reaching up to it as it reached down to him, Marek's thought leapt, and his cry followed, ringing like a bell…

"OZIRA! … OZIRA! … OZIRA!"

It was as Marielle had promised. The Sun had given to him his name. He was no longer just Marek; he was OZIRA.

He turned the boat towards the coast and the wind filled the sail, speeding them along, clearing a snowy pathway of foam through the dark water. Where he was headed for ultimately Marek did not know yet, the simple journey of the moment being only to return the boat to its proper place and do it safely. What else he thought of was dim and distant, and overshadowed by Silene, but he pushed it far away. The moment was much too beautiful, this moment where he was OZIRA and the day was fresh and new, and the sea sparkled with a million diamonds.

At the sheds he hosed the boat down and hoisted it to its proper place. The sheds were as deserted as they were the day before and Hal's estate was large and isolated. Few inhabited the place in winter and Marek saw no sign of life except the gulls which foraged around the sheds and, remembering that the summer people often came with picnics or cleaned fish they had caught under the taps, approached him hopefully. Marek spread wide his arms and shrugged. "Sorry, but I'm empty-handed, and just as hungry as you are." He could hardly wait for his next meal but he would have to; civilization was at least two hour's walk away.

The city of Alsea was one of the largest ports on the coast. Part of it was a sailors" nest filled with bars and rooming houses, cheap eateries and clubs offering bawdy entertainment, but for the most part it was a busy metropolis, and the palaces of commerce and avarice were crystal towers reaching to the sky. Marek chose the sleazy side of town, not because he liked it but to avoid the streets paved with money, where, in spite of his well used clothes, he might still be recognized. He could not change the face he wore and its nearness to Silene's was a problem still to be solved. He had the beginnings of a beard though, but it was slow in coming.

Anonymity was everything to him now. And the desire to vanish for a while. On the road towards the city an uncomfortable feeling had impressed itself upon him. The sensation of being watched where there were no eyes to be seen was strong and growing stronger. Silene knew – Marielle had said he would. It had begun: Silene's renewed appraisal of him, and it meant an increased threat.

Silene was treacherous, he had already proven that. At first he had regarded Marek as indulging in youthful folly, or the kind of pointless rebellion a young man finds seductive for a time. Then he had realized the seriousness of Marek's intent and had perceived the possible danger in it. Yet even so there was still the element of a game in all that Silene did, for he was so very sure of his power of control that he never doubted eventual success.

Then, he had been dealing with Marek, who was still struggling to find his way out of Illusion – not a difficult combatant for the Master Silene. But now, he was dealing with Ozira, and it was a very different proposition. Did Silene know at last what would happen in the end? Did he finally understand?

After rejecting six beer houses and several greasy looking food halls

Marek stopped at a place by the docks called the Jolly Anchor. It didn't look too bad and the food as it turned out was tolerable, but the company was rough and moody looking. He chose a simple meal of fish and noodles that couldn't be spoiled by having too much done to it, and a place of comparative isolation in a corner behind the room's single large fireplace. In shadow he sat and listened to sailors talk in accents that spanned a globe. Alsea was a port for ships coming from and going to everywhere. Marek wondered what it must be like to wander the whole world.

Light was kept to the minimum in the Jolly Anchor with nothing but a dirty yellow-stained light bulb above the bar and a few candles for atmosphere. More likely though it was so that patrons couldn't see what they were eating exactly, Marek decided. Or else it was because the Jolly Anchor was a place where its inmates chose the protection and anonymity of shadows. In that way he was one with them, although he was aware that he had not gone unnoticed and that from one direction at least he was the object of a surreptitious interest. From two tables away, a man watched him intermittently with a sidelong scrutiny. An old man with a grizzled face and dark, weather-browned skin, sitting and drinking with three of his mates.

Two new patrons arrived, sliding in through the door of the Jolly Anchor with an air quite foreign to that of anyone who had come before. At the sight of them the other patrons visibly stiffened, and Marek shrank back into his dark corner. Only this and the shadowy atmosphere of the rest of the place had made it possible for him to see the newcomers before they saw him.

Two men with snake-like, impassive faces and expensive, dark suits, as out of place in the docks as two pedigree cats in a dog pound. They ordered nothing, but stood and cast their slitted, unblinking eyes around the room, slowly, with great concentration. Marek guessed what they searched for, if not who or what they were, and there was no way he could exit the Jolly Anchor while they studied every corner.

The snake eyes passed over Marek once, to examine other scowling faces. Then, subtly, they returned, and settled. Marek did not move, but under the cover of the table he took up his few belongings, gripping them tightly. He was not afraid; however, there was no sign of human feeling in the gaze which lingered upon him. He readied himself to run; he would fight if he had to in order to get away. Last time Silene had only been able to take him by stealth and deceit; this time it was different.

The Jolly Anchor was suddenly as silent as a tomb. It was as if the whole establishment held its collective breath. Not a table squeaked, no chair leg scraped, the sputtering candles were steady. Sure and confident, the two interlopers started to glide forward, when there was a sudden stamping of boots, a curse and a shout, as a fight erupted at one of the tables. The shouter raised a fist and leapt over the table to attack the curser, spilling beer glasses and scattering men and chairs in his wake.

Other men joined in the battle and the curses and punches flew like thick darts. The nattily dressed suits, caught up in the turmoil, tried to extricate themselves, but fists and kicking boots were flying everywhere. Everything seemed to happen in the blinking of an eye, and Marek caught a flash of someone half behind him. Someone plucked at his sleeve and beckoned, and without waiting any longer, Marek fled.

He was in the back of the Jolly Anchor, running down a darkened passage towards a dim light that was a half opened door. He seemed to have lost his beckoner, but guessed there was only one way to go. He ran past an empty urinal and heard feet clattering down the passage after him. He launched himself out the doorway, into daylight and the Jolly Anchor's back yard.

He was stunned for a split second, by solid blank walls and the fact that the one who led him out had simply vanished. The yard was blind at three ends, unbroken by any door or arch. Since he could not scale sheer brick or walk through stone, only one choice remained, the lane way leading back to the street. Marek knew, if his pursuers had any brains at all they would not both be following; one of them would be waiting for him as he dashed into the street.

He had to run. He started into the lane, but halfway down there was an iron door in the wall of the opposite building, and it was open a crack. As he hesitated, a hand pushed open the door and dragged him through. In absolute darkness someone fumbled with a great bolt, sliding it across metal. The hand grabbed him again. "Come on," a deep, rough voice said.

Led by an invisible hand, Marek stumbled along through near blackness. The passages wound tortuously and since he could not see much more than a short space in front of him, Marek had no idea of where he was or where he was going. Then, by the slim light that chanced through a few broken slats and cracks, he realized he was treading a maze of half a dozen connected buildings and that his rescuer was the old

66

man who had studied him in the Jolly Anchor.

Finally, they stepped through a warped old door which was no better than a piece of rotting timber into a cavernous room which looked like a cellar. Barrels of whisky lined the walls amidst cobwebs that draped halfway to the earthen floor. The only light was pallid and natural and it came from a stairway leading above, making the room shadowy and gloomy. Not until the old man switched on a cobweb covered light bulb could Marek see his face properly.

"Thanks," Marek said. "But why did you help me? How do you know?"

"Know what? What's t'know?" the old man replied. A long table with a bench stood to one side of the barrels, a shelf on the wall behind. There were tin mugs on the shelf. The old man snatched up a couple in his brown, leathery hand. "Want a drink? It's good whisky, not cheap."

Marek shook his head.

Tapping off a mug full from the nearest barrel, the old man took a seat. "Well, sit down," he said. "Not a drinking man, eh? Ah, you're young yet, so there's still time. Me, I need it, after that rough run. You're not so beat though."

Marek sat. "I'm curious. I'm a stranger, yet you helped me."

The old man took long, deliberate sips of the whisky, as though it was a medicine he relished. He stared at Marek with a frown. "The moment I saw you, I knew you was in trouble. An' when those two weevils turned up, I says t'others it was you they'd come looking for. We don't like those types down here an' we certainly don't go encouraging them by giving 'em what they want, so we organized the little riot."

"You did that just for me? And you don't even know anything about me. I'm sorry," Marek said. "T'isn't important." The old man grunted in between long swigs. He got up and refilled the mug. He grinned, a gap-toothed smile, through teeth which were astonishingly white. "An" don't apologize. The mates love a good tumble anyway; you weren't no more than a good excuse." With half closed eyes he seemed to be studying Marek. "I've been a'looking and now a'listening hard t'you, an' here's what I see an' hear. You come from Uppers, like the weevils work for, but you aren't like one of them. Hiding down here, you've got t'be running from something."

How far could he trust someone in a place like this? Marek wondered. Yet, in spite of his roughness, the old man's light was clear and clean. "Yes. It's certain Uppers that don't want me around," he replied, using the same quaint phrasing to describe the social cast he had gladly left behind. "So I have even more to run from than just those creeps, whatever they are. I'm running for my life."

Raising one grizzled eyebrow, the old man swallowed his last draught. He cleaned his mouth with the back of his hand. He appeared astonished. "You don't know what they are?"

"No."

"They're Gover'mint men, you can always tell. They come down here a bit, but we always shift "em off, or almost always."

"Why do they come here?" Marek asked.

The old man raised the other eyebrow. Clearly, Marek had surprised him, by his ignorance again as it turned out. "Excise men, mostly, or Immigration. Looking for this whisky an' other things." He chuckled. "Sometimes they're after drugs an' illegals. Sometimes, well … even we don't know what they want. Often they just like hassling the mates. They're bad stuff; that's why I pulled you out of the Jolly Anchor."

Not Excise or Immigration, but Government Security, Marek thought then. To say that he did not know what they were was not a lie, yet he could hazard a guess. They were probably Agency creeps, but because they were after himself and by the look of their ultra-expensive clothes, they were more likely working extracurricular hours for Silene, on his secret, though very generous payroll. Marek decided to keep this suspicion to himself. "Well I'm grateful to you. But now I've got to decide where to go next."

"Town too hot for comfort?" The old man led him up the stairs through a hidden door that came out into a Ship's Chandler. Marek was fascinated by the profusion of shining brass, the copper, white knotted rope and sail, the instrumentation, both mechanical and electronic, the polished timbers and the pictures of great ships. No matter that this was modern times, the sea and all things connected with it always held a romance of its own.

"The whole country's becoming too hot for me." "You'll want t'be getting out then?"

Marek nodded. "For a while."

"I see by that crest on your kit, you're able with the fixing of what ails. That so?" "Yes."

The old man offered Marek a gnarled hand. "M'name's Kenu an' I'm shipping out in two days.

There's a spot on my ship, the Crescent, for a mate who can do the fixing, and more work besides, if you're up to it. The captain's an old mate o'mine; he'll be more than willing t'slip you under the net. Reason I say that is because he ails a lot with bad belly trouble an' he can't never get any of you lot t"go t'sea. Best way t'leave Telaia, invisibly, as they say."

Marek knew that secret departures from Telaia were just as illegal as secret arrivals. "I'd appreciate the help, really. But won't it get your captain into difficulties?"

"Cap'n Jimson? He knows what he's doing. He part owns the ship, he doesn't have t'answer t'anybody. D'you think you're the only man in the world t'ever vanish when things got too hot? Don't worry about it, we're old hands."

"Well, okay," Marek said. Leaving Telaia was a big step, however it seemed to be the only path at present. That Silene had managed to track him down so easily, he wasn't sure; maybe Silene was simply covering every point of exit and the two "weevils" had just gotten lucky. He wondered how he would manage invisibility somewhere else; it should be less of a problem. Well, maybe. And maybe not, he had his doubts. He wasn't naive and he wasn't deluded either. Silene and the Brotherhood had a long reach. Like an octopus, their arms went everywhere. If he could find somewhere that existed beyond their interest, but their interest stretched even to the stars.

Chapter Ten

The Crescent was not one of the larger ships. It was a small freighter which usually plied the sub tropic and tropical waters of the Great Eastern Sea and visited the kinds of ports which barely rated a mention on important maps. It carried stores and oil barrels and small vehicles and home furniture and took away produce and other items of trade and the occasional cash strapped passenger who couldn't afford expensive rides, or anonymous types like Marek who'd rather no one knew where they were going.

It was not often that the Crescent shipped as far north as Alsea or even to the south of Telaia; it did so only once in every few years. The captain had bought a cargo of coffee and rum at bargain prices and he wanted to offload it where he'd get the best return. When he'd met Marek, Captain Jimson was buoyant with success and big profits made him generous. He offered Marek the chance to cure him of his belly then and there. Smiling to himself, Marek mixed a potion, and the captain's ugly stomach eased. Marek was now an indissoluble part of the crew.

As Kenu had promised, he and the captain knew what they were doing and, for a sum of money which emptied Marek's wallet entirely, they were able to get him false papers and a fresh identity. He was now someone called Matt Best, although everyone seemed to have decided upon calling him Doc, in honor of the captain's stomach. They treated him with a practised discretion, ignoring his accents and accepting him without questions.

Then, the night before they sailed, old Kenu took Marek to a party, a sailor's party that was more of a wake for dead dreams and passionate farewells to week-long girlfriends than anything to celebrate, yet the men seemed to enjoy it in their unique way. Mostly it was a case of getting drunker than usual and Kenu matched it with the best of them. As stubbornly as he could, Marek battled to hold off the constant offer of every kind of booze, and tried to stay sober, but it wasn't easy. When the long night came to a close it was Kenu who hoisted Marek up the gangway and like an indulgent, fumbling father, rolled him into his allotted bunk.

Marek had never been so drunk in his life before. He lay in the swaying bed and was everything a drunk could be: verbose and cheerful to the point of madness; maudlin; depressed; sullen; nauseous. In other words, a perfect subject for his own potions. If Kenu had listened to Marek's unleashed rambling, he would have learned enough to make him wish he'd never met with his new cabin mate, but fortunately for him he snored above the noise. For a short time, during an interval of partial coherence, Marek worried about Silene. Which he shouldn't have, because he dropped off to sleep in the middle of an unwise thought and that thought became a door for Silene to enter.

Normally, before he slept, Marek shielded his consciousness from intrusion by casting a light around himself. This night, though, he was incapable even of thinking about it. He plummeted into unconsciousness like a stone rattling down a deep well and it was not until nearly morning that he began to dream:

He was thirteen, and his mother had asked him not to go with Silene, but he went anyway.

Silene explained to him about women, and especially mothers. "You see, they like to keep their little boys at home where they can smother and control them. They don't want you to grow up and they don't want you to be thinking for yourself. Women are all like that. A man is a little boy forever if he listens to women. If you want to be a man, you must stay in charge, always."

In his sleep, Marek wept.

"In this world you can have anything you want," Silene said. "You have that right; you are better than the rest. The world and everyone and everything in it was made to serve you, and me, because we are its Masters."

Silene showed him the Great Hall of the Princes. It was ornate and gilded with every luxury a country's taxes could afford. It had been built long ago for regal overlords during a time of famine. Emperors, kings, princes, presidents, only the titles had changed, the separate seats of power and poverty remained the same.

In a foreign country they drove in sumptuous vehicles to visit a palace and a great long wall built of stones and cemented with the blood of rebels and slaves. A palace designed for one man which could house a thousand families or more, and a wall of ancient times which crossed halfway over a land where dissension still stirred and objections were still buried under bloody stones. "We are more civilized," Silene whispered to him privately. "Outright murder is not to be tolerated in Telaia; it doesn't look good. Sophistication is our watchword; there are many ways to control a nation and the populace is more content if it believes that it is free to dissent."

In a secret meeting-pyramid hidden behind the facades of modern commerce, Silene introduced him to some of the Brothers. Most of them were unseen forces in the world, contemptuous of the elected fools who thought they had been chosen to rule and of the people who believed in the quaint notions of representation and choice. Very few of the Brotherhood were like Silene, though, who enjoyed outward eminence as well. But then few held the degree of personal power he did; he could handle the attention.

Restlessly, Marek turned in his sleep. In the dream Silene raised the regalia of the Grand Master of the Brotherhood above the boy Marek's head. "One day this will be yours." Marek groaned and turned away.

"What's going on?" Silene asked. He was affable, friendly, uncomplaining, even though young Marek had done something wrong. "Are you all right, little brother? Let me help you. Tell me what the problem is; I am your best friend, remember."

"You know I only want to help," Silene said soothingly. "If you've made a mistake, it doesn't matter. You can come back. Come back, little brother, I miss you. Let's be together again, like the old days. We had good times then; you had everything you wanted, didn't you. We can do it all again."

Feverish, as the alcohol dissipated through his bloodstream, Marek tossed to and fro in his bunk. "NO! NO!"

The real Silene spoke through the slits of a smiling mask. "I'll find you. There's nowhere you can run that I won't follow. You know that the Brothers are everywhere, and they are not as forgiving as I am. Better you come home to me while you still can. Remember, the Brotherhood controls the entire world; there is no place that is free. We own the world. It is Ours."

A sweat broke out all over Marek's body. The drunken blood pounded his brain like a hammer. But he could not wake.

Silene's impassive face grew into a snaky grin. Where his eyes should have been were two lidless lumps of coal as black as jet. When he looked at Marek, the coal shot forth two bursts of heat, like burning breath. The taint of the Dragon's Breath, thought Marek. Poisonous. And Silene bathes in and drinks It's Blood. It is that which makes him inhuman.

Marek tried to rally some defense. "You can be free too, if you want," he said to Silene.

'Really?" Silene smiled ironically. "You are on the run; do you call that free? And We will pursue you until you drop from exhaustion or die. We are patient. We don't get tired."

"But you're running out of time," Marek said. "You realize, don't you, that soon it has to end. The world you have so artfully put together is a sham, and it will soon end. Humanity will turn away." He watched a shudder pass through Silene's narrow frame. The coal eyes glinted, contracting to a point, then flared.

Silene laughed. "Ah, little brother, what a fool you are. Don't you know that you are alone? Not a soul in this world wants to share in your foolish fantasy of freedom. They all worship this world you call a sham. Pain, pleasure, disaster, dream – they still want it all. They believe in it like no other.

Even the after-life they cling to is fashioned to match it, and the Gods and Devils mimic the patterns of their desires. Brother, don't you see where you are? You are the loneliest man in the world."

Wars, hatred, subjugation. Family battles, misery, illness, alienation: is that what people really wanted? Sweat gathered on Marek's forehead like dew. "No, you are wrong. I'm not alone. There are others."

"An insignificant few. Not enough to turn a tide."

Suddenly, in the dream, they had company. Beings walked in procession across Marek's line of vision. Men in expensive black suits, young men with handsome faces and believable airs. Yet Marek saw behind their smart suits and plausible smiles, the trailing tails of crocodiles or dragons.

Swarming at him, the mask of Silene's grinning face grew huge and engulfing. "Come back, little brother, you are forgiven. Come back and I will give you all the world." He breathed on Marek with the hot breath of a furnace. "All the world, my brother. All the world."

"Join us, join me, don't turn away," Silene exhorted. His influence flooded over Marek like a slur of molten iron. It clung, it wheedled; its effect had the cloying stickiness of too much heat and luxury, of satiation, of excess. It nauseated him. He twisted away, groaning, in the throes of a vomit.

Marek woke, draped over the edge of the bunk like a limp, wet rag. He was nauseous but, thankfully, he had not actually been sick in the bed. Dawn had just arrived by the look of it, for a pale grey light stole in the tiny porthole and the gulls were about, crying in the sky. Kenu snored in the other bunk, oblivious. Marek's head was pounding, his whole body shook with the chill of sweat and the cold morning air. He dragged himself back into the hollow of the bunk and pulled the blankets over him. A little rest and he would survive, he decided. He was annoyed with himself, though, for having let Silene in the door. But alcohol in excess did that, opened the psychic gates for any rubbish to enter. It would not happen again.

He crouched in warmth and felt the relaxing of aching, tightened muscles. The dream which was no dream had managed to work him over like a prize fighter. Under the blankets he studied the jewel in his ring; he had just thought of something more, an idea that, if it worked, would keep Silene out of his head forever.

In his sojourn in the tower, Marek had considered the problem of the ring, but without finding an answer which satisfied. He knew that as well as reflecting his physical well being, the ring reflected his moods. Marielle had spoken to him about moods, as they revealed themselves in his eyes. She had said, "You are undisciplined as you search. You shift, you wander, you dream carelessly, and you let old fancies and hurts take hold. Like that, you become the prey of anything stronger, anything or anyone with a stronger intent. Intent is the key. Where there is no intent you are like a cloud which can be blown this way or that. If your brother sees the lack of intent in you, he doesn't have to try very hard to control you; it's easy for him, because he is expert at this. So banish those moods, my boy, and replace them with a clear intent. Do this and you will banish your brother's influence from your life."

The ring was a dull red brown at the moment, which was not the result of a mood. It was his body's semi parlous state which colored the ring now. Had he been dead, the stone would have become a flat coal black, like Silene's dream-eyes without the fire.

When he healed, he was all intent ... no mood intruded. Then the ring's stone turned a glorious emerald, his favorite color nowadays. And he knew that his eyes did the same. In fact, since he had not fallen prey to any sort of mood for a long time now, the ring was generally a stable entity, which, like his eyes, reflected only a purity of feeling and directed thought. But even this was a window for Silene, and Marek did not want his brother knowing anything more about him, much less the direction of his heart or mind.

Underway, the Crescent was on a slow roller coaster ride through heavy swells. It was bearing north-east at first, bound for a small island country before it turned for warmer, more equatorial waters. After he had thrown up a bit and then settled his quaking stomach with tea and dry toast – it was the night's after affects mainly and not so much the rolling sea – Marek went above.

He said hi to Captain Jimson who stared at his pale face and laughed. Above decks was another world where the open sky, with its snowy clouds heaped up like ice-cream mountains, the clearing, invigorating wind and the brightening sunshine made him want to shun the cramped confines of the cabins forever. He stood on the foredeck to face the sun and cared not if anyone watched or wondered. He removed the concealing gloves and opened his arms to the light.

Three times he called, Ozira … Ozira … Ozira. Not aloud, of course, for that would be tempting too much curiosity from the mates.

The voice of his heart, truer and more passionate and more potent and louder than any cry, would carry this message to the Sun of his Being. In Its Light he stood, at one, arms outstretched, hands reaching. His ring was on fire with a single intent. No longer would it reflect anything but the one Light. The ring blazed, a diamond in sunshine, a pure, bright, white light reflecting the experience of being only the NOW.

If his intent remained pure, the jewel would reflect it constantly, with the intensity of a flawless diamond, and if Silene tried to seek it out, he would be forced to recoil. Silene could not face either such intent or such light, for they were the antipathy of his purpose. The link was broken at last.

"Bit of a sun worshipper, eh, Doc?"

Kenu joined him at the rail. In raw daylight the old man appeared younger, less grizzled and more vigorous. He was hardy and brown, reminding Marek of Marielle. Marek turned and laughed. "I am, especially after last night."

"Then you'll like it when we head south. Plenty of sun down there, and women as sweet and as golden brown as honey. And dark rum too, with a taste t'match."

A poet as well as a drinking man, Marek thought in amusement. Ah well, they often went together.

He liked Kenu although he would never agree with him about the virtues of excess booze. "Is that where you hale from?"

"No, I'm a Southern Ocean man, but I haven't been home fr"a long time.

I'm island born ... you may o'may not have heard of the place ... Te Tanaa ... my people are Tanu."

Tanu – Marielle's people – so she had told Marek. His hands gripped the rail. The ring glinted in the sunlight and shot off shining sparks, which leapt out from the ship and over the waves to meet the dancing diamonds of the sea. Kenu noticed them too and although he said nothing, his eyes widened and fixed themselves briefly on the ring.

"So the Crescent doesn't go near there."

"No. You'd have t'make other passage, after we reach Arpay. Why, does Te Tanaa interest you?" "I've met someone else from there. Is it heavily populated? Would you recognize a name if I told you?"

"Aye, probably. T'isn't so big that all the family names can't be counted."

Marek frowned. "It's not a family name, just a given name. I never found out the other one."

Kenu nodded. His brown eyes twinkled. "Ah, lass is it? You might as well tell me then. I know a lot o'the lasses, or their mothers at least." He grinned. "A lot to'the names get handed down."

Marielle was not exactly a "Lass", but Marek didn't enlighten him. He just wanted to discover all he could. "Her name's Marielle and she's from your island, that's all I know."

Kenu stared at him, hard, as if he wasn't sure about something. His fingers drummed the rail. Marek wondered what he'd said wrong. Finally Kenu cocked his head on one side and gave Marek a sideways grin.

"You young rascal, you're putting me on," he said. "An I didn't even see it coming. You know a lot more about m'people than you let on; guess that comes fra' having an ed'cation."

What was this? He had said something untoward, but what the devil was it? Marek shrugged. "No. I just asked if—"

"You like a game. I can appreciate that, I like a joke myself," Kenu answered reflexively. "Well, I'll play along. Marielle is not a name any Tanu would give t'his daughter ... it's a sacred name, not for common use, and we say it as Mari-E-ele. It's the name we give t'our Goddess. It means Beautiful One From The Sun and The Sea – She who made our island and is our Mother."

"Oh," Marek said. "I'm sorry, Kenu, I wasn't trying to be smart, though. The truth is I didn't know that. It's what I was told."

Kenu chuckled and slapped the rail. "Then it's you who's been had, not me!"

"Marielle, who are you? What are you?" Alone, Marek studied the waters, lit to a turbulent deep blue-green by the sun. "Mari-E-ele," he repeated, phrasing it the way Kenu did. He had not been "had", he knew. Marielle ... Mari-E-ele ... was real. She had rescued him, cosseted him when he was hurt and healed him of it. She had counselled him and let him pour out his pain, and healed him again, in spirit. She had opened him, heart and mind, to the wonder of his being. She had given him the love of a mother and yet had not been soft with his initial reluctance to move out of illusion. His feeling self had been liberated from Silene's suffocating teachings, from that overbearing belief of his brother's that a man must always be right and in control. Marielle had shown him that real power came from the heart, for the only power lay in the loving self, and all the rest was fantasy. Marielle had brought him alive when he had thought that he was dead. What else would a Goddess do? What else was a Goddess for?

Rainbow light sparkled on the waters, a flash of memory travelling from there to him. On his finger the ring shone, now a reminder of all that had gone before. Yet there was more to come, much more. Everything was contained in this moment of NOW – past, present, future – the liberation of himself and of an entire world.

Marek looked up from the rail. A shout came from aft; he was wanted and there was work to do. "I'm coming," he called.

PART 2
Six Years Later

Chapter One

Night was a shimmering veil across the restless sea as the moon poured its cup of silver upon the water. Alone on the beach, Marek waited for the call.

It came at last, as an echo faint above the thundering waves. The subtle pounding of a drum; a gentle, serpentine rhythm rolling steadily upward into the discernible, strident beat of an excited heart. Marek shivered in expectation, the whole length of his spine tingling. He felt every hair on his body rise. The drum call always affected him this way.

There were other drums used in these night-time meetings, but this first was the charm, the most thrilling of all, and he who played it was the master player, the best. Resonance was the key this player understood and he fit his beats to match the human heart exactly, from all its perturbations to its moments of deepest tranquility.

Te Tanaa itself was like the drum, an artfully played instrument that resembled the world outside, although subtly askew. Coming at first to Te Tanaa, Marek had looked for a land of dreams, only to find that it was much like any other land. The sea raged round it, the wind blew and the sun shone, and people lived and died as others did elsewhere.

Yet there were differences, and mostly these were discovered in the drum and the night. Some aspect of Te Tanaa was hidden from ordinary eyes, for the native Tanu kept their secret selves for after hours entertainments to which they did not invite strangers or others of the island, Marek excepted. The call was for him to come. Marek walked back along the beach to join them – "his people".

So they had styled themselves; it was not his doing. Not long after he'd arrived in Te Tanaa, it happened. "My people shall welcome you, for they shall know who you are," Marielle had said. They were first and foremost the Tanu, children of their Mother Goddess, Mari-E-ele; now they were "his people – Ozira's people", as well.

He walked up over a dune fringed with whispering grasses and hollowed by shadows of ink and passed through coastal shrubbery to a dense forest of palms. This he negotiated carefully in moonlight, although he was used to the paths by now. He exited the forest and descended a small hill to another dense overhang of trees illuminated however with the brightness of orange flares. From a distance the trees of sticky sap, with their huge trunks and gargantuan root systems, looked like some sort of eccentric building, a temple perhaps with columns gone all awry.

He knew what would happen the moment he entered the circle of flares. This evening was special: a night of songs and dancing, of feasting and of story telling, with certain particular reminiscences.

And afterward, if he wished it, one of the beautiful girl dancers would join him in the house he had been given to live in. He was not sure which one it would be and it did not seem to matter to the Tanu, as long as he was happy.

The attitude of the Tanu to love, or rather, love making, had astonished him at first. Nowhere else in the world was it so free and uninhibited. When he'd become known to the Tanu, and chosen by them, he found himself thoroughly alarmed by what followed. It seemed that he became instantly magnetic to the women, almost so that he had to fend them off at times. Although he was flattered, he didn't understand it, until one day he found out why. It was considered to be good luck for an important stranger to father a Tanu child. And even better luck when that stranger was the Messenger they had been waiting for. That brought him swiftly back down to earth. So, he was not exactly the greatest lover in all the islands, he was just a good luck package.

The Head-man of the Tanu was a man of giant proportions. From within the circle of lights the world outside seemed to be only darkened space where nothing existed and the Head-man was the central sun around which the rest of them rotated, like dedicated planets. When the Head-man spoke, the people listened, the children most of all, with open mouths and wide, wide eyes.

He spoke first of their new happiness, acknowledging and honoring their guest with a bow of his own great head. "A year ago today, the hope we have long held in our hearts was realized when our beloved Messenger came to us. To celebrate this and to remind you all of what this means, I will tell the story of our people."

A shiver of anticipation ran around the circle and mothers settled their children into their arms. No longer so embarrassed by the open adulation of himself yet still disapproving of a worship that he knew was not right or healthy, Marek sank back into a shadow. Yet he wanted to hear this story in full, having only caught parts of it before.

The Head-man began...

"Long ago, when there was no land but only ocean on the globe, our people were born from out of the mouth of our Mother who lived in the Sun. She was Mari-E-ele, but she was not called that then.

When the first people were ready to descend from the Sun, Mari-E-ele went ahead in order to prepare a way. She descended into the sea and found there a land which she raised up to be their home. It was a beautiful land where everything was bountiful and good. This land was Te Tanaa, the land of our forebears, and our land, which our Mother made for us.

"Mari-E-ele stayed close by, in the sea, to keep an eye on her children and to make sure that they behaved themselves. When necessary she would rise up and come ashore to instruct the people. Then one day, Mari-E-ele decided that the people had learned all they needed to know about their home and that her task was done. On beautiful streams of golden sunbeams, she returned to the sun to take a well deserved rest.

"But not long after Mari-E-ele left, dissatisfaction grew amongst some of the people and they began to argue. They argued night and day about who owned the fields and vegetable patches. They argued about the animals, all of which were wild and free, saying they wanted to tame them, and claiming that it was the people's right to rule everything that lived. Others tried to keep to the principles laid down by Mari-E-ele, saying that no one owned the land or the animals, but that the people had been put on Te Tanaa only to enjoy it and care for it. Thus began a battle, first of words, then of fists and weapons.

"While the wars raged there were some who realized the advantage to be taken of their warring brothers, and they set themselves up as peacemakers, claiming a fee of land or property for every settlement they made. This made them rich and powerful, and resentment grew amongst those who, afterward, had nothing left.

"Because of this greed and the anger and ill feeling it created, the people forgot the wonder of their origins, and sickness spread across the land. They had forgotten their Mother and their own beauty and that they had been Sun Beings once, and they became dark and ill, and so they died.

"Into this darkness came others then. They were the Ones Who Dreamed – they were not Tanu – but were great Black Magicians from afar. They told the People that Mari-E-ele spoke to them in their trance states and that other, greater Gods spoke to them also. That they had been given laws by Mari- E-ele and these Gods, and the people must obey those laws if they wanted peace and order in Te Tanaa. They told the people that when they died, the Gods would receive them in a place of paradise. All the people had to do to receive this reward was obey and live useful lives.

"This made a kind of peace at last, and yet the people were not happy. They had lost something and now they had even forgotten what it was. Te Tanaa had become a dull and lifeless place, and nobody knew why.

"From her place in the sun, Mari-E-ele saw all and she was sad. She had thought her people would be strong enough on their own, but it was not so. They needed a Messenger to help them remember.

So she sent from out of her mouth once more, a ray of light into the waters of Te Tanaa, which, blending with the moving light of the sea, instantly turned into a beautiful woman.

"The name of this woman was Re. She was so beautiful that the sun seemed to shine out of her, and through the streams of her hair which was as golden as the sun's light, and when she came upon the shore, to the villages of the Tanu, the people all thought that the world had suddenly been filled with rainbows. This was because the eyes of Re were special too, for they changed color constantly, like the sun's light when it shines through water. Thus the people knew that Re was the child of the sun and the sea and that she had come to bring them a reminder of their true origins.

"Re stayed with them a long while, until they all became well. But after she had left, called back to her mother for other duties, the people grew slip shod again and the same old fighting and nonsense returned. The people became even worse this time, because other nations had arrived in Te Tanaa, adding their own ignorance and alienation. A great war occurred and much of Te Tanaa was destroyed, sinking below the sea.

"The world of the Goddess was all but destroyed; only a few Tanu remained who remembered her.

New Gods ruled the scene, Gods which were cruel and unforgiving. A beautiful woman such as Re meant nothing to this new world, and women were treated like cattle. From above, Mari-E-ele saw it all and wept. Was there anything she could do?

"'I will send another Messenger,' she said. 'But this time it will not be in the form of a woman. The world is too cruel for woman-kind and the people will not care to listen to anything from that direction.' So Mari-E-

82

ele sent her Messenger in the form of a handsome man with rainbow eyes who spoke to the People of love and who had magic also in his hands, so that when he touched people who were ill, they were healed.

"The people listened to this Messenger briefly, but the world had grown too cruel even for him.

Only some of the Tanu, who still kept Mari-E-ele deep in their hearts, wanted him to stay. Egged on by the Black Magicians who still controlled them, the rest set out to destroy him, and destroy him they seemed to do. But not before he had opened a way home to Mari-E-ele, a rainbow stair of stars which cut a great roadway through all the evil, as one of our boats parts the waves as it flies on the wind through the sea.

"The roadway remained, even though the Messenger had departed, yet the world descended into more and more darkness, for most of the people had forgotten what they ever were and those in control continually told them lies, so that they believed they were not worth saving or that they would be saved, one day, as long as they obeyed the rules.

"Thus, this is the world we have today, and we Tanu who are left and still remember Mari-E-ele are very few. But our Mother has not forgotten us, for she put into our hearts, along with the remembrance, the knowledge that, one day, when the time was right, a Messenger would return. A Messenger with the rainbow eyes of sun and sea, and magic hands which healed, and this time the light of the Goddess would prevail."

A poetic description of the reality of Mankind, and fairly accurate in its own way, Marek thought. He wondered what the Tanu would think if they knew that their present Messenger had also been one of the Black Magicians they so despised.

By the end of his long story, the Head-man's voice had dropped to a hoarse whisper and he lowered his gaze to the ground. He looked exhausted and without any sort of directive that Marek noticed, his wife ran up with a large mug of beer, to revive him. Every eye in the place was filled with dancing orange fires and they had turned from the Head-man to Marek's direction. They expected him to say something in reply.

In order to speak, he stood – that was expected also – and their eyes lifted with him. He felt shy in these moments even though in one year there had been many of them. He did not like the attention particularly and knew that such devotion was not the best thing for either the Tanu or himself. And it was this which he had been thinking about for several days and now must speak of.

83

Marek moved into the center of the circle so that all could see him with ease. He started with a thank you, praising the Head-man's story for its interest. Then he said,

"The world of Mankind as it is today has never changed for many thousands of years. What your story says is true; the people have forgotten who and what they are. Instead, they believe in a Great Lie told to them by those who pretend to be gods or the spokesmen of gods. The people think that they are not good enough as they are and that they must have intermediaries to help them find salvation. But this salvation is a lie. There is nothing to be saved and there is nothing "out there" which will save you – that is, there are no saviours or intermediaries necessary. Every human being is his or her own Light, there is no other. You come directly from the Source of All to give Light to this planet – that is your purpose. You are not fallen or imperfect or evil, as the priests of all religions would have you think, but on the way you have gotten a little lost in all the illusion which has been built up by the False Ones: those who lie to you in your dreams, and by their servants in the world.

"Every time one of us gets lost in forgetting what we really are, the world's illusion gets a little stronger. Then people make it stronger still because they keep on doing and thinking the things which make it more and more difficult for them to escape from it. Life after life, we strengthen the illusion in ourselves, and this makes us very unhappy and angry and unkind to one another. Then we feel dark, as if the Light never did belong to us or we to it, and we believe in the lies and think we are bad people who don't deserve to be happy or healthy or loved.

"Our bodies get sick because we are not giving them enough Light. And we also get our understanding all mixed up, because we believe we are the bodies we inhabit, but at the same time we hate the body when it is ill and we blame it for all our suffering. This is confused thinking, for how can we be both? Our bodies belong to the Earth, not to us, and we are supposed to give them Light, the same as we are supposed to give the Earth Light.

"Do you see what I mean? The Earth was not made for us. Not to possess it or to rule it or to take from it or to hurt it. The story of Mari-E-ele tells you that the people came to Earth, through the Sun, to live in the Earth and give it Light. And you are those people, the first people; there have never been any other. If you want to call anything God or Goddess, call your own Light that, not anything else."

Marek turned in the circle and gazed at the Lights, which were so

84

much greater than any fires. "I see you all and you are beautiful," he said. "I want you all to see it too. Before you sleep tonight, please meditate on this."

Alone in his house afterward, Marek listened to the outside sounds of a village preparing for the night. Dogs barked, children chattered and some cried from over-tiredness and the parents quietened them. No doubt some would be discussing the evening's revelations and, Marek hoped, understanding what they meant. He would not be alone for long, he guessed, and clad only in shorts, he stretched out on the bed to relax. He certainly didn't mind the occasional visits from one or other of the women, and they always seemed to happen after a meeting like tonight's.

Insects buzzed in the stilled, night-time trees. It was hot and airless in the house and he thought he would rather sleep on the beach, under the stars. A breeze wafted suddenly over his face as the front door opened. He heard the soft steps of somebody coming across the matting of the living room and a young woman was at the bedroom door. Seeing who it was, Marek was surprised; even more than that, he was dismayed. It was not a woman but a girl.

"Lani! What are you doing here?"

The Head-man's daughter, Lani. She was small and very pretty, in love with the Master Drummer's apprentice and they were going to be married soon. She couldn't have been more than sixteen, but the Tanu paired early. She was a regular visitor to Marek, but not for sex. She came to listen to the stories of his travels; she loved to hear about other lands.

Why had she come for more stories? Hadn't she had enough tonight? It was Lani who had asked him the pertinent poser, "Why must you move from place to place? Why not stay where you are happy all the time?"

Marek had never told her the real reason for his wanderlust. Sometimes, after six months in a place, he would sense or actually catch sight of the Brotherhood's operatives as they hunted for him. Sometimes he lasted a year before they caught up with him again. For five years he had wandered in this way, as an itinerant medicine man with no place he could call "home". To throw off his pursuers, he changed his appearance as often as possible, being long haired and bearded one minute, clean shaven the next, and bearded again. He had a kit full of fake papers too, although he often found his way about by secret means. From Kenu he'd learned to be street-wise, and experience taught him even more.

Then, a year and a half ago, he had seen an operative who truly unnerved him. A man, or rather an automaton of a man, whom he had known about in the old Telaian days. It was the Vorken – he had no other name – an assassin and a bounty hunter employed secretly by Silene, although usually only outside of Telaia. The Vorken was skilled in the use of all sorts of strange exotic weaponry. He had a success rate which was awesome and Silene boasted of him once that he had never brought a quarry back alive.

Things were clearly hotting up; Silene was getting serious, deadly serious. When Marek found himself running to Te Tanaa, he shaved clean and cut his hair. Six years roaming the lands of the Southern Ocean had given him a natural tan and a wilder, outdoors look. He looked very different from the pale young aristocrat of Telaia now.

Te Tanaa was sanctuary. For a year he'd felt safer than he'd done in a long time. Yet how long was it going to last? He believed that, soon, he would have to leave.

"Lani?" he asked again when she did not reply.

She closed the door behind her and stood gazing at him. "The Grandmothers said you will be leaving us soon."

He had said nothing to anyone yet, but there it was, plain as day: the fact. He shrugged.

What little she was wearing, Lani took off in front of him. She came naked to the bed. "They told me to come to you now. I am ready to conceive. They want me to bear the Messenger's child before it is too late."

She was slim and delicate, like a beautiful doll. Around her slender waist she wore a narrow girdle of fine, pearly shells, the signature of her unmarried state. Marek could not deny the sudden pang of carnal desire he felt; but, no, it was not enough.

"Is it what you want, though?" he asked.

"Yes. I want the Messenger's child. It will be a wonderful thing."

"What about your marriage to Raool? I thought you were in love."

"I am." She lay down next to him, but sensing his reluctance, she was puzzled. She touched her small hand lightly upon his chest. "You are our Messenger. You are Ozira. Do you not want to leave your blessing here in Te Tanaa?"

The Tanu were the only people who had recognized him, the only people he could be himself in front of. Even so, they did not fully understand. "I thought what I had to say tonight was blessing enough," Marek said. "I can see now that it wasn't. Lani, you don't need to bear the Messenger's child, no woman does. I'm not special, you know. I'm not different from you or Raool, or your father, or the Grandmothers, or anyone else. We can all be messengers; we all have that Light and power inside us. Any child you and Raool make between you will be a messenger for the future."

Lani's hand travelled down to his. Delicately she fingered his ring, then she lifted his hands and lay them over her naked belly. "But Ozira, these hands, they're not ordinary hands. They are magic, healing hands. How can my child inherit these if you are not the father?"

"My hands!" He lifted them in surprise. "Lani, my hands are just like yours! They've no special magic in them. Healing comes not from these but from the Source of All. You could heal if you wanted; what you need to know is how."

Lani sat up. Her eyes were wide. "Is this true, my Ozira?"

"Do you think I would lie to you?" He propped himself up on one elbow. "You, yourself, are a beautiful light; I thought I made that one thing clear tonight. Lani, I wouldn't take from you what isn't mine to claim. I wouldn't break your girdle of shells. Go to the man who loves you. When you are married you two can make as many messengers as you like together."

"And you will teach us how to heal? So that we may teach our children?" she asked.

"Exactly. Now, you understand," Marek answered. "I'll teach you all. But if there are any who cannot understand; if the Grandmothers are annoyed and ask why I sent you from me, you must not worry. Just tell them what I said. The young are the future of our world; you and your children will bring your people further into the Light."

Lani dressed, but she did not leave right away. Instead she wanted to stay, to talk more. She perched on the side of the bed and played with Marek's hair, curling it in her fingertips then smoothing it out. The Tanu were such a relaxed people and so easy in their intimacy that such behavior meant not what it did in other worlds. Simply, Lani loved him, though not as a lover, but as one adopted into her family circle. Without embarrassment or any trouble, she had accepted his pronouncement and had immediately returned to their old relationship.

"When you go away from here, Ozira, will you teach others what you have taught us?" she asked.

"I will try, yes, somehow. It's not so easy, out there," Marek said. "For one thing, they don't know what Ozira means, and for another, many of them don't want to know."

87

"They will not listen?"

"Many won't. Also I don't want to draw people to myself; they need to see what is in themselves not me."

If it were possible, Lani's eyes opened wider than before. "Oh! Then Mari-E-ele will have many messengers, all over the world!" She laughed, pleased with her own understanding.

"Exactly,"

Marek did not show Lani the journal he had been writing over the years since he'd left home. It would mean very little to her anyway, for although she spoke and read Telaian with ease, as so many races did nowadays, for it was a dominating culture in the world, yet Lani herself was not a patient reader. She preferred the spoken word where she could listen and ask those difficult questions she was so fond of, and she learned better that way. As well as writing the journal, Marek had put down all that had come to him through the revelations of Ozira. One day soon, he decided, that would be his anonymous message to the world, and it was this, he realized, that Silene and the Brotherhood feared.

"You have been to many places, but were you ever in love?" Lani asked him before she left. She's good with the hard questions, Marek thought. But this one is relatively easy. "No."

Then he remembered Faran, so far away in time and space. Of all his encounters in Telaia and throughout these six wandering years, and apart from Marielle, she was the one he thought of and longed to see again. Her face and the Light she shone often haunted his dreams and sometimes he woke from them with an aching heart and with feelings of loneliness and loss which nothing could erase. "Well, I could have been once," he said. "Except that the girl was way too young, younger than you are now."

"How long ago was that?" "Six years."

Lani stood up. "I have to go, it's late. I wish you sweet rest, my Ozira. Six years is a long time, isn't it. That girl is probably grown up by now."

Marek lay back in the bed. He was sleepy and relaxed, but his mind was alive with speculation. Lani was right, six years was a long time, long enough. And it was time the running was over. He knew now where he was bound to go.

Chapter Two

Te Tanaa was the major part of an archipelago of twenty two islands, the remnants of a drowned mountain range. Some of the islands were too small to be lived on and most of the others had, for some time now, been populated by other than the Tanu. The Tanu had been pushed gradually and culturally into a corner of Te Tanaa and had lost their historical sovereignty over the rest. Only the tiny islets and one island of greater note remained under their total control.

From a grassy hill that rose above the high cliffs of Te Tanaa you could see the brace of islets and their one larger companion which loomed from the sea like a single mountain of cerulean and ultramarine soaring through foam-capped clouds.

Marek stood with the Head-man on the hill. "What's the name of that island there?" Marek asked. "That's Ompalo – Mari-E-ele's Garden."

"Why is it called that?"

"It is the Tanu's birthplace, where Mari-E-ele set the first people. The Tanu lived only there for a long time, before they spread out to other places."

"So there's water there?"

"Yes, plenty. There are many streams and waterfalls, and fountains spring from beneath the mountain. It truly is a garden; it's a very beautiful place, with plants and animals that have disappeared from the other islands."

"Has anyone ever tried to take it from you?"

"Oh, yes." The Head-man waved his arm in the direction of greater Te Tanaa. "The powers that be in Tana City have always wanted it, but fortunately for us, one of our wiser Tanu leaders made sure about a hundred and fifty years ago that Ompalo would remain forever in Tanu hands by a formal sale covered by Statute and Decree. At the time, the outsiders who'd taken over thought that it would be a good bargain to trade Ompalo off for control of almost everywhere else, and I guess it was a bargain at that for them. But nowadays there's a few in government and business who wish it had never happened. To them it's darned good real estate just going to waste. We've had quite a few offers to buy it."

"And you always turn them down?"

"Of course. They don't understand. Ompalo is more than real estate to us. It's sacred, and absolutely taboo to outsiders. We'll never let go of it."

Marek wandered part way down the hill, as if by doing that he could get all the nearer to that lovely mountain of blue. It reminded him somewhat of the little island where he had met Marielle, although this mountain was a lot higher, the surrounding sea a lot deeper, the sun above a lot warmer. The

Head-man followed him, dutifully.

"When I come back," Marek said, "Do you think the Tanu would give me permission to visit Ompalo and spend some time there?"

The Head-man's face was alight with happiness. "You will come back, Ozira?" "Yes, I intend to."

"Then, Ozira, you must go to Ompalo, if that's what you wish. It is the Garden of Mari-E-ele, and you are her Messenger. I will tell the people; they will be glad. We will wait for your return, Ozira, eagerly."

"You have been happy here, Ozira?"

Together, Marek and the Head-man took the forest trails back to the Tanu village. The trails dipped through valleys of palm-filled shadow. Birds of brilliant colors sang and whistled high in the fronds where the sea breezes waved. This place is paradise, Marek decided. If paradise be possible, as it ought to be. "Yes, I have been happy. I love it here." He stopped for a minute, sniffed the salty air and sighed. "Marek would never even leave at all, but Ozira must, for the whole world needs the message of freedom."

"Marek? Who is he?" the Head-man asked.

Marek laughed. He had forgotten that he'd never been called anything but Ozira by the Tanu. "That's my birth name, my Telaian name."

"Ah." The Head-man nodded. "I had wondered upon that occasionally. And your family name, may I know it too?"

Marek shook his head. "I'd rather you didn't. It's not a name I'm proud of."

"And yet I think I know it," the Head-man said suddenly. "When you first came to Te Tanaa, I thought your face was familiar to me, that I'd seen it somewhere, a picture perhaps, maybe in a newspaper."

Marek shuddered and for a moment the valley shadows seemed to drop the temperature of the air.

But it was only himself feeling cold with the old dread, he knew. The nature of Tanu daily life, the village simplicity had made him forget that it was a chosen way, not a predetermined or imperative one, and that

90

Tanu like the Head-man were not simpletons or primitives. In fact the Head-man was a well educated man who had travelled, and knew the world outside as well as Marek did. "I've never had my picture in any newspaper, so it wasn't me."

"No," the Head-man said thoughtfully. "Not you, but someone resembling you. I'm sorry, Ozira. I see by your expression that I've stepped into something I should have kept out of. Forgive me."

Marek started back along the trail. "It's okay. Forget it, no need to forgive. The past doesn't matter any more. Who we are or have been in the illusory world has no meaning once we've turned to what we truly are. It's just that I don't like to advertise my connection with the past because it could make difficulties for me. But so you'll know and not let it bother you, I'll tell you."

"That's not necessary, Ozira."

The forest trail had ended in sunshine and open spaces. Marek stopped and turned. Even though Marek was reasonably tall himself, the Head-man towered above him. Set against the sharp blueness of the sky he looked like a dark tree carved as a man. "I think it is, for your protection as well. When I came to Te Tanaa I was on the run from someone. I've been running for six years, for my life. The picture you saw was of my older brother, although I don't think of him as a brother now. He is very afraid of Ozira, he wants to kill him."

"Yes." The Head-man understood. "Such men that hate the Light so. They are what we call Black Magicians."

"I know."

A deep frown creased the Head-man's broad forehead. He said, "Then by leaving here you are taking a great risk. You must be wary, Ozira. We want you back, you know."

When they reached Marek's house he asked the Head-man inside. "I've something I'd like you to see." He took out his journal and the big man handled it gingerly, turning the pages slowly as he read some of it.

"These are wonderful words, Ozira," he said.

"I want you to look after this for me," Marek said. "I don't want to take the risk of having it on me… if something goes wrong. These are Ozira's words for the rest of the world and they must be published one day soon, but if I take them with me there's always the chance that they might get lost. I know they'll be safe with you and when the time is right I'll call for them."

"I'll take good care of them, Ozira."

Two weeks later Marek left Te Tanaa. He went first by sea under a false passport to a nearby country, then, incognito and illegally, overland across half a continent, through jungles and near- deserts to the latitudes closest to Telaia. In that time, two months in all, he spied not one operative of the Brotherhood, although he could not dispel the feeling that, somehow, his progress was monitored. He told himself that he was being foolish and paranoid, but the feeling did not go away, nevertheless.

The sensation of being followed had begun halfway through the second month, when he had arrived in an inland city. The city was a pest hole for every kind of down and out, for every kind of sin and low behavior. It was the sort of place where even the law was heavily involved in crime and corruption. It was a good place to lose oneself in, as far as avoiding authority was concerned, but it was also a situation which made it difficult to detect a watcher and to stay safe. There were so many sly, watching faces, and not an innocent one between them, and it was ironic that the worse they were themselves, the quicker they were to single out a stranger on their patch, in the fear that any newcomer might be competition.

Marek was glad to get out of that seedy town in one piece. In two more weeks he had made the coast which bordered the narrow sea between it and Telaia's southern shore. Now he had only one more thing to work out. How to get into Telaia without Silene or the Brotherhood finding out.

Considering the considerable risk that lay in return, he had asked himself, over and over, why on earth he was going back there. To this there were two answers. One was simple: he was sick and tired of Silene running him like a fox, into hole after hole. If Silene wanted to kill him then he would just have to try. In relation to his brother and all the Brotherhood Marek felt more equal now, if opposite. More than equal, for he knew that the Light was his ally, his strength. It was not just foolish, cocky confidence which made him feel this way, and Ozira's words were safe with the Tanu, but the years of wandering had made him stronger and more self reliant. And then there was the Light, it was a power deeper and more vast and permanent than any illusory force the Brotherhood might present.

The second answer was more complicated and had to do with feeling a certain lacking in his life and knowing that Telaia was somehow the key to his next step, whatever that next step was. He was still uncertain about some things, but there was one thing he had already done which would affect a change in the world at large. The day before he'd left Te Tanaa, he had returned alone to the hill overlooking Ompalo. It was more than a beautiful sight, that island. It was a center of physical, planetary power, and he placed around it a great white light which enveloped the whole mountain with a cone of attractive, conductive energy. It was not just for himself, although its power would call him back; it was for the whole world.

To get into Telaia legally was the best way. Marek decided on the oldest set of travelling papers he had, the ones Captain Jimson had gotten for him to leave his old home. He had used them only that once, to get out of the country, for the Crescent's ports of call, and to enter Arpay, the country he was now in. Where he had been in between was unrecorded, so the papers suggested that he had not been anywhere else at all. Arpay was a good country to have gotten lost in, big enough to be anonymous in and so poor and badly managed that individuals were born and died without anyone caring or taking account. A place without the tight, watch-dog rules of Telaia and nations like it. When the poor were so poor and the rich so few but exceedingly prosperous, what did human life matter as long as it did not impede the flow of capital or events?

Downtown, in the same waterfront city of Vargas of six years earlier, Marek rediscovered the port headquarters for Entries, Exits and Excise. He remembered that these derelict rooms which served for government offices had not even a pretended grandeur and that they always seemed to be filled with long untidy lines of mostly ill fed men wanting to get away from their ruinous existences, to work in the paradise of Telaia. For the majority of them it was wasted time hanging about the offices, but they lived in hope anyway, spending half their lives in line. What became of the women or any children, Marek didn't know, for you never saw any. Perhaps they just stayed home.

Marek was privileged; he possessed Telaian papers and had only to wait three hours on a hard bench. The exit officers worked at snail's pace, taking frequent breaks for coffee and socialization. They completely ignored the waiting men, as if they were invisible or did not even exist. Marek was in line behind sailors and various suspicious looking cut-throats, but who were considered as superior beings if they were from anywhere but Arpay. Even so, the officers ignored them with the rest.

"Papers," the moustached officer said lazily, in Arpayan, and stretching out a hand. His fingernails were chewed black and his wrist was banded with a tattoo of a blue serpent, and except for the distinction of a grubby uniform, he looked more like one of the hopeful emigrants he was supposed to serve.

Marek handed over his wad of false credentials and waited. They included a faded color photo of him with the shabby beginnings of a beard and an eye patch over one eye which the photographer had added for effect and, Marek thought at the time, was a pathetic attempt at disguise which he had not really wanted. It was unfortunate, that patch, because Marek had lost it somewhere a long time ago and so he was standing before the official with two good eyes.

The officer scanned Marek's face without much interest, mentally subtracting the beard and reconciling the similarities of the image with the man of flesh before him. But he noticed the subtle difference. "What happened to your eye?"

"Got it fixed," Marek drawled, also in Arpayan. Luckily, although Arpay existed nowadays in the realm of the down-and-out countries of the world, it had not always been that way. A hundred years ago and Arpay was a power to be reckoned with. Well, that was Arpay, just another example of history gone wrong; but, because it had once been greater, Marek had learned the classical version of its language in school. Which was more or less good enough for him to get by on.

The man studied the papers one more time. "What? Here?" Marek kept a sombre face. "Best surgeon in the country."

The black moustache twitched as the officer stifled a guffaw. He realized Marek was having him on, and his own lax slant on life helped him appreciate the irony. He knew his country was on the slide, but he didn't care all that much. The same as he didn't really care who entered Arpay or who left it. He had a job and that was to stamp papers, it wasn't hard and the pay was regular. He was employed to do nothing else and he wasn't paid extra to carry out inspections. As long as the shifty types were leaving Arpay and not coming in, it didn't matter to him if they wore a patch or not. With a grunt, he affixed the stamp.

"Next."

Three hours waiting had made it too late to look for passage on some outgoing ship, so Marek went in search of a room for the night. After covering the mazes of several winding blocks north of the Exit Office, he discovered a miserable sort of pension run by an old woman who was scruffy but not too unpleasant. The place wasn't up to much; plaster shuddered from the ceiling at the slightest vibration and the taps dripped long lines of rust down the wall. But Marek was trying to save money in case the ships" crew lists were full and he had to buy passage rather than earn it.

Just on dusk, he stepped out to look for the best place to eat. Experience in so many of these not-so- salubrious downtown environments had taught him to be careful about eating houses and the company which frequented them. There were eateries in the main road near where the offices were but to get there from the pension required that he negotiate the maze once more. This time he chose another route where the streets were wider – he did not trust the alleys at dusk. A quicker route, he hoped, than the wandering one he'd taken before. On his way he passed by another lodging house, two run down shops and a bar and several abandoned buildings covered in graffiti and slogans reading things like, "Freedom is a Gun" and 'Rampage!" and "Bullet Proof." One building, that appeared empty from a distance, proved to be some sort of medical center. The falling down sign said, FREE CLINIC, in Arpayan and Telaian. But the windows were boarded up and he could see no indication that the place was open. He wondered what sort of medicine was dealt out there and guessed it would be the usual kind. Hospitals were generally not free and if the poor could not afford treatment, then they didn't get it. The number of times he had given his services free to desperate poor people when he could barely afford his own next meal, he could not count.

A hundred yards ahead he could see that the street opened out into a square with a kind of dusty park in the middle. He checked his bearing and knew that at the square a right turn would send him almost to his destination. Thinking of eating at last, he began to feel quite hungry.

A sound behind him caused him to turn. Footsteps in the growing dusk, which stopped as he stopped. Was he being followed? He wondered. Until now he'd felt relatively safe, but had someone been watching him all along? Perhaps, if it was true, then someone even knew of his visit to the Exit Office.

Marek kept walking and he was sure that he could hear someone behind him who kept out of sight.

His best chance for losing them, he realized, was to reach the main thoroughfare, there to blend in with the night crowd and, hopefully, disappear.

At the square he paused and looked around. He could see no one, yet the sense of a presence was strong. Then, as he crossed the corner of the square, he was suddenly surrounded by men who seemed to have appeared from nowhere.

There were six of them, all youths in their teens, all cold and warrior like. A local gang, Marek decided, stalking him for literally anything he might possess. He considered that he did not look particularly prosperous, but in places like these it did not matter. When alienated young people were desperate enough and hardened by their desperation, any passing stranger was fair game.

He was almost relieved that they were only young hoodlums, except that he was in big trouble, he knew. They circled him, and he saw the glint of knives. He had no idea what he was going to do next.

It all happened very fast. One, probably the leader, approached him at a rush. Marek swung his kit bag as protection, missed, and felt the slice of metal across his side and a flood of heat beneath his jacket. He felt no pain and had turned to defend himself from the rest, when the air around them all exploded into flame. From somewhere, who could tell where, another man leapt into the space, firing, as he leapt, a weapon strange in its silence but devastating in its effects. Every one of the hoodlums fell to earth on fire, their eyes and mouths wide open in scorched surprise. Marek saw the one who had cut him fall, rise up to his knees and stare white eyed through blackened flesh before he died, as if he could not believe that life was so unfair. Then he tumbled forward onto his smouldering face.

Struggling upward, Marek turned. He still had the strength to rise, although the searing pain had caught up with him and his jacket was rapidly staining red. He turned to see that the hoodlums" assailant was no rescuer at all. The Vorken simply grinned at him, slung his flame thrower over his shoulder, took a small, modest looking pistol from his coat, aimed and fired.

The missile only entered Marek's left shoulder. Next it would have to be a bullet to the head, Marek decided as he dropped. Yet it was not much of a shot for a trained assassin, he thought, surprised by the Vorken's inaccuracy.

But no further shot came and as he lay at the feet of the bounty hunter, he saw the Vorken's cold face press near. He was still smiling.

"I'll be off now," the Vorken whispered, like a friend offering a fond

96

goodbye. 'Don't try to get up. I'll tell you this, just so you understand before you die. That is no ordinary bullet inside you. It's not even metal, it's a plastic which reacts with body chemistry and gradually dissolves and it's filled with a poison that will work its way slowly through the shell and into your nervous system. It's death by creeping paralysis, and it never fails. With something like this it doesn't really matter where I hit you, although some places are more quick acting than others. In your case it shouldn't take too long.

However, by the look of that knife cut you will probably bleed to death first."

Marek closed his eyes against the Vorken's sneering face. When he opened them again, the assassin was gone and the square was silent and empty, with only the smouldering ruins of men who were already turning to ash.

Although he struggled against unconsciousness, Marek knew he had to survive. He cast the Light around himself and it gave him the strength to get to his feet. The numbing action of the drug had not yet begun to take effect. A knife cut he could deal with, but the unknown was about to occur. He had to find help. In the back of memory was the place he had passed earlier. FREE CLINIC – the words shone in his mind like a beacon. If only someone was there.

Walking was more a case of staggering sideways until he had got up enough momentum to break into a perilous, stumbling jog. With a gradually weakening hand he pressed against his torn side; his good hand he needed, for his meager possessions and to support himself on walls whenever balance threatened to desert him. Marek knew that he did not have much time. The ache in his shoulder was already progressing to a feeling of growing stiffness down his arm and he wondered where it would extend to next. His brain probably, he decided. A certain mental fuzziness was beginning to creep in there, a lack of mental control. That was it, most likely, a gradual shut-down of the brain, bit by bit, neurone by neurone, until the whole system collapsed.

How he got finally to the clinic doorstep, he didn't really know. He found himself there, his good hand thumping feebly on the door, then dragging the peeling paint off it as he collapsed. The stone step felt as cold as ice under him and there seemed to be no answer from inside.

Chapter Three

Even from halfway down the street, through the gradually thickening shadow of streets which were never properly lit at night, Nikola Langan could see the bundle which covered the top step, blocking access to the clinic door. She groaned and said to her companion, "Not another drunk or drug addict! Oh, damn! God, I hate Vargas, Dan. I'll be glad when Dad returns and I can go back to Telaia."

Aidan Coel, or Dan as he preferred to be called, shook his head. Nikola was not like her father, whose clinic this was. But, hell, Vargas was no place for a sensitive woman, he thought, and although he knew that Nikola cared about the pain and suffering she saw and dealt with, she ought not really to be here. It was that she couldn't distance herself from the grinding misery and the cruelty of life in Arpay, that was the problem. Dan was in love with Nikola, even though he was seventeen years older. Old enough to qualify as her father himself, and often he felt nearly like it. And that was another problem too. Nikola saw him in the same way he was sure, as a great big, gruff, overly protective father figure who sometimes got on her nerves.

"It's the hopelessness of this place, Dan. That's what I can't accept," Nikola had explained to him once. "It doesn't matter what you try to do, the brutality goes on and on, nothing ever changes. Men drink and beat up their wives and the women go back to them all the time; the kids are all doomed to be drug addicts or cut up in gang fights or turned into prostitutes just to survive. I don't know how Dad can stand it."

"I guess he just has to try," Dan replied. "He's got guts, your father has."

That had made Nikola hostile, Dan remembered. She was ego centered enough to think he was criticizing her, but he wasn't. She had plenty of guts herself, he thought, for she ran a hospice for the very ill and dying on Telaia's southern coast. It took guts to watch people slowly expire when all you could give them were pain killers and a little comfort. So, there were different kinds of caring and courage, Dan thought. And everyone had to find their own way through this mess which they called the world.

"I suppose we'll have to get the poor devil inside and do what we can. Sober him up, or whatever," Nikola said as they got nearer.

"I'll see to it. You just get the door open." Dan was not only big, he was also very strong. He was an ex-cop who, for his own private reasons, had turned night club bouncer for a while, but who now loved the job he had in Vargas, despite what Nikola said about it. He was Doctor Langan's employee, and his friend of many years, and he had watched Nikola grow from girl to woman in Telaia. While the Doctor was away, he had left Dan behind to look after Nikola and keep her safe. Dan was a nurse- assistant, a strong right arm and a bouncer again when necessary. And now a bodyguard. To come to Vargas, Nikola sailed with one crew on her own motor yacht from Telaia. She lived on it in the bay because she preferred water around her rather than slums. Every evening, for the clinic was open only in the hours when most disaster happened – the night, Dan escorted her from there to here and back again in the morning.

"Oh, God!" Nikola said when they reached the stairs and saw the blood. She bent over the prostrate figure and felt for a pulse. "He's not dead. Get the door open, Dan, quick!" She fought to free the unconscious man's wrist from the tangle of a bag strap and when Dan opened the door she held the bag along with the door while Dan carried the man inside.

Dan carried him, and on the small examining table, stripped the clothes off him, while Nikola washed and got together all the things she was going to need.

"Young male, white, late twenties or thereabouts. Not from around here, I'd say. One knife cut, fairly deep and very long, on the right side just above waist level; one gunshot wound in the left shoulder, no exit point, so the bullet's still in there. Nothing else that I can see yet," Dan said, sounding to Nikola as if he was cataloguing the inventory of a corpse instead of a live patient. It was his policeman's training – always objective, generally cool, and always reliable, Nikola knew. Then Dan added, sounding almost amused this time, "Knife wound and bullet hole. That's variety. What has this guy been up to?"

Last of all Dan peeled off the gloves, observing that they were strange things to be wearing in a place as warm as Vargas in the spring. One of the gloves was soaked with blood, the result of the young man clutching at his side, Dan reasoned. The left hand and arm were strangely limp, more flaccid than they ought to be, but that wasn't what surprised Dan most. He whistled. "Nikola, look at this! What a decoration! What stone is that, d"you know?"

Nikola was too preoccupied to pay much attention to a ring, but she glanced at it briefly. "I don't know. Carnelian? Maybe jasper? No, it couldn't be. Dan, will you get washed and prepare saline? This guy's going to need a whole lot of help." She lifted the patient's eyelids. His eyes were bloodshot, inflamed. In fact even the brown irises were streaked with dark red. The pupils were dilated – he had been drugged. Well, that wasn't a surprise; around Vargas it was practically a certainty. And he was almost out of it now, she thought.

In fact, Nikola was as wrong about her patient as she was right. He had been drugged, however not in the way she thought. But he was not out of it. Although nothing was showing in his eyes, Marek was not comatose. He was aware of where he was and he hoped that his body was in competent hands.

Marek felt the burning sensation in his side, but of itself it was nothing. Not so the increasing numbing coldness creeping from his shoulder to his neck and chest. It would go on growing, spreading, like something icy and tentacled and parasitic. It was already beginning to affect his powers of concentration so that he could barely steady his mind enough to direct the Light. If he did not stop it soon he would be finished.

Contact had to be made with the woman who was seeking to help him. If she wasted time on the knife wound first, it would be too late. Marek's eyelids felt like two great pillows of stone, so it required a huge effort to lift them. He fought them open, at the same time focussing all his intent upon the woman. Please. Please! he thought.

Marek must have also made a subdued noise, for the woman's eyes flew to his face. They stared at each other for a few seconds, she and Marek; then Marek could hold the moment no longer. Nikola, poised with the needle in her hand and ready to make the dozen or so stitches needed in the side, put everything back in the dish. 'Dan, get a cold pack on this, will you? I think the bullet hole's more important."

Dan was surprised. He'd never known Nikola to be so dithering before. But he shrugged and obeyed. He might sometimes have to play the surrogate father, however unwillingly, yet when it came to this sort of thing, it was her baby and he did what he was told.

Nikola worked on the shoulder while feeling a strange sort of urgency inside her mind which she did not understand. The hole was so small that it made probing too difficult, an incision was necessary; but the wound was cleaner and the surrounding tissue damage much less than she would have expected. It was as if the missile had been slipped in place so neatly and smoothly that but for the entry hole and the slight evidence of bleeding, you wouldn't have known it was there at all.

As soon as the Vorken's bullet left his body, Marek felt the effects of the poison beginning to clear. Now he could focus his body's healing powers and recover. The speed of the woman's response had pleased, even surprised him. It seemed there was some special resonance there, between himself and her. Now that his mind and senses were untangling, he became aware of other things: the chill wash of antiseptic, the pricking of a few stitches in his shoulder, the now dull ache of his side. Then another bath of coldness at his waist, and the longer, harder to endure sewing up of the knife slash. Something sharp was put into his arm and he had to fight an oncoming lethargy. He had to stay awake just a little longer.

The man and woman were both Telaian. He heard them talking, as from a distance far away. "Odd sort of bullet," the man was saying. "In fact, it's totally weird. I'd like to find out a bit more about it. Do you mind, Nik?"

"Okay, if you want to, Dan. Once a cop, always a cop, eh?"

"Not exactly." The man sounded to be offended. "It just intrigues me, that's all."

Marek heard the rattling of a dish. He felt the sheets tug around him as if he was going to be moved.

He was – this place was a working clinic, not a luxury hotel room. They had to clean up the examining table to be ready for the night's events.

They put him in a small side room in a warm bed; the big man carried him as if he was a child and tucked him in with a mother's care. There was a drip in his good arm and the feeling of drowsiness was proving stronger. He heard one interesting fact and thought one more important thought before he fell asleep. "Heck!" the man called Dan said loudly from the other room. "What the hell's going on?

What's happening to that bullet?

"What do you mean?" the woman replied.

"The damn thing's vanishing before my eyes! The damn thing's melting! Hell, it's gone!"

Marek's thought was briefly about the Vorken and Silene. The Vorken believed Marek to be dead. Well he would be by now if everything had gone to plan. And that was a good thing because it got the bounty hunter off his back. As long as the Vorken believed that, Marek was safe. Only when he was told the truth by Silene, for Silene would know by the ring that Marek was not dead, would the problem arise again. Marek hoped it would not be soon.

Around about midnight Marek woke to the sound of rain, and of noises in the next room which broke through the muffling of the closed door because they were so loud. "Cool off!" Dan's voice was saying in rough Arpayan, "You're patched up, now get out of here!" There was the hint of a scuffle and the sound of someone being carted about bodily, probably out through the front door. Then it was quiet again.

Marek stared around him. A lamp turned to low was on the wall beside the bed and made enough light so that he could just see the shadowy corners of the room. The room was small and shabby but clean, no other objects in it but the bed, a portable drip and himself. Marek lifted the bed covers to look at the evening's damage. He was naked under the sheets. Wads of gauze were taped across his shoulder and side. The drip in his arm was taped down too. It had been changed once by now, he guessed. He didn't really need the drip, he thought, but it was doing no harm and most likely it was giving him useful fluid. So he left it alone, and, instead, tested his shoulder by reaching up tentatively at first and then turning the lamp-light higher so he could see better.

He unstuck part of the gauze and squinted down at his shoulder. Four neat evenly spaced stitches, a tidy expert job. The wound at his side was more impressive, running from the ribs down towards the navel. Marek counted fourteen stitches and winced at the memory of their putting in. They still stung a little when he moved.

What had they done with his clothes? He could not see any of his things. Well, it didn't matter for the moment; there were a lot of hours yet before morning, and he wasn't going anywhere. He lay down and got comfortable again. Time to use the next hours to best advantage.

Beginning with the aegis of his Light burning strongly and brightly around him, Marek reached inside and out – it was all one thing anyway – to make the step, to fly across the invisible spaces of a universe surging like a pile of soap-suds down a drain. That was his imagery mainly, but it served.

He came into the place of peace and there looked down upon the world floating in a soap bubble. Or a sphere of shining dew hanging on a spider web in a silvery dawn – a diamond on a thread of crystal light. And a web which no spider had made or owned; it was endless and eternal and complete.

It was marvelous that he could see – from outside – the universe and

102

right down into it, through it to the galaxy, thence to the little sun-centered world, to the planet and the place of his physical body lying in the room. This was how he healed, his own body and others. He was a Light separate from the ego and the body of flesh. As Light, he poured the blessings of love and harmony through that ego to the body, and, in resonance, it healed. This was what he had taught his beloved Tanu.

How well this worked, for himself or others, depended a lot upon understanding and upon the clarity of the flow from Light to earthly body. An ego impeded by doubt or fear, a mind without heart or sympathy, a personality corrupted by vanity and selfishness, could not allow the flow of Light to the body. And so many people believed that their bodies were themselves that they did not know they were Light at all.

Chapter Four

That's one night that's well over," Dan said. He stretched his big frame and yawned. The last of the reprobates had been shown the door and Dan was glad to see the back of them. Not that he was always throwing people out, he wasn't as callous as that, and there was genuine suffering to deal with almost every night. But tonight had brought with it more than its fair share of trouble-makers and liberty-takers. Too many drunks looking to get out of the rain. Too many punks wanting a fight or to see what drugs they could score for free, by pretending to be ill.

They'd even had a visit from the militia, Vargas's pathetic excuse for a police force, asking if they'd heard or knew anything about a dinner-time skirmish in the nearby square. It was something that had the militia totally bamboozled: six piles of greasy, smoking ash with the only evidence that human life was somehow involved being some charred shoes and rags and bones and a scattering of weapons and a deal of blood on the cobblestones. Of course, there were no witnesses; there never were. People around here had their own dramas; they didn't want to get involved in anyone else's. Dan had looked at Nikola and Nikola had looked at Dan and both of them said, No! The militia was not only pathetic, it was thoroughly corrupt. Whether the man in the next room had been involved in the trouble in the square or not, it wouldn't have mattered to the militia officers. One look at that expensive ring on his finger and they would have killed him as soon as question him, just to get the ring for themselves.

"Are you okay?" Dan asked Nikola. He thought she appeared strained. Tonight was the first time Dan had ever seen Nikola so filled with distraction. It was as though she could hardly keep her mind on the job. He guessed it had something to do with the man in the next room; Nikola had been in there so many times, Dan couldn't count them.

"I'll just check on our patient," Nikola said, yet again.

"If you think so." Dan shook a puzzled head, wondering at her behavior. Each time she returned she seemed more and more distracted, Dan didn't know why. He'd been in there a couple of times himself and although still comatose, the fellow seemed stronger with every inspection. That ought to have pleased Nikola.

"He's still out of it, but I think he's only asleep now," Nikola said when she came back. "What are you going to do about him, Nik?" Dan asked.

"I'll have to stay here today and look after him." Nikola massaged her tired eyes. "It'd be a help, Dan, if you could go out and get something to eat. I'm starved."

"I could stop in at a hospital too, have him picked up. Would save you any more trouble," Dan suggested.

"NO!"

Dan did a double take. The vehemence of Nikola's blurted out reply startled him. "What's the matter, Nik? The guy'd be better off in hospital—"

Nikola cut him off. "No!" Her face flushed to a rosy hue and Dan knew from experience that her next words would be logical ones, to cover some complicated emotion or thought. "We don't know anything about him, Dan. He might not be able to afford a hospital. If he can't they'd only turn him out. Then where would he be?"

"I suppose so," Dan agreed. "Now why don't you tell me what's really bothering you?"

Under her breath, Nikola swore, but Dan heard it. Her face was red again. "There's something about that man, something that makes me want to find out more. If we send him off to hospital, I might never know."

"Know what?"

Nikola didn't answer, so Dan said, "There's a bag and a bunch of bloody clothes. If you want to find out more, why not take a look? At least he might have some papers on him, and if we're lucky we'll know that much."

"What? Poke our noses into his things? Dan, we can't!"

The policeman still in Dan roused. "Why not? You put him back together, didn't you? I reckon he would have died without your help. At least you deserve to know what you're getting into, wanting to keep him here."

She blushed so much that Dan wondered if she'd suddenly gone soft in the head. Or was it that she was actually sweet on this guy, unconscious and unresponsive as he was? But wasn't that a bit like falling in love with a dead man? And besides, she was older than he was by the look of it. She was thirty-seven, he couldn't have been more than thirty, if he was even that. Nevertheless, the age difference wasn't all that great, a hell of a lot closer than thirty-seven and fifty-four. Better a young, good looking lover than a cranky old guy old enough to be her father. Nikola could never fall in love with himself, Dan thought miserably, and he was only kidding himself by considering it. Yet even so he would keep on doing it, he knew. While there was life there was hope, even for a fool.

Dan snatched up the bloody clothes and rifled through them. His thoughts were so stupid they embarrassed him. He told himself surely that he was making something out of nothing, and what Nikola did or didn't do was really none of his business. But why, if now he was being reasonable, did he feel the twin pangs of jealousy and possessiveness all the same?

From the jacket he pulled out money and papers. "Cash, a reasonable amount, so he's not broke.

And yeah. See, Nik … Telaian, from Alsea. A ship's deckhand, name of Matt Best. Exit papers stamped yesterday. Must have been getting ready to ship out."

"Might have missed his sailing, this happening," Nikola said.

"Yeah. Well, at least he's not one of the wandering unemployed. I'll check out the bag." "No. Leave it."

"I think we ought to."

"No!" Nikola's voice rose to nearly hostile heights. "We know his name; isn't that enough? Why Dan, what's your problem?"

Dan was taken aback. What's her problem? he thought. He'd never seen her like this before, so uptight. What had happened to his Nikola? Where had she disappeared to? He felt the irritation of having to defend himself. Damn it! Didn't the woman realize he was only trying to protect her?

"Look, Nik, this man's a deckhand. Since when did a deckhand earn enough to afford a ring like that? Come to think of it, who do you know in Telaia that could either? Did you see the gold work? It's the most expensive bit of jewelry I've ever seen. Who knows how he got hold of it, or what deals he's been making on the side?"

Nikola made a guess. "You think he's a drug dealer." "It's likely."

"Well, I don't." Nikola went to stand by the door connecting the two rooms. It was partly open. She pushed it all the way and stared into the room. "It doesn't make sense."

"What? Drugs?"

"No, not that; the ring."

Maybe he just didn't understand women, Dan thought. But what was she talking about now? 'Something else is bothering you?" he enquired.

She turned. "I feel a bit stupid, saying this." She hesitated. 'Remember when you asked me what stone was that in the ring, what did I say?"

Dan struggled to recollect a whole night-time away. He wasn't familiar with the more obscure names of gems. "Um, jasper, I think. Or, or carn-something."

"Carnelian."

"Yeah. But you said that wasn't right, in any case."

"Yes, I did. Because those gems are never faceted the way this one is. And they're not transparent either. It was just the color I was trying to get at. But now I'm totally confused."

Such fuss about a ring. "Why?"

"Because the gem in the ring is no longer that brownish-red color. During the night our patient had his hand out on top of the covers and when I turned up the light I saw. It's green, Dan, as green as grass! And what's more, this morning, if you look at it, you're going to swear that it's an emerald!"

Is that what had taken Nikola so constantly into the room, a ring that changed color? Well, it was unusual, Dan decided.

"But it's not all," Nikola said.

"What then?"

"His eyes. I know you didn't get a look at them yourself, but I promise you I'm telling the truth. They were brown when I examined him first, and a bit reddish too, but that might have been because they were so bloodshot. However, they weren't that color the last time I examined him."

Eyes which changed color too? Dan shook his head. The night had been too long and difficult; Nikola was surely exhausted. But he had to ask. "What color were they then?"

Nikola frowned. "Green, like the ring. I thought I must be dreaming."

Marek woke this time to the scents of hot coffee and food. His stomach groaned and he felt his dry mouth begin to salivate. In the last few hours before dawn he'd been so deeply asleep he hadn't even dreamed, but now it was morning and he was wide awake. He flexed his shoulder and moved in the bed. There was no pain, but the stitches prickled, especially at his waist. They would have to come out or they'd drive him crazy.

The door was open and he could hear voices. Marek called out, "Hi!"

There was a scrape of chairs and two figures filled the doorway, the woman in front, the big man towering behind her. The woman came forward. "You're awake. How do you feel?"

"Hungry," Marek replied. "I haven't eaten since early yesterday, and I'd like my clothes, please. I want to get up."

"But—" the woman began to say.

"Your clothes are all bloody," put in the man abruptly.

"Well, I've got spare ones in my bag," Marek told him. 'Maybe you would get them out for me." In the other room Dan put on his policeman's hat again and did a rethink. This deckhand from Telaia sounded the least like a deckhand that he'd ever heard. And he didn't seem bothered by the idea of a stranger rummaging about in his possessions either. It was as if he had nothing he wanted to hide, except a true identity. That made Dan suspicious; however, he wondered if the drug dealer notion was way off line.

He found the clothes and returned to the other room where Nikola was trying to talk her patient into staying put, in bed. But she was failing, miserably.

"Thanks." The young man sat up and took the clothes, and Nikola's protests died. She beat a retreat out the door.

"I've upset the lady," the young man said as Dan went to follow Nikola. "Tell her I'm sorry but not to worry about me. I'm okay, really."

In the examining room, where they had pulled chairs up to a table to have their breakfast, Nikola flopped down angrily. "He wouldn't take any notice."

"He said he was sorry he upset you," Dan reported. He was feeling quite bemused; nothing was making sense. "But it's possible he's really strong enough, otherwise he wouldn't have been so sure."

"After that? How could—?" Nikola shut her mouth. Her patient, who no longer considered himself that, was walking in through the door as if nothing had ever happened to him. Nikola had seen quick recoveries before, in young men who looked fit and strong, as this one did, but more often it was a case of patients disregarding their bodies messages, and suffering for it. This man was just too confident; without wishing it, Nikola waited for the possible collapse.

Marek did not want to upset anyone, however his thoughts immediately upon waking had been to get his things and leave, quickly. It wasn't grateful and it certainly wasn't polite, but he felt the need to get out of Vargas and back to Telaia even more strongly than he had before.

Then he recalled something important which sleep had temporarily driven out of his mind.

Resonance – he'd thought he felt it here – and wasn't that what his quest was all about? Resonant, sympathetic souls to open up the hearts of the world. He'd found them in Te Tanaa, so why not here, even in a place as destitute as Vargas?

So he reconsidered. The first thing to do was assess his rescuers, find out something about them, then decide if he could trust them with some of the truth, if not all. He had already seen suspicion on the face of the man, but since they were here in Vargas, any suspicion was to be expected and, in a way, it was reassuring. It meant that the man at least was cautious and careful about who he dealt with.

He got dressed but left his shirt undone and not tucked in. At some point he was getting those stitches out. He didn't care when as long as it was soon, and he didn't care for more objections either. Stitches weren't necessary any more, for his wounds had already healed themselves to a great degree.

"Hello," he said, coming into the next room. "Your breakfast is making me drool. If there's any left, could I have some?"

Nikola seemed struck dumb so Dan gave Marek his chair and fetched coffee from an alcove. "Hot off the stove. And we've got rice and onions, still warm – Nikola's vegetarian. I'm Dan, and you are…?"

Who am I? Marek thought. Yes, Matt Best, deckhand, otherwise known as Doc. He extended a hand. 'Matt. But some people call me Doc."

Gingerly, it seemed, Dan shook hands. "That a title?" "Sort of, but my medicine is a bit different from yours."

"Better, I suppose!" put in Nikola so suddenly and passionately that Dan started.

Marek smiled at her. He knew she was mad at him for going against her advice. "Nothing could be better than what you did for me. I'm more grateful than you know. I owe you my life."

That softened her, and she smiled a little smile. She opened the can of rice and onions and its contents steamed forth, a heavenly aroma to Marek.

Nikola said, "You had better eat then, before you starve, or else all our careful work will have been for nothing."

Chapter Five

"I'd always wanted to help people," Nikola explained. "And my father being a doctor, I thought that was the best way. Dad's father was a doctor too, and his before that, and so on; it was like an unbroken line."

"So you came here?" Marek asked.

"No. This is Dad's place. He has several around this region, and he has two in Telaia. Well, he had two, now one is mine; he gave it to me for a birthday present. I'm just here to help him out. He had some problems to sort out with one of the other clinics."

Quite a birthday present, Marek thought. He wondered that he had never come across Nikola in the old days. The dynasties that made up the historically professional families like hers often moved in similar circles to his family. They were generally rich privileged people, powerful: a consenting part of the Establishment.

So something did not quite make sense to him. Establishment types did not bother with free clinics in poor, disaster riddled areas like Arpay. That was more for the charitable types, those who spent as much time trying to scrounge money from unwilling governments and pay their rents as they did actually helping people.

"What brought your father to a place like Arpay?"

"Why bury himself in dirt, isn't that what you mean?" Nikola said perceptively, staring at Marek with a frown. "My father's a rebel. He doesn't like the road his profession has taken. And they don't like him; they rejected him a long time ago."

"'And so he came here?"

"Yes. He wanted to help people who couldn't help themselves. Fortunately, there was plenty of family money for him to do what he wanted. My grandfather was a very wealthy man and left Dad everything. But it was Dad's own grandfather who inspired him. He was a country doctor, and that made him many things to many people: surgeon and medicine man, psychologist, confessor, sometimes even a baby sitter. And most of all a friend. He didn't have a fancy house or elegant rooms and he didn't charge fancy prices either. Sometimes he didn't charge at all. Also he knew when to quit, when to let a patient go; he wasn't afraid of death. I guess Dad is a bit of a throwback to the old man; he never could see the point in learning to fix broken bodies just to end up doling out drugs to neurotic rich people, or lining his pockets with the profits of drug subsidiaries."

"And you share his feelings on that, otherwise you wouldn't be here," Marek guessed.

"Yes, that's about right. I must be a throwback too, except that I can't stand this place. I don't like Arpay and I can't stand Vargas. Dan could tell you how much, I'm always ear-bashing him about it. I suppose that makes me a bit less than noble compared to my father, but it's how I feel." Nikola flushed and looked at Dan, who throughout the conversation had been conspicuously silent.

Marek realized that Dan's silence was deliberate; so that he could listen better, observe better. And Marek was the subject under the spotlight. "Are there rules about how a person has to feel?" Marek said. "If there are I'd like to know who makes them up. You have your reasons, I'm sure."

Nikola's eyes grew wide and over bright. She looked from Dan to Marek and back to Dan, then back again. "Yes, there are. I hate the dirt and the misery, but not for myself. It gives me pain to see the people here, especially the children. They have no future in this place and even though my father has had this clinic for twenty years, not a thing has changed. All we do here is patch up damaged lives, and it seems that there's no will, not even in the people who suffer most, to change it."

Marek thought she might be going to cry. Dan must have thought so too, because he was wringing his hands slowly, and Marek could see the pain in his eyes also. But the pain Dan felt was chiefly for Nikola, not Vargas.

There was an awkward silence then and Marek's other questions hung unasked in the emotion- charged air. He had to make a decision, he told himself. He had to follow the lead of his intuition which had told him from the beginning that resonance lay here. These were truly good people, not selfish or vain. Perhaps they would understand his predicament and help him. Perhaps they could even understand the rest.

"I really ought to tidy up, or the clinic will never be ready for this evening." Nikola got up and began putting things away in cupboards.

"Give it a rest," Dan said. "You worked all night, I'll do it." "So did you."

Dan emptied her hands of tablet jars and cotton. "All the same, I said I'll do it," he asserted. Gently he pushed her away. "Sit down. Rest. You should be back at the harbor, in bed and asleep by now."

It was raining outside, heavily, pouring down like an upturned river upon the filthy streets. Spring in Vargas was always the same, nothing but dust for weeks, then a deluge of sticky rain that sometimes went on for days and washed all the dirt down to the shore. "Couldn't go out there anyway," Nikola replied. She sat next to Marek, close enough that her hand almost touched his on the table. "I worry about you. Are you sure you're not feeling weak or tired? By rights you should still be a cot-case."

"I'm fine," Marek answered. "Once you got that bullet out of me I knew I'd survive. Then I could hurry up the healing, as usual. It was close, though. The bullet was made from a dissolving plastic and it actually held a poison which attacks the nervous system. It would have finished me off if you hadn't been here to help."

The silence that followed this speech was heavier than the rain. "What?" Nikola said finally, and Dan had turned and stared. "You mean you know what that bullet was all about? Do you know also that it actually evaporated in the dish afterward? It simply vanished without a trace?" Dan asked.

"Yes to both questions. The man who shot me told me what it would do, and I heard you say the bullet had melted."

"And who cut you? The same guy?"

"No. That was a gang of young men. Kids really. They just wanted to rob me, but they got more than they bargained for, I'm afraid."

Dan was in policeman mode again. The trouble in the square, he thought. "What happened to the kids?"

"They're dead," Marek said. "The one who shot me killed them."

Dan remembered the sickening description of the square given him by the militia. "What weapon?" "Some sort of flame thrower. I don't know much about weapons."

"How horrible!" Nikola winced. "But why did he only shoot you, with that poison thing?"

Marek looked away from her intense eyes. He could almost see reflected in them the image of burning boys and of the one who had lived just a little longer than the rest, staring up from a blackened, smoking face and white eyeballs in disbelief at his own demise. Marek shuddered. If anything had the power to make him feel ill, it was this memory in particular. "He wanted me to know. He wanted my death to take some time, so I would know."

Nikola was horrified. "Oh, God! Know what?"

"That he had been sent after me, to kill me, and that he'd succeeded."

"Okay, that's enough!" Dan interposed, coming over to stand above

Marek. "You've just told us that an extremely dangerous murderer is on the loose and that he's been hunting you. Now I've been listening carefully to everything from the beginning and I noticed how apt you are at asking questions. Nikola has practically told you the story of her life, but this ... tale of murder is all we've got from you—"

Nikola interrupted. "Dan, you're being a bit hard—"

"No, Nik, let me handle this." Dan glared at Marek. "Either you tell us everything or you leave right now; I'm not having Nikola put in danger. And don't tell me you're a deckhand named Matt Best either; you look and sound as much like a deckhand as I do somebody's maiden aunt. Now take your choice."

"Dan!" Nikola protested.

"No, he's right," Marek agreed. "I'd like you to know the truth, although I don't expect it will give you much comfort. My problem in the past has been knowing who to trust. You see, I've been on the run for six years."

Nikola stared. "On the run. From whom?"

"From the law?" Dan asked, with narrowed eyes. "No, from my brother."

There was silence again.

Rain poured down the window in long greasy streaks. Arpay was worse than this in the summer; then it rained every day and was so hot that mushrooms grew like large fleshy ears out of cracks in the walls. The phrase that walls have ears meant something entirely different and literal in Arpay.

Marek had to speak above the pounding of the rain as it hit the roofs of tin and broken tiles. "My real name is Marek De Ravana, and my brother is a powerful man in Telaia. Just over six years ago I did something he could never forgive. I went against him, not politically or in any way that matters to most people, but to him it was a situation he wasn't prepared to tolerate."

The air had the pressure of a giant's heavy hand. Not only that, both Nikola and Dan were listening with the intensity of fascination. "What did you actually do?" Nikola asked.

"I denied him. That doesn't sound like much, I suppose, but Silene had brought me up to be a perfect carbon copy of himself. He wanted me to take over from him one day and when I denied him he knew his plans had failed. So he hunts me down to this very day. He's afraid of what I know about him, and of what I could tell the world."

"Silene De Ravana? His high-and-mighty Lordship, eh?" Without humor, Dan smiled. "Hunting down his brother. So, he's not the lily-white aristocrat. What a surprise. When I was on the police force I heard rumors about him and his lot that would curl your hair ... well, they wouldn't yours, I guess. None of the rumors ever got to be anything more, of course. Too many of my lot were in the pay of his. That's one of the reasons I left the force. A cop trying to be honest doesn't last long in a situation like that."

Nikola poured fresh, hot coffee into china mugs. "Fancy, your own brother being your enemy. That's sad." Dan had left them for a while, to clean up some messes in the hall. It was the usual kind of thing they had to deal with after a busy night; somebody had bled against the wall, or had been sick on the floor. The stain of Marek's blood decorating the front step had been easily dealt with by the rain.

"Is this the first time he's caught up with you?"

"I've managed to stay out of sight, yes," Marek answered. "The Vorken, that bounty hunter, thinks I'm dead. He was so sure of himself that he won't suspect I'm alive. It's Silene who's the problem though. He'll know. And I have to go back to Telaia."

"How will he know?" Nikola enquired. "If we don't tell him, no one else will. And why go back to the place where he's most likely to find you? I don't understand."

Marek sighed. "It's a difficult thing to explain, however I'll try. But first I'd like a favor. These stitches are driving me mad. Would you take them out, please?"

Nikola was dismayed. "But I only just put them in! If the stitches come out, you'll just open up again, especially that wound in your side. Surely you realize that!"

"Just have a look at them." Marek pulled off his shirt. "If you can accept what you see then I'll tell you more about my brother and me and what I have to do in Telaia."

Nikola gazed at him skeptically, sighed and shook her head, then peeled back the gauze first at the shoulder. Her facial expression was one of shock and surprise, almost of disbelief, and very quickly she stooped to his side. With extra care she lifted one piece of tape, peered under the gauze, and then lifted off the other end. She studied the long

114

dark stripe with a fixed concentration, as if she was trying to convince her brain of the evidence of her eyes. "Lift your arm up high," she ordered. "That is, if you can."

Marek lifted his arm and Nikola's eyes opened wide. "That doesn't hurt? No feeling of strain?" "It's a bit tight, that's all."

Nikola leapt up. She called, "Dan, stop what you're doing and come in here for a minute. Come and look at this!"

"I'm finished, anyway." Dan materialized with bucket and mop in hand. "What?"

"Stand up, please," Nikola said to Marek. To Dan she said, "Look. Stitches put in only fifteen hours ago or thereabouts, and you'd swear they'd been in for nearly two weeks!" She stared at Marek. "How do you do it? I've never seen anything heal that fast! Have you done it before?"

Marek touched his fingers along the line of stitches. Their cut off ends tickled. There were four stitches in his shoulder too and that was better healed than the side, probably because it was so much smaller. "Not for myself, not something like this."

"You do it for other people?" Dan asked. He squinted and bent closer. Actually he needed his glasses but he never wore them in the clinic. Vanity, he supposed, for they made him look older and less of a fierce proposition.

"Yes. That's my medicine. I said it was different from yours."

Nikola's face reddened. "It's amazing, but wonderful. If only ..." Her words trailed off into a dazed expression, as if she had left the world and was somewhere else far away.

"How long have you been able to do ... it?" Dan said. He did not quite know how to describe what he saw.

"As long as I've been away. Six years plus a couple of times when I was on the run in Telaia. My brother knows nothing about it."

"It's a wonder you didn't cause an uproar everywhere you went. That sort of thing's likely to attract a crowd."

"I never let anyone know how I manage to help them. I carry herbs, and I use them too, because they always work well. Not every condition is as dramatic as this. Sometimes people need more cosseting than cure. They need to feel cared about so they will care about themselves. I give them

115

the right herbs and they take them and we talk. Over the days or weeks I listen to them talk and hear what they're saying about themselves, then I set them straight about what their illness really means and about what their body should mean to them."

Nikola joined them again, but she must have been listening because she said, "This is wonderful, Marek. My place in Telaia is not like this place. It's a hospice for people who are either very ill or terminally so. Not rich people, but those who can't afford fancy sanatoriums. We do what we can for them, but it would be so great if you could come there. You said you had to get back to Telaia and I could take you. I've got my own yacht in the harbor and you can exit here legally as Matt Best and enter Telaia the same."

"Hold on, Nik—" Dan objected. However Nikola was not hearing him. She had eyes and ears only for Marek, waiting for his reply.

"I can't bring dead people back to life. Neither can I help people who are determined to die," Marek explained.

"No, no, I didn't mean that," Nikola replied. Her face was lifted to him and her eyes were alight with excitement. "You could help them though, couldn't you? Some of them live in such terrible pain, the sort of pain no drug can ease. But couldn't you do something?"

In Te Tanaa, Marek's introduction to the Tanu had been to help the Head-man's old mother die, by accompanying her to the gate of death in peace and happiness. It was she who had given him the title of Messenger before anyone else. Marek nodded. "I would try."

"Then you'll come with me?" Marek nodded again. "Yes." "Nik ..." Dan tried to say.

Once more she ignored him, not for any other reason than because her thoughts were racing so far ahead, and objections meant so little. "Get on the exam table and lie down," she said to Marek. "I can't take those stitches out while you are standing up."

116

Chapter Six

Nikola had decided. "I'm not going to reopen the clinic."

Dan agreed. "Good idea. You need the rest. You haven't slept in twenty four hours. Matter of fact, neither have I."

"No, Dan," Nikola explained. "I'm closing it. I'm going back to Telaia first thing tomorrow morning and taking Marek with me."

"Closing! But what about your dad?"

"He's going to be here in a couple of days, and the clinic has been closed before."

Then what about me? Dan wondered. Was he supposed to watch Nikola leave Vargas in the company of a stranger? A dangerous stranger at that.

Did Nikola not realize the trouble she could be getting herself into? Or was it that she did not care? Worried and unhappy, Dan said to himself, She's smitten with this man. She's only known him one day and already she's wanting to mean something to him. But what does she mean to him? A lift back to Telaia? Safe haven for a while? A sympathetic ear?

It was not that Dan disbelieved Marek's story. God and the Devil knew he wasn't surprised that a ruthless man like the Baron De Ravana would hunt down his own brother because he knew too much. Dan was not naive, he knew what evil went on in the world, but it seemed that Nikola was, or that deliberately she was blinding herself to the facts. Why won't she listen to me? Dan thought. She listens to a man she's only just met. I've been her friend for all of her life, but she turns me aside, just like that. She means everything to me, so why can't she see it? I care about her more than any stranger is going to, so why doesn't she understand?

Dan decided to give it one more try.

He could speak freely at the moment because the stranger was in the other room, however he dropped his voice to a whisper. "Nikola, please listen to me. I know you like Marek, and I think he's okay, in himself. But you're not just dealing with him if you get involved. He's dangerous goods, Nik. For heavens sake, there's an assassin after him, a madman with a flame-thrower running around out there looking for him, a cold blooded murderer, Nikola. Not some natty gentleman with a purse and a pocket handkerchief!"

Nikola pinched her lips in a tight expression of defiance. She whispered back, "Then he needs help all the more. And besides, that assassin thinks Marek is dead. He won't be looking now, will he? He's probably left town already."

"Nik, You may not realize this, but bounty hunters generally like to get paid for their services; it's their trade. Marek said so himself that his brother would know he wasn't dead, although I don't know what he meant. That bounty hunter's going back to Telaia with a grin on his face and his hand out for his money. Then, if what Marek says is right, all he'll get is a knock-back. How do you think that's going to go down with a madman?"

Nikola's mouth opened and dropped. Ah, a doubt. A question at last, thought Dan. But just as quickly she shored up the crack in her tight armor and her mouth returned to its thin line.

"You don't have to patronize me, I know what a bounty hunter is."

"Then you understand that the danger isn't over. That young man next door may be nice, but for the people he comes near he's just one big risk."

"A risk I'll take," Nikola asserted. "I think he's worth it."

Dan could have shaken her. She had always been fairly stubborn, even as a child, but he had never thought of her as stupid before. Had her brains suddenly turned to mush, and was this what infatuation did? He could not bring himself to use the word "love", nor even consider it. If it was true, then that would be a thought too hard to bear.

Although the roads and paths were rivers and mud caked their shoes, rain was the best cover for making way anonymously down to the harbor. Upturned collars, hoods and heavy rain capes made good disguises and what people there were on the streets rushed by, their heads down so as not to mis-step and take an unwanted bath in dirty water.

At the dock Dan and Marek waited in a dilapidated shed with no front door or wall while Nikola paid the local boatman to ferry them to the yacht. The boatman drew his dinghy out from under the dock itself and bailed it out; he hadn't expected a fare all day, and his grinning smile was broad and obsequiously grateful. The dinghy was a small, faded specimen of ageing timbers. Most likely it leaked, but who could tell in all that rain?

Marek gazed out across the bay. Rain poured down in sheets, blurring the images of ships and boats. There was no way of telling which of the boats was Nikola's. "You'd sail in rough weather?" he asked her.

Nikola explained. "It's a motor yacht. As long as it's only rain, we can."

The boatman was ready, his grin still holding strong under a dripping hood. "Get in the dinghy," Nikola told Marek. "I want to say goodbye to Dan."

Marek sat on the wet seat; his boots dabbled in a puddle at the bottom of the boat. He could see Nikola and Dan, and they were still arguing. He pulled the rain cape around him and ignored the boatman's idiotic grin, and waited.

The motor yacht Rhona was larger than Marek had expected. It was an ocean cruising vessel of impressive dimensions with four staterooms, two bathrooms, a spacious saloon and aft deck dining area, galley, and a wheel house with literally everything necessary and useful for modern navigation. Nikola's sole crew was the Captain, a man named Boddy, who treated her respectfully and called her Ma"am even though she was a doctor and unmarried. Marek thought that made her sound somewhat like a grand lady or a queen, and he was a bit surprised. He wondered how she managed to run such a ship when her main business in life was to provide charitable help to the poor.

They were both drenched by the trip from the dock, so after a quick tour, it was to the bathroom where Marek had his first hot shower in many days. Six years away from Telaia had made him forget what luxury was like. The soft white towels, the steaming water, the scent of spice and flowers of Nikola's soap. It was enough to make him almost sentimental for days gone by, but it was only the physical comforts he was remembering which made him feel that way.

Nikola had shown him to a guest stateroom with walls upholstered in heavy fabric to match the pattern on the cover of the bed. Captain Boddy had provided nautical looking clothes for Marek until his own were dry again. When Marek finished showering he found them laid out on the bed in orderly sailor fashion, so he knew it was not Nikola who had put them there.

How did Nikola afford all this? Besides its double bed, the stateroom had a banquette for an additional sleeper. If he assumed that all four staterooms were similar, that must mean the yacht had berths enough for ten people. Why did she need a boat this big when there was only herself plus the Captain?

All the floors and the walkways inside were carpeted and soft underfoot. Marek went barefooted to the saloon to see that he was the only one there. He found himself surrounded by warm polished wood and shining brass. The seating was plush upholstered armchairs, color coordinated to match the floors and lamps. Very tasteful. In a tight ship every square of space was utilized to the maximum. Where the vessel's heating unit and drive shaft were likely to be housed, a concealing wall unit of cupboards and shelving and a copper-clad bar with a mirror behind and rows of every kind of liquor formed an elegant entertainment area. Did Nikola drink a lot? Or maybe it was the Captain?

Marek went forward and up to the wheel house, to find it empty. He lingered a while to examine the amazing cornucopia of gadgetry and equipment. Then, smelling a scent which was fragrant and appetizing coming from aft, he followed his nose and found Captain Boddy in the galley, stirring something in a silver pan. The galley had the same atmosphere of efficiency and order as the wheel house, so Marek guessed that the Captain was also the cook.

Captain Boddy was broadly built though not tall. He laughed at the sight of a taller, slimmer Marek swimming in his clothes but with wrists and ankles well exposed. It was in his nature to be relaxed and easy going, Marek gathered. A friendly man who liked to laugh; quite a different proposition from the other man in Nikola's life, Dan.

"I always wanted to go to sea," the Captain told Marek. "But I started off my working life as a professional chef, before I took to sailing. This job suits me just fine because now I get to combine both."

The Captain's words proved to be one more puzzle in the mystery of the Rhona. Marek did not think that cooking for one person and oneself would constitute a satisfactory challenge for a professional chef; but then who could say what ought to satisfy another?

He left the galley and waited for Nikola in the dimly lit saloon. He spent the time thinking briefly of Silene, then he looked at his ring. The hue of the stone was blue, like a sapphire, and he knew without looking in a mirror that it was the color to match his eyes. He was not pleased about that.

All that had happened since the Vorken's attack had caused him to lose focus in that regard. Briefly, if Silene was watching, he had become a partially open book. Yet there was every chance that Silene may not have seen. It was time to return the focus to its point of light.

But before he could do anything, Nikola arrived. Her coppery auburn hair, which had been tied back in a practical plait for the clinic, was loose and full around her shoulders and damp from the shower. There were dark circles under her eyes and her skin was pale, she hadn't slept for well over twenty four hours; but, in contradiction of this, her spirit was bright and alive and it shone from her face with a glow of genuine bonhomie. For the first time since meeting her, Marek was able to appreciate how attractive she really she was. He wondered how old she might be and took a guess at thirty five. She was actually quite warm and womanly, he thought, now that she was freed from the doctor-posturing of the clinic and that shapeless white coat she had worn.

Nikola greeted Marek eagerly. Tiredness, it seemed, had not dulled the excitement in her but enhanced it. She was on a high; perhaps it was the lack of sleep, but her consciousness felt to be heightened and her mind was incisive and alert. And peculiarly sensitive. In the half darkness of the dusk and the rain outside, she saw Marek in Captain Boddy's blousy, oversized clothes, saw the flash of the ring on his hand and caught the azure brightness of his eyes, and one part of her was not surprised even while the other part marvelled.

The excitement came from a source Nikola recognized but did not comprehend entirely. She had already traced it back to that moment of astonishment when Marek had first opened his eyes and their minds had met. That was it exactly, there had been a contact of the kind which she could not describe, even to herself. A contact of mind and feeling which had opened a door in her consciousness. It was this which she could never explain to Dan, for he had not experienced it. And she was sorry that she could not, because her insistence on keeping Marek with her, no matter what, had been the thing to drive a space between them. How could Dan understand her feeling about Marek when she could barely understand it herself?

"Poor Dan," Nikola thought then. "He's so gruff and bossy at times, but also very sweet. I wish I hadn't upset him so."

She switched up the lamps, and the saloon and Marek burst into brightness. She felt her face grow almost feverish as she sat opposite. "We'll have dinner soon. The Captain said it won't be long. Are you hungry?"

Marek nodded. "It won't be too soon for me. And you look exhausted. You need rest." "It's been a long twenty four hours."

"Can I ask you a personal question?" Marek said.

"If I can ask you one too," Nikola replied. Marek grinned. "Mine's only short."

Nikola grinned back. "Mine's complicated. Go ahead."

"I'm curious, and I know it's none of my business, but the Rhona is what I'd call real luxury. How can you afford it, much less keep it up?"

"That is personal," Nikola said. "And it could be that I have a very rich lover who lets me keep the boat in exchange for favors." She smiled at Marek's bemused face. "But, unfortunately, I don't. As I told you earlier, my father has what some people call "independent means". I don't, but Dad has been generous. He bought the boat originally for my mother; that's why it's called the Rhona – her name.

But now I maintain it. I use it for myself only when I need to. The rest of the time I hire it out for charter to people who like to impress, you know, business types for entertaining, parties for cruising, things like that. They get a luxury craft and a very nice host and gourmet chef in the Captain. We also do a package tour of the gulf islands, with an experienced pilot, nice accommodations and splendid meals, and the proceeds help pay for the hospice. In many ways the Rhona is more Captain Boddy's and the hospice's than it is mine. It serves the hospice, and the Captain is in charge and spends nearly all his time on board."

"Tell me about your ring. Then tell me about your eyes," Nikola asked. "Dan thought you might have stolen the ring or got it in some awful way. That's when he thought you might be a drug dealer."

"A drug dealer!" Marek laughed. "Well I suppose that was a reasonable assumption considering the circumstances." He grew thoughtful, and to Nikola's mind, seemed sad.

"Actually it was awful, the way I got the ring, although I didn't think so at the time. I was just sixteen and Silene had it made for me as a perfect copy of his own. It was a much too expensive gift for a youth, even for one who was used to rich things. My mother was angry with him, but for other reasons as well – I won't go into those. I was only flattered; I thought it made me look important.

Some of my school friends taunted me about it though." "You wouldn't have liked that," Nikola reasoned.

"No, I didn't. But Silene said they were only fools, and that they did it because inferior minds were always prone to jealousy and spite."

"Did you believe him?"

"In a way. I didn't like to be teased, so I decided that his answer was the best revenge.

"I thought the ring was the best gift in the world. When Silene explained to me that it was a special kind of stone, one which changed color with my moods, I believed him. After all, he had one just like it, so

122

why should he lie? And in a way he wasn't lying, because it was a mood ring. However he didn't tell me the whole truth, that it showed the state of my health and intent of mind, and that his own ring was resonant with mine. All he had to do was concentrate on his ring and think of me and it would show him how I was and the mode of my thoughts. To him I couldn't lie; I couldn't hide from him either. It took me a long while before I knew I was being monitored and then longer to figure out why."

Without actually questioning how such a thing could be, Nikola wondered why herself. And why Marek still wore the ring. "Can't you take it off? You could sell it to a pawn shop or even give it away, or throw it in the sea."

With an effort, Marek turned the ring on his finger. "See how tight it is. If I could get it off I would toss it overboard right now. Remember, I said I was sixteen. I was a light-weight, pretty thin and scrawny. By the time I was twenty-five and wanted it off, my hand had grown in size. I've never been able to get it over my knuckle; it's too big, although I've tried, believe me."

"So your brother knows your mind even now and that you are alive, not dead, as the bounty hunter thinks."

"That's about it. But Silene hasn't known my mind for six years. I found a way to shield myself and the ring from his snooping. When I got shot that messed things up a bit. I'll put that right later tonight."

Although Nikola would have loved to know how, she didn't ask. Instead she said, "Your eyes fascinate me. They seem to change color in sympathy with the ring. Does your brother have eyes the same?"

"No. His eyes are grey, a bit like yours, only darker. I'm the only person I know with eyes like this. 'Chameleon Eyes', my father used to call them. But they're not that changeable. If they match the ring, it's because they reveal similar things. If I'm ill or hurt as I was, they generally look a dark reddish brown. When I'm actively healing my body or helping someone else, they go green. When I'm calm and relaxed, or talking with someone as I am now, they're blue or blue-green. But I don't think about them all that much, otherwise I'd go crazy."

"It's a wonder you don't, what with people asking you about them all the time." "Most people don't even notice."

On reflection, Nikola agreed. "Yes, that's more like the reality. I just noticed because I had to look closely. And…" she smiled here, "you interested me. Tell me, Marek," she continued, as her smile grew more mischievous. "What color would your eyes be if you were in love?"

"I don't know," Marek said. "Do you think dinner would be ready yet?"

Before he prepared to sleep Marek had Ozira focus on the ring. The gem flashed and dazzled and turned to diamond brightness, briefly lighting up the stateroom with white fire. Silene may know he wasn't dead, but that was all he would know.

After their talks over dinner and the probing questions asked by Nikola, Marek was tired of thinking and reliving a history which was meaningless to him now. He just wanted to rest, and the bed was luxury itself, and the boat seemed to shift sleepily in the water. The rain, though lessening, drowned out all other sound; as a blessing from Mother Nature, it even drowned out thought.

Marek closed his eyes and breathed deeply, glad of the isolation of the rain. But he was not really alone. A single idea, planted by Nikola, would not leave him be.

"What color would your eyes be if you were in love?"

"I don't know." He had never been in love … why was that?

Bringing a scent of tropical flowers and salt breezes, Lani joined him in the bed. "You have been to many places; but were you ever in love?"

No … but there had been that one …

Lani got up to go. "Six years is a long time. That girl is probably grown up by now."

The rain beat its monotonous, sleep inducing rhythms on timber and water, and Marek spoke to himself one name: Faran. Lani was right. Six years was long enough to turn a girl into a woman. His heart seemed to ache with a deep pain when he thought of her. He wondered how she would be. Had the years and the world been good to her? He hoped they had. Although he thought of her and could contact within himself the brightness and clarity of her Light, her face and form remained that of a child.

Then he slept and during the night, dreamed of a wild, high country inhabited by the spirit of a fair, young goddess with threads of gold and silver for her hair, and a heart that waited for him to come home.

Chapter Seven

The Rhona docked three days later at a shared mooring beneath a coastline which soared almost perpendicular above the water. A road ran along the narrow shore just a stone's throw from the gravel beach and followed the cliff side upward in corkscrew twists and leaps until it vanished over the top. This part of the southern coast was different from the other, for it tumbled down to the sea from the vast distance of the inland heights and was the tail end of Telaia's giant backbone of mountains which formed a long tapering isthmus which ultimately drowned itself in the sea. For the rest of the wide south coast, the land dropped smoothly and gradually until it finally reached sea level and the popular holiday resorts so beloved of Telaia's wealthy populations. What the rich saw in those tacky, glitzy, swampy towns, Marek had never understood even when he was a boy. He saw even less to attract him this time as the Rhona had passed them by.

The way up to the top of the hill was by riding in an ancient, decorated carriage drawn by two tough little ponies plumed with pink and blue feathers. "For the tourists," Nikola explained as they climbed inside. "It's not comfortable but it's quaint, and they like it. The carriage runs the coastline on the bottom road too. Just around the corner, a little way on, there's a village which reaches from the water to halfway up. That's where the tourists stay. The little hotels there charge outrageous prices. Have you ever been here before?"

"No," Marek said. "How far is your place?"

"Not far. The top of the hill, across the coastal reserve and on the other side of the road. You can hear the sea from it sometimes, when the wind blows the sound around the cliffs."

Nikola's hospice looked more like an old style, double storey country manor house with modern, single storey extensions. The new had been made to blend in with the old, but the gardens were all vintage, full of spring flowers and leafy walks under ancient drooping trees. In fact it had been a hotel once, and a bit of a derelict when Nikola's father bought it, and had come cheap because of the mess. "The patients live mainly in the extensions. It's easier for them to get out into the gardens that way.

There's nothing like nature for bringing peace and acceptance to the suffering. It seems to harmonize them and it doesn't demand anything," she explained.

She put Marek upstairs, in a couple of rooms not far from her own. Since he had so little luggage she talked about buying him clothes in the nearby town. Marek had not thought about clothes, other more pressing things concerned him. In three days he had told Nikola a great deal about himself, excluding all of Mari-E-ele, Ozira, Te Tanaa and the journal. That would come later, maybe. Nikola knew the risk she was taking in having him there; even so, he thought he ought to remind her again.

"You will have to call me Matt, not Marek. And if I'm to help your patients it will have to be in the same way that I've done for the past six years. I can't draw attention to myself, I can't afford the notoriety, and neither can you. My brother is not a forgiving man and he doesn't care who he steps on. Your hospice and all the people you help mean nothing to him or his kind."

Nikola nodded glumly, her satisfaction in having settled Marek in so neatly and without the suspicion of the authorities suddenly lessened. Reality was reality, not always nice to know, but fact. So, she had to call him Matt, but that didn't spoil things. However he meant it when he said he had to keep a low profile, and that was a shame.

In her eagerness to be seeing just what Marek could do, Nikola had put out of her mind the danger which his presence posed. She had even been thinking to herself, speculating really, of how a man of his unique talents could be a good draw card for the hospice. However, yes, she had been foolish to even consider it, for she could not afford to publicize him any way beyond that of a simple, if successful user of natural medicines. Still, all was not lost. The main thing was that she had him here, with her. That was what mattered most, she told herself. She said in answer to his intent, serious face, "I understand, yes I do."

126

PART 3
Spring, One Year Later

Chapter One

Just north and slightly inland of the Telaian seaside town of Minerva, plantations of banana palms spread like battalions over the low red soil hills and waved their wide fringed leaves like green flags to passers-by on the main road. Dotted along the road were makeshift stalls with signs reading, "BANANAS – Large Hands at Wholesale Prices," and similar. Also, at irregular intervals, there were little shops and tea houses. The tea houses filled jaded travellers" stomachs; the shops filled their pockets with bric-a-brac and useless novelties.

One of these shops, however, sold items which were more worth taking home. Things like delicate crystal jewelry and home made perfumes and salves, and unusual jams and savory spreads, and, once a week, fresh baked bread. The shop was called simply The Sisters" Shop and it was popular even with the locals who knew it to be run by a commune of women living up behind the plantations in the forested hills of the hinterland.

To one side of the shop a road of red dirt ran back between the palms. Each day, seven days a week, along this road, several of the women would travel down from the hinterland to act as custodians of the shop. They styled themselves as Sisters belonging to a loosely grouped Sisterhood, and since no one around the area had ever seen their home or exactly how they lived, they were considered by most to be peculiar, even while the goods they sold in their shop were widely appreciated and, when spoken to, the women seemed as normal as anyone else.

On the first day of spring three of the women arrived at the shop with a truck load of the season's new fruit wines. These were always pressed during autumn and fermented over winter and were very quick sellers. Usually they sold out in the first two weeks, so they provided the commune with a good financial start to the new year.

Two of the women were nearing middle age; the third was twenty-one. The youngster, as the others thought of her, was a girl with long wavy hair of the color and fineness of spun gold. She was not a big girl and was finely made, even delicate looking, but she was capable and willing to work. She had large blue eyes which seemed always a shade too wistful and prompted silent questions in those who considered themselves her friend. But no one ever asked the questions, for it was the agreement of all the women who joined the group that no one ever questioned another's life unless invited. The commune was not religious, nor did it have any official rules beyond contributing in some way to the whole and respecting the life of another. It was just a group of women tired of the world outside who were trying to find a better way to live together.

That was how it had started out, at least, with an ideal of happy, companionable living. But Faran was finding out that ideals rarely survived the turbulence of personalities and neuroses and the desire to dominate or rule which most people fell prey to. She was beginning to feel isolated in the Sisterhood, as the youngest and as one who could not help but observe the fallacies of their daily lives.

Faran had come to the commune in search of peace mainly and some sort of purpose. But a number of the women there were jaded and bitter and were turned against the world of men because of their own bad experiences. In fact, men were never invited to the commune, to prevent the inevitable conflict they would cause. Well, that was the stated reason, whether it was true or not. And that, thought Faran, is just one more silent rule to add to the rest. Two years in the group had revealed a dozen unspoken laws which she must not break. In many ways, this world was the same as the one she'd left, except there were only women in it.

"We'll put the boxes in the corner then you two set the bottles out on the shelves near the front window, in nice neat rows, and color coordinated, mind, not all over the place." As she always did in any activity, Thea considered herself in charge. And Betti, her limp, overly adoring actual sister, bleated an obedient mew that meant agreement.

Or so it sounded to Faran. She began to feel worried. "Now I'm getting bitchy," she told herself.

The silent criticisms of women she had once admired were increasing with every day and she wondered how much longer she would last in the commune. Of course she could go back to her aunt and uncle's house in Hanna Harbor. Young Will was at a boarding school near there. But that would mean throwing herself back into Aunt Moria's idea of society, and that she couldn't stomach.

She felt so unsociable today. Perhaps it was the spring, for it had seemed that the first breeze of the morning brought with it a restlessness of spirit and a desire to be anywhere but where she was. She found herself wishing she was back in the high country. There was a place which knew what spring was all about. Down here there was no spring at all, just degrees of heat. Faran missed the change of seasons, that sense of rebirth as Mother Nature woke from her winter sleep and blossomed.

"I'll take the truck back," Faran said. It was a good excuse to get away since the truck was needed in the commune. Thea and Betti wouldn't object; they preferred each other's company in any case.

Driving the truck wasn't easy. It was an old bomb of a thing with gears which stuck, and it jerked and leaped about on the road and rattled your bones as if they were loose inside your body. But Faran was pleased that she'd mastered it. That was one good thing about the commune, it had taught her a lot and made her self reliant. To be a useful functioning member of the group you had to learn to do everything yourself. If something was broken, you fixed it; if there was building to be done, or renovating work, you learned how to do it and did it. And if something had to be driven, you drove it. That suited Faran; she liked knowing that she could look after herself.

As she negotiated the long rough road, the restlessness of the morning returned, and had the truck not been so decrepit, Faran felt she might have by-passed the commune and kept on driving. But to where and what for? Not only would she have run out of fuel eventually, but she had no direction in mind. And besides, the truck wasn't hers to take.

At the commune shed she parked the truck then began unloading the empty boxes by herself. She wasn't alone for long though. One of the women came running out of the big house to help. Her name was Kay and she was thirty nine, which made her much nearer to Faran by years than either Thea or Betti and less domineering because of it. Faran quite liked Kay, although they had never shared more than superficial conversation.

"Faran, guess what! Jan is back from Tempah Springs! She caught a lift up from Minerva. It's a wonder you didn't pass her on your way down to the shop. You should see her, Faran, it's amazing! She looks so well!" Jan was Kay's particular friend. They were twins in age and also very similar to look at. They had both been Sisters for a long time and of the two Jan was the hardest worker. Only she had been laid up by a serious inflammation of the joints and it bothered her that she could not contribute. So she'd made the journey to the town most famous for its mineral springs, where she hoped she would find a cure.

Faran stacked boxes one by one onto a pile in the corner of the shed. "So the springs did her aches a lot of good, then?" Kay added to the pile. "No, the springs hardly helped at all, she said. Then someone told her about a healer living somewhere nearby. You should listen to her go on and on about him. She reckons she feels great after seeing him!"

"A healer? What sort of healer?" Faran asked. She was suddenly interested. "Maybe it's someone who could help Rezia? No one else has been able to, so far."

"Rezia? Oh, I don't know, Jan had bad rheumatism, but—" Kay turned away. She knew that Faran and Rezia were close. In fact Rezia was Faran's one real friend in the commune. Rezia was elderly, not young, older than Faran's Aunt Moria, however they had blended well in an instant resonance, recognizing in each other qualities they both possessed and understood. Rezia wanted freedom as much as Faran did, and she hated pretence. Yet of late, pretence was mostly what Rezia had to deal with as she and the other Sisters struggled to come to terms with her creeping illness. As yet, no one had admitted that Rezia's disease might be terminal, but they all thought it.

Jan was ebullient. She showed Faran joints formerly red and swollen which were now nearly normal in size and not inflamed. Jan said, "He gave me a herbal concoction to take and when I told him how difficult it was for me to get from here to Tempah Springs he even showed me how to make it myself when this lot ran out! And he didn't charge me anything for the medicine. He works from a hospice run by some woman doctor, not far from the Springs. You have to pay her but it's not a lot. It's a lovely place, but it's full of old people and people who are actually dying and can't be helped. A bit depressing actually, I thought."

"Is that all he did? What's he like?" Faran asked.

"No, we talked a lot, of what I felt about the pain and other stuff, like how I felt about life and so on. He told me a few things about myself which shocked me because I hadn't thought I was so transparent." Jan blushed. "You know … personal stuff we're ashamed of, that we all like to keep hidden from the world. It was as if he saw right through me but didn't dislike what he saw, and that none of the awful stuff mattered. It made me feel better just knowing that. And he held my hands while we

130

talked. I was rather embarrassed by that at first; but, well, it was really nice. He's very sweet and gentle … for a man."

"So, he's nice," Faran said. She considered how Rezia would feel, holding hands with such a man. "He sounds to be a kind, understanding old chap."

Jan laughed. "Did I give the impression he was old? He's not. He's a whole lot younger than I am.

That's what was so hard for me at first, to sit there, holding hands with a good looking, young guy, while I bared my soul to him. I never would have believed it if somebody had told me I was going to do that."

"Have you seen Rezia yet, Jan? Do you think this man could help her if she went there?" Faran asked.

Jan grimaced. "Rezia isn't too well. It's a long way to travel, if you're not well." Faran persisted. "But if she did, could he do something?"

"Probably. I can't put my finger on it, but he has some feeling of power about him. The doctors have all given up on Rezia, haven't they, so he's her best chance. If he can't do something then no one else can."

"Let's go talk to Rezia then," Faran urged.

Rezia had lived with severe pain and illness for nearly a year, but she had not given up quite yet. Nevertheless, the idea of uprooting, even for a while, and travelling, when every day was a trial of pain and struggle, did not attract her exactly. "It's so far to go. I don't know that I'd be able to make it," she said to Faran.

"I'll go with you," Faran promised. "It's not really so far, and I'll look after you. Please, Rezia, you've got to give it a try."

Rezia vacillated between thinking she might agree and rejecting the whole idea, while Jan sang the praises of the healer, trying to convince her to go. Faran watched her friend's tortured face and understood. It was not the prospect of a journey that actually bothered Rezia, and she truly wanted to be well, but she also knew that seeing the healer might only confirm what, in silence and suffering, she feared most, that she was dying. It frustrated Faran to watch her dither between hope and hopelessness, mainly because, to Faran, it seemed like surrendering to fear. She remembered the words of another healer, years before, "Fear won't help your brother", and sighed, also for reasons of her own. But it was true, fear helped no one. It was the greatest prison for the human spirit of all.

"Let me talk to her," Faran said quietly to Jan, and understanding the signal of Faran's raised eyebrows, Jan left the room.

Faran wasn't certain if she ought to be gentle or hard in dealing with her friend. So she opted for honesty, which was the best in any case. 'Rez, you've always said to me that you want freedom more than you want anything else. So if you go to the healer and he helps you, then you'll be free of your trouble. If he can't help you, then at least you'll be freed by the truth. Isn't it worse for you to stay here and keep on playing the game of pretending and seeing us all play it with you, than it would be to know for sure?"

Rezia buried her face in her hands and for a long time she did not speak. When she looked up there were tears in her eyes, yet she also smiled. "How did you get to be so wise in only twenty one years?" she said, without really requiring an answer. "You're right, my dear little friend, freedom is what I've always talked about, and now it's about time I put some faith in all my words. I'll go to Tempah Springs, as long as you come with me."

Faran hugged her. "I said I would. And I'll look after you properly; you won't have to think about a thing, I'll do it all."

It was Jan who drove Faran and Rezia in the truck down to Minerva. She wanted to do it, she was so proud of her functioning hands that she just had to show them off somehow. "Be safe," she told them before they waved goodbye from the bus. "Don't lose the address I gave you, but if you do you only have to ask someone in Tempah Springs. They all seem to know where the Langan Clinic is."

"I will," Faran assured her. She made the two steps of the bus in one energetic jump. She was more eager to go than even Jan could have imagined.

Rezia was already in her seat by the window.

"Are you okay?" Faran asked her. The jolting truck ride had seemed to take a lot out of Rezia. Her face was pale and strained. "Do you need a pain killer?"

Rezia summoned a wan smile from somewhere but she nodded. "Maybe, yes. And a sedative too. I think I'd like a little snooze, so I'll be better later on. You won't mind if I go away for a while, will you?"

"No, of course not. I've plenty to think about." Faran leaned across Rezia and opened the window slightly to let in a breeze. The bus was vintage, but was not uncomfortable. Had the Sisterhood been able to spare more cash, then they could have taken the inland express and got there within eight hours. As funds were tight, that meant they had to take the coastal bus. It also meant a journey of one day stretched into two with a stop at Hanna Harbor. Faran hoped she might get time to go and see Young Will, but her aunt and uncle were not on her list of desirable people to visit; she would avoid them like the plague.

Rezia lay her head on a pillow and quickly began to doze. No, Faran didn't mind being left to herself. She closed her own eyes but she did not sleep, there was too much in her head; and too much turmoil for rest.

Hope and excitement. Faran could hardly sit still for thinking about her destination. As they were driving to Minerva, Jan had told them more about the healer, Matt Best.

"I liked him right away, although I was surprised at his being so young. And there's something a bit odd about him; you'll notice if you look closely, Rezia. His eyes, they're unusual. I had the distinct impression that they changed color at some point in our talks, and not once but several times. Isn't that odd?"

Faran had to suppress an exclamation. A shiver ran up and down her spine and she felt her heart thumping madly. "What does he look like? Is he fair … dark … what? Is he from Telaia? Or somewhere else?" she said in a controlled voice, for she wanted the questions to sound casual.

"I think he is Telaian, but I did hear him speak in Arpayan to one of the staff at the hospice, so he could be from there. When he speaks Telaian his accents are cultured and I would say he is very well educated, so either he comes from here or was educated here. He has dark hair, near enough to black actually, and a pretty good tan, which makes me vote for the Arpayan option. Or maybe he just spends a lot of time outdoors. Who can guess? At least he's not the wishy washy sort; you know, like the ones from the east coast that you see around here on holidays, looking like they've been manufactured out of cold porridge."

Faran forced a laugh; however, she hid her sweating hands in the folds of her dress and surreptitiously rubbed them dry. "What else?"

"What more do you want?" Jan glanced at her curiously from the steering wheel. Faran affected a nonchalant air. "A bit more detail than that so we can find him okay."

"Yes, more detail," Rezia put in. "I'd like to have a rough idea of the person I'm going to see."

Jan shrugged. "Uh-uh. Let me see then." She thought for a moment as she re-made the healer in her mind. Visual memory was not Jan's strong suit and her descriptions of things always left something to be desired.

"Okay … nice looking and quite tall, but not big … you know, not bulky with it. But not skinny either. I'd say he's taller than average but averagely built." Jan sighed in frustration. "I don't know; what else can I say? He's intelligent and kind and his name's Matt. Don't worry, girls, you won't miss him in the crowd. They're very nice at the hospice. Once they know why Rezia's there, they'll put you in contact. Just tell them I recommended you."

Faran and Rezia looked at each other and shrugged too. This was all they were going to get.

However Faran's spirits fell a little. Could it be him? she wondered. What Jan had said about his eyes... surely no one else ... But it was possible that others could have such eyes, wasn't it? Oh, please, let it be him, she moaned silently, all the while telling herself not to get her hopes up too high.

Jan parked the truck by the bus station entrance and after Faran had taken Rezia to sit down inside, she returned to help Jan with their luggage. Jan handed Faran her bag and turned her back to lift Rezia's from the truck. She said, "Oh, one thing I forgot. You'll know Matt easily by the fact that he wears the most amazingly beautiful ring on his left hand, a gold ring with a fabulous stone in it." She turned, "Hey, Faran, watch out!" she cried, as Faran dropped the bag on her foot.

Chapter Two

The bus pulled into Hanna Harbor at five o"clock in the afternoon. The bus company had an arrangement with a small, low budget hotel to put up such of its passengers who were travelling on and who wanted to stay somewhere reasonable. It was an arrangement which pleased Faran and Rezia for it meant that they didn't have to go looking for accommodation. Faran led Rezia up the stairs to the room allocated to them. Although she had dozed on and off for a great part of the journey, Rezia was exhausted.

The room was a might spartan, but clean, and it had a tiny bathroom attached. Faran helped Rezia wash and change, then she settled her into bed. "They have dinner at seven, downstairs, but I'll get something brought up so that you can stay in bed," Faran decided. "But in the meantime, if you don't mind, I'd like to go out. I want to see my brother, if possible."

Rezia didn't mind. "I haven't been much company for you so far, have I? It's fine with me, you go ahead. Wake me when you come back."

At Hanna College boys were just finishing their day and getting ready for dinner. It was an expensive school where boys with freedom in their heart of hearts had to barricade it under uniforms and rules and strict behavior. Faran felt sorry for them all. She sympathized because she had experienced the prison of such a school herself. Almost immediately after the Crafters" arrival in Hanna Harbor, Aunt Moria had insisted that Faran should enrol in the 'Right school". "But I can't afford it," Will Crafter protested. "Never mind that, Josh and I will pay for it," Aunt Moria said. "Indulge me, brother; I've never had any children of my own to spoil. And Faran must have the chance at a good life, mustn't she. You've kept her as ignorant as a native up in that wretched place; now it's time she learned something of the real world."

Which wasn't the truth to say that Will had kept his daughter ignorant. Faran discovered when she entered Hightop House Quality School for Girls, that the girls knew no more book information than she did and all they thought about was how to make themselves pleasing to predatory males, in the quest of husband hunting. They neither knew nor cared to know anything about the Earth itself or the wide world beyond them. Neither they nor the school impressed Faran one bit.

Faran had to endure the curious glances of the fresh faced young males as she went to meet Young Will. The Head Teacher, although somewhat put out by her unannounced visit, directed her to a room where she could wait. She waited nervously, which was ridiculous, however she hadn't seen Young Will in a year, although they wrote to each other every month. I'll bet he's grown, Faran thought. And I suppose I should stop calling him Young Will now, since Daddy's been gone for four years. She felt tears sting her eyes when she thought of her father. Dear Will, the space that his passing had left in her heart would never be filled.

"Faran!"

Young Will Crafter burst into the room and bowled Faran over with a hug. She gasped in his strong arms and felt dwarfed by his size. No, she must not call him Young Will any more; he was getting close to being as big as his father had been, even though he was not quite sixteen.

"What a surprise!" he said as he collected himself. It seemed to Faran that he was trying to marshal some relic of masculine dignity. Evidently it was not right behavior for College Boys to mangle their big sisters so enthusiastically.

"You look pretty good," Faran said. "You sure have grown this last year. What have you been eating to get so big?"

"Not just eating! I'm doing weights and fitness classes, and they really make you hungry." Will's eyes shone and he became a little boy again. "You want to see my muscles?" Proudly he pushed up a sleeve and Faran obliged by squeezing the bulge presented. She was genuinely impressed.

"Is school okay? Are you happy?" Faran asked.

Will grimaced. "School is school. Only some things are okay, the rest I can do without. I'd rather be with you though, and back home."

By "home" he meant the Towers, Faran knew. However it surprised her that he still thought of the place, since it had been seven years. But then such a place was not easily forgotten. "I think of our old home too," she said wistfully. "One day we should go back there together, just for a look."

"Do you ever think about the man in the tower? I do, but I never did know what that was all about, and why we had to leave," Will said.

Faran looked away, out the window. Boys were running like ants across the quadrangle. Somewhere a bell rang.

"That's the dinner bell, Faran. I'll have to go or I'll miss out." Will grasped her hands with a compulsive gesture. "I wish you had come earlier, there's been no time and I haven't even asked you anything! Will you come back tomorrow?"

"Oh, Willie, I can't," Faran said, lapsing into her old fond name for him. She could see the disappointment all over his face and she shared it. "I'm on my way to Tempah Springs with a friend who is sick. We have to leave first thing in the morning."

Will put his arms around her one more time. "Then when you come back, please." His arms seemed to be capable of crushing her, so tightly did he cling. Faran wondered at the desperation she thought she felt in his embrace. His voice, soft and low now, echoed it. "Faran, you've got to get me out of here, please."

"Are you so unhappy? Is it such a terrible place?"

There was nothing of the boy in Will's voice this time. He answered solemnly, "It's just a school and no worse than any other, I guess. But they give you no peace; they don't let you be. Faran, I'm suffocating here. I feel like I'm in a prison and I just want out. I want to be free, like you."

On the way back to the hotel Faran stopped at the harbor to look at the ships. There were three freighters in dock and one was Arpayan. It made her remember that Jan had said the healer also spoke Arpayan, but she was sure now that he must be Marek. Her heart told her he was; she just knew with every ounce of her feeling that Marek had come home at last.

Where had he been all these years? She let her hand slide along the rail of the harbor wall in tune with her wandering thoughts. As if following Marek on his travels, she boarded the Arpayan ship in imagination and watched Hanna Harbor vanish in the distance. How many times had she escaped the oppressiveness of her own school to come down to the harbor to watch the ships and dream? How often had she stood at this very spot and dreamed of running to faraway places and thought that one day, on the journey, she would turn a corner of some foreign street, or walk through the door of a shop somewhere, and there he would be, the man she dreamed of every night. She still dreamed of him, but, now, was she soon to know the reality?

In the shadow of the bows of the big ships the water was mysteriously dark. Its surface was slicked with oily rainbows and reflected nothing and revealed nothing. Further down the harbor and a world away, was the huge marina of the rich. There, the brighter, cleaner waters shone and sparkled with gilt reflections and the glossy sweep of painted hulls. The

137

yachts bobbed gently in their moorings and waited for the days of summer to liberate them.

Faran glanced up at the clock on the customs house across the street. She still had plenty of time if she wanted to walk down to the marina. She enjoyed looking at the yachts with their sleek lines and their shining brass just as she enjoyed sailing on the sea. It would be relatively safe to go there this early in the year; it was not likely that anyone she knew might see her.

She had only walked a little way when the memories began to return. In the distance the yacht club stood like a guardian of the boats behind. The doors would be closed but Faran didn't need to see inside to know what luxury was there. She stopped and gave a little involuntary start. In a way she did not understand, the memories began to transpose themselves into pictures of a future, and she saw her brother in place of herself.

Young Will was growing so attractively. He had his father's strong build and the best of his departed mother's handsome looks. In a few years, if he had not escaped his posh school and his aunt and uncle's control, he would be thrown into that world of parties and yachts, and would be prey for every greedy, prowling female on the marina. Looked at superficially, it was not a fate most young people would decry, and many, Faran knew, would envy it. But Faran knew better. Will's spirit was too bright for her to let it be tarnished by what could happen to him there, for they would eat him up with their greed. "No! No!" she said out loud to herself, so that a passer-by stared at her. "Once is enough. It won't happen again."

Dinner in the room with Rezia was a quiet affair but Faran preferred it that way. She hadn't wanted the sociability of the dining room with its long refectory tables which meant almost compulsory conversation with strangers. Besides, she was too tired herself and only wanted a bath and a good sleep. For a little while after they had eaten Faran and Rezia talked desultorily. Rezia was unusually quiet but Faran knew it was because this journey was still such a challenge for her and that she had not entirely eliminated the specter of fear from her consciousness. If only I could reassure her, Faran wished silently. Jan had been right when she spoke of the healer's power. If only I could tell Rezia that the most wonderful man in all the world is waiting to help her.

After kissing her friend goodnight, Faran ran a hot bath. She lay in the steaming water and let herself daydream. Of course the dreams were all of Marek, as they usually were. Even when she had convinced herself years ago that they may never meet again and life had to go on without him, she still longed for him and dreamed of him, nevertheless.

Toweling herself dry, she caught the movement of herself in the mirror and remembered another time when a reflection of herself had made only a galling reality. This time she turned full on and studied what she saw with greater confidence. She was a woman now and not a child. The body had grown to match the person within and it was not unattractive at least. She didn't count herself as beautiful, she'd seen far better looks on other girls, but her body was neither thin nor fat, and her one and only vanity, and she supposed it was a vanity, was her hair. She touched herself absentmindedly here and there and wondered what Marek would think of her.

Would he remember her? Would he even recognize her? For seven years they'd lived worlds apart, so who knew what he'd done and where he'd been. He might even have someone he loved.

At Tempah Springs Faran and Rezia left the bus but not the bus station. Posted on a board in the waiting room were timetables for other areas, but not being familiar with the names of the towns this far west, Faran had to ask.

"Where exactly do you want to go to?" the woman clerk enquired.

"The Langan Clinic."

The woman eyed her then glanced over at Rezia who sat on a bench and waited. She nodded as if she understood. She smiled. "You're in luck then. There's a bus leaving which goes by there in half an hour. It takes about forty minutes."

It was five thirty in the afternoon. Faran calculated. They would arrive just after six thirty and they were coming unannounced. It was not a good idea just to turn up and expect someone to accommodate you without notice. Faran looked at Rezia; she was very tired. As much as Faran herself was eager to go, it was best to wait.

"I think we'd be better travelling in the morning. What time is the first bus tomorrow?"

The clerk consulted her schedules. "Ten in the morning." She gazed sympathetically at Faran. "I tend to agree with you. Your mother, is it? She looks quite done in. Do you know where you want to stay tonight?"

"No, not yet."

"Well, dear, there's a little place just down the road, only a short

139

walk. They have reasonable rates.

Can I give you the address?"

The little place was a lodging house and since it was on the very outskirts of town, it was not as expensive as those near the springs. Even so, it was overpriced for Faran and Rezia until Faran mentioned the hospice. "Are you patients of Doctor Langan? If you are I'll put you up for whatever you can afford. Doctor Langan is a wonderful person, she helped my old father when we couldn't afford expensive treatment," the landlady said.

"Well, my friend is not actually a patient yet. A friend of ours had great success with the healer who works there and recommended him. We're going on the off chance; we've come a long way."

The woman pulled a doubtful face. "The healer, eh? From what I heard he's rather busy. Why don't I call the hospice for you, you don't want a wasted journey. Sometimes they're quite full up and people who only want daily help have to go back and forth from here."

Leaving Faran and Rezia waiting in the sitting room, the landlady vanished into her office. In five minutes she was back. "I spoke to the Doctor herself. She's a good lass; she's got room and she'll put you up."

"Then we can see the healer?"

"Looks like it, my dears. But you might have to wait a while, he's much in demand it seems."

Chapter Three

The Langan Clinic was hidden from the road by a wall of high green hedge which kept out the strong winds from the sea. As they had driven up in the bus Faran had seen the ocean on one side and very far down, and emerald covered fields on the other. Although as far south as Hanna Harbor and Minerva, the weather around Tempah Springs was like a bathe in fresh, cool water. Faran tossed out her hair in the breeze. For the first time in years she felt she was in a place akin to the high country, except for the presence of the ocean of course.

"What a lovely spot," Rezia said, obviously agreeing and made agreeable by the sudden freshness of the air. They walked slowly down the avenue of trees to a manor house which looked like a large old hotel. A fountain and a pool with pink lotus rising up out of it faced the front door which was open to let in the sun. All the front rooms seemed washed in sunlight. Even if this was a place where people came to die, it had the most cheerful aspect, Faran decided.

As they approached the steps a woman in a pink coat came out to meet them. "Are you the people Mrs. Wrenn told me about?"

Faran nodded. So this was the famous Doctor Langan! Faran was surprised. She had expected someone much older, but this woman was about Jan's age and no more. She was also fairly attractive in an efficient and serious looking way, although with her hair loose and undone she would be quite beautiful, Faran thought. Faran recognized instantly the poise and accents of a class she had come to be familiar with, but she didn't see the Doctor fitting in with the shallow philosophies and entertainments of the yacht club world exactly.

Doctor Langan led them inside, into the airy vestibule where a receptionist in a blouse the color of daffodils took down Rezia's details on a form. Then Rezia was invited into the Doctor's office while Faran had to wait outside.

"Sit down, please, they're going to be a while, so you might as well relax," the receptionist said, with a smile. "My name's Marie. Is that your mother?"

Faran sat down." No, we're not related, Rezia's my friend. I'm Faran."

Marie apologized. "Sorry, my mistake. But I should have guessed; you don't look anything alike." "It's all right." Faran shrugged. "A lot of people have been making that mistake. It's probably a natural thing to suppose." She stared long and hard down the several halls which led from the vestibule to places unknown. The floors in the halls shone, reflecting even the colorful pictures on the walls. "Everything is so bright and cheerful here. It makes you happy just to come in."

"That's the ticket. It's Nik– er, Doctor Langan's idea. If people are sick and suffering, they don't want surroundings which are only going to make them feel more depressed, so we cheer them up with color and light. Not one of us dresses in uniform ... you know, stiff old white starchy stuff and all. It's a friendly place, or we try to make it that."

"Yes, it seems so," Faran said. She stared harder down the halls, wondering where Marek might be. "The healer Rezia came to see. Where is his office?"

"Oh, Matt? He doesn't use one. Generally he sees people in the garden, that's how he likes it, except when it's cold or it rains of course, then it's in the Conservatory. And if patients are too sick to go out, he goes and sees them in their rooms. He's pretty casual and he can't stand forms." Marie giggled. "The Doctor tried to get him to do them, but he'd always forget, or not bother. So now we do it all, whether the patients are his or ours."

"How long has he been here?"

"A year. Doctor Langan brought him with her from Arpay. I don't know how they met up." "Does he live here or somewhere else?"

"Oh, he lived upstairs for a month or two, but then he moved out. There's a gardener's cottage in the grounds, right at the other end of the property; Doctor Langan had it fixed up for him. I guess he likes his privacy and some peace and quiet away from everything; but then we all feel like that after a long day. Although we like our jobs and all, you need to get away. The Doctor lives upstairs though. After all, this is her house."

The door of the Doctor's office opened and Doctor Langan came out. "Marie, will you get someone to show Miss..." She looked at Faran and smiled.

"Crafter," Faran said.

Doctor Langan nodded. "To show Miss Crafter where she and Rezia will be staying, then when I bring Rezia over she can settle her in. That okay with you, Miss Crafter?" "Okay with me," Faran said.

The room was in one of the long extensions. Although it was not huge it had its own bathroom and was very prettily done out, flowers everywhere, even as patterns on the bed quilts. It had a picture window which overlooked the gardens behind the house and Faran could see how beautiful and extensive they were. While she waited she stood at the window and studied all that could be seen of the garden beds and walks. It wasn't flowers she was interested in; she just hoped she might see Marek.

Then Doctor Langan and Rezia arrived. Before she left them to settle in, the Doctor summoned Faran outside. "You know your friend is very ill," she said quietly.

Faran nodded.

"I would like her to stay here a while, but she says she's only come here to see Matt, then she's going back to Minerva."

Faran explained. "She's just afraid of knowing the truth, that she might be going to die. I won't let her leave prematurely, I understand. She'll get her fears under control, once she's seen the healer."

Squarely and with interest, Doctor Langan eyed Faran. "You seem very sure."

Quickly Faran covered her near mistake. "I know Rezia; she'll be fine; she only needs a good rest. We've been on the road for two full days and it's worn her out. But one thing worries me, Doctor, and it's probably worrying her too … we don't have a lot of money to afford a long stay."

The Doctor smiled. "This is a charity hospice, Miss Crafter, and those who can afford some payment do pay a little, but those who can't we're happy to help. I've already told Rezia that."

"Oh," Faran said, feeling that she had been corrected, though not unkindly. "Will Rezia be seeing the healer today?"

"Well, yes, and it must be good luck for her because we had the day all booked up until someone had to cancel this morning. Matt's after lunch space is free so she'll see him then." The Doctor looked at her watch. "It's eleven fifty and lunch is at twelve thirty. Matt is at one fifteen. We'll bring you some lunch to your room so Rezia can rest in between."

Faran was content to spend time with Rezia in the room although her heart would not seem to stop thumping so loudly that she thought Rezia must surely hear it. The two of them used the time to freshen up and choose clean clothes for the afternoon. Faran showered and washed her hair which felt stiff and dusty from two days of travel. She didn't have many dresses, since she wore mostly shorts or pants when working at the commune, but she chose the one which was the least crushed. If there was any chance of her seeing Marek, she didn't want to look like a frump.

Then they ate lunch, both nervously, with little appetite and only picking at the food, but each for different reasons. Rezia confided in Faran, "I feel a bit scared, but glad all the same." "You'll be fine," Faran assured her.

"Doctor Langan said that the healer won't see a patient with anyone else in tow, unless they request it."

"Do you want me to be?"

"No. I need to do this by myself. But when they take me to him, will you come along and be somewhere nearby?"

"Yes," Faran said. "That I will. Don't worry; I intend to be not far away, that's for sure."

A nurse dressed in a long loose gown of multicolored flowers came to fetch Rezia. She okayed Rezia's request to have Faran tag along. "The gardens are so beautiful; I even wander about them on my time off. I'm sure you will find it a pleasure to wait for your friend," she said to Faran.

Beside the colorfully dressed nurse Faran felt somewhat drab in her plain white. The nurse looked to rival the real flowers herself, but it was true, the gardens were a delight. Faran hoped she would be able to get near enough to see Marek properly, though; it was not just pleasure she was after, for it seemed to her suddenly that her whole life was riding on this one day.

They walked down a small gravel path between blossoming hedges and into a miniature grove surrounded by silver barked trees with lime green leaves. One side of the grove was open to a park like space with flower borders which reached up in tiers of color. This was where Faran had to leave them because the nurse directed Rezia to one of the seats under the trees. Faran stayed hovering behind the flower bed since the top tier was as tall as she was. The flowers smelled sweet, they were a blend of gold and purple blossom and the bees were busy at them.

Then Faran saw the healer coming through the trees and she gave a little tremulous sigh. Without a doubt, it was Marek. Even from a distance she knew it was him, by his walk and straight posture, by the way he extended his hand to Rezia, and by the shining waves of his dark hair which he had grown a little longer and now which curled slightly at the ends. And before he sat down it was as if he had felt the heat of Faran's eyes, or the intensity of her thought and feeling, for he looked up and glanced briefly at the flowerbed.

But then he became all concentration, devoted to Rezia and her

144

troubles. Faran saw how he took her friend's hands in his. She saw the Light which grew and blossomed between them, reminding her of the time with Young Will. And of other times of her own when she had felt that such a Light existed for herself. Often, beneath the ancient, towering trees of the rainforest hinterland, Faran had seen and sensed the wonderful healing energies of Nature, and felt them as they flowed directly through her own being. As in the high country too, where the powerful pull of Nature's forces had been so pure and active that they drew one's spirit upward like a bird in flight. This Light, too, was an element of Nature as much as it was of Marek. It seemed to fill the sky and warm the heart, like sunshine, Faran thought.

So now Faran knew for sure what she had often speculated upon. She knew how, primarily, the healer worked his magic. Yet no one else had ever commented on the Light, not her father, not Jan. Perhaps they had not been aware of it? And was she the only one? She had dreamt so often of that Light and Marek that, in her mind, he and she were indissoluble from its presence.

So, it was real to her but not so to others, perhaps. She had guessed as much. It was only logical, she decided then, since a Light like that would cause a sensation if it was universally seen, and the healer's fame would have been spread everywhere in Telaia by now.

Did Marek's awful brother still search for him? Faran wondered. He wasn't using his real name, so that told her he didn't want to be recognized. Then, if Silene still hunted him, why had he come back to Telaia? The receptionist, Marie, had said that Doctor Langan brought him from Arpay. Why then did he walk back into danger, and stay?

For a long, speculative hour Faran stayed in her place behind the flowers, then Rezia's consultation seemed to be at an end. At a command Faran did not observe, the nurse returned. Possibly she was not far away either. She had told Faran and Rezia on the way over that she would escort Rezia back to the room so that she could rest quietly by herself for a while; apparently that was the done procedure at the clinic and extraneous family or friends were encouraged to give the patient some space when it was needed. Faran didn't mind that at all.

Rezia and the nurse left, but Marek stayed where he was, sitting on the bench, in contemplation it seemed. Faran hovered nervously. She wanted to run out of the flowers and throw herself into his arms … well, that was her dream. But she was afraid. Would he even know who she was?

Then Marek stood up as if to go. Faran's heart was pounding but still she hesitated. Don't be a fool, said a voice inside her head. Here is the man you've been dreaming about for seven years, and you hide here, like an idiot!

Marek walked a few paces away then abruptly he stopped and turned back. His eyes riveted themselves on the garden bed. GO! GO, YOU DILL! GET OUT THERE TO HIM! Faran's inner voice screamed at her.

She stepped out dizzily from behind the garden of flowers. Marek stood frozen, his eyes on her.

Faran was trembling as she came nearer. Her eyes were filled with the image of him, but it was gradually blurring with tears. What an idiot I am, she thought to herself. He doesn't recognize me, he doesn't!

There was a moment, which was also like forever, as something passed between them on the air. A ripple; the sound of bells chiming or of endless, sweet singing. Rainbow arcs flashed in the atmosphere; a streak of blue-white light blazed across the sky; stars came out in the midst of day.

A salt breeze wafted in from the sea and picked up Faran's long hair, waving it across her face. She pushed the hair aside. Marek's hair also ruffled in the wind as he started to walk towards her. He reached out his hands and his voice sounded strange as he said, "Faran … Faran."

She stopped her feet from running though they wanted to. She trembled so much and felt so unsteady that she didn't want to trip and fall like a fool at his feet. "Marek!"

She could hardly focus on his face because there were so many tears in between, but she thought that his eyes were just as full as hers. When he took her hands and held them she felt a great energy there, like a powerful charge of electricity passing from him to her. Healer's hands, she thought.

Marek smiled down upon her and she returned it. The energy had passed from him to her, but she sent it back to him with her smile.

Chapter Four

I thought you wouldn't recognize me," Faran said.

They stood with their hands joined, as if both of them were frozen forever to that spot of garden filled with trees and flowers and the breezes of the sea.

Marek smiled. "Well Faran has changed size, Faran has grown. And Faran is older. But YOU, I would recognize YOU anywhere."

Did he mean her Light? By now she understood what she already shared with him. Perhaps she had always shared it. "You recognized my Light? Is it the same as the one you gave to Rezia?"

His eyes widened with surprise but also with pleasure. At first sight they had been blue-green; now they had deepened into a blue warmer than the sky, maybe ultramarine. "You are the friend she spoke of? So you saw that? Yes, it is the same. But I don't actually give it to anyone . I'll tell you about that later."

Passing by the grove on the way to the house, a gaily dressed nurse paused when she saw them and stared curiously. Then she hurried on.

Marek said, "Let's take a walk."

"I thought you had patients to see," Faran said.

"Not now. I have one day and three afternoons off a week, and this is one of them. I need the time off because I've got other things I want to do."

He took her by one hand as they walked. He seemed not to be wandering but to be leading her somewhere in particular. They crossed gardens and were well away from the hospice when they came to a hedged fence. Faran saw the road between a gap in the hedge where there was a stile. Marek led her over it and they crossed the road.

They had entered the coastal reserve and followed a track so narrow that it had only been carved by the tread of feet. The hedge grasses rose up on each side to above knee height and at times higher, above Faran's shoulder. Marek went ahead at a deliberate pace. Evidently this was a walk he knew well.

Then suddenly they were at the coast. The cliffs fell away below them, but in terraces which were like wide paths, so it was possible to climb down them a way. Marek led Faran carefully downward until they came to a place overhung by the rocks of the cliff. He pointed her to a seat of sand and tufted grass and they sat down. Faran looked up. To anyone standing above they were invisible. Only to ships would they appear as two tiny spots of human color painted on the cliff face.

"I like this place," Marek said. "No one else seems to ever come here and it gets me some solitude." He leaned forward, arms hugging his knees. His gaze drifted out to sea.

They hadn't said much to each other and Faran could feel the pressure of so many feelings and their attendant words building in her that she didn't know how she was going to control them if she didn't express them soon. What was Marek feeling? She must not assume the same intensity for him, she told herself silently. He was not likely to have dreamt of her for seven years. "And now I'm here and your solitude is broken," she said tentatively.

Quickly he looked at her. He was very close and in his eyes was an expression Faran did not understand. There was some pain in that look, she thought, and something else hard to grasp, and his eyes, still blue, had gotten even bluer. And darker and warmer, if that was possible.

"Faran," he began. His voice sounded strange again. "Why did you come looking for me?"

I have to be honest with him, it's the only way, Faran thought. 'Rezia and I, we have a friend – Jan. She'd just come back from seeing you, she had inflamed joints." Marek nodded. "So I wanted to bring Rezia. Then Jan described you a little: your eyes. And I thought … I hoped … it was you. It wasn't until we were at the bus leaving Minerva that Jan mentioned your ring. Then I knew for sure."

Marek appeared downcast. "So you didn't really come looking for me."

Faran thought she would not be able to control herself much longer, but she tried. "Marek, I did want to find you, so much! I've been wanting to find you for seven years, hoping I'd see you somewhere, dreaming of it. If I'd known where you were I'd have come right away."

"You would have?"

Faran nodded. To her, at that moment, he was as she had not seen him before, almost like a little boy, like Young Will at his most vulnerable and pleading.

He said, "When I left the Towers I went east to the coast. Then Silene almost trapped me again so I had to leave Telaia altogether. After that I kept on the move. I had to. Silene has so many eyes and ears everywhere. I used to last in one place for six months or sometimes up to a year, then

I'd see one of his agents, or what looked like one, and I'd have to move on. After five years I did find a place I felt safer in; it's actually a place I want to return to. But everywhere, no matter how nice, was still running away. I didn't want to run any more, and there were things I needed to do in the world, and still do. So I decided to come back. I was lucky to meet Nikola – Doctor Langan, in Arpay. She brought me here."

Faran listened without interrupting, but to her there was something incomprehensible in what he said. If what he needed to do was in the world, why do it in the place which offered the most danger of all?

Marek continued. "When we arrived here, the first thing I did was to get Nikola to try and locate you and your family. I couldn't do it openly myself, on the chance that Silene might find out. But you seemed to have vanished, you'd left the Towers and disappeared. I asked her to keep on trying, but a whole year went by and no luck. I was wondering what to do next. I thought of going and searching for you myself. Then, suddenly, here you are."

"Yes." Faran spoke softly and kept control, even while her eyes were on fire with suppressed tears. "Daddy didn't want to work for your brother any more, and he was afraid, I think. We went to Hanna Harbor, where his sister lives, and we changed our name, like you did. Young Will and I got enrolled in school under our uncle's name. That's how we disappeared. But why did you want to find us?"

"For the same reason I came back to Telaia because you dreamed of finding me and that drew me unconsciously. And I came back because of my own dream to find you, Faran."

Did that mean what it sounded like? Faran trembled with suppressed emotion. All she could say was, "Marek."

"Let me tell you something," he said then, more steadily. He sat close enough so their shoulders almost touched but he kept his arms wrapped around his knees. "It's like a fairy story.

"There was once a young man who was in big trouble, and locked up in a darkness he wasn't sure he was going to get out of. He wasn't afraid though, and he wasn't unhappy, because he had discovered some wonderful things about life and about himself and the Earth. But he was alone. Except for one grandmotherly old lady who had loved him and taught him once and she seemed very far away, he was totally alone.

"Then, into his darkness came the loveliest Light he had ever met. It was a goddess of the high hills who set out to free him. However this

149

goddess inhabited the form of a young girl, a girl too young for a man and therefore unattainable. So even though it saddened him to leave the goddess, the young man went away, but he never stopped thinking about the goddess and he always dreamed of seeing her again and of being able to love her in the way of a man loving a woman. All that he worried about though was that she might have found a different way in the world and was in love with someone else. She might not be able to return his love.

"Then, one wonderful day, the man saw his goddess again, and she stood before him, and she was the brightest Light in the world. He said to himself, "Now I have found my love," but he still wasn't sure how she felt about him.""

Faran sighed a great, shuddering sigh. She set her small fair hand over Marek's larger, browner one. "But now you know, don't you? When you went away I thought I'd die of unhappiness. I understood that you saw me as a little girl, but I was actually older than you realized; I just hadn't done much growing yet. I was fourteen, still too young for you, I know, but old enough to fall in love and feel the pain of losing you. I never got over it, not ever, and Daddy used to worry about me. I'd see him looking at me so sadly sometimes, but there was nothing he could do about it."

Marek grasped her hand and held it tightly. The strangeness in his voice returned. He said only two words: "Faran, love," then, without conscious intent, they were in each other's arms. Faran laid her head against Marek's chest; with one hand Marek caressed her hair. Faran wrapped her arms around him and let the waiting fountain break. Why were there so many tears? She pressed into him and felt the heaving of his chest. He was crying too. His cheek was pressed on top of her head; his hand trembled in the threads of her hair.

Too many tears for passion to follow. So many tears. They both were fountains. Why?

Sinking into him, as if their two bodies could meld with the uniting power of tears, Faran began to understand. Two spirits, two Lights that once, long ago, were One, separated, torn apart by the cruel world of Illusion. Now they had met each other again. Now they were one again. Tears were for the pain and sorrow of loss, just as that look in Marek's eyes she had not been able to define before was loneliness. He found his lost love, then had wandered for seven years, alone and lonely. So she understood, his pain and hers, and now that pain was ended and they would find the ultimate freedom together.

Faran tasted the salt of her own tears, but the crying was over. He was quiet and still too and they lay together for a while, not moving or saying anything. But though tears were cleansing powers in their own right, they did make your nose run. And the hard ground was no feather bed either. As if in concert, they each felt the discomfort of their bodies at the same time and sat up, looking at one another.

There was so much joy in both of them that they laughed and made fun of each other's red noses and puffy eyes. Faran's inadequate rag of a handkerchief was soon too wet to use so Marek offered her his. But instead she wiped his face for him and smoothed his hair as she used to do for Young Will. She was very tender towards him and felt that, now, they were properly equalized. And like a little boy, he let her do it, then buried his face in her neck and held her. And then, and only then, their embrace evolved into a kiss.

The kiss was long, slow and went so deep that Faran hoped it would never end. No one had ever kissed her like that before, but then there was no one quite like Marek, was there. But it was the only kiss, for Marek lifted her to her feet.

"It's lovely here, but it's not very comfortable." "No, it's not," Faran agreed.

"Will you come to my house? It's not far." Marek asked.

"Wherever you want to go, I'll always go," Faran said, with feeling.

Marek's house was only small. It had one bedroom and adjoining bathroom in the attic and the other living areas were all downstairs. It was centered in the clear space of a coppice of leafy trees, and faced south to a wide open walk which led back to the hospice, which was out of sight over a grass covered rise. At the back of the house the coppice had grown itself close up to the wall and was kept back only by the width of a square of flagstones serving as a dry area by the door.

Marek led Faran through the trees and quickly under the porch of the back door. He opened the door and just as quickly got them both inside. He explained his haste by saying: "If it seems like I'm sneaking in through my own back door, it's true."

Faran said, "Is that because of me?"

"No. It's because I don't want anyone to know I'm home. This is supposed to be my time off, but often someone will just 'drop by' for a chat. I'm not unsociable, but I think I deserve some time to myself when I want it." Marek turned the key in the lock and hung it on a hook. He explained further. "When I first arrived at the hospice with Nikola I got to stay upstairs in the main house. Although it was very comfortable, I didn't like it much because in a situation like that you are always at everyone's beck and call. No one seemed to realize that occasionally I might want a little peace and quiet, and I spent almost as much energy trying to deal with the staff's curiosity about me as I did in treating the sick people. Then the rumors started flying around that I was Nikola's lover."

"And were you?" Faran asked, without expression.

Marek had led her by the hand in through the kitchen to a single front room with stairs leading up to the attic. A dark floral carpet similar to the one in the room she shared with Rezia was held down by an assortment of comfortable loungers, a small table and a settee with two clean pressed shirts lying across it. At the table was a high-backed chair; the table itself was strewn over with bouquets of dried and scented herbs and several sheets of written on paper. Marek moved the shirts off the settee to the high-backed chair and they sat down. He did not appear resentful of Faran's question although it had clearly surprised him. He said, "No, I wasn't. But they thought I was, so it was time to move out. Nikola agreed to fix up this place for me; however, I don't think she was very happy or pleased with my decision to leave. She said this place wasn't good enough. But it suits me fine."

"Maybe she wished she was," Faran said. "What?"

"Maybe she wished she was your lover."

Marek started. Faran was just supposing, yet it was possible that what she said was true. He knew that Nikola had some feelings for him, but he had believed they were mostly of good friendship. But had she wanted him then? He was a little shocked by his own blindness; however, he had never sought anything from Nikola but her friendship and the resonance they shared as sympathetic beings in their hopes for the betterment of the world.

He said, "If Nikola wants true love, she has it already waiting. There's someone in Arpay who would give his life for her, if she would only open her eyes and see the truth of him. His name's Dan, and he loves her, but she doesn't see it."

"Poor Dan," Faran said sympathetically.

Such talk drew them both now to their own thoughts of love. Marek put his arms around Faran and kissed her with the same long held intensity as before. It was a kiss which went beyond their meeting lips; it entered her heart, it swept through her spirit, and she gave it back again in the same measure. It was a kiss which joined them forever.

The kiss became other kisses. Marek held her close; his mouth was warm against hers. Faran could feel the accelerated beating of his heart, an excited rhythm to match her own. His hands caressed her, growing ever more intimate in their touch; he murmured in her ear, "I want to make love to you. I want to take you upstairs and make love to you, now." Then he pulled away a little and added, sounding uncertain and apologetic all of a sudden, "Oh Faran, I'm sorry. Am I rushing you? Is it too soon?"

Faran lifted her face to gaze into his worried eyes. Gently she drew his head closer again. She touched her mouth on his, feeling him tremble as she held him. She whispered, "I've dreamed of you for seven years, wanting this very moment with you more than I've ever wanted anything. Believe me, it's not too soon."

Chapter Five

My love, how wonderful you are, Marek thought as he lay with her. Her body had the same quality of delicate beauty as the younger Lani's, but Faran was no flower perfumed doll to toy with. Nor was she some love offering either but met him full on as herself, as his mate of flesh and blood and spirit, and there was great strength in her because of that and an intensity which matched his, in love and desire.

Her hair fell over her shoulders and breasts like a waterfall of the purest gold. Between his fingers it felt like running silk. When she rose above him to kiss him with her own passion, it fell around his face like a protecting veil. It also tickled his face and hers, and that made them laugh together. As her kisses travelled to his chest and then the length of him, he closed his eyes and felt the slip of her hair under his hands. She was not inexperienced in the mechanics of making love, he realized later, when the power of thinking returned to him, but then neither was he.

Mechanisms meant nothing but knowing what pleased and what did not, whereas making love, real love, and expressing it, came from the heart. Faran was all heart and she was uninhibited in expressing her heart to him. Together they blended not just like lovers but as old, old friends. That was their secret – they had belonged together from the oldest of times – and now they were reunited. If Marek had not understood that regret was a pointless waste of energy, he might have wished they had never been parted. Even so, he wondered now how much of his pain and anger as a youth had been also caused by the sense of loss originating in the sundering of this most profound of relationships. How long had he sought for this one love without knowing what he sought for? How many false paths had he trodden because of it? How many idle diversions and illusions had he fooled himself with in trying to assuage the feelings of emptiness? To find Faran and know her was akin to finding and knowing himself. Where there was one Light now there were two, and yet they were both One.

Afterward he rose and put on a robe and went downstairs to make them both some tea. He felt invigorated and alive, more alive than he had ever been. He chose the tastiest tea he had and searched for something nice to eat. Rarely, if ever, did he eat in the middle of the afternoon, but now he was as hungry as a lion.

154

As he waited for the water to boil and the bread to toast he wandered into the sitting room, thinking he would take his clean shirts up with the tea and hang them in the wardrobe before they got too creased. On the table, amongst his scattered work, was a small garland of creamy flowers tinted with pink and yellow. Puzzled, because he had not remembered either collecting the flowers or leaving them there, he picked them up and smelled a perfume which filled his head with strange exotic memories of Te Tanaa.

This is odd, Marek thought, this wasn't here earlier. Had someone just wandered in and left the flowers like a calling card while he and Faran were upstairs? The thought disturbed him so he checked the front door. It was locked, as was the back.

He studied the flowers again. They were blossoms of the simplest type, a whorl of creamy petals without frill or ornament or stamens to disrupt the purity of the spiral. He would almost call them primitive had not their perfume almost made him delirious with pleasure. They were not flowers he knew, however, and he'd never seen them anywhere before, and certainly not here.

Then from nowhere he heard a gentle musical laugh and the image of Marielle swam before his eyes. She was laughing with him, not at him, and she said, "Greetings, dearest heart. Did I not tell you once that when you free the Goddess in yourself and give her her due, then will she come fully into your life, and you shall be whole?"

"Yes, I remember," Marek said to the air. Marielle had explained that what people often called the Goddess was really the Feeling Power of the awakened Self, that power of heart without which no ego could be what it was meant to be. "Marielle ..." Marek started to say, but Marielle was gone as swiftly as she had come, and the kettle had boiled and Marek could smell the distinct aroma of toast turning to a cinder.

While Marek strove to rescue his burning toast, Faran lay back in his bed and thought only of their love. How, once they found each other, they had quickly come together. Though not in haste, since found was incorrect and rediscovered was the true word to describe their meeting.

Marek's bed exhaled the fragrances of sandalwood and cedar spiced with the scents of his manliness. Faran breathed them in. How beautiful his body was, she thought. In seven years it was still as she had remembered it from the tower, still smooth skinned and athletic, though rather browner and perhaps even fitter. His body seemed to express perfectly the essence of him. There was not a superfluous thing about it.

155

And it was strong. He had strength and gentleness both. When, at first, he had come to her, she had reached for him and clung to him for the strength which was in him and the power of his love, as a flower reaches to the sun and clings to the earth for light and life. Though strong, his lips were so soft on hers, his kisses so tender and his hands so sensitive. He was so sweet and loving towards her, and so vulnerable in his own desire that she turned from clinging to him and seeking his strength and power to giving him all of her own. This then was the essence of their physical love, expressing outwardly what was deep and vast and permanent between them.

Marek came up the stairs and into the room carrying a loaded tray. He set down the tray on the end of the bed. Beside the plates and mugs was a garland of flowers, and, ceremoniously, he lay the garland over Faran's head, setting it delicately across her shoulders.

"A gift, from one dear heart to another," he said, without explanation.

Then he apologized. "Sorry I was so long, but I burned the toast and had to think what to do because I've run out of bread. I scraped off the worst burnt bits. Do you like grilled cheese? It'll help to cover up the charred taste, I hope."

Faran had always hated burnt toast, but she didn't say so. Instead she laughed. Why should she grumble when the taste of Marek was so sweet?

Eating made her think of other, forgotten things, like Rezia. She was appalled. She said, "Marek, I haven't even thought about Rezia once this afternoon! And I was supposed to be here as her friend, to help her if she needed it!"

"Well, Rezia is probably resting at the moment," Marek said.

"What, still resting? It's over two hours since you saw her. Don't you think she'll be wondering where I've got to?"

"Maybe. But Faran, your friend is rather ill. Nikola talked to me about her before I saw her and she doesn't usually do that with the people I see. She wanted to do some tests of her own because I don't think she believes I can help Rezia all that much."

Faran bit her lip. "Do you agree with her?"

"No. Rezia can be helped, but it's largely up to her. Do you think she wants to get better? I got the impression that she does."

"Yes, she does," Faran said vehemently. "Why is Doctor Langan being so negative?"

Marek reached for the last slice of tindered toast. "Do you want this?" Faran shook her head.

Marek grimaced. "No, neither do I." He lifted the tray and set it on the floor. "I don't know what's going on with Nikola. I wondered myself about that. I thought Nikola had more faith in me, considering what she saw in Vargas…"

"What did she see?" Faran asked quickly. She reached over and opened his robe to the scar on his side. The scar was fading fast but was still visible in all its length. "Was it something to do with that?"

Marek looked down at the scar.

"I wanted to ask before, but I figured you'd tell me when you got around to it," Faran said. "Yes. The scar is how I met Nikola, at a clinic in Vargas."

Faran was incredulous. "You had an operation?"

"No." Marek frowned. 'Vargas is not a nice town, not healthy and not safe. I met up with some unpleasant young men with knives. I guess they thought to rob me."

"Oh, Marek, they could have killed you!" Faran gasped. She put her hands on his breast and kissed him once on the cheek. Then, very deliberately, she pushed aside the robe from his left shoulder. "And that?" she whispered as she touched the white mark on the soft spot there.

As if he was being asked to eat burnt toast again, Marek pulled a face. "You do notice everything, don't you. I got that at the same time, but not in the same way."

"Tell me," she said intently. "Tell me it all."

He looked as if he didn't want to, yet he said, "The young hoods were just bad luck, but I was being followed and I didn't know it. Silene had sent someone after me, a bounty hunter. He was sent, not to bring me back but to kill me, and he thought he had. He's a smart one the Vorken; he doesn't rely on ordinary means of murder. He pumped something into me that I wouldn't have been able to overcome except that Nikola got it out of me. I owe her my life for that, but it also gave her the chance to see what I can do, even with my own body. She was so excited to think that healing could be so swift. I think she thought I was some kind of miracle worker, although there's actually no miracle about what I do."

"Perhaps it's not miracles, but it is wonderful." Faran bent and kissed his scarred shoulder. She lay her head against his chest and held him close, as if by her love she could be his shield from further attack. "Why is your brother so determined to hurt you? Daddy never could explain; he said he didn't understand it either. He put it down to an awful case of jealousy, but I felt it was much, much more. When you left us I was so afraid for you. Every morning and every night I used to pray, not to anything in particular, maybe to the stars or the wind or something. I prayed just to keep you safe and happy."

Lying against him, she heard him make a kind of hiccuping noise and felt his chest heave. Looking up, she saw that his eyes were filled with tears. And love, so much love. And she had not noticed before but his eyes had changed color again. This time they were the most beautiful violet hue, and as warm as the feelings of her own heart.

"Your eyes have changed color," she said. Marek swallowed tears. "What color are they?" "They're exactly the color of violets."

Marek smiled down at her. "Ah, then now I know." "Know what?"

He kissed her and she tasted his salt. "Someone once asked me what color my eyes would be if I was in love. I didn't know the answer to that then. But now I do."

Three hours was long enough to be away when Faran worried about Rezia. They rose to get dressed and Marek lent Faran a brush for her long hair. But after a second he took the brush from her hand. "Here, let me have a turn; you have such lovely hair." He twined his fingers through its silken threads and lifted her for a kiss. "I don't want to let you go, not even for a while, though I know I must. But come back with me tonight, and bring all your things. You have to stay with me, now and forever."

"I'll never leave you," Faran said, even as she peeled him away from her so that she could fix her hair in its clasp. "But I shall have to explain it to Rezia. However I know she'll understand. She knows about you."

"Knows what about me?"

"I told her once that there was a man I loved whom I hadn't seen in a long while, and how I still wanted him, if only I could find him again. She will be surprised but she'll understand."

Marek buttoned up his shirt and tucked it in his trousers. "Good, I'm glad. Then she won't mind if I take you away. Nikola will have dinner sent over to the room. I'll come by to fetch you after and have a talk with Rezia too. I've already told her that I'll see her again in the morning so this will be a social call."

"What about you? There doesn't seem to be much to eat in your pantry. What are you going to do for dinner?" Faran enquired. She noticed that he had knotted a blue and white scarf such as sailors wore around his neck to go with the shirt in the fashion of a tie.

Marek pulled on his boots. "I usually eat with Nikola in the evenings, but that's going to change after tonight. I don't know how she will react when I tell her about you."

Faran was worried somewhat. "Might she resent me? I can't stay here with you and be a burden on her. But I'm very handy, Marek. I know how to do lots of things. I'm good at gardening and I can even fix a truck motor."

Marek raised one surprised eyebrow. His smile was amused. 'Really? You'd be no burden anyway.

I work for Nikola, but ask no fee except a place to stay and enough food and time to myself. The Langan Clinic only used to be a hospice for the very ill and dying, and most of them couldn't pay much, if anything at all sometimes. But in the year since I've been here outpatients have come to see me, and Nikola charges them for the time. She's philanthropic, Nikola, but she's also a good businesswoman, and I'm providing her with extra income for very little cost. And she has other means."

"Is she rich? How much does she know about you?"

Marek nodded. "She's well off, yes. And she knows my real name and the reason I don't tell it to anyone. She brought me here knowing she took a risk, so I respect her courage. She also has some understanding of what I'm about and what I want to do in the world, and she's sympathetic to that."

"Did you tell her of the Towers? And why your brother wants to kill you?" "Yes, most of it at least."

"Then she knows more about you than I do."

"She knows more facts. But she doesn't know me, not like you do."

Before they parted on the path near the hospice Marek promised to tell Faran everything about himself and the last seven years when they returned to his house.

And I will have to tell him everything about me, as well, Faran thought dizzily. In her heart of hearts she knew that history meant nothing to Marek, in fact he scorned it. However she was nervous all the same. She was not proud of her own more recent history, there was too much in it to be ashamed of, so she believed.

When, quietly, Faran opened the door of the room, Rezia was waiting for her, set in the only armchair with knitting in her hands. For the first time in a long while Rezia's cheeks were not pale. She glanced up at Faran with a flushed smile. "Hello, dear, I thought you must have dropped off the edge of the world."

Exactly, Faran thought. Off and out of it, into another more wonderful one. She said, "You didn't miss me too much, did you? It's just that I met someone."

"Someone you know?" Rezia shook her head. "No, Faran, I have to confess, I didn't. I've not been awake very long. After I saw Matt I came back here and slept like a log. I haven't slept so well in more than a year."

"So he's helping you already. I knew he would," Faran replied.

"Did you really? He's such a lovely man, Faran. He said he'd see me tomorrow morning, and I'm looking forward to it. I feel loads stronger already."

Faran stifled the urge to jump up and down with glee. "Well, actually, you'll see him before that. He's coming over here after dinner," she said calmly, but she could not contain herself any longer. She rushed to Rezia and fell at her knees, exclaiming, "Oh, Rez! Remember the man I told you about, the one I was in love with who had to go away?"

Rezia gazed at her quizzically. "Yes. The man you dreamed about every night. I thought he was just part of a fairy tale you enjoyed telling."

"Did you?" Passionately Faran grasped her friend's hands. "No, Rez! I never made it up, it was all true! And your healer is him; he is the man I love!"

"Matt is your young man?"

"Yes. I've been with him all afternoon. We love each other, Rez. Will you mind if I don't stay here tonight?"

"Faran, I'm your friend, not your mother. It isn't for me to mind what you do. Besides I see how that sad look had left your eyes at last. It's about time too, I say."

Oblivious to Rezia's knitting and a number of dropped stitches, they hugged each other.

Chapter Six

Marek took a roundabout route to the main house, skirting the flowerbeds and avoiding windows and doors still open to the afternoon light. He entered the house through its rear door and went straight up to Nikola's rooms by the back stairs. If he went out of his way to shun company or sudden meetings with the staff, it was because even after a year there was still a lot of curiosity in their minds about him and any chance for gossip was always an added danger.

A year in a place seemed to be his limit, he thought, but he was not going to run this time. With Faran coming into his life again something potent and destined felt to be on the move. Seven years was a cycle, perhaps, at least in that world of constant circling about illusion. He had come to put an end to all of the illusion. So was the confrontation looming near? He felt the presence, not of Silene or the Brotherhood and their nasties, but of some operation of power. Maybe it was the power in himself and in all the others he had touched in seven years, for they were all involved, and every day their numbers were growing.

Nikola was not in her sitting room, so he stood by the window and stared out at the garden and waited. It was nearing six, her regular dinner hour, and she was somewhat a creature of habit. Marek guessed that in her job she had to be; when one had to organize other people, it was fairly necessary to be organized oneself. Staff in the kitchen always had dinner ready for them exactly on time, they never had to wait. This was something like the bad old days in the De Ravana household where there were servants to cater to every whim, but Marek didn't care to dwell on the comparison. His life was about to change yet again. From now on he and Faran would look after themselves and each other.

"Hello! What a lovely evening it is!" Nikola bustled in through the door. She stopped suddenly to give him an interested and appreciative inspection. "My, you do look chipper tonight. What have you been up to? Dinner's about to go on the table. Go in, I won't be a moment." Her hands went hurriedly to pull out the pins from her rolled up hairdo and she disappeared into her bedroom.

Marek sat at his place at the table and waited yet again until Nikola arrived. She came in dressed in summery attire and with her hair loose. She always seemed to dress up in the evenings whether the occasion demanded it or not. They were served their meal and Nikola talked while Marek listened.

She spoke only of the day's events, as if talking helped her unwind. It wasn't until they were beginning on dessert that she glanced up and commented, "You're awfully quiet this evening, Matt. I don't think you've said two words since we started!

Marek shrugged. "I was waiting for the right moment. I've got something to tell you." Nikola put down her fork and looked at him with sudden concern. "Is something wrong?"

"No, on the contrary. Remember the family I asked you to help me find when we came from Vargas?"

Distractedly, Nikola stabbed at a piece of melon and put it in her mouth. Thinking, she chewed. "Um... yes. The Crafters."

"That's right."

All Nikola's patients were dealt with on a first name basis by herself and she was terrible with remembering last names. "I've heard that name recently, I think. Haven't I?"

Marek nodded. "It's the name of the young lady who came with Rezia."

"Oh, yes!" Nikola paused in mid bite of her melon. Hastily she chewed it down. "That girl is related to them?"

"Not related; she's actually Faran, the daughter of the man who helped me. Or rather she's the one who really set me free. Remember, I told you about her."

Nikola remembered. How could she not, when Marek had told her how he had felt about this girl and how he hoped to find her again? She also remembered that she had not tried very hard to find the Crafters after the initial failure to do so, and why. The guilt she had felt then over her own reluctance to share Marek with anyone else faded as the year passed by. Now it was back in full force. "I don't know what to say," she blurted out involuntarily.

Marek looked at her strangely. "Say whatever you feel. I don't mind."

No, he doesn't mind, Nikola thought, seeing in his glowing face a look she had never observed before. She knew what that look meant. He was over the moon, full of the sort of joy she had never experienced or felt; he was in love. No, it wouldn't matter what I said, she told herself amidst a sudden jolt of pain and disappointed jealousy. He'd hardly hear it anyway. "You must be very happy," were her lame words.

"I am," Marek said. "And I want Faran to stay here with me, in the cottage. It's big enough for both of us. I hope you understand, Nikola.

She's more important to me than you know. We belong together, forever."

To Nikola's smarting ego this statement sounded less like a request than an order. But Nikola nodded, knowing that at least in the depths of her caring heart she understood Marek's truth even while her ego railed against the man.

As always, Marek was just being Marek. Which meant that while sometimes he sounded as though he'd never put lordliness behind him and knew very well how to give orders and expect to see them obeyed, yet it wasn't like that. Marek had always accorded her the respect of being open and honest with her. He never pulled his punches, nor prevaricated, nor dallied with her feelings, and she always knew where she stood with him.

In the beginning, at the time of the bad gossip, he had come right out and said what he believed and felt. He was not her lover and he didn't intend to be. He said, "I'm sorry, Nikola, I can't stay here with this going on. It's not good for you or me. I'm your friend and I want it to remain that way. I don't want to let stupid gossip spoil that." There were other reasons too, such as the staff pestering him with prying questions. However, even then, Nikola hadn't wanted him to go. But she was less capable of outright honesty, for her complicated feelings would not allow it. So she didn't tell him how she truly felt, afraid that the knowledge would drive him away altogether.

But that was all over, and, now, a year later, it was final. Any hope, however vain and illusory, that Nikola might have cherished once, was gone.

"I only spoke to Miss Crafter briefly about her friend. Will you bring her to meet me properly?" Nikola ventured bravely.

Marek smiled. "Of course. Tomorrow morning." He pushed back his chair. "I'd better go. I told Faran I'd collect her after dinner and it's been a while."

He rose halfway, to leave then paused, saying, "About Rezia: I don't want you to give her any tests; they won't help the way she is. I think I can do something for her, but she needs to have confidence in me and in herself, and the tests would only undermine that."

For Nikola to collide with Marek on any point of consultation had never happened before. Nikola never interfered with Marek's work nor he with hers. But, for Nikola, these words and what was said earlier seemed to combine in one huge feeling of rejection. Before she could stop herself she barked back, "She's much too sick! She's beyond you! You said to me once you couldn't bring people back from the dead. Now do you think you can?"

Marek's face wore the sudden look of somebody who had been slapped without any justification and by a dear friend. He stared for a moment then said quietly, without emotion, 'Rezia's not dead yet, and she wants to live. I'm not ready to give up on her if she isn't." Then he left the table and the room.

Nikola slumped in her chair. She covered her smarting eyes with her hand and wept silently a little. "Damn it all, I'm such a fool!" she said, and cursed, over and over. "Damn! Damn! Damn!"

Marek knocked on the door and it opened. The old lady, Rezia stood in the doorway. She smiled at him. "May I come in a moment?" he asked.

"You're welcome," Rezia said. "Faran is busy taking a shower, I don't know why. She looked clean enough to me."

Besides two beds and a small table, there was space in the room for only two chairs, a comfortable one and a hard-backed variety. Marek waved aside the comfortable one which Rezia politely offered and took the other.

"So you are Faran's young man. I could hardly believe it when she told me. But it makes me happy to know it. Dear Faran, she's such a lovely girl, but I've always worried about her so much. She always seemed a little lost, you know, as if her heart was somewhere else," Rezia said.

"Have you known her long?" Marek asked.

"Two years. I was at the commune a year before she came, so I looked after her at first. She was so young then, like a little lost child, I thought. I didn't know what she was doing in such a place at her age. But she settled right in. She proved to be a great worker, very clever too, very capable."

The commune. Marek hadn't heard about the commune except in relation to what Rezia had told him of her own experience. Somehow he hadn't placed Faran inside it either, not really thinking how she and Rezia had come to be friends. So why was Faran not with her own family? What of Will Crafter? And Young Will? So far, he and Faran had hardly spoken of anything but their own love. Now he saw that there was much to know, for he sensed, not only from Rezia's words, but from the movement of his own feeling towards Faran, that something in her young

164

life had gone very wrong indeed.

However he wasn't going to question Rezia about Faran. Instead, he said, "We'll have our proper talk tomorrow, but tonight, before you sleep, Rezia, I'd like you to think about something in particular."

Rezia nodded.

"It's simple really," Marek continued. "It's to consider your relationship to your body. I want you to separate your idea of your self from the body. Try to step outside and look at the body objectively, as if it was someone else's, then see what you feel and think about it. Don't criticize it; just observe it and your own feelings. Can you do that?"

"I'll try, but it's not easy to get away from the pain. It feels like a prison to me," Rezia replied forlornly. "I wish I could, but—"

"Don't worry about that feeling. Don't let it stop you from trying." Marek left his chair and knelt on the floor beside Rezia. He took her hands in his. "Close your eyes for a minute. Relax. Breathe. The trick is in breathing, you know. Make the breaths steady and deep and slow. That's right." His tone had dropped to soothing levels. He felt the warmth in his hands transfer itself to Rezia's colder ones.

Opening the bathroom door, Faran saw that the little room was alight with a glow which came not from lamps or the moonlight streaming in the window. She smiled down fondly on Marek and Rezia. She knew what Marek was up to. She dared not break the moment so she stood unmoving until he finally looked up and saw her.

Across the room they spoke to each other silently through their eyes. "I love you," they both said.

Then Rezia roused. She sat more upright and said, "I don't know how you do it but you always make me feel better." She noticed Faran. "Dear, you've finished. That was one long shower, but it gave me the chance to talk to Matt. Have you got your things all ready to go?"

Faran pointed to her bag beside the bed. "All ready," she said. "You really don't mind, do you, Rez?"

Rezia considered her friend's flushed face. Then she gazed on Marek's long and steadily. He was still kneeling on the floor beside her. This time she took his hand. "Get up, young man. Take her with you, where she belongs. I can see it in both your eyes."

'Rez thinks you're wonderful, and so do I," Faran said.

Marek laughed and shook his head. With one hand he carried her

165

almost weightless bag; with the other he held hers. To negotiate the paths in darkness was not easy, although the full moon helped and he knew the way well.

The breezes had dropped and the air was clear and just slightly sharp and damp with the tang of the sea. Marek felt the damp air creep through his thin shirt, but Faran's dress was thinner. He felt how her hand, warm from the shower, was starting to chill. He stopped and put the bag down, then undid his shirt, taking it off, and before she could protest, he had dressed her in it. "No arguments, please. I want to get you home."

Faran fought her hand from under the long flapping sleeve to take his again. She squeezed it tightly. "Home," she said. "Home. That's such a lovely word."

After several more minutes they reached the entry to the coppice. As they passed under the darker shadows of the trees, moonlight fell upon them in dappled pools of silver. Faran regarded Marek in the moonlight. "You should never wear clothes," she said. "You look like a beautiful god of the forest as you are right now."

Bemused, Marek could only laugh again. "A frozen one though, if it got any colder."

"You remind me of the time in the tower, when I brought you the water and soap for a wash. I was so ashamed of myself then because I couldn't take my eyes off you."

Marek unlocked the cottage door but he did not open it. He turned to Faran instead, saying intensely, "Faran, what happened after you left the Towers? The so few things you've said about your father make me feel that something awful happened. Am I right?"

Faran turned her face away. She stared out into the shadowy night. Marek thought he saw a tear in the corner of her eye. She swallowed and replied so softly that he had to bend close to hear.

"We went to Hanna Harbor and it was very difficult for Daddy. He tried so hard to support us but he couldn't do it alone. My aunt and uncle said they'd help but what they really wanted was to take us from him. He fought them for three years, then ..." At this her voice choked and she began to cry and Marek just held her in his arms. "Then he was working at a building site, it wasn't much of a job, but it paid the bills. But there was an accident and Daddy was killed."

Marek carried her upstairs. She was so light in his arms, and she pressed herself against him, clinging to him, so that he was reminded of the child she had once been. Perhaps now, remembering her dear father, she felt child like, even with him.

But in the bedroom she was warm and womanly again, although subdued. "Will you be all right while I take a shower?" Marek asked and she nodded solemnly. "Get into bed, get under the covers, you need warming up. I won't be long," he told her.

Thinking only of her, he raced through his shower. He wanted her very much but he decided he would have to wait. Some things needed sorting out in Faran. Pain that needed to be cleared. Well, if there was anything in this world he was good at, it was this, thanks mainly to Marielle and seven long years. Perhaps that was what the time had been for. He had worked through his own pain and had cleared it all away. Now nothing stood between himself and the Light. He was Ozira, he was the Light.

He came to her in the bed and she snuggled close and snuffed him. "Mm, you smell lovely," she said. "So warm and nice."

Well, I have to be a little less nice in a moment, he thought. As Marielle had done with himself; it was necessary.

He put his arms around her and stroked her hair but he did not kiss her; one kiss would be his undoing, he knew. He said, "You have a lot of pain still inside you, my love. All that crying we did together on the cliff still hasn't cleared your tears. Is it all for your father, or is there more?"

"I thought you wanted to make love with me, not talk," Faran said.

"I do. I want you, but I want you clear and free as well. Don't you want that too?"

Faran sniffed and nodded. "I don't know where to start, but yes, I want … I have to tell you it all."

Now Marek felt safe for just one little kiss, so he kissed her. "Start at the Towers where it all began, or at Hanna Harbor … wherever you feel is best."

Chapter Seven

I'll begin with the Towers, and it has to do with you," Faran decided.

"I think it was from the beginning that Daddy saw how I felt about you, and that made him afraid. Even though he didn't know anything about you he guessed enough to make him worry. Well, after he did know he was even more concerned. When you'd left us we had to wait for your brother's men to come back and do as you said and pretend, so that we would be safe. Daddy was ready to run too.

He'd decided that, whatever happened, he was leaving the Towers for good. His older sister had always wanted him to come to Hanna Harbor so he thought it was best to go there, even though he didn't like the cities.

"When the men came, your brother was with them, and that scared Daddy a lot."

Marek felt both appalled and apologetic. "Silene came to the Towers? I never suspected he'd do that. I'm sorry."

"It wasn't your fault. Anyway, Daddy was really great, considering. Your brother seemed to accept his lies and even his resignation, and they went away. But we never did feel safe after that, not in the high country. We had no money much and Daddy worked on the way because His Lordship hadn't bothered to pay him for the long service he was owed."

"That bastard!"

"You sound angry," Faran whispered. "Do you hate your brother?"

Marek shifted uneasily in the bed. Did he hate Silene? If he'd hated Silene once, now he'd gone beyond that or any other feeling for the man. Monster, not man. "I hate what he does. I don't think of him as a brother any more."

"Well, I won't call him that any more either," Faran said. "In any case, he doesn't come into the rest of the story except as a reason for us changing our name."

"That would have made it difficult for Will, to get work I mean," Marek said. "I understand that myself. When you assume a false identity you can hardly call on your past for references."

"Yes. Daddy had to work at all sorts of low paying jobs, and they were always changing. That's when Aunt Moria and Uncle Josh stepped in. They wanted to send Young Will and me to school, pay for it I mean. Daddy said yes to that because he didn't like leaving us all day in the

168

suburb where we were staying. It wasn't the best of places.

"But then Aunt Moria, it was her mainly, showed what she really wanted. She said that since I was nearly grown up I should be put in the 'right school' – 'So Faran can have a chance at a better life,' she said. Daddy wasn't happy about that, because by the 'right school" Aunt meant the best and snobbiest. But it was that or nothing and after a lot of arguments, poor Daddy gave in."

"So you ended up at Hightop?" Marek asked.

Faran started, surprised. "How do you know that?"

"It's the top girl's school in Hanna Harbor, isn't it? When I was a boy of about fifteen or so, my family and a lot of my friends" families used to vacation around there. The Hanna snobs, that's what we boys used to call the local gentry, but we were worse than they were, a real ghastly lot, very superior and condescending. Anyway, they always invited us to the school dinner dances—"

"They were setting you up as potential rich husbands for their daughters," Faran said.

Marek nodded. "And we hated the dances , couldn't stand the girls, but our families made us go. A lot of us used to beg off or sneak away early and go down to the sleazy side of town to ogle the street walkers. They were much more stimulating to the imagination of teenage boys."

"I wouldn't blame a boy for begging off. I know how awful those dances were too, I went to enough of them," Faran agreed. She tried to make herself sound suddenly light hearted but in truth her heart was growing steadily more morose and heavy. It was at one of those dances where she had met Brock for the first and fateful time. He was not as young as Marek had been though, he must have been nineteen or twenty then. "But street walkers! Did any of you boys ever … you know … go with them?" she added.

"Me, you mean?" Marek stifled a laugh. "Some of my friends paid up, the precocious ones. But I was never that forward, and besides, I can't remember any girl ever being attracted to me except if it was because of my father's name."

Faran thought that unattractiveness and Marek made an unlikely combination, however she didn't say so. She continued, "I hated Hightop, it was so phoney. I felt it was a prison, but no one was going to let me escape, not even Daddy. But I understood his dilemma so I made the best of it and didn't complain. I missed him though, and Young Will."

"What about your brother? What was he doing?" Marek asked.

"He went to day school, a 'good' one, but it wasn't so awful for him then. The trouble with Young Will started nearly three years later. I think it was my uncle's turn this time. Aunt and Uncle have no children of their own and Uncle had always wanted a son. He offered to adopt Young Will, then when Daddy said "NO!" he got really nasty for a while. Daddy and he fought and fought; it was awful; it really got Daddy down. Uncle Josh kept trying to make him feel guilty for all sorts of reasons; he knew we'd come from the Towers because of some trouble with the authorities, otherwise why did we change our name? But he didn't know what it was exactly, yet he tried to hold it over Daddy, like some sort of threat.

"Then Daddy came to see me at school and he was talking about us leaving and going somewhere else. I agreed and I wanted to go." Faran paused. Her voice began to waver. "Oh, Marek, he was so unhappy!" she said. She pushed her face into Marek's shoulder and began to cry. Through the sobs he could just hear coherent words. "The very next day, oh, Marek! H-he was dead!"

Marek held her and let her cry. He could feel no hint of great guilt in her tears; it was mainly sorrow. The pain she expressed at this moment was for her father's situation primarily and not her own, but was it all? He thought not.

For nearly half an hour they lay together in the bed. Outside, the darkness grew more silvery as the moon rose higher. Clinging to the open window, a climbing plant of green leaves and pale purple bracts had lost all its color in the subtle light. A salty breeze blew, lifting the gauzy curtain like a veil of mist. The plant crept across the window shelf and wandered indoors. It brought with it the fragrances of a sunny day, tempered and softened by moon glow.

Calm now, Faran continued:

"I stayed at school. What else was there to do? Then Uncle got his way and adopted Young Will.

They called him WILLIAM; I had no say in it, no legal claim on him, I wasn't old enough. I hated them for that. It was like they were flaunting their success at my father and going behind his back. But they always said, over and over, how they were doing everything just for us. I knew it wasn't so, though; they were just being selfish; they had wanted children and now they had them... well, Young Will, at least."

At these words Marek felt an awful disquiet. Faran did not seem to realize what this implied, he thought. He knew enough of the law to understand that it would not be possible for an uncle to adopt a child with a false, unauthorised name, so it followed that at some time the uncle must have revealed Young Will's true identity to the authorities. Just when had the uncle done that? he wondered. After Will Crafter died or before …?

"I couldn't do anything but accept the fact," Faran was saying. "And I was stuck at school, with a year to go. Young Will is nearly sixteen now. He's at Hanna College, and he hates it. He's like Dad and me; he just wants to be free. When I saw him at school just the other day he begged me to take him away."

"Do you want to?" Marek asked.

Faran nodded. "I do. But I don't know that I can, not legally anyway."

"That's true, not until he turns sixteen, at least."

Faran sighed. "There's more stuff to tell, but now it's going to get really personal; it's all about me.

Are you sure you want to hear?" "Yes. Especially if it's about you."

Faran sighed again, more deeply this time. "It's stuff which makes me ashamed." "Well, we've all been through that," Marek assured her.

"My Aunt Moria's idea of the fit place for a young woman is in a good, preferably well off marriage. That's what she wanted for me, or rather, for her so she could social climb a bit higher. She had him picked out, you know, the guy she set her sights on, long before I had any idea of what she was up to. She 'arranged' for us to meet at the school. My first reaction to him was dislike, but I was only seventeen and Daddy had just died and I was at a loss and didn't trust my own judgement, although I should have. As time wore on he laid on the charm and paid me such attention that I began to fancy I liked it. After I finished school Aunty pushed me into the yacht club scene where she and Uncle Josh liked to mix. Of course the guy was a summer regular there too."

"He wasn't from Hanna Harbor?"

"No. He was very much from that upper class, like you were before," Faran said. "It's ironic really that Daddy had been so afraid of me getting mixed up with you, because you came from that part of society, then Aunt goes and throws me right into the same pot. Some of the people in that class were really nice people, but a lot of them weren't. He wasn't nice, so I found out later.

"Then he said he wanted to marry me. I was almost nineteen, and Aunt Moria was overjoyed." "How did you feel about it?" Marek asked. He felt Faran shiver against him. "Are you okay?" "Y-yes," she said tremulously. "I didn't love him, if that's what you want to know. How could I, when every night I dreamt about you? But I didn't know if I'd ever see you again ..." She paused and he felt her quake, as if recoiling from something which horrified her. "I never actually said "yes", but I didn't say "no" either, and that was my mistake. Everyone decided that it was going to happen, him most of all, and he started pressuring me for..."

Faran turned her face from Marek's. "He didn't really want marriage. He just wanted sex, and as soon as possible. The first time he tried, it was awful. He wheedled and persuaded, and I was too naive to think that all I had to do was make a fuss. Aunt Moria would have thrown him out then and there, I'll credit her for that at least, she was always one for upholding that sort of morality, but I always felt kind of powerless in her house. He waited for Aunt and Uncle to go out then he came around. He wouldn't take no for an answer. Marek, I couldn't stop him!"

She began to cry softly. Marek swallowed tears of his own. "Did he hurt you?" he whispered. "Y-yes. Oh, he didn't hit me or anything, nothing like that. But it hurt like hell and when I begged him not to keep on he took no notice. So I had to endure it. That's what makes me most ashamed, I didn't put up a fight like women are supposed to. Part of me was kind of excited by his attentions ... you know, I sort of wanted to find out what it was like, but then I didn't. I didn't love him or want him, but something in me wanted to know. It was so confusing that I didn't know how to react, so I let it happen, and it still shames me to remember it."

Marek turned her face to his. "Don't hide. Look at me," he said gently, but firmly. He held her face in his cupped hands. "So what are these tears all about? Shame? Anger? Do you feel cheated? Like a fool? Did he spoil a dream for you? What?"

Faran stared at him, wide-eyed through tears, as if shocked by his sudden hardness. "I-I-I don't know! I felt spoiled, trashed. All my dream was to find you one day, and come to you p-pure. For it to be perfect: you and me ... pure. Oh, I DON'T KNOW!"

She tried to avoid his eyes again but he would not let her. Her whole body shook as he held her. "Yes, you do," he said. "Don't run away from it, face it!"

He watched her struggle, as he had struggled once. He felt compassion for her but he would not let her give up. Then she burst out, eyes flashing, angry at last. "I'm not ashamed, I'm not! He did it! HE HURT ME! But I was stupid! I let him! I let Aunt and Uncle take Young Will! I didn't help Daddy enough, I should have made him take us away from Hanna Harbor from the beginning! I could have, I could have made him do it! He might still be alive, Marek, if I'd been smarter or stronger. Oh, damn it, I'm angry, I'm mad at myself! I hate myself for having been so weak! I hate myself for letting things happen to me and for doing things I didn't really want to do!"

She collapsed in Marek's arms, sobbing feebly. "Well," Marek said, while he steeled himself to keep the same gentle firmness in his voice. "That's a whole lot of "I's", isn't it? So many wicked "I's". What about the others then, do they have no responsibility in this "I" world of yours?"

Faran pulled away, staring at him. "W-what do you mean?"

"I mean that this whole mess seems to center around you. But does it?" Faran looked stunned. "Oh!"

"Look at it this way. Here you are, a weak, tarnished, stupid, errant creature in a world where everyone else is either non existent or without wills of their own. They all depend on you for their behavior or their satisfaction, and no one is responsible for what happens but you. Is that it?"

"Oh, Marek!" Oh, no, it's not!" Faran replied, shocked. "What is it then?"

Faran looked this way and that. Unconsciously she was wringing her hands. Marek felt himself grow hot and feverish with love and compassion, with hope. Soon the dam will burst, he thought.

Faran held her forehead. Her breathing was growing heavier and heavier, deeper and deeper. She would not look at Marek, in fact she could not. The only place she could look must be within. She must look into herself now, for the truth.

And it broke. With tears came the release. The pain, the misery, the guilt and anguish of a meager twenty-one years, buried under that mountain of so many other lifetimes lost in illusion. It was the same as it had been for him, and it needed release.

"Daddy always wanted freedom," she said after the anguish was ended. "And so did I. We sought for it in the high hills, away from the hard world, but it isn't there, or anywhere, is it. It's here, inside, where you don't worry any more about all the things you've done and the mistakes you've made.

Where you put it all behind."

"That's right," Marek said softly. "All you have to do is turn your face in the right direction. Not backwards, to where history will constantly try to drag you down, but to the Light which you are and have always been.

History is only a catalogue of mistakes, so why would we want to bother with it? People like to say that they have to learn from their mistakes, yet they keep on making them, the same ones, over and over. That's because they focus on the illusion which says they aren't pure and that they're bad and weak and stupid. But they are pure, essentially. You wanted to be pure for me, and you are. You are pure Light, my love, and nothing can outshine you."

"Is this your strength, this freedom which you know?" Faran asked.

"Yes. And it can be yours. The Light is our freedom, as long as we face It and be It."

"I'll finish my story now," Faran decided. "I never told you the guy's name, it was Brock. He tried to force me a couple more times but it always ended in tears and frustration. My tears, his frustration. I couldn't let go, I didn't want to, and he'd only hurt me. He got fed up but he didn't intend to give up. I don't think he wanted his friends to find out that he was such a lousy lover, so he kept on sucking up to Aunt Moria, saying he was going to marry me. That's when I decided to run away. A girl I knew had a cousin in the commune near Minerva, so I went there. I didn't have to worry about Young Will. At least at school he was relatively protected, so I left and never went back."

She lay in his arms, at peace. They didn't make love that night because the release of so much emotion had drained her so that she was weary by the end. Instead, Marek asked for her hands and she gave them willingly. Was it healing he was offering? she wondered to herself. She felt to be still in need of something, although she did not know what.

"Close your eyes," he told her. "Just relax and be with me."

Faran closed her eyes. His voice came softly to her. "Everything has been cleared away, the Light is you, you are the Light." An energy seemed to come from his hands to hers. Then the words became faint to her ears, as from a far distance away. A slight humming sound began in her head, rising to a buzz which matched a tingling along her spine. She felt as if she was at the very base of her own spine and rising with the buzzing. Her whole body tingled with energy; it was not like anything she had ever known before. The tingling increased and rose the length of her spine. She felt that she was the energy, not just that the energy was there and alive. The most tremendous urge to breathe, so deeply, came upon her. She breathed, and it was as if her breath and her consciousness were drawn up out of the very Earth itself. She breathed from the Earth, from the Earth's core, and rose up with the breath, her consciousness singing in tune, rising in resonance.

The whole length of her spine, she breathed and rose, then her consciousness surged through her head and shot out into space, as if at the top of her head there was the opening for a fountain which wanted to play itself into the universe and beyond. By then, body consciousness had departed, although strangely the body was still a part of the whole flow. Yet she was not that body any longer, she was free. With another great, primal breath, her consciousness rose, tingling, alive, fountain-like, the blossoming of a great infinite flower in the infinite sea of energy and remembrance. Now she knew the freedom she had always wanted, that desire for freedom which had so often expressed itself in the high country as she watched the birds. "Oh, why are my feet so solidly planted on the ground?" she had often said to herself in those days. "Why can I not fly too?" But one did not need to fly, not bodily, when one was truly free.

Her consciousness surged, rose, then also like the fountain, cascaded back down, darting and dazzling like shining water. Back into the body again it poured, a flowing, healing stream of Light and Life. The body it poured into rejoiced, the Earth rejoiced and Faran rejoiced. The Light was once more connected and whole. Yes, she was free.

The tears which came now were tears of joy. This had been given to her by another, or it was that Love itself had been freely given and she was ready to receive it in full measure. The freely expressed, unimpaired flow of love of one Light for another was a beautiful thing, the most beautiful of all things…

That night she slept beside Marek in the deepest, sweetest sleep of all and only dreamed one dream. Somewhere in the depths of night, when the moon itself had gone to bed, she woke and remembered it, and it was very vivid and alive in her mind. She dreamed that she was between earthly lives, not in this one, not in the one before. Her time was then a time to choose the way, and not so much to choose as to remember and re-affirm. Three cards appeared and on each a name, and, taken together, these expressed her full Self, her Light. She took the cards and named herself: RAI-A- ELE.

Chapter Eight

Just as dawn broke up the shadows in the room, Faran woke up. She opened her eyes and forgetting for a moment where she was, lay unfocused on anything but the name in her mind. It was still there, shining like a trio of three little stars which together made one bright light, clear enough and sharp enough to rival the sunrise. She breathed and said the word silently, Rai-a-ele, or that was how it sounded, she thought.

Then she remembered the night and Marek. She turned in the bed and smiled upon him. He lay on his side, facing away from her. He was still deeply asleep.

Faran propped up on one elbow and studied him. He was so beautiful, she decided, yet again. She laughed at herself and her own indulgence in such open worship. So, if she said it too often and he was embarrassed … well, that was just too bad; it was the truth as she saw and felt it. But then the beauty was also his Light which shone from his face and radiated power from his touch. She felt beautiful herself now after what had happened last night. Would it show in her face too?

She wanted him to wake up so she could tell him of her dream. He knew about the other experience. How could he not, when he had been instrumental in bringing it about? But neither he nor she had a name for what it was or meant; they just understood how it felt.

She felt so full of lightness and joy that she wanted to share it with him. She leaned over him and her long hair fell across his bare, brown shoulder. She took a piece of her hair and began to tickle his cheek with it. "Wake up, wake up," she whispered, in delight.

Marek stirred and with his hand he pushed the hair away. He made a noise something like, "Mm … mnn …" and whatever that meant it was not agreement to wake up. Faran tickled him again, laughing to herself. "Lazy, lazy … time to wake."

Marek groaned and opened his only visible eye. "It's not even light," he murmured sleepily. "Yes it is. Listen, you can hear the birds." Faran attacked him with the hair once more.

He rolled further away, pushing his face into the pillow to escape. "No sun yet," he mumbled. "Too early … damned birds."

Faran put on a voice of mock dismay. "Well, some lover you are. Less than twenty four hours and the romance is all gone. Here you are, with a

176

naked woman in the bed beside you, and you don't even want to know! I suppose that's what I get for taking up with an old guy of ...?"

Face buried in the pillow, Marek grinned. "Thirty two."

"Thirty two? Good grief! So that means I'm going to have to try harder, I guess." Faran slipped down next to him, hugging his back. She reached an arm across to hold him then let her hand wander.

Marek sighed and groaned and sighed, but not because of sleepiness. Eventually he turned in the bed and smiled at her from dulcet, violet eyes. "So much happiness in you, it's making you mischievous."

Faran smiled back. She kissed him on the mouth. "So much happiness in me, it makes me want to love you all the more, if that's possible."

They gravitated together, skin pressed against skin, mouth meeting mouth. Love sharing love. Now they came to each other, both clear and free, as the sea birds wheeled and cried in the blue and the sun rose higher in the sky.

Before they got up she told him, in wonder, of her dream and the name.

He was very interested. He said the name aloud, three times, pronouncing it very carefully as she had done. 'Rai-a- ele ... Rai-a-ele ... Rai-a-ele." Which Faran thought was a curious thing to do.

"You don't happen to have ever learned Tanu by any chance, do you?" He asked her. "What's that? What's Tanu?"

"It's a language, a very ancient one. And the Tanu are a people who live in the Southern Ocean." "Why did you ask?" Faran wanted to know.

"I was there for a year, before I came here. The Tanu took me in and made me a part of their world.

It's a beautiful place, Te Tanaa. Your name is so similar to two Tanu words, although I don't know about the 'a', that I can't believe it's just coincidence. To the Tanu I am not Marek but Ozira." He nodded at her wide open eyes. "Yes, I have a name too. I got it not long after I left the Towers, when I reached the coast."

"How?"

Marek sat up. "It's a long story, too long for now. We have to get up; I've got to work this morning." "Okay," Faran agreed. "You did promise before dinner yesterday that you would tell me everything about yourself, but instead you let me take over." He studied her. "Aren't you glad you did?"

Faran reached for his hand. "Yes, but I still want to know about you."

Marek lifted her fingers to his lips and kissed them. "You shall. Now I had better get washed and dressed. I'll be seeing your friend Rezia at ten, but before that there's someone else."

"Then I'll make us some breakfast," Faran offered, getting up herself. "You do have some food downstairs, don't you? You didn't use it all up yesterday, I hope."

Marek headed for the bathroom. "There's cereal and eggs, but no bread. I burned the lot making afternoon tea. I'll get supplies today, so we can have all of our meals here from now on, unless Nikola wants us to dinner, of course."

Faran pulled a face he couldn't see. "Would you want that?"

Marek turned on the shower and talked to her through the steam. "No, not really. Maybe once or twice, but not too often. I just used to have dinner over there because it was easier. I'm not actually a very good cook, I haven't had enough practice over the years, so I've been taking the easy way out."

"Is that so? I would never have guessed," Faran said, remembering, with irony, the dreadful toast.

She slipped into Marek's robe. Her bag was still at the bottom of the stairs where he had dropped it in order to carry her up. She would unpack it later, when he'd gone, she thought. She realized now that she would have to wait to see Nikola, or Doctor Langan as she still thought of the woman. She wasn't so sure how that would turn out but she had every confidence in Marek making it as easy as possible.

With enthusiasm Marek attacked his eggs. "I remember the last time you fed me. If I think about it I can still taste it."

"It made such an impression on you?" Faran said incredulously. "I can't even remember what it was."

"It wasn't the food which made the impression, my love, it was you." The light in his darkness: this was how he had thought of her, even though she was a child then. And now she was here, a woman, the light in his life. "Do you want to stay in the house while I go out, or go to Rezia?" he asked. "Either way, I'll take you to visit Nikola for lunch. Then after I've seen one more patient, we'll have the afternoon to ourselves."

"Oh? Is this another of your half days?" Faran was pleased. She considered. "I'll stay here. I have to unpack my things. There isn't much because most of my stuff is still at the commune, but I need to freshen it up a bit. Can I wash something?"

Marek finished up his tea. "This is your home now, Faran. You can do anything you like in it. All right?" He jumped up and headed for the

178

stairs. "I'll just tidy myself up and then I must go. I've never been late for a patient yet and I'm not starting now."

In ten minutes he was downstairs again. He bent and kissed her and she tasted his sweetness and snuffed that same tantalizing scent of sandalwood and cedar and unknown herbs with which he and all his possessions seemed infused. It was a pity he had to go at all, she thought, feeling for that moment, intensely selfish.

At the front door he turned and in parting, said, "I'll be back just after twelve. If you get bored waiting for me, there's something in the bedside chest which you might like to look at. It's on the top shelf."

"What?" Faran started to say, but he only smiled and then was gone.

Faran hurried through every task she set herself. She made the bed and washed up the dishes, swept and cleaned up the kitchen and washed her clothes and found a line outside to hang the clothes on. She inspected his house in general and saw that, whilst it was clean, it wasn't very tidy. Well, that was a man for you, she said to herself. She had been quite used to tidying up after her father and Young Will, so it didn't bother her very much. But she hesitated to put anything away lest she put it in the wrong place. She picked up his clean shirts which were still laying over the chair and took them upstairs. As she hung them in the closet she thought about what he had said. Her eyes went to the bedside chest, but she controlled the urge to look just yet. There was something else she wanted to do first.

She opened her bag and took out all her other clothes and looked for a place to store them. There was plenty of room in the closet and half a dozen spare hangers on the rail. Like herself, Marek did not seem to have much in the way of possessions.

The last thing in her bag was folded and stored inside a cloth bag of its own which smelled of lavender and sweet thyme. Thoughtfully she drew it out and lay it on the bed cover. The coat. His coat. She wondered if he would remember it. It looked better now than when he had given it to her father, since then it was stained and scuffed by the rough treatment the men had dealt out to him. She remembered how pained it had made her feel to see on it those marks of his torture, and how carefully she had sponged it clean, even adding some of her tears to the soapsuds. The memory returned vividly now as a painful convulsion inside her as she thought also of the scar on his shoulder. Why should anyone want to hurt him? she thought. A man like that, so good and gentle? She could not understand it.

With a tender gesture she smoothed her hand across the soft velvety fabric which never seemed to wrinkle no matter what you did to it. So many times had she gone to sleep at night with that coat clutched in her arms. For the dreams of Marek, and later, for a comfort, when she felt lost and alone after Will had died. Wherever she went she was never without this coat; it was her talisman of hope. But now it could be Marek's again, and from the humble look of Marek's clothes hanging in the closet, it would still be the best thing he owned.

Still puzzling over what must be in the chest, nevertheless she took a shower and dressed herself in an ankle length dress of fuchsia colored silk which she had hung out in the bathroom while she showered, in order to take out any wrinkles. This was actually her best dress and one she rarely wore, if ever. It had been one of her aunt's choices, and in spite of disliking the woman Faran couldn't deny that she certainly had an eye for charm and good taste in clothing. Faran had hated to take such clothes with her when she ran away, but had she not she would have been travelling practically naked.

Hastily she towelled her hair then went straight to the bedside chest. What could it be? She wondered. She opened the little door and looked in. There were two shelves cluttered with bits and pieces: some crystals which were very pretty; a piece of coral, once pink but now bleached almost white; some dried flowers of a type she did not recognize; a collection of documents which she did not look through; a small clock which did not seem to be working at all; a pen and a blunt pencil. But on the top shelf where Marek had said to look there was only one thing, a book. Faran took it out. It was not a commercially produced, printed book such as one might buy in a store, but a handwritten one. She opened the cover and saw written on the first page in an elegant hand, Journal of Marek De Ravana, and below that, From OZIRA, and underneath all, two dates enclosing a space of just five years. The first date began seven years before, two months after Marek had left the Towers. The second was two years ago, before he came home to Telaia.

Faran closed the book and held it to her breast. Marek's book, and he wanted her to read it.

Chapter Nine

In the little coppice outside, in early morning sunshine was a garden bench with a wooden table beside it. Faran took the book, settled herself down in the sun, and commenced to read.

It began with an introduction, as a retrospective description of the events of a time before the journal's starting date. Marek's amazing life. Faran read with awe of an incredible past, and discovered in his words a world which made her sit open mouthed as she read. She learned that his family was the end point of a long line of powerful controllers of the world, and one of the dynasties which propagated themselves, again and again over aeons of lives, in order to keep the reins of the world in their hands. Constantly, they were the same beings who replicated themselves in positions of power, and Marek acknowledged himself as having being one of them at one time.

"When I was a small boy of about five," his journal said, "My father took me to a place where there were a number of other important men, although not one of them was anyone I knew or had ever seen before. I don't remember a lot about this meeting, only that the men questioned me and studied my eyes. Apparently, when I was two years old, my eyes suddenly developed a propensity for changing color with my moods. This caused a great sensation in my house because it was a phenomenon never seen before but which had been predicted long ago as the indicator of a being of enormous power and mastery who could change the world or order it in any way he desired. What this actually meant could only be surmised, but the males of my family, with their narrow focus on worldly power and control, decided that it was my destiny to make them and their dynastic line even more almighty than before.

"When I was twelve years old, my father met an unexpected death and my older brother, who succeeded my father as Baron, decided to take charge of me. He was, as I found out later on, the Grand Master of a world organization known as The Brotherhood. It is really these men who order all the workings of the world, not politicians or heads of state, nor royalty or the great religious leaders, although very occasionally they can be one and the same. Such as my brother, Silene, Baron De Ravana, who manages a high profile in Telaia.

"It was through Silene, although at the time accidentally and without his intent, that as a young man, I discovered that the Brotherhood itself was not the real power in the world even though it ruled it.

The Brotherhood takes direction from elsewhere, as an organization of beings who have sold their souls to something darker in return for worldly power. It is an ancient story, this, but a true one. It is the reality behind all the demons and gods and heavenly prophets, the old priest kings and the more modern divinely inspired rulers and pontiffs. Religion in all its forms is its servant and all manner of human traditions are its slaves.

"This darker force I called the Dragons, for want of a better name and because the name describes somehow their essential character. They do not exist in our physical world and cannot act in it directly, which is why they need the cooperation of greedy men. Unknown to Silene, I have seen them, these Dragons, and smelled their tainting breath, but unlike Silene I have not drunk the poison of their black blood, that is, not for many lives, at least.

"I acknowledge that once, in other lives, I was as my father and brother. I sought for power and mastery and learned to wield them expertly. Too expertly, which explains how it was I who fulfilled the prophesy of Chameleon Eyes, as my father used to call me. After he discovered that, he never called me Marek again.

"I did not realize at first, but it was the Dragon Force which really intended to snare me and the power I held, for the strengthening of their position in the world. The petty ambitions of my family were nothing to them, although they were seen as useful for keeping me under control. Our world is, at this time, at the point of a great change, which means that any new focus of human consciousness can be responsible for a radical alteration of existence here on Earth. The Dragons know only too well that should the focus turn away from their elaborately constructed illusion of reality, in which so many people do believe, then their days are numbered as the Lords of the World. The Earth will be free of their damaging influence and so will Mankind.

"This potential as a catalyst is what they saw in me, and they knew that I must be carefully schooled to keep my own focus pointing in their direction. So they chose the Master most able to order and direct me, my brother. Since he was so much older, it could be done from my earliest days and within the extra advantage of a powerful and rich family. The Dragons know well what a lure privilege is, and how easy it is to foster corruption in a soul amidst luxury and ease.

"Now I must speak of my mother, who had no part in all of this except to bear me, yet who was ironically the greatest and truest influence in my life. From the age of twenty on, my mother bore my father six children in twelve years. The first child was a son who died at age nine, then came four daughters, then Silene. I was not born until some fifteen years later, so I was the child of her maturity.

"My mother was an opposite force to the others which surrounded me. From my birth onwards she was determined to keep me from the corruption she saw in the rest of her children. It must have been a sad thing for her to observe and accept the deviant nature of the De Ravanas. Although she came herself from one of the highest families in Telaia, she obviously married my father without understanding the sad truth of the world she was entering.

"It was a fortunate thing for me that I was born in her later life. She was no longer a girl with unformed ideas and was strong in her desire to save me. Her heart had always been a true one and had guided her head. She strove to inculcate in me the same sensitivity to my feeling self, and to the world at large. She taught me, by her own example and by the right words and actions, that I was a being born to love myself and others, and not to hate and despise the unhappy world, as Silene did.

"I often think with sadness of my mother when she found herself watching Silene inveigle himself into my life, and I, still an easily influenced boy, followed his grand example in many things. For a long time I lived with the guilt that I had hurt my mother deeply by following Silene, then not so long ago I understood her better. Never once had she shown me resentment for my betrayal of her ideal, but that was because in her heart she knew that her influence had been strong enough to turn me back when I'd had enough of darkness. She said to me once that there was a great good in me, and that it would always win, no matter what the dark threw at it. In short, my mother had faith in me, a faith which she never let go of.

"When Silene found in me a tendency to waver between his world and hers, he decided on stronger tactics. He took me ... I was twenty one ... on a Grand Tour of the world's ancient centers of rule and culture. I think he reckoned on the majestic nature of such places to impress me with the worth of being at the seat of power. What it did, though, and this I did not tell him because I was somewhat afraid of him then, was to have the opposite effect. So much grandeur, so much luxury and excess, it nauseated me. I knew it was bought and built by the blood of ordinary humans, the humans which Silene so despised, and it nauseated me.

"My life became very difficult for me then. It was like trying to swim across a river with two conflicting streams flowing in opposite directions. One stream was on the surface where Silene dragged me along behind him, trying to convince himself that I acquiesced to his ways at last, while the other stream flowed in the depths of my being where I ached to rebel and find my own way.

"Then Silene stepped up the pace of control, for I think now that he was secretly worried that he would fail with me. When I was sixteen he had given me the present of a ring identical to one he wore. It is a ring of very special properties which I still wear because I'm unable to get it off. The stone is a resonator, that is it has the power of resonance with another, like stone. It is also influenced by psychic forces and changes color when impressed by thought. Not only that but the wearer of one can tune his stone with the other and by observing the color changes, can know much about that other wearer's state of mind. In other words, Silene had me monitored and I didn't know it, and that was how he guessed my uncertainty and saw that possible trouble loomed ahead.

"For two years he watched me like a hawk and tried to do only those things with me which he felt would not repel me. But he was also getting desperate himself for he had to put up a shield against the prying of his masters. He did not want to fail himself or them, nor even let them know of the possibility of failure. They were urging him to bring me deeper into their influence but he was wary of what would happen if he did. Nevertheless he decided to proceed, but with caution.

"Silene is a magician – an unpopular and dubious word these days – but that is what he is. He knows how to influence the minds of others, how to manipulate thought and create illusion. He has the power to unlock energies in situations and in people which he then uses for his own purposes. He also knows how to steal energies, which he never gives back to the unfortunate victim. All this he taught me, although under a veil of dispassionate science and omitting the acts of thievery and hiding the truth from me, so as not to alienate my mind. I took it all in, and because the practice of these arts and skills came easily to me, I did not reject what seemed at the time to be plausible or harmless. He was pleased and impressed by my prowess. He said that one day I would make a greater magician than he was. I only half believed him; I did not know then that, for once, he was being sincere, that he was telling me the truth, as he saw it.

"In my twenty third year my mother died and it was a terrible blow for me. Silene saw how I was affected and he must have decided that I was not in any mood to be pushed for a while. So he let me off the leash temporarily and I went to the coast, to stay at a friend's home for a month. In retrospect Silene would say now that he shouldn't have, since that trip became the moment of my beginning freedom.

"Ironically, my mother's death brought me back to her all the way. My heart opened, but I was still confused and lost more than ever. I did not know where to turn for help; there was not another on this Earth who could understand my position, or so I thought.

"Then one day, when I was sailing alone off the east coast, I got caught up in a squall and wrecked my boat on an island reef. After escaping drowning and getting safely ashore, I fell on the rocks and broke my arm and cracked my head. I thought to myself, this is it, because the small islands around that stretch of coast are all uninhabited and are generally lacking in fresh water. I thought I was going to die and, frankly, I didn't much care.

"That was when a strange old woman appeared, as from nowhere. Who she was or how she happened to be on the island, I didn't know, and she didn't tell me. But she fixed my broken arm and, even more wonderfully, she helped mend my broken spirit. I shall not name her. She was an old, old lady and was a healer from the Southern Ocean somewhere, and she showed right away that she knew me and understood my life. It was she who showed me the Light in myself that turned me forever away from Silene. That was when I discovered that all the power in me could be used for other than Silene's twisted aims. It was also an irony that it had been he who helped me unleash it, for now I could use it to go contrary to his way. I wanted to be a healer too, like the old lady, and she taught me many things about the art.

"I stayed with the old woman for many weeks, while on the mainland there was a frantic search set up for me. Apparently, and this I found out later, Silene made an awful fuss, blaming my friend and his family for letting me go out sailing alone. He practically mobilized the whole armed forces of the east coast in search of me and wouldn't give up even when the pieces of my boat were found washed up on the coast. How the searchers never seemed to come near the island I was on, not even for a look, I'll never know, but it was as if there was a ring of exclusion around the place and that I was never meant to be found, so that I could stay on the island unmolested until I was fit and ready to leave.

"How I got off the island is another story in itself, but it is not really relevant to anything that followed. Suffice to say that, when the old woman and I came to an understanding that I was strong enough in myself to face Silene again, she bade me goodbye and I got picked up by a passing freighter, which just 'happened' to see the signal we set on the beach. Silene was glad to get me back, but he was also curious about where I had gotten to and annoyed because of the trouble I had caused him. I told him that I had been hurt, and the arm was a proof, and that I'd found shelter with a hermit who had no means of communication with the outside world –all essentially true and Silene had to accept that.

"I had left the island, and I was a changed being. Without telling Silene a thing, I began to make a serious study of Nature's laws and cures, looking to transform myself into someone useful for a change. But of course Silene knew something was afoot … the ring, it was that told him … and he was forced to watch me again. Then he confronted me and I told him simply that I wanted to be a herbalist. He laughed; I don't think he'd ever heard anything which sounded so ridiculous to his mind.

"I persevered and he ridiculed and watched me. I gave no hint though that I was thinking of anything more than simple herbalism. But now that I was older and more sure of myself, I was not afraid to argue with him. So we argued rather a lot for a long time before he began to get more wary of me and less certain that I was only following a foolish whim.

"It was the damned ring and my own lack of caution which finally gave me away. Just before my twenty fifth birthday he and I had a final showdown. I told him what I thought of the Brotherhood and the ways of the world they ruled, although I never let on that I knew anything of the Dragons. He was very cold with me that day, then, surprisingly, by the next he had mellowed. It seemed to me that he had simply given up his hold, as if I was a lost cause and a disappointment, but that he would finally accept it. I didn't really believe he would give up so easily, however he was so mild and almost friendly that I foolishly dropped my guard. He said that whatever I chose to do, I was still his brother and he loved me. Liar!

"On my birthday he asked me to his city apartment for a celebratory drink. I had doubts, but I went. While I was there Silene had visitors, but they were actually his own men, the ones who always did his dirty work for him, and I was their next assignment. I suddenly realized that something unpleasant was in the air and that it had to do with me, and I tried to bolt. However there were too many of them and they stopped me

186

and beat me up. Then they held me down across a table while Silene firstly crowed about how stupid I was to think I could ever go behind his back. He spoke of the ring, of the truth of it, which his men did not understand but which I had already guessed. Then he gave me a lecture about the foolishness of crossing him. He ended it by saying he would forgive me if I would come back into his world and behave myself. Whether it was a wise act or not, I practically spat in his eye.

"Silene got very angry. He said he would teach me a lesson I'd never forget. He made the men hold on to me while he forced some liquid down my throat and one of them hit me to make me swallow it. I lost consciousness soon after that and didn't wake up until we were on the road to somewhere. They drugged me again and when I woke up next I was in complete darkness and silence, and I was chained.

"It took me a whole day to work out that I had been left for dead in some ruin far from help or civilization. And another to realize that it wasn't quite like that. Because, although Silene had left me without food, he had left water, a great big pitcher full, enough for many days, and had also left me with all of my things: wallet, ID, and every bit of my money. That's when I finally understood.

"Silene had heard my determination to turn my back on everything he had ever taught me and he was wise enough to comprehend the real meaning of that. It made him desperately afraid, knowing I was consciously against him and it was no whim or fancy of mine, and that once turned from himself and the Brotherhood I was the greatest threat to their existence which they had ever faced. He knew also what the Dragons would say: "Get rid of him", but he was still arrogant enough to think that he might be able to take control of me again. All he had to do was to make me behave like him, just once. In other words, if I used power to save myself, I would return to his ways. So he put me into a situation of dire need, where either I could starve to death or play the magician again. Either way he would win, he thought.

"I could almost hear him mocking me: "Come on, Magician, Breaker of Chains. Show me what you can do to get out of this one!"

"Then I discovered there were other people involved in my dilemma. Silene had me put in a tower in a place where only decent people lived. He was cunning. He realized that if I wanted to be a breaker of chains, then I could use the powers of manipulation to induce someone into letting me out. Which is the worst sorcery actually because it involves taking over the minds of others for one's own ends. I didn't know what I was going to do but I was determined not to play this game."

Faran lay the book on her knee. She stared into the sky, which helped to keep back the tears which threatened. What a life Marek had endured. It was a life so strange and different from most others that it was almost beyond ordinary comprehension. So, he had come to the Towers in that terrible way, but it had not turned out as Silene had hoped. She opened the book again, to see what he had to say about his time in the Tower.

"The man in charge of the Towers was a good and honest man, the kind of man my brother counts as a fool. Silene had him pegged from the start, I would say, and knew that he would be unable to stand by and let another man starve to death. Which, to Silene's way of thinking, meant that such a man possessed the amenability to be easily and unconsciously influenced beyond giving succor to a prisoner to that of freeing him entirely. In Silene's mind such men are merely dupes, and are all the more easily manipulated because of their impulse to be kind. That is his philosophy, but it is not mine.

"Silene calculated that I would become so desperate that I'd try anything to get out of the hole I was in. The tower was certainly not comfortable. For most of the time it was dark and freezing cold, enough to daunt me, and I must admit that, for a while it did. What Silene did not count on though, and probably didn't know about, was that the caretaker had a daughter who was rather special. From the first time I met her I felt that she was to be the light in my darkness; and I clung to that from the beginning, with the hopeful feeling that something unexpected was just around the corner. It was, and I was able to escape the tower by absolutely honest means.

"There is a power in this world greater than all the manipulation and deceit which Silene worships so completely, and that is love. Because I helped the caretaker with his sick child, he was willing to let me go. It took no coercing, or twisting of minds; it was simply the giving of a gift and the gratitude which followed. I know Silene would probably say that I still manipulated the man, but I know it is not so. The man responded from his own goodness. That is how I got out of the tower.

"But I was certain that Silene would believe otherwise, that I had used tricks to escape. I didn't care if he thought so; in fact, it was safer for my rescuers in any case, for Silene expected nothing more or less from them or me.

"My journeys then began. I was on the run from Silene. I knew it would take a while before he'd realize that I was not coming back. I marvel, though, at his self confidence. Did he not think how I would hate him for what he'd done? So what did he expect from me? It was that the experience was supposed to teach me that cooperation with power was the only way. He expected me to come back, subdued, but ultimately reconciled to his way, and he did not really care if I hated him or not, as long as he snared me for the dark again.

"After several weeks of running, I made my way to the coast and it was then that Silene began to actively hunt me down. I was nearly trapped again, but got away, and decided it was time to leave. So I left Telaia. I won't say how, yet it was easier to do than I would have reckoned.

"But before this happened I had made a little trip to the island of two years before. It was deserted now, and that disappointed me, however I hadn't really expected to find my old friend again. But I stayed one night and relived the experiences of the past, so vividly that it was as if time did not exist for me on that island. I relived the release of lives of guilt and pain which my friend helped me through, how I had turned my back on all that Silene stood for, and how the Light had come into my heart and mind. I also experienced something more, which brought to me the name Ozira, which is my own true name, the name of my frequency of Light."

Here the introduction to the journal ended and it became a series of dated entries, not day by day reminiscences, but as and when Marek had felt urged to write them. Faran read of Marek's travels away from Telaia, and as she read she shared their visions but also felt the loneliness through the words. Here and there were vague, haunting references to his thoughts and feelings in the tower, and sometimes her name appeared as an isolated thing, as if Marek was merely noting a sudden feeling or emotion. This touched her deeply, realizing that he had thought of her, even as she had wept and dreamed and believed that such a man would not remember a little girl like herself.

Then there were other entries, brief and to the point and bristling with irritation, which showed a Marek still on the run from the brother who hunted him relentlessly.

Marek spoke also of his growing understanding and use of Light, especially for healing. In his travels he became a herbalist-healer and this was how he had subsisted for most of the time. The journal entries ended at an intriguing point, just as he was beginning a voyage to somewhere, which he did not name.

Then, following this, on a new page, came the words of Ozira. Faran put down the book. Although she wanted very much to read more, she felt suddenly exhausted. She looked up to realize that the sun had risen impossibly high in the sky. How long had she been there, absorbed in Marek's life? She glanced at her watch; the time was five minutes after twelve. She could scarcely believe that two hours could have passed so swiftly.

Marek had said he would be back just after twelve. Faran stood and watched the distant rise, waiting for the first sight of her love. And he appeared, several minutes later, striding over the rise and down the little slope towards her. Or was it him? She could only see a figure bathed in a great light, as if the sun was a super nova exploding around and through the form in nimbuses of darting flame. It was Ozira, coming towards Rai-a-ele on a pathway of fire.

Chapter Ten

"Hello, Sweetheart, you look stunning in that dress," Marek said. His eyes travelled from her to the book on the garden seat. "How far did you get?"

"To the end of your journal. I wanted to read more but there wasn't time." Faran said. "Ah, then you know everything about me. It's only a pity it's such a miserable tale."

"It made me want to cry," Faran confessed. "But it isn't everything; there's nothing about the last two years."

Marek smiled. "I have another one which I'm still writing, and now that it will have you in it, it's bound to be a whole lot happier."

They went into the house. Since they were going to the hospice for lunch, Marek wanted to lock up first.

"Can we go upstairs a minute?" Faran asked. "I have something up there I want to give you." Marek nodded. "Sure. I have to put the book back too. What is it?"

"Wait and see."

The coat had been put away in its protective bag, which still lay on the bed. Faran handed Marek the bag. "Open it."

Marek sniffed at the perfumes of lavender and thyme and looked puzzled. He pulled the drawstring and peeked inside. He glanced at Faran strangely then drew out the coat. It unfolded itself in his hands, the soft, velvety fabric slipping heavily over his arms. He gasped, astonished and remembering. "Good Heavens, you kept it all this time!"

"I made Daddy give it to me. I wanted it; it was all I had of you," Faran explained.

Marek's expression grew strange again. He was staring down at the coat in his hands as if it was something foreign and unknown. Faran felt suddenly that she might have done the wrong thing in returning it. She said, "Don't you want it back? Does it remind you too much of all the awfulness?"

Abruptly he dropped it on the bed. It was a deep, rich, very dark blue, almost shading to indigo, and it lay against the white cover like a patch of night sky amidst clouds. Then he pressed his fingers against his eyes, as if brushing away tears.

Nervously Faran squeezed his arm. "Marek, what's wrong? Shouldn't I

191

have …?"

"Nothing. Nothing's wrong," he said tremulously. He sat on the bed and fingered the coat. He seemed to touch it with a pained tenderness. He looked up at Faran, and his eyes were a wet smoky grey. "My mother gave me that coat for my twenty-third birthday, not long before she died. When I realized I would have to get rid of all my expensive clothes so that I wouldn't look too conspicuous, I gave it to your father because I didn't want to just sell it off to some second hand merchant in a town somewhere."

Relieved, but also touched because she knew now what his mother had meant to him, Faran sat down beside Marek. She took up the coat and held it up against him. "It might still fit you, by the look of it. You haven't put on much extra weight in nine years, have you, although a bit more muscle maybe. Try it on."

Marek slipped his arms into the sleeves and Faran settled it around his shoulders. It fit, although only just. Suddenly Marek realized something and he said, "I thought you didn't know I was Matt Best until you were on the way to here. How come you brought this with you then?"

Faran blushed. "The truth is that I brought it with me because I've never gone anywhere without it, not ever. There was no way I was going to leave it behind at the commune, even though I thought I would be going back there when I packed my bag."

"Well, I'm glad you brought it, and it's very sweet of you to give it back to me even though I'm not likely to wear it all that often here." Marek smiled as he pulled it off. "Thank you," he said, and the coat slipped onto the bed as he kissed her, and his eyes became violet once more.

When they walked up the rise he had his arm across her shoulders and she had tucked hers cosily around his waist. Since reading his journal, Faran felt even closer to him now. Only one other person had read this journal, Marek said, although he did not say who it was, and Faran got the impression it was not Nikola. However he had written the book for a purpose. The words of Ozira, he told her, were written for the world, and he intended that one day soon they would be read.

Faran did not know what they were as yet. "And your journal too?" she asked.

"Some of it," he said. "The relevant bits. But the latter communications are what's important. When you read them you will understand why."

"Has Silene been pursuing you all these years just because of what you speak about in the journal? I mean, is he afraid of what you will tell the world about him?" Faran wanted to know.

"Hardly," Marek said. "Just think about it. If I was to tell publicly what I know about him and the Brotherhood, all he would have to do is say to the world that I am insane, and who do you think would be believed, a man of worldly substance and power like him, who has proven himself in society, or a runaway like me? In most people's eyes I would be a mad younger brother who couldn't handle the real world and ran off to go wandering. Imagine, a young man who has everything, wealth, position, power, luxury, who trades it all in for ignominy and relative poverty. No, they would definitely see me as unhinged. And besides, I have no concrete proof beyond my own experience and assertions.

"Then what is he afraid of?"

"It's what's in the rest of my book. When you read it you'll understand."

"Have you talked to Doctor Langan yet?" Faran asked him. She was feeling somewhat nervous about the impending meeting.

Marek shook his head. "I only saw her briefly, to organize lunch." He stopped to study her face. "Does the thought of seeing her worry you?"

"A bit," Faran admitted.

"Don't let it. Nikola's not an ogre, you know. Actually, she's a very fine person. I think she really understands in her heart how I feel about you, so she'll get used to it. Any problems she may have are mainly ego ones. By this I mean that, like most people, she feels hurt at times when things don't go her way, and her pride sometimes gets in the way of her relationships. We had a bit of a tiff about your friend at dinner, although I didn't let her carry it on. She let her emotions take charge when I told her I didn't want her to interfere with Rezia and she said some things I'm sure she already regrets."

To Faran, listening to his words, the truth was now suggesting itself, and she wondered that he didn't see it too. Nikola – Doctor Langan was most likely in love with him.

But Faran held her peace. Until she had met this woman face to face and seen what there was to be seen, she wouldn't make judgements of that sort, not yet.

"How is Rezia getting on? I should be spending more time with her than I am," she said.

"You'll see she's much better, in herself, that is," Marek said. He bent to explain, taking Faran's hands in his. "You know that it's her heart which is giving her the most trouble, don't you? Well, the rest is attendant upon that. We humans can be so awfully complicated and confused at times that we end up by giving our bodies hell. A lot of Rezia's trouble stems from a problem of heart which isn't even physical, but since our talk this morning I think she's beginning to see that."

Faran stared up at him with wide open eyes. "You amaze me," she said to him. "That you can see so much in another person from only two meetings. How do you do it? It took me half a year to find out from Rezia what made her most unhappy in life, and then she never told me it all."

Marek shrugged. "Just a skill I've got, I guess. We all have to be good at something." He grinned at her playfully. "Didn't you say that you could fix a truck? Well, when it comes to mechanical things like that I'm just one hopeless duffer."

To fix a truck, or to mend a human heart? Faran did not think there was any comparison.

They walked again. Once in sight of the hospice, Marek offered Faran a gentlemanly arm. Which was a more dignified way of entering a public place where one was about to advertise a connection without actually flaunting it. Clearly, he's thinking of Nikola, Faran realized. And why shouldn't he? She recognized by this that Marek was actually quite fond and certainly respecting of this woman and that he didn't want to cause her public hurt. So perhaps he did understand her heart, after all, Faran decided.

Marek led Faran up the back stairs, not the front, and straight to Nikola's personal rooms. A simple but elegant lunch was already on the table and Nikola was waiting for them. It was obvious to Faran that Nikola had gone to some trouble either to impress or to make her feel welcome, Faran wasn't sure which at first. But after the first five minutes she knew that it was the latter, and she was greatly relieved.

Nikola had come, by degrees, to acceptance. After Marek had departed so swiftly from the dinner table, leaving his dessert half eaten and his coffee untasted, she had rued her unfortunate words for half the night, and had tossed in her bed, wishing she could undo the mistake and return things to the way they were before.

Also, she was racked with guilt. To know how happy Marek was in finding Faran, to see his face alight with love and peace now that he had found what he had been searching for, and to remember how carelessly she had treated his wish to locate the Crafters, passing it off as less important than her own desire to have him by her side at the hospice. All

194

this compounded in her mind to make her miserable and self condemning. She had never believed she could be as selfish as that, she told herself. He wasn't in love with her and he never would be, but he had always been willing to be a friend, and a good one.

She reasoned then that had she been in love with him as much as she'd convinced herself she was, would she have acted in this way? As the night drew on she tried to understand, by separating her heart from her head, in order to make her thoughts more clear. When that did not work, she got out of bed and wandered to the window. She gazed out and upward, studying the stars. But they gave no answers either and she was not comforted. Restlessly she paced about the room until exhaustion drove her back to bed. In all things Nikola was nothing if not practical, and she knew she would be no good to anyone the next day if she did not get some rest.

She lay in the bed and closed her eyes, but before she drifted off to sleep she had decided upon something which was honest and worthy, at least. When she saw Marek again, and his beloved young lady, she would forget the past and put aside the guilt and be gracious. It was not for her to detract from his happiness with bad grace, not that it probably would, she calculated. But she could add to it by being kind and, perhaps, in behaving that way she would actually become it.

When Nikola saw Faran for the first time, she had thought briefly, That's a pretty little girl. But nothing more. Now she saw the girl differently, as in the reflection of Marek's eyes. She saw also that Faran loved him purely, without reservation, and that he returned the same, so that there was an almost palpable, an almost visual flow of feeling between them.

This made her reflect upon herself later. Had she ever loved anyone so well? She didn't think so now. It wasn't true to say that she had never been romantically involved with a man before. She'd had her chances. However, too often she mixed together feelings with expectations and heady opinions, so that somewhere along the line she was bound to be disappointed in love. The only man she had never expected anything from, but that he be what he was essentially, was Dan Coel, however he and she weren't romantically inclined towards one another. They were just the best of friends, even if they did grouch at each other sometimes.

The three of them ate lunch together, quietly and somewhat awkwardly at first. "You mustn't call me Doctor Langan," Nikola said to Faran. "We try to stick to informality as much as possible here, especially amongst friends. Please, call me Nikola."

Faran nodded. "I said to Marek that I don't want to stay here and do nothing to contribute. I'm sure there's work I can do."

Hearing the unfamiliar name of Marek, Nikola started. She'd been so used to calling him Matt that she'd almost forgotten it was not his real name. Beside Faran, Marek grinned. His eyes, so warm and bright with a color Nikola hadn't observed before, seemed full of mischief and delight. "She can fix a truck."

"Well, we don't actually have a truck," Nikola said, smiling, and Faran blushed. "But I'm sure there are plenty of other things. Something is always in need of fixing around here."

When lunchtime ended and they were ready to leave, Marek took Nikola aside for a moment. "Thanks, Nik," he said sincerely, with a smile. "Thank you for making it easy for her. I'm very grateful."

Nikola nodded, feeling weak and devastated in the way which she always did when he smiled at her just so. Easy for Faran! she thought. I was just trying to make it easy for myself most of all.

Before they parted near Rezia's room, Marek said to Faran, "Now you're here there's one thing you have to remember, and that is I'm not Marek in the hospice but Matt. Only you and Nikola know who I really am, and we want to keep it that way."

Faran apologized. "I forgot. But it won't happen again. As long as I can call you Marek at home." He laughed. "At home you can call me anything you like!"

Rezia had pulled the easy chair close to the window, which she had flung wide open to let in the afternoon breeze. The luncheon plates were still on the little table and Faran was delighted to see that only scraps remained of the meal. Which meant that her friend was certainly feeling better.

"Hello, love," Rezia said. "I've never seen you in that dress before; it makes you look like a little bright flower."

Faran blushed. "You're looking happier too. How do you feel?"

Rezia raised her eyes to the window. "Improved, and heading towards some feeling of peace, I believe. In fact I'd like a walk in the sunshine, now you're here."

On Faran's arm, Rezia wandered about the garden beds and smelled the flowers. She had always been a keen gardener and knew all the names and attributes of the plants she observed. She touched the waxy petals of a flower which was almost the color of Faran's dress. "This one's unusual for so far south," she said. "But I guess the winters are cooler here than in Minerva. From what I've seen of some of the flora here, I think this area has a little micro-climate all of its own."

Faran remembered the small clumps of violets she'd seen under the trees in the coppice around Marek's house. They were like the delicate reflections of his loving eyes. Reminded of him, she said, "Matt has been helping you then?"

"Yes. Plenty." Rezia stuck her nose in a cluster of yellow blossom. "Mainly he's been helping me sort myself out. It sounds silly, I suppose, that a woman of my age could still be confused about life, and he is so young to understand it all." She shrugged. "But that doesn't matter. What matters to me is that I've realized what I've got to do."

Faran smiled. She had not seen Rezia this bright and purposeful in a long time. "So what's that?"

Rezia's eyes were moist when she looked up. "Make my peace with my daughter first, then get on with living instead of worrying about dying."

Faran knew that her friend had gone to the commune following an estrangement from her daughter who had tried to put her in a home for old ladies. Why the daughter had done what she did, Faran never understood. What had always been clear to her though was Rezia's disappointment in her daughter and her resentment of the fact.

"I always believed that, one day, I would find it in me to forgive Rene." Rezia grimaced. "Big of me, wasn't it?" she said, somewhat sardonically. "I reckoned that she was in the wrong, and acting selfishly, and I still do. But, as Matt says, that's her problem and her reality, not mine, and I'm not responsible for someone else's point of view, even if it is my own child who's involved. He made it very clear to me that forgiveness is not the issue here. In fact he said that forgiveness is only an illusory step towards something more real. And that the reality is love. "All you have to do," he said, "is dig deep inside and open your heart to the love which you truly feel for Rene." And as soon as he said that, I knew he was right. I've so often felt that love, especially remembering Rene as a child, but what she did made me feel betrayed ... you know? Well I realize now that she doesn't see herself in that way; she probably doesn't see herself at all. I don't know how he did it, but Matt helped me stand outside of my self, not my Self, but all that collection of hurt and anger that I got so mixed up with that I thought it was me. I was always a bit guilty too, about Rene being the way she is. I thought it was my fault, you know, that I'd brought her up wrongly or something."

After this long speech, Rezia smiled sadly at Faran. "You know, when I met you I thought, " Now here is the daughter I ought to have had," which wasn't very fair to Rene, was it? She is my daughter and I do love her and that's really all that matters. Whether she loves me is up to her, but I think she does. She's just confused about life, and no more than anybody else."

Faran felt close to tears of happiness. "I'm so glad you feel this way. Will you go to see your daughter now?"

"When I leave here," Rezia replied. "First, I'll go back to the commune and settle in again, then I'll make the trip to my daughter's home. It isn't actually very far from Minerva."

Rezia must be feeling much better, Faran gathered. She's talking about travelling when before she could barely face the prospect. "I'm going to stay here with Matt," she said. "Although I'm not letting you go back to the commune alone. I'll come with you, and then I can get the rest of my things and return."

"No." Rezia shook her head. "You don't need to leave your young man. I'll go on my own. I know I can manage—"

"But, Rez—" Faran protested.

"I've thought about this," Rezia said. "I've been thinking about it since last night. You can stay here and I can use the spare bus fare to take the express back to Minerva; it's only a day that way. Then I'll pack up all your things and freight them down here to you."

'Rez," was all Faran could say.

Rezia smiled. "I saw how Matt looked at you. He won't want you to leave, not even for a while." "Yes. But he wouldn't object if I had to. He would want you to be okay most of all."

"But there's no need, because I will be okay by the time I'm ready to go, I just know it. And you know me, Faran, always Mrs. Independence, that's how I've been all my life. One trip alone on the bus is not going to hurt me, now that I'm feeling my self again."

"Okay." Faran did not demur, for she hadn't really wanted to leave Marek, although she would have for Rezia. But it was wonderful to hear her friend talking this way, with the old gallant spirit of the past. "I'm glad you feel so strong again," she added.

Unconsciously they had strolled in the direction of the grove where

Marek usually conducted his sessions. From a distance Faran could see him through a low sweep of lime-covered leaves, how concentration inclined him towards the other person on the bench – this time, an elderly man. She steered her friend away … they must not intrude … but Rezia had seen him too. She nodded at Faran, comprehending. "Doing his wonderful work again, I see. He really is a remarkable young man. So insightful."

"That's because he has a special view of the world," Faran explained. "Because he's realized his freedom. And he knows what love truly means."

Rezia regarded Faran with an interested eye. "Yes, he spoke to me of freedom, and what it means.

You know how often we've talked about it ourselves, but his ideas go deeper, don't they."

"Yes. And they're more than ideas," Faran said. "We only talked about it then; he has actually experienced it."

Rezia's scrutiny became closer. "And you, my little friend, what is it that I see in your eyes?" She took Faran's hands in hers. "Love, certainly, and I didn't expect anything less. You're brimful of that, and joy, the same as I saw in Matt's eyes today. But what other magic has been working in you?"

Faran threw her arms around Rezia's neck. "Oh, Rez, you're not the only one who has been healed.

That freedom which Ma … Matt knows and is, I know it too!"

Chapter Eleven

A sudden burst of heavy afternoon rain and a rhythm of dark clouds piling in from the sea transformed the day instantly from an outdoors one into an indoors one. But it was cosy really, Faran decided, just to perch on the settee next to Marek while the storms ran round and round the sky and, in between, the sun came out, making the whole wet world shine.

She tucked her legs up under her and hugged her knees. "What do you usually do on your free afternoons?"
"When it's due, my housework," Marek said. Faran laughed. "No need, I've done that."
"So you have. Thanks. Well, I also write, as I told you. And I like to go for a walk along the cliffs or a run and a swim, to keep fit and in shape. And also I make up any medicines I need. There's something I want to make for Rezia later."

'Rezia certainly is happier." Faran threw her arm around him and kissed him on the cheek. "Will she be able to get properly well though? It seems to me that she's not so concerned about her health as she was."
He took the kiss and returned it lightly. "She will have to look after her body better: treat it with more respect and do what I told her to do. But Rezia will do okay, as long as she concentrates on living truly. When the heart is clear of its confusion, the rest usually follows. So many of the people I've seen are simply dying because they've never unlocked the emotional pain inside. And they exist with such a distorted image of their own true nature that their body gets affected by the distortion and consequently gets ill."
Faran considered his words. "That sounds like an important subject for a book. I hope you're writing about that."

"Among other things, yes. And you're right, it is important, very important."

Another storm rolled across the sky, darkening the room and dipping the lights briefly. Marek jumped up and went to the window and threw back the curtains to give more light. Outside, the world was purple and dark grey. Lightning darted from earth to heaven and back again.

"Would you like to read the rest of my book?" Marek asked.

Faran felt a prickling of excitement inside. Eager to do so, she nodded.

It seemed to Faran that the atmosphere of the day was just perfect for reading about the turbulent history of Mankind.

This was how Ozira's story began, detailing the loss of Light to the Earth and its populations as the egos of men and women fell prey to a seduction of mind and a denial of feeling which then created an artificial world filled with only pain and separation. Part of the illusion which Mankind believed in was that It (Mankind) was an unworthy and helpless thing which needed guidance from "Above".

The "Above" was presented to the human race in many forms, as gods and angels and "Special messengers", as spirits and creation beings; even as departed ancestors who, somehow by their dying, attained a knowledge by which they were supposed to know better. The creation of "One God" topped it all, as a "Father" being who was as two faced as he was single minded, as cruel as he was kind, as elitist and favoritist as he was all encompassing, and as pathetic and spiteful in concept as he was all powerful.

"You are not helpless creations," said Ozira. "You are not souls in bodies needing to be redeemed by higher powers which exist outside yourself. You are not even the bodies you inhabit, although so often you believe in this limitation along with all the other falsely created ideas and ideals that you cannot see or move outside the walls you build around your lives.

"If you choose to believe in manufactured ideals and mental concepts, then you deny yourself the right to exist without freedom from outside control. When the source of your understanding is not the Light, not from the flow of Light, which is in you and is you, then your understanding is useless, to you and to the Earth. Worse, such understandings which come from the twisted minds of those who believe in illusion, and this includes your own mind, can actually damage your existence and the life of the Earth.

"The Earth is a huge, mighty organism, a being of tremendous power and beauty, with its own consciousness, and it can take its own steps to recover balance, and it possesses the added strength of all its wonderful natural forms. The forms of men and women are just as wonderful as the rest and are as much a part of Nature's expression as anything else on this planet. However, you have so distanced your consciousness from even your body's mother, the Earth, that you cause much damage to your body, and this is called illness or disease.

"There should be no disease. What you are in actuality is Light, and that Light Consciousness moves straight from the Source of All to this Earth. It projects here for a purpose, and its purpose is to give Itself to all that It enters and to experience the multifarious joys of all Creation. If the Light moved through your ego unimpeded, then your body would be living in perfect joy also. There would be no disease.

"However, your ego acts to cloud and distort the flow of Light. The ego has been so blinded for so long that it can see only a constant reflection of itself as it is sunken into the mire of manufactured beliefs. And this reflection it considers as the truth of its being. It is not; it is only an altered reality, and since there are so many ego experiences with so many different realities, little wonder that the human world is fraught with chaos!"

Faran sighed and lifted her eyes from the book. Marek was at his table, writing. Seeing how his dark head bent so assiduously over the pages, Faran was moved to tenderness and love. The storm had abated temporarily and the light of the window was alive with rainbows and diamonds. Outside, the trees glittered with a million gems. A world filled with Light and Beauty and Peace; wasn't that what everyone really wanted in their heart of hearts? Along with the freedom to know that it was a fact, came the surge of Love so necessary to make it happen. But how to create such a world?

She returned to the pages of Ozira. His next words gave the clue.

"You can do nothing for another except BE your essential self. No one changes anything by trying to make over or rule or control, or by attacking or exerting against the thing one wishes to change.

Blindly, you think you must seek to change the world, when all you need to do is change yourself. This is a concept well known even in the illusory world; at least it is often proclaimed and espoused. But without real understanding.

"Changing means re-orienting. The illusory world is unmistakably there outside, and you cannot go like a hermit into a forest and hide from it and pretend that it does not exist. Well, you can try to hide and deny, you can become a hermit if you like. However, you will shortly discover that the illusory world never left you, for it lives inside your mind just as strongly as elsewhere. To change means to turn completely from this illusion, but the process is not denial or a "turning away"; it is, rather, a "turning to". That is, one turns to one's Light, because that is all one desires. You recognize that you are Light first and foremost, that there is nothing else but Light. You align your consciousness at last with what you are and you become your Light. This then is all you can give to others, the beautiful, magnificent glory of your Light. Is that not enough for this world?

"Know that you are Light. As Light, you are everything the Earth needs; it needs no pompous gods or great masters, or saviours from beyond. All it needs is your Light – YOU.

"Be the Love which you feel in your heart for all the wonder which is outside and inside you. If you think you cannot find any love within you, then seek to discover why. Realize that the hurts you experience which cause you to deny love, are the hurts of your ego, which has always told itself that it is very special and better than anybody else and, therefore, it gets very pained when others do not treat it with the respect it thinks it deserves. Remember how I spoke of the myriad of realities created in this world by the many experiences of ego? Your present ego reality is not the same as another's, so other people do not see you as you see yourself. In fact, you are lucky if they even see you at all, since their own egos are so busily introspective and narcissistic that they see only what they want to see, the distorted image of themselves bent in the mirror of illusion.

"Can you understand this? Pain is something your ego creates, like a picture in that distorted mirror.

Others seem to give you pain. They appear to attack you. But what is it that feels so pained? It is not your Light, your true Being; for nothing illusory can touch that."

Through all the darkening and brightening of the storm, Faran read on. She felt her heart and mind opening themselves within the flow of the words, as a lotus pushes itself up through the gentle water to take its place in the sun, petals unfurled, to show its beauty to the earth and to give and receive sustenance. All this had been inside her, she knew, and was only waiting for its release. She thought then of the things Rezia had said, and saw by that how the healing of her heart and the realization of love for her daughter would also become, in time, the release of her Light. If only Rezia could read this, she thought. If only the whole world could read it!

There was more, so much more, and it would all take longer to read and absorb than in the space of one wet afternoon. However, from what she had already read, she now perceived what Marek had meant when he said that these were the words which Silene feared. Faran thought to herself, Imagine, if all the peoples of the world turned their faces to their Light, what would be left for the men like Silene? How could they deceive and manipulate beings who were free? Where would their power be then? It was a possibility which was almost unimaginable, so used to the twisted world in the mirror as they all were. Yet it was possible, otherwise why did Silene try so hard to destroy his brother?

How many would it take to lessen the power of evil men, to ultimately destroy it? She could not be sure. Yet she could think of this: people like Rezia re-connecting with her feelings of love and going to make her peace with her child. That was real healing, wasn't it? It was for Rezia. And if her love was great enough and pure, how would it affect Rene? Not knowing Rene, Faran could only speculate, however there were few children in this world who did not want the sincere and unconditional love of their parents.

Perhaps this was all it would take: real people willing to face their innermost conflicts, to admit them, to see the fallacy and illusion of them, and then to have the courage and the perseverance to turn away from them and to admit only love in their lives and their relationships with others. Perseverance was the key, Faran decided then. It was all very well to say that one was Light and that one loved others, but it required work, real work, to overcome lifetimes of blind habit. It also required an honest willingness to observe, to see when you were descending again into illusory behavior, for the truth was that habit was an unconscious thing, and difficult to overcome if one did not try.

Faran glanced up to see that Marek had finished writing and was turned in his chair, gazing steadily at herself. There was on his face a kind of distant absentminded smile, as if he was lost somewhere amidst contemplation of her.

Faran felt herself grow warm. "What is it?"

His eyes were as soft as violet smoke and his look was dreamy. "I was just thinking how purely beautiful you are."

Faran blushed. "And I was thinking about all this." She lifted the book from her lap. "It's wonderful, but I understand now why Silene hates you so. Marek, how many people would it take to change the world?"

"That I don't know. You and me? Nikola? Rezia? A hundred? A thousand? A million? We don't have to worry how many, as long as we focus on our Light. Your world is changed when your reality changes and Silene's illusion becomes as nothing to you."

"But you would want this to be read by as many people as possible?"

"That's the idea. I can only see a few, talk to and help a few directly. The rest will have to make it on their own. So that's what these words are for, as a help to many. Even though they're only words, they have the power to open what is already boiling up inside so many people today. This is what Silene and those like him hate and fear, not Ozira's words as they are, but what they will unleash.

Because it's the people who have the power inside them, each one of them, and so many already feel it there. All they need now is the catalyst to open them."

Reflecting, Faran said, "The people whom you actually contact are lucky. What if you could draw hundreds ... thousands? I mean, if you could go public, show what you do, what you are, tell them everything, teach them?"

"No." Marek was adamant. "Think of what would follow if I did that. The chaos: people running after me, wanting me to heal them. Even after I'd told them Ozira's words, that they are the same Light and can heal their own ailing minds and bodies, do you think they would want to do it for themselves when they had me to run after? Then it would be me who was the focus of their lives instead of what really ought to be, their own Light."

"I hadn't thought of that," Faran said. "All I was thinking of was how lucky I was really." Marek smiled. "I'm the lucky one, now that I have you."

Faran blushed again, but she was thinking less about herself now and more about him, for something was troubling her. "Marek, in your journal you said about your ring that Silene had given it to you and that it was a monitor but that you didn't know it until later. When you were at the Towers I saw the gem in it change color, but now it never does. Why is that?"

Marek rubbed his thumb across the dazzling diamond-like facets. "Yes, I never said in the journal what I did about the ring, did I. Well, let's just say I made it so that Silene can't look into it any more. It just reflects pure white light ... not the sort of thing he can manage to take with his consciousness the way it is."

"Then he can't monitor you any more? You told me about that, that bounty hunter, he thought he'd killed you. So does Silene think you're dead now?"

"No, he knows I'm not dead. If I was, the gem would look dead too, coal black. Silene can't look into the ring but he knows by this fact that I'm deliberately holding him off. That's probably got him madder and more worried than ever."

Faran felt a tremor not of excitation but of fear. She knew she ought not be afraid but she couldn't help it. She knew also that it was confession time again and guessed that Marek would not approve her fears. "And more determined to find you," she said. "That's why I was thinking of your going public, so it would be harder for Silene or any of those other monsters to do anything if you were a public figure."

Marek tilted his head to one side to consider. Not necessarily, he thought. Neither Silene nor the Brotherhood would have any trouble in turning such a situation to their advantage. The thorough damning and destruction of a public figure had been achieved successfully many times before.

He frowned and stood up. "Is that what's bothering you?" he asked as he came to sit beside her. "Are you afraid?"

Faran had been busily studying her fingers and was reluctant to look at him, but Marek tipped up her chin with his hand. "Are you afraid?"

She had to look into his eyes even though her own were threatening to spill over with tears. "For you, I am," she whispered. "I'm afraid they might hurt you, and I-I don't want you hurt, that's all."

As he bent his head towards her, understanding, Marek used gentle fingers to brush away the tears from her cheeks. He had already admitted to himself that confrontation was probable rather than merely possible, but the thought did not make him afraid. He had gone beyond fear of Silene long ago and even while he ran across half a world with Silene in pursuit, it was not capture which had driven him to run so much as the desire to buy more time in which to unfold his own awakening in peace and without interference. Silene – he could manage him, he knew, and all the dark forces of Silene's world were only that – dark. They were without Light and would soon sink into their own morass of illusion, caught, if they did not turn away themselves, in the degenerating coil of their own trap.

But how to tell Faran that, when she had only just found him again after so long a time? And all the memory which she had carried with her since the Towers was of himself, in trouble. He understood; she did not want to lose him again.

He held her in his arms. "You mustn't let yourself be caught up by fear, Sweetheart," he told her. "Fear is the strongest weapon they have and they will try to use it against you. But don't you know how much stronger the Light is? I think you do, but you've let yourself forget momentarily. The Light has protected me for seven years, and now I know I have an even greater shield than before."

When she looked up at him her eyes were as bright as twin blue stars. "What's that?"

"You, and the knowledge that you love me. Your love, and I feel it with me always; that's my shield. I even felt it in the tower although then I wasn't able to realize it as I do now. Your love is stronger than anything they can dish out, and they know it too, that's why they would like to encourage fear in you, because they are afraid of your power of love."

Marek held her closer. "Whatever happens, you will never lose me, and I will never lose you. We can never be separated again because now we know who and what we are, and we are Light; we are One."

Outside the day had become bright once more, and the thunder, if it rolled at all, was very distant.

PART 4
Early Summer of the Same Year

Chapter One

Silene De Ravana rubbed his dry, burning eyes. He had not slept properly in three days and was experiencing a drain of energy such as had not occurred for many years. Energy, he'd always had it in abundance; that was when he could glean it from others during times of special need. There was always a need for the boost to a body which often suffered from the results of excess or for the psychic activities he was wont to maintain on this earthly layer as well as in the realm of his Dragon brothers.

In more ancient eras energy, both psychic and physical, had been more directly forthcoming. Since his many past lives were an open book to him, Silene remembered easily the days of the willing or captured slaves who brought his life to him in offerings of devotion and obeisance, who doted on him bodily and fed his desires psychically without the liberty or understanding to murmur or resist.

Sometimes he longed for those simpler times when the world was more sharply divided into owner and owned.

Growing steadily more restless and irritated, Silene prowled about his chamber. Oh, what it had been like as a guru or a great religious leader; he had done both several times. A religious leader commanded great respect and power over the masses he controlled and during feast days and occasions of organized celebration the energy of the masses – their combined expending of emotion – was the true feast for him and his kind. What did they know, these foolish humans, of the forces which gorged themselves on the outpouring of so much unconscious desire? Not a wit, thought Silene, with a sneer.

He reminisced on his lives as a guru of mysticism and spirituality. The experience was not so different from religious power, but was sweeter because it was more intimate. There, he fed directly from the devotion of the bedazzled. They also catered to him bodily, giving him their energy through their hands and in other ways. Their eyes worshiped him, and their minds followed, like lambs after a herder. They knelt at his feet and would do anything he asked of them. Now that was truly worth cultivating.

So what had he come to in this life? In many ways his power was greater than ever before, since the world had grown wider and the stage bigger, as modern life moved, through easier communications, to a more global existence. And yet the world had also grown progressively colder and more cynical, as people, over burdened and hardened by almost too much suffering, questioned old values and ways. There was definitely a change in the air, Silene thought, and the demise of an era was upon them all. But that did not have to mean a lessening of power for those like himself. It had happened before, as the circle of history closed in upon itself and humanity rode the swell of a great discontent. But, as always, they would never find the solution to their discontent, for they did not know where to look for it.

In how many instances at such a point as this had the Dragon Lords turned the tide of possible human awakening back into illusion and therefore in their favor? And each time his power grew stronger, his place more assured in the scheme of things. And he was not going to let go of it now.

As he prowled in the sallow glow of his midnight chamber, Silene looked upon the things of his present existence. It was a strange life, he decided. A life more powerful than any other, yet without houris or devotees, and even without friends. Friends: he did not believe in those in any case, and in place of devotees he had obedient servants who would do anything for the right encouragement and who feared him as well as any cringing beast would fear the man with the gun and all the power. And yet, you could not always trust such servile creatures, for even in their greed and ignorance they could sometimes still be treacherous.

Energy could not come from these lackeys, at least not much, but the world at large always managed to furnish a good supply. Religion still flourished and encouraged war after war, conflict after conflict, division after division, and one did not have to be involved in order to draw what one needed. And then there was the main supply line of energy – fear – the greatest and most successful source of all. The world lived in continual fear of one thing or another; sometimes the fear changed daily; but the most abiding fear was the constant of illness and disease, and of late this had become a world wide preoccupation. The philosophy of fear and the syndrome generated by it, made fear the chief cause of increasing illness. The more afraid they were of getting sick and the more they focused on it, the sicker they got, and so on.

The satin sheets of Silene's bed had a rumpled look as he tried again to lay down and rest. How his eyes burned! He was disconcerted. It was not usual for him to be so discomforted and out of focus.

His close source of energy – the contact with his brothers on this plane and the other – seemed oddly inadequate for what discomforted him. It was as if what ought to have been dispensed in his favor was being held back or denied. Yet he could not accept such an idea; it was beyond him to think that things might be about to change.

Rather than just try to bring on sleep and fail, he put himself into a meditation first, centering his mind in a wordless way on that point of power in his own consciousness where the will was most active. It was like entering a hermetically sealed room and finding there at the core an altar with a searing flame upon it. Though it was a fire of sorts, that flame burned with the hardness of a diamond, yet without a diamond's brilliance or flare. That fire was his will and it burned closely and fiercely with a great heat. It did not radiate beyond the closed walls and its energy returned constantly in a loop as the fuel to feed itself. So his will was concentrated and powerful; there was no one on this Earth who could match it.

Silently, he passed into the temple of fire, and stood in worship of his will. This was his sacrosanct place; it was always quiet and focused here. Too often the world outside could be a bore, especially when foolish humanity sometimes spoiled his plans, not by any cunning of theirs but through sheer stupidity.

Take the Vorken as a case in point: his arrogance and vanity equal only to his failure to understand.

Longer than a year ago it was now that the Vorken had let vanity overrule his common sense. "Find him and kill him," Silene had ordered. But, no, the Vorken had to play his little games. A bullet straight to the head would have done the job, but he just had to gloat and play the victor. And therefore, in some way that even Silene had not comprehended, he had failed.

Silene had given him an almighty slap for that mistake, and one final chance to redeem himself. But it had been more than a year!

On the bed, Silene's body shuddered and twitched, reflecting the sudden convulsion of rage which swept through his consciousness. His meditation was broken! Never before had he allowed the sanctity of his temple to be invaded by such errant thoughts! He jerked himself to attention and closed the breech, determined to focus again on the purity of his will fire.

The breech had been closed. Or was it?

Sealed inside the integrity of his psychic walls, Silene became aware that he was not alone. It was a scent of something which alerted him, a scent which he knew well and accepted elsewhere. But not here!

The Dragon stench; it had never upset him before. But then, before, he had been the one to choose a meeting, and not this invasion of his most absolute personal space. If he was not the Dragon Lords" equal exactly, neither was he their slave. They were cohorts who were supposed to come only when invited.

Silene uttered a damnation. But such things did not move the Dragon mind. Entirely without feeling themselves, the petty curses of humankind were meaningless to them, and were not even a provocation.

So Silene fumed in vain. The Dragon Lord: it was only one, with the outward name Syriaxis, manifested only briefly, but with enough time to bully Silene once again over his own major failure, about which he was exceedingly sensitive.

"Why have you not bought Us the one We seek?" uttered Syriaxis. Silene glowered. "I don't know where he is as yet."

"He is close by, within your current sphere. We feel his force and We are not pleased. You must bring him to Us soon!"

"I thought you wanted him dead?"

"Death. What is that to Us? We who know it not? You may see him bodily dead, if that pleases you.

All We want is his Consciousness in our grasp. This way he will be Ours forever." "If he is here, in Telaia, and you know it, tell me where he is," Silene said.

The Dragon, Syriaxis, replied coldly, "Telaia is nothing to Us; it is your domain not Ours. We only feel his frequency at hand, in relation to you. It is the intrusive force of the Light Being, Ozira, which runs counter to yours and to Our purpose. Ozira is building great energy in the ethers which We cannot abide. A channel has already been opened and threatens Our position. He must not be allowed to continue. Do not fail Us, Ravana. To fail Us is to fail yourself."

Silene took the warning like a blow to the face which was so fierce and deeply shocking that it managed to eject him from his meditation. He sat up in bed, trembling and cursing. Black fury swam like poison in his veins. The earlier sense of being denied his due became a reality as he understood his new position. It was an ignominious one such as he had never known before: fail, and the Dragons would discard him.

His head felt to be splitting in two; one of his black headaches was coming upon him. He cursed loudly and roundly, "Damn you, little brother! Damn you!" His whole ire was directed to this one source of trouble. Was the boy, now a man, to be the single cause of all his lives" undoing? That bane of a child whom he had nurtured and cultivated so carefully; what gratitude had the young wretch ever shown him?

Then, oddly, through all the ire, Silene felt an unaccustomed twinge of sadness and regret, which, however, only made his headache burn deeper and his stomach turn with nausea. "Marek … Marek…" Silene moaned and clutched his pounding head. "My brother, my brother, I even loved you once. Why have you done this thing to me?"

Next morning, although he had slept hardly at all, Silene rose early, bathed and dressed quickly, and with the usual fastidiousness. He was always a very careful dresser, for he was conscious of the power of the right appearance. In this world, men judged so shallowly that facades were important, and the beautiful and elegant were always worshiped above the plain and ordinary.

Letting himself rest for a minute before setting off to his office, Silene stood and studied himself in the mirror. He was not quite satisfied with the overall effect of himself today so he took up a brush to tidy up a rebellious bit of hair which kept looping down over his forehead. He needed a haircut, he decided. He liked to keep his hair short and sleek in order to emphasize its glossy blackness. He was forty seven and not one grey hair had appeared yet; he was rather proud of that. Age had not caught up with him, he thought, except in a certain increase in girth, which, he believed, suited his height and the substantiality of his position in society.

The hair would not behave and it fell over his forehead again and Silene realized he would have to resort to stronger means of control. Just like life, he thought, as he reached for the hair gel. Neither Nature or mankind were any good as they were; they had to be ruled and ordered, otherwise only chaos would result. The hair stayed, glued back in a severe sweep, and Silene regarded it with approval and, unconsciously, he smirked. He liked the distinction of handsomeness his dark hair and brows gave him. It was a legacy of the De Ravana's foreign origins, just as was his skin, which would color readily to a tan when exposed to sunlight, if only it was given the chance. But Silene would not let it. He disliked the sun; it made him uncomfortable, somehow.

Silene's mirrored face stared back at him and he smiled at it. He was proud of his Arpayan ancestry, of the great De Ravanas of history who, in their time, had ruled half a world between them. They had nothing to do with the deteriorated Arpay of today, though, with its weak decadence and disgusting poverty. They were nowhere near the powerless Arpay of now, but represented an Arpay of many generations past, when Arpay had been the glorious center of world control.

His hair tidy, Silene touched his shaven cheeks and with a careful finger, smoothed away some lines appearing under his eyes. That was the problem, he realized then: his eyes. They were red from lack of sleep and would give him away today and spoil the perfection. So he slipped on his favorite gold rimmed sun glasses. The image in the mirror pleased him now. Yes, the image was sufficient unto the day, and superficiality was satisfied.

Silene lay his hands, one over the other, against his chest momentarily. A reminder, he thought, of what he was ... especially necessary after last night. Under his sumptuous though elegantly understated clothes: the fine white shirt with diamond cuff links, the rich but conservative tie, the plain dark suit of silken luxury, Silene, Baron De Ravana, wore the mark of the Dragon Lord on his naked breast. But he never showed it to anyone. Regarding it earlier, when shirtless, the thought had crossed his mind that it resembled mostly a mark which had been burned there by a branding iron, as if he had been a steer, hobbled and thrown in the dust for the operation by some unfeeling cowboy.

The thought instantly shocked him, coming, as it seemed to do, from nowhere in his consciousness. That mark of the four reversed crosses had been his chosen mark, induced by his own desire. It was his stigmata of worthiness, his proof of divine favor, and if ever the rule of the Dragon Lords should manifest openly on the Earth, this was to be his designated seal of Over-Lordship, as One of Them.

Dressed as he was, Silene was every bit the master of his Earthly troops. He was quite famous in Telaia for the wizardry of his administrative skills and his sharp negotiating in international affairs, and he was thought by most of the population to be at least partly responsible for Telaia's continued economic triumphs in the world. At best, Silene was considered to be a brilliant man and the perfect bureaucrat, albeit an

214

aristocratic one. At worst, Silene had a shoddy reputation in certain circles.

Some, who thought him slimier than a slug and more secretive and dangerous than a poisonous snake, would never have said it though, for fear of becoming a death statistic. Those who suspected these things of Silene, feared him from a distance and kept their peace. The few who knew them for a fact, kept their peace also, and lived in the shadow of a terror so great that oftentimes the idea of death looked more attractive.

Silene's last act before leaving his chamber was to take up a pearl grey silk handkerchief and polish the stone and the gold mount of his ring. This ring was his personal seal, and the public one of his worldly authority. He used its resonant powers sometimes to addle the brains of those he wanted to control. Its other use, as an eye to watch his rebellious brother, had, long ago, been scotched by Ozira. Except for that one occasion in Vargas. But what had Marek been doing then? Silene had watched the stone change too abruptly from the dark blood-red brown of physical trauma to a vivid emerald, and all in the space of several hours. Such a vivid and powerful green – it was not the color of a mood, and it was a color Silene had never manifested on his own ring before. So what did it mean?

In search of an answer, Silene had questioned one of the Dragons, this time Xuoster. But the Dragons did not like questions and Xuoster prevaricated with words which were only a riddle. "That one deals in frequencies which do not harmonize with Ours," It said. "That one is Our enemy." Which was only what Silene already knew.

"Send for Klider," Silene said to his private secretary. "I have to go out briefly, but I'll be back soon. Tell Klider to wait in my office."

Klider was classed officially as Senior Clerk in the Records Section of the Department of Administration and Finance, a dull, retiring sort of job thought by those who judged only the outside of a man as suitable for one who was dwarfed and twisted nearly to the point of deformity.

But Klider was much more than a clerk; he was Silene's secret eyes and ears in Telaia.

Silene returned to his office where Klider waited for him, like a puppy panting and slavering on a mat.

"You have that report I asked you for last night?" Silene said.

"Yes, Sir." Klider offered up a folder covered in brown leather tipped with brass corners. Silene waved it away. "Just the details, Klider. The Bolton boy is still where he should be?"

215

"Yes, Sir." Klider flipped open the brown cover and read, "William Bolton, formerly Crafter, age fifteen and eleven months, student at Hanna College. Considered a better than average pupil by some and unresponsive by others. He—"

Silene silenced him impatiently. "Enough. I don't want to hear the young fool's scholastic history. Is he still receiving letters from his sister?"

"Yes, Sir. But not from the same address as before." "She's moved? To where?"

Klider a-hemmed and shuffled. "We have a problem there, Sir. The most recent letters, three of them, have each been posted from different locations."

"Where?"

Klider reeled off three names.

"Curious," Silene said. "So, what is your opinion, Klider? What do you think our little Miss Crafter is up to?"

"Travelling, Sir?"

Silene frowned at the obviousness of the answer. "Perhaps. But don't you think that these towns are unusually far apart? Is Miss Crafter such a restless spirit?"

"I don't know, Sir," Klider said.

Silene sighed. "Klider, either you are being deliberately obtuse or you are merely stupid. Which is it?" He fixed the little man with a glare. "And be careful of the answer; your neck may already be a bit wry but I can always arrange to have it twisted further."

Klider's pale face reddened to the roots of his thinning hair. He cringed. "Stupid, Sir. I'm being stupid."

"That you are." Silene pressed white fingertips against his burning eyes. "The little Crafter minx is playing games with me, Klider. It's obvious she does not want to be found."

"But, Sir, she couldn't know you're watching her. Why would she suspect?" Klider blurted out before he could think better of it.

"Stupid … stupid." Silene shook his head in disgust. "Why do I employ you, man? Think, will you?

If it is at all possible. Originally, we kept an eye on the father, because of what…?" "Because he lied to you, Sir. You said so, Sir."

Ignoring Klider for a moment, Silene thought back to the time of the

216

Towers. When Marek had not come home with his tail between his legs, Silene was forced to reassess the circumstances of his brother's escape. He considered the Caretaker again. The man had lied ... and how! It was not the lie as such but the nature of it which alerted Silene back then. The Caretaker had lied too well, proving to Silene that he was not the ignoramus he made himself out to be. Had it been a case of Marek simply beguiling an ignorant man into setting him free, and that man realizing later that he had been made a fool of, and in fear of discovery, lying to protect himself from punishment, why then, Silene would have only been pleased to disregard him. But it was not. Crafter was intelligent, Silene had known that the minute he heard the trace of irony in the man's tone. Crafter had been in a league of complicity with Marek, and this worried Silene enough to initiate surveillance. A man who knew too much was a man to be watched, and, if necessary, removed.

But back to Klider ... Silene tapped the desk, making Klider shift his feet about nervously, twisting up the rug under him. "Go easy on the carpet," Silene said. "Then, after Crafter's unfortunate demise, we transferred surveillance to the daughter. Why was that?"

"In case the father had told her what he knew, Sir."

Silene threw up his hands in mock delight. "Praise be! And now we keep an eye on the boy for the same reason. He is the key to finding the girl, and I want her found, do you hear? Now get out!"

"Yes, Sir, yes, Sir." Klider backed out the door at top speed. "Found!" Silene called after him. "Found. But no interference."

How was he going to find a wayward girl? It was like looking for a needle in a haystack, Georgi Klider thought. She had always been a bother, since she seemed to want to choose a lifestyle which went beyond the norm. By now, a girl of that age and education ought to have been either in a regular job somewhere or safely married to someone easily traceable, someone socially respectable who paid his taxes and kept his nose ostensibly clean. There were thousands of potential husbands like that, men with bank accounts and mortgages, whose lives were circumscribed by the rules and who only cheated a little.

In many ways he was such a man himself. He was a husband and a father, and he had a mortgage. Which described him almost as a normal person, except that, try as he might, the bastards he worked with and the social set his wife's family belonged to would never treat him with

217

respect. Always, he was sneered at and looked down upon, and he knew it was only because of his deformity. He could not compete with normal men, so he had chosen the secret way of revenge. He had a dozen dossiers on men he knew, those who considered themselves so superior to him. He even had dossiers on his own wife's relatives, for they were such a snobbish lot.

The only person in the world Georgi Klider cared for, and who loved him unconditionally in return, was his daughter, Jenevra. She was eleven years old and it mattered not to her that her father was different. She had some of his deformity herself, having been born with a congenital weakness of the lungs, but it was not a thing which was outwardly spectacular, as was his bent body. The doctors, however, had given her up, saying that only time would either cure her or kill her; they could do nothing but pump her full of expensive drugs and hope for the best.

He would never let his daughter wander off like the Crafter girl, he decided. This girl, this nuisance of a girl, just had to run off and join a bunch of wacky women whose whole existence seemed to flaunt the rules. Some day, when he got the chance and enough dirt on that commune, he would see that it got closed down. But now the girl had left the place and vanished, and Klider's only option was to step up surveillance on the boy.

Klider hated jobs like this. They seemed so petty to him, and right from the beginning he hadn't understood why the Baron would want to know the details of such unimportant lives. Of course, he knew it was tied to the events of the Towers. While all the Baron's men involved in those events, himself included, were sworn to secrecy, the Caretaker of the time was the wild card. And the Baron had said that the Caretaker lied. So, it was reason enough for what had to follow.

Klider did not like Silene, Baron De Ravana. In fact he hated him. And every daily taunt and insult simply drove his hatred deeper. It was a hatred that also went beyond just one man. Klider hated all of that aristocratic class who were his masters. Which was why he had enjoyed the little affair of the tower so much. The Baron's beloved brother! Well, who would have thought it? But it was a pleasure to see their falling out, and even if he had less reason to hate the younger brother than the older, the satisfaction of being given permission to mistreat one of the class he so despised, was a joy.

One thing he truly did not understand however, was why Silene still searched for his brother. Obviously, to Klider, the young man had decided that life anywhere else, maybe even a life of poverty, was preferable to bullying at home, in luxury. A wise move, Klider thought, and showing some character after all. It did not occur to Klider, though, that he might have made such a choice himself. To him, his job was the only niche he was able to inhabit, the only place in the world available to him where he felt like a man, that is at those times when he was not the object of his boss's scorn.

Returning to his own office, Klider contacted the relevant agents to set up an increased watch over the Crafter boy. From now on they were to open his mail before it got to him instead of merely noting the postmark. Naturally they complained about the boring nature of their duties and were offensive to himself as usual, so Klider retaliated by telling them that their lord and master had a special punishment worked out if they did not show a result soon. Although they hung up in his ear, Klider felt their fear. "That's put the wind up "em," he said to himself with a bitter smile. His own ego still smarted from the Baron's dressing down. When he remembered how Silene had gotten him to call himself stupid, his blood fairly boiled with resentment and hate.

Halfway through the afternoon, Klider's wife turned up at his office door. This was something she had not done before, for she did not go out with him in public usually. Klider had always believed that she hated to admit her relationship with himself and so avoided being seen with him. So this visit was a total surprise. It had to be an important reason then, to bring her into his domain.

Instantly, with fear, Klider thought that something terrible had happened to his daughter. He pulled his wife in through the door and shut it behind her. Almost as if he was ashamed of being seen with her.

"What are you doing here?" he asked roughly.

"I came to tell you that I've decided. I'm leaving with Jenevra this afternoon."

There had been between husband and wife a running battle about one thing: Jenevra's health. Klider was willing to pay anything to get his daughter better, but he was a conventional man who accepted only the pronouncements of medical authority. His wife, though, had her moods and fancies, and had taken it into her head to try more unorthodox solutions. For the sake of his daughter, Klider stifled objections and let her have her way, however when none of the "cures" seemed to work, Klider had put his foot down.

But to no avail. Mrs. Klider could be obstinate when she wanted to be and Klider insisting that she cease only made her try harder than before.

"All right." Klider nodded and sighed. He had given in, again. He could not stop her and he was tired of fighting. "Do you have enough money?"

"I do," Mrs. Klider said briskly.

"Good." Klider was trying to be gracious about defeat. "If you have any problems or need anything, just let me know. It's a long way to Tempah Springs, and accommodation is bound to be expensive this time of year."

Mrs. Klider's facial expression went from set and determined to soft, as if her face was granite turning suddenly into blancmange. "Georgi," she said, and in her voice was a surprising note of appeal. "Georgi, I'm doing the right thing, I just know I am. I feel it in my bones. This healer Jenevra will see is supposed to be so very good. The reports are excellent. You have to understand."

Klider nodded his head in mute assent. He knew she meant well, that she loved their daughter as much as he did.

"Thank you!" Mrs. Klider bent abruptly and kissed him on the cheek, and Klider was so astonished by the kiss that he let her get out of the door without so much as another word or even a goodbye.

How strange he felt then, after that, and the thought crossed his mind of how nice it would have been if he could have gone with them.

Chapter Two

The sun was a blaze of light and heat in the sky. Or was it a great eye, perhaps, of golden, wide awake awareness which looked on all below it with a gaze of love?

The summer sea was bluer than the sky above it, as if the mirror not only reflected what it saw but added its own deep and mysterious quality to the image. From the high cliffs, the sea appeared as the moving breast of the Earth, the Earth's feeling self, and, as such, it hypnotized, drawing you in through the rhythmic ebb and flow of your own feeling nature. The sea breathed long, imperturbable breaths which the human body matched in its most responsive state, and you followed easily, becoming so alive and aware, as if you were the froth on the crest of the wave, or the wave itself, or the wide, wide rolling waters.

Together, on this day of sun and sea, the Sun, the Earth and the Earth Body were one, one expression of conscious and unconscious harmony, as the mind of the ego, quiet and without desire, yielded to the feeling part and opened wide. The opening of the ego, as the opening of the lens of another eye, made all clear and understandable on this bright day. The Light flowed unimpeded and the Earth rejoiced; it was as simple and as beautiful as that.

On one of Marek's half days, Faran and Marek took a picnic lunch to their secret place on the cliff. They had spread a rug over the bent dry grasses and patches of sandy soil, and there they reclined and ate their fill, glasses of chilled white wine in their hands.

"I'm too full even to move," Marek groaned. Nevertheless, he poured himself another half glass of wine. "These past few months you've done nothing but spoil me rotten."

Faran laughed. "And you object? I think it's about time somebody did spoil you a bit; you've done enough for other people. Anyway, I don't call it spoiling, I call it taking care, and it's only what I want to do because I love you."

"You are the most loving and glorious being on the face of this Earth." Marek said. He felt sleepy and a touch poetic today; most likely it was the wine speaking. He took sip after lazy sip, relishing the flavor of fruity grape. "And, well, I have to be honest with you; the truth is that I enjoy your "taking care". I admit it, I love every minute of it." He leaned towards her and laid his lips on hers, and the taste of the wine mingled with the sweeter taste of her.

Faran stretched back into the crook of his arm. "I love you. I love this place. And I love the sea," she said. "The first time I saw the sea was once when I was five years old, then I didn't get near it again until we went to Hanna Harbor. But I always felt it in me somehow; it was a memory which never dimmed with time."

"I love the sea, too." Marek drained the glass and sighed. That was the last of the wine. "When I was eight years old I learned to sail, with some cousins of mine who were about the same age, and at Hanna Harbor actually. We learned on the smallest craft, and we had to stay in the cove by the yacht club and couldn't even go past the point. It made pretty tame sailing, the water's generally a mill pond in that little cove, but it got us through the summer without anyone drowning at least."

Now, it was such between the two of them that they could talk about the past without any of it intruding or meaning anything for the present.

"I went sailing a few times myself," Faran told him. "But I'm not really a sailor. I was more of a passenger. When I came to Hanna Harbor I didn't even know how to swim so I had to learn first, before anyone would let me near a boat."

Marek played idly with her long silky hair. "Wise people. The most useless person on board is the one who can't swim. Nobody wants to have to dive in for a non swimmer, especially during a race.

Would you believe it though, but I've actually met sailors who can't swim. All their working lives aboard a ship, and they never learned how."

"Would you dive in to save me?" Faran asked.

"To save you I would dive into the pit of a fiery volcano," Marek said in a tone of absolute seriousness, although in his mind was still poetry.

Faran laughed. "How romantic! But I sincerely hope not." She lifted up to kiss him. "Are there any volcanos in Te Tanaa?"

"Not on the island itself, but there is one on another island not too far away. It's temporarily dormant though, has been for several hundred years."

"Tell me more about Te Tanaa."

Marek thought he had told her everything there was to tell about the island he hoped to take her to some day. He'd even told her warily of

222

what the Tanu women had wanted of him, but her reaction was unexpected. For she had stared at him for a moment with an incredulous look on her face then had laughed and laughed until he was laughing too, although with a degree of uncertain embarrassment.

"I didn't think it was funny, at the time," he said, somewhat mortified, after.

Her eyes were full of wicked lights as she played with him. "No," she said. "I'm sure you and they were very serious about it. So, of course, you refused them all?"

"Um, well …" he began, until he saw her laughter bubbling up again.

"I'd tell you about Ompalo, except that I haven't been there yet. We will have to discover it together," he promised.

"I look forward to it," Faran said. "But there's one thing I wonder about: the people, the Tanu, how do they really see you?"

"See me?" Marek was not sure he knew what she meant.

Faran explained, "From Ozira's writings I get the understanding that it's most important for each individual to express fully their own Light, that we must be only that and not project out our desire for Light on to someone else … you know, like a god or a guru, or something. We have to avoid worshipping another, because we are the Light ourselves, and that is enough. Now, I know how you want to avoid being put at any kind of center … you told me so yourself, so how do you deal with the Tanu when they call you their Messenger and come running after you?"

"Well, yes, it was a problem at first, but only a slight one. The Tanu are unusual. Although they have their regular society they're also very relaxed about life. They did come running after me, as you say, but mainly it was because they were fascinated at first. When they got to know me and I got to know them, and they found out that I didn't want to hold myself separate, but wanted to be a part of life just like them, they just treated me as one of the family. I worked with them, doing what everybody else did, except when they wanted me to speak to them at their special celebrations. Then I did my darndest to show them that they were all "Messengers" and that it wasn't just down to me."

"Do you think they accepted that?

"Most did, I believe. The Tanu aren't the kind of people who want much from other civilizations, they're rather a self sufficient lot, as personalities I mean. And they like life to be casual and easy, they don't want to be formal and organized. The Head-man told me how the Tanu disliked the religions of the outside and how they resisted them coming into their culture."

"But they have their own?"

"Unfortunately, yes. It's a different kind of religion, though. It doesn't have any system, which is a good thing. I suppose most would call it primitive because it only deals with the things of nature. It's not the sort of religion the Dragons would get much out of; apart from recalling the conflicts of history, which every race seems to have, there's no degree of conflict in it and no real guilt, and very little assigning of rights to higher powers. Even so, it is still a step away from the truth because they do revere a Goddess – Mari-E-ele."

"And Mari-E-ele has sent her Messenger," Faran said significantly.

Marek gave her a wry smile. "Yes, I see your point, and, as I said, I tried my best to counter that. I know you're right, but I still want to go there. I believe I can make it work there. And besides, I want us to go to Ompalo; it's important that we do. If we can manage to live in Te Tanaa and fit in, we shouldn't have much of a problem with the 'center thing', at least I hope not." Marek's forehead creased in a sudden worried frown. "You do want to go with me, don't you? I thought you did. Was I wrong?"

Half seriously, Faran gave him an admonishing thump on the shoulder. "How can you ask that? Of course I want to go with you! I'd go anywhere with you, or for you. Don't you know that, silly?"

Marek grinned foolishly. "I'm an idiot then, aren't I."

Faran turned the thump into a warm caress. She smoothed his tousled, windblown hair from his eyes. "The idiot I love," she said, kissing him.

From high above them, the big rock threw a long cool shadow across the rug as the day lengthened.

Although he was comfortable and content, Marek found himself growing restless and uneasy. "Something is wrong," he said at last, sitting up.

Faran followed. "What do you mean?"

Marek stared blankly out to sea. "I'm not sure, I just feel it. Something is very disturbed, back at the hospice. Something's happened there." Without any further delay they packed up their basket and the rug and headed back to the hospice grounds. As they were approaching their cottage they saw someone running across the brow of the hill. The long tail of a soft pink open jacket streamed out behind the running figure, and her hair was in disarray, coming out of its combs. It was Nikola.

"I was right," Marek said. He dropped the basket where he was and strode out in a half run, leaving Faran to catch up later.

He reached Nikola as she descended the hill. "Nik … I had a feeling—"

Before he could say more or ask anything, Nikola had blurted out her fear. As she was nearly out of breath, she was almost incoherent. "It … it's Dan!" was all she managed to say at first. Her face was streaked with the remains of tears. "Dad just called. He said Dan was attacked, in the street!"

He isn't dead, is he? Marek thought. Instead, he asked her, "How bad is it?"

Nikola wiped away the stains on her cheeks. "He has several knife wounds, Dad said, but only one of them is a real worry."

Marek could see how she struggled to hold herself erect and aloof as she tried to cover her fear and upset with the calmness of fact, so he resisted the impulse to put his arms around her. Let her tell her story first.

Nikola continued, "He took a hit in his back and it went very deep, close to the spine. A fair bit of damage, Dad said; he didn't give me all the details, but I gather that Dan is suffering some sort of lower paralysis. Dad has had him in surgery, and the repair work's all been done, but I don't think Dad's confident about a good prognosis. He doesn't think much of Arpayan hospitals so he's bringing Dan back here as soon as he's strong enough to be moved."

"To where in Telaia? Brentore? Or here, to Tempah Springs?"

Nikola looked up at Marek and blinked away new tears. "I asked him to come here." Her lip trembled and her eyes opened wide. They had a look in them of hope and pleading. "To you."

The tears spilled over and Nikola was ready for comfort. And confession. "I-I didn't realize how much I really cared for Dan until, until

225

this. When Dad said he'd been attacked, I thought at first that Dan was dead." Nikola buried her face in Marek's shoulder. "And I just couldn't bear the thought of never seeing him again." She glanced up into Marek's eyes. "Why didn't I know before how I felt about him, Matt? Why did it have to take something like this to make me understand?

Marek held her. "You're the only one who can answer that, Nikola. But one thing I do know is that Dan loves you too. I saw how much in Vargas. I think he's probably been in love with you for quite a long time."

"Do you mean it?" The question only helped Nikola to find fresh tears again. "Then, if that's so, then both Dan and I have been such fools, haven't we. Oh, I hope it's not too late. Will he believe that I love him after this, though? I mean maybe he'll think I'm just saying it because …"

"Don't worry about that yet," Marek counselled. "Just be your honest loving self with Dan and wait till he gets his strength back. You can do no more than that at present."

"But you, you can?" Nikola's voice pleaded. "If he's paralyzed. I mean … oh, Matt, you will try to help him, won't you?"

"I will. I'll do everything I can," Marek said. He gazed over Nikola's bent head to Faran who had been standing there quietly for most of the time. The two of them exchanged sympathetic glances.

Even Faran guessed how difficult a healing this might chance to be, but Marek was sure of it.

It was a week and a half before Dan and Doctor Langan Sr. arrived at the hospice. Nikola had them both put up in rooms near her own, Dan in the ones which Marek had occupied formerly. Nikola seemed at a loss to know how to approach poor Dan, so she was very quick to seek out Marek and bring him to the main house.

But first Marek went to see Nikola's father.

During his time at the hospice, Marek had met Nikola's father on two fairly brief occasions, but it had been enough for them both to establish a rapport and an understanding. Doctor William (Bill) Langan was a man of unique qualities in his profession, for not only was he remarkably selfless in his whole way of being, but he looked on life not as something to preserve at all costs, but to savor while it was there. This made it possible for him to deal with the tragedies of Arpay and elsewhere in a way that Nikola could not. Nikola had not yet learned to let go of control, to surrender to the flow of life, tragedy and all. She still struggled with the idea that she must make a better world, and therefore she suffered from remorse and self reproach when it did not happen, whereas her father knew that a better world was only to be made in oneself. On meeting old Doctor Langan for the first time, Marek realized that the resonance he had felt in the clinic in Vargas was chiefly because it was the father's domain, not the daughter's.

Although Marek felt comfortable with Nikola and had shared with her many of his thoughts and feelings, he had never yet shown her the first journal with its attendant words of Ozira. But the father was another matter. During the second of Doctor Langan's visits, Marek had asked him if he would like to look at the book. The old man had come back to him the very next day describing how he'd sat up all night to read the words because he had not been able to put the book down until it was all read.

"This is so wonderful!" the Doctor had said. "It expresses everything I've always felt inside myself. And the things I've suspected about the world, how it's manipulated and changed from what it ought to be. I could never quite figure the world or Mankind, or why things are as they are. But you've straightened me out, my boy, you certainly have! I think this book ought to go public, and I'd like to be the one to help you do it!"

Marek was very gratified. "I've still a lot more to write," he'd explained. "Then I would be more than happy to set it on its way."

William Langan extended a friendly hand. "My dear young fellow! How good it is to see you again! Only a pity it has to be under such unfortunate circumstances."

Marek shook hands. "Good to see you too, Sir. How is Dan doing?"

The Doctor shook his head. "That I can't quite figure. Dan has me puzzled, I have to admit. He's always been such a tower of strength and I never would have guessed that even something as serious as this would have knocked him over in the way it has."

"Nikola says he can't walk. Was the injury so great?"

"Pretty extensive. The wound wasn't clean, it went everywhere. I don't know what the bastard who gave it to him was thinking of; just to do the most damage possible I guess. But the wound is one thing, and its Dan's attitude which really bothers me. It's as if he's decided that life isn't worth living any more."

"It would be a hard thing to accept for a man like Dan, paralysis, not being able bodied any more?" Marek suggested.

"Yes, it would be if it was likely to be permanent. But I've already told Dan that, in my opinion, time and the proper care ought to bring him back to full mobility again. And this is what I can't figure, he just doesn't seem to be listening."

"Will he listen to me?" Marek wondered.

Doctor Langan made a doubting gesture, then in contradiction, nodded. "Nikola seems certain that he will. So give it your best try, my boy, that's all anyone can do."

What did it take to make the lame walk and the disappointed heart believe again in love? Which was the easier to repair? The physical damage of tissue and nerves, or the stubbornness of an ego locked in pride and self delusion? With Dan, Marek had both to deal with. With Dan, they were one and the same thing.

Marek walked in through the door of his old bedroom. Dan lay in the bed, reclining against two fat pillows. Stretched out to his full length he seemed to Marek larger and more monumental than ever. A fallen, stony faced colossus, if ever there was one. "Hello, Dan. It's been a while."

In fact they had not seen each other since Vargas.

Dan grunted a greeting which did not sound wholly unwelcoming. Maybe there was a chink somewhere in that wall of stone, Marek thought. Perhaps Nikola knew better than any of them.

He decided on directness as the right approach, since Dan was not one for subtlety usually. "Are you in much pain?" he asked.

Dan shook his head. "Not a great deal, not now. And I can't feel anything below."

Marek dragged an armchair over to the side of the bed. "You remember what I did in Vargas, don't you? I could do the same for you, but only if you want it."

Dan glared at him. "Why wouldn't I want it? At least being able to get out of this confounded bed would give me back a bit of self respect!"

Marek leaned back in the chair and rested his chin on his hand. "Only a bit? What about the rest of it?"

There was a space of grumpy silence while Dan considered his next move. Then he said, "I think I like you better than I did in Vargas. No shilly-shallying around, no mystery any more. You're being direct; I appreciate that, not like Nikola who has barely said boo to me."

228

"Nikola has her own problems in dealing with what's happened. You're not the only one to be suffering," Marek said. He saw Dan flinch at this, saw the look of surprise come into his eyes. "Now tell me what's driving you into such a funk."

Dan glowered. "You've got the lousiest bedside manner I've ever encountered. I don't know why Nikola and Bill make such a fuss about you." He frowned. "Okay, I'll tell you, because you know what it feels like to be attacked and they don't; how helpless it makes you feel. It seemed to me that I just let it happen ... me, an ex-cop! And it made me feel old all of a sudden, like I'm way past my best and there's nowhere to go but down. And I know this'll get round Vargas, it probably has already. So what use will I be to Bill any more, if I can't even hold up my end in a fight?"

Marek leaned closer to the bed. "I understand what you mean," he said sincerely. "And knowing Vargas, I think you're probably right about the clinic. Doctor Langan will have to get someone else to play the heavy; a younger, fitter guy."

As if searching for something other than honesty in the blunt words, Dan stared hard into Marek's eyes. But finding nothing else, he turned his face away and swore, "SHIT!"

Marek waited. He knew that he could not cosset this man, that Dan would not accept healing from him as would a hurting child or most of the wounded souls whom he saw daily. Dan had too many walls, too many defenses and too much pride for simple surrender.

Finally Dan turned back. The look on his face was one of grudging acceptance of an unpleasant fact. He grimaced. "Hell! So what am I supposed to do now?" he said.

"That's up to you to decide," Marek told him. "But if you want any advice, I'm willing to give it."

Dan folded his arms and frowned. "Advice." He glared again at Marek and humphed. "Advice from a puppy?" he said, rudely. Then he unfolded his arms. "Okay, give it to me."

Marek had to suppress a smile. "My advice is for you to lay here and think about what self respect really means. And to think about your years of friendship with Doctor Langan, and what that means, to you and to him. And to think about Nikola, whom you love more than you love yourself." At this Dan stared then looked away. Marek heard him growl softly, like a bear in pain.

"Anything else?" Dan barked out the words.

"Yes. Ask yourself what is it that you are: a bag full of bones and big muscles, or the being which lives inside the bag and would like to be free to love and to simply be. Ask yourself if you're laying here like a grump because you want to punish your body for the fact that it isn't as young as it used to be. Ask yourself who the hell you think you are."

"That all?"

Marek stood up. "That's enough for now."

Dan scowled. "I've changed my mind about you, I don't like you any better than I did in Vargas. Don't bother to come back!"

Marek closed the door behind him and came face to face with Nikola. Nikola's fair skin was paler than usual and there were dark smudges of shadow under her eyes. However her eyes themselves were bright and she attempted a smile. Even so Marek saw the anxiousness in her eyes.

"How did it go?"

Marek sighed, thinking to himself that he might just have failed with Dan. But he said, "He's a stubborn man; he needs time to sort himself out. Don't go in there for a while; he's not in a very good mood."

Nikola's face fell. "I don't know what to say to him," she said. "I want to tell him that I love him, but I'm sure he'll take it the wrong way. What shall I do, Matt?"

Marek considered that he had given enough advice for one day, nevertheless Nikola wanted and needed something. "Wait a while and when you do go to see him just forget about how upset you are and follow the feelings and instincts rising from your heart. Don't think and don't worry and calculate. You love him and you know it, and he loves you, so don't worry about the complications, you'll get those sorted out in time."

"When are you seeing him again?" Nikola asked.

"When he's ready for it. When and if he calls," Marek said. Dan called, but not for three days. This time he had dragged himself more upright in the bed and had four pillows behind him instead of two. The expression of his face was still as gruff and as sombre as before but when he spoke to Marek his first words were ones of apology.

"I was way out of line, I'm sorry," he said grimly. "And I knew it then but I didn't want to admit it. I thought I was tough, but you were tougher. I didn't like that."

Marek pulled the chair nearer to the bed. "So, you've been doing some thinking."

"Yeah. I've been thinking about my life. You know, I was always big, even as a kid, and the other kids, my friends and my little brothers and sisters, used to look to me to protect them. It got so that I saw myself as this big guy who was supposed to be some sort of guardian of the world. I joined the police force with that in mind, but I soon saw what a mistake that was. When Bill asked me to help him in Arpay I jumped at the chance to do something useful, but I still saw myself in the same way.

"Then there was Nikola. I've known her since she was born. She looks a lot like her mother did, but Rhona was a totally different sort of person, not over serious, like Nikola is. Sometimes I wish Nik would let herself unwind a bit and be relaxed more, as her mother was; but you can't make one person into another, can you." Dan reached for a flask and a glass from the bedside table. Into the glass he poured a dark, golden colored liquid which looked suspiciously like something alcoholic. He took a sip and pulled a face.

"It's not what you think it is," he said, reading the curiosity in Marek's eyes. "Some sort of iced herbal tea, I think. Nik won't let me near anything stronger. I won't offer you any; it's not that great, believe me."

Marek smiled. "Tell me about Nikola."

Dan nodded. "Yeah. She sort of grew on me, Nik did. One minute she's a kid climbing all over me, wanting ice-cream and all that, and the next thing she's going out on dates and I find myself worrying about her like I was her father instead of Bill. Then I didn't see her so often for a few years, when she was in college and medical school. But when I did I hardly recognized her, she'd gotten so smart and self assured. I knew I didn't have to worry about her any more, but that didn't stop me. And somewhere along the line I realized that what I felt for her had changed into something more, more than it should have been.

"I find this hard to explain. One minute I'm Uncle Dan who feels like a father to a little girl, and the next minute I'm seeing a lovely young woman in front of me and experiencing desires that embarrass me. I wanted her, Matt. I'd always loved her, but now I loved her and wanted her too.

"It was a difficult time. I got confused. I had always tried to protect Nik, and now I felt like I had to protect her from my own desires! So eventually I made myself stand apart from how I felt. I decided just to love her from a distance but still look after her." Dan heaved a great sigh.

"Damn it all! Years and years of telling myself I couldn't expect to have her, especially when I knew she was involved with this or that boyfriend. But it was odd that she never got married. I know for sure she had a couple of offers. Still, I never saw myself in the running at all."

"But you do now?" Marek asked.

Dan laughed bitterly. "What … like this?" He shrugged. "Just let me keep talking. I've got to get all this off my chest. If I stop now I might run out of steam.

"So, then along comes you, and I worry about Nikola all over again. I didn't know what was going on in her head about you. I still don't. She seems to like you a whole lot, but she tells me you have a wife now. That so?"

Marek nodded. He and Faran were not married in the official sense, because while Marek had to keep a false identity it was not possible to do anything legal. However wife was what Faran was to him and he was husband to her.

Dan shrugged his big shoulders. "But things seemed to turn out all right with you, and Bill reckoned you were okay, so I stopped worrying, more or less. I even thought I might get up the courage to ask Nikola to marry me. Then this damned business had to happen." There was a pause while Dan considered his next words, then he continued, "I thought about what you said, self respect and all and what I really am. I know I'm not the guardian of the world, I never was, and I'm not just the big tough hulk everyone thinks they see. Bill knows me, the real me, and he's not been my friend for all these years just because I was big and useful. I remember when he suggested I go with him to Arpay, it was because he knew I was unhappy with my life as it was. I guessed that was what you meant, wasn't it? Self respect is knowing yourself and not mixing it up with outside stuff. I did that for too long, and when my body couldn't hack it any more, I thought I was finished."

Marek said then, "I also meant that self respect is loving your Self, and that you then have to extend the love to the body you live in, instead of resenting it for what it can't do. That's the only way healing will occur, Dan. If you can love the whole of you as you love Nikola, you will be well on the way to recovery. And maybe you can tell Nikola how you feel."

Dan rubbed his chin doubtfully. "I don't know. How would she react to that?"

"You might be surprised," Marek said. "Talk to her, Dan. I know for a

232

fact she wants to talk to you."

"I got the feeling she's been trying to say something, but—hey, where are you going?"

Marek had stood up, as if to leave. "Unless there's something more, I have to go. I've got work—" "There is. You did offer; remember. You said, if I wanted …"

Marek perched himself on the edge of the bed. "Give me your hands then." He smiled at Dan's reaction to such a request. "It helps me focus on the frequency of you," he explained. "It's just a contact, probably not absolutely necessary, but it helps me all the same."

Marek hurried downstairs to the lobby. Today he was seeing people indoors because it was raining outside. Summer storms only, they did not last very long but came down in bucketfuls, and this made sitting in the garden impossible.

Nikola met him by the receptionist desk. Her face was anxious. "How was he this time?"

They moved out of earshot of the two women at the desk: Marie, the usual receptionist, and a new plump looking assistant who was still learning the ropes.

"Much better," Marek told her. "He's ready to talk. He wants to and needs to. If I were you I'd go up there straight away."

"Did he say anything about me?"

"Plenty. He wants you, Nik, but he has to know that you want him."

Surreptitiously, so that the women would not see, Nikola wiped a tear from her eye. "At this moment, more than anything, I'd like to give you a great big hug, but I don't think I'd better, not here. I'll go up to him." In replacement of the hug she would rather have given, she touched her fingers to his hand. "I do love you, you know. Thank you," she whispered.

Nikola ran upstairs and Marek went to the receptionist desk. He was due to see his next patient in five minutes and all he needed to know was the name, for it was someone new.

"It's a child," Marie said. "A little girl, eleven years old. Jenevra Klider, from Brentore. She's already waiting in the Conservatory."

Brentore, Telaia's capital and Marek's home city. "Are the parents with her?" Marek asked.

Marie simpered. "Just the mother. They're staying in Tempah Springs. They're quite flush by the look of them."

Marek frowned slightly. He was not overly fond of Marie, considering her to be too interested by half in other peoples" affairs, even for a receptionist. The other woman hovered behind Marie, evincing a similar degree of interest and obviously waiting to be introduced.

"Oh, this is Trudy. She's going to be doing afternoons," Marie said, as though remembering the other woman as an after-thought only.

Marek said hello and stretched out a hand. Trudy offered hers reluctantly, as if she thought his welcoming grip might break it.

Although Trudy's wrists were well padded with fat, the right one looked larger than the left and was discolored. "Is there something wrong with your wrist?" Marek asked.

Trudy grimaced. "I slipped over in the garden at home this morning, in the wet. I think I must have sprained it a bit."

"You should have gotten Nikola to take a look at that when you arrived; it probably needs strapping." Marek reached over the counter and took Trudy's wrist between thumb and forefinger, palpating it gently. Even so, Trudy winced in pain. He said to Marie, "She shouldn't be working with that unattended to. Get one of the nurses to see to it right now, Nikola's going to be busy for a while."

Marie's self satisfied smile turned into a chastened, embarrassed grin. "Of course, yes Matt, right away."

As Marek left, the two women watched him hurry down the hall. Marie was somewhat disconcerted and piqued by what she felt was a correction of herself for not looking after her charge better. "He's not usually that brusque and unfriendly," she said to Trudy.

Trudy raised querying eyebrows. "I didn't think he was brusque, or all that unfriendly. Hadn't we do something about my wrist, though?"

"Yes," Marie said, in irritation. "I'll page a nurse, then you'll have to go to the infirmary."

After the nurse had tested for damage and then strapped the swollen wrist, Trudy made her way back to the front desk. Passing by the Conservatory, she caught a glimpse of the healer and the child as they sat together on a wicker couch. The child's mother was seated some distance away and had fixed her attention on the rain outside, as though she strove to keep out of the proceedings. Trudy saw how the healer held the hands of the child, and she touched her wrist thoughtfully. She had heard about this man before, not from Marie or anyone who worked at the hospice, but from her next door neighbor who had been treated by him a year ago.

"He had the most wonderful touch. It was like I could feel an energy coming from his hands," Trudy's neighbor had said.

Had she felt something herself? Trudy wondered. Perhaps. However, the touch had been too brief to really register anything. Nevertheless, she was interested in this man, for she had a great curiosity about people who were unusual in any way.

"Where is Matt Best from?" she asked Marie.

Marie was not sure. The most she could say was that he had come from Arpay, with Nikola. "But he's not Arpayan, is he? I mean, he sounds Telaian."

Marie nodded. "He does. I always thought he was very much East Coast … you know, Up There, where ordinary mortals don't dwell." Marie was angry at being corrected and also somewhat annoyed with Trudy for not agreeing with her earlier and it was making her feel bitchy.

Trudy didn't seem to understand the gibe, for she said seriously, "You could be right. He certainly has the accents." She stared in the direction of the Conservatory. "There's something familiar about his face, like I've seen it before, but a long time ago, a younger face."

Marie sniffed. "I don't know where. You've never lived anywhere but down the road from me. Or have you spent secret time as an East Coast socialite that I don't know of?"

Marie's little stab at sarcasm went nowhere, for Trudy had grown so thoughtful that she didn't seem to hear.

Chapter Three

When Nikola went up to see Dan she did not go into the bedroom immediately but stopped outside the closed door, resting her hand on the doorknob. Why is it that I'm so nervous? she asked herself. She was aware of feeling all fluttery inside, like a sixteen year old about to embark on her very first date. But she was not sixteen, she was mature woman getting close to forty … so why the terror and the nerves? This is ridiculous, she thought. It's only Dan, the Dan I've known all my life. Which was part of the problem, perhaps, that Dan had always been a friend and Nikola ought to have known all there was to know about such a long acquaintance. Yet it was clear to her now that there were hidden depths of feeling in Dan, depths she had never chosen to plumb before.

It was almost like throwing wide a door to another kind of life, like crossing a threshold to meet a stranger, not knowing what to expect. But she would never find out if she did not go in. Nikola turned the knob and opened the door cautiously.

Dan appeared to be asleep, for his eyes were closed and he breathed deeply and slowly. Nikola took the opportunity to observe him for a while. It was not done objectively, not with her physician's eyes, but warmly and reflectively. Actually, for his age, Dan was an attractive man, if you overlooked the gruffness of his usual manner, which Nikola knew was mostly only for show and not his real nature. Before the attack he had been very conscious of keeping himself fit and strong, as it was necessary to be for a job that often involved manhandling inert bodies or ejecting troublesome clients from the clinic. It was that strength and power which always made Nikola feel safe and protected when she was in awful Vargas.

But when her father had brought Dan here how shocked she was to see the sudden change in him. He seemed to be wasting away, as though a spirit which was no longer sure and confident was in control of the flesh it inhabited and had requested that it lay down and die.

Yet here Dan lay now, and it seemed to Nikola that color had come back into his cheeks and that the lines of his face were smoothed away by an attitude of peace. I shouldn't wake him when he looks so restful, she decided, and was about to creep away.

Dan's eyes shot open. "Nikola! Boy, am I glad you're here. I've been

236

lying in this bed, trying to keep calm and wishing someone would come in soon. My right foot, Nik, it's itching and it's driving me nearly crazy!"

"Your foot? You can feel your foot?" Nikola said excitedly. She threw the covers off his legs. "You're getting back some feeling already?" The physician in her jostled the excited woman aside and she took a pen from her pocket and ran its point along the side of his right leg. "Can you feel that?"

"Yes … yes!" Dan growled, a bear with an itch he could not scratch. "Damn it all, Nikola … the foot! Just scratch the itch first, and then you can play doctors!"

Dan had slight sensation in almost all of his right leg and partially in the left. He was overjoyed, but no more than Nikola. "How did this happen? Dad said it would, eventually, but this is great! I must get Dad! He'll want to do tests," she decided.

"No tests, not yet," Dan said with sudden forcefulness. "I don't want you running off now, I want to talk to you."

Nikola stared. In all the excitement she had almost forgotten what she had come there for. "Cover me up again, I want to look decent for this." Dan sounded as if he was giving orders to a staff member. "Then sit down here." He patted the bed beside him. "Yes, Dan," Nikola said meekly.

Dan pulled himself more upright, waving away Nikola's attempts to help him. "I can do it," he affirmed. "You just sit where I put you." Even had he added "My girl" to that, he couldn't have sounded more in charge. Nikola was amazed. Such a change in him already; it was like having the old Dan back, and fighting.

"First things first," Dan said. "I want you to get that young fellow back here as soon as possible." "Matt? He was a help to you then?" Nikola asked, for she hadn't yet realized the reason for Dan's speeded up recovery.

Dan knew she did not understand. He grinned at her. "The other day he asked me if I would want him to do for me what he did for himself in Vargas. I said, "Yeah, why not?" but then we got into some heavy stuff and I was pretty unpleasant. I told him not to come back."

Nikola was surprised; Marek had not told her that. "I didn't know."

"Yeah, well, he's one up front guy and he didn't beat round the bush, and I'm not proud of the way I behaved. Anyway we got on better today. He's okay, is Matt. In fact I would say that your healer is about the most amazing guy I've ever met."

"Healer ..." Now Nikola comprehended. She had asked Marek to help Dan but she had been thinking more of Dan's overall health and state of mind than the temporary paralysis. She had gotten so used to the more public persona of "her healer", as Dan called him, the one who used herbs as a way of treatment and who drew his patients into an understanding of their problems so that they more ably healed themselves, that the other aspect had seemed to fade a little in her mind. Although she had seen for herself the astonishing speed by which Marek had healed his own wounds, it was not a thing she had observed since, although it was certainly the invisible part of the healer's cure. But of course, to Dan, who knew all about it, he could offer more direct help, and this he had done.

I can hardly wait to tell Dad about this, Nikola thought, before bringing her mind back solely to the present moment.

Dan took her hands in his. "Nikola, I have something to say, and it isn't easy for me, so promise me you'll just listen and not interrupt or anything."

Nikola bent her head. Dan was holding her hands rather too tightly and the fluttery feeling in her stomach had returned. "I promise."

"Good." Dan was nervous too. "We've known each other for so long, we ought to be able to say the things we mean, and not fool around uhm-ing and ah-ing. Like Matt, I want to be upfront. Nikola, I've loved you for many years. I mean, I've been in love with you for a long time." Dan swallowed the lump of nervousness which seemed to have stuck in his throat. "I ... I know I'm a lot older than you—"

With lowered eyes, like a maiden all overcome by modesty, Nikola said, "I love you too, Dan. I want you."

"You do?"

Nikola raised her face to him. All the while as he had made his little hopeful speech, she had been trying to fight back tears. Now the pressure of emotion was just too great to resist. Tears slowly spread over her cheeks. "Yes." She pulled one hand away and scrabbled in a pocket for her handkerchief.

Dan's hands were trembling around the hand he still held. He said tenderly, "Don't cry, Nik, there's a good girl, or you'll make me cry too."

He sounded as he had done when she was only a child, all the gruffness gone, replaced by that great gentleness which she had so often been the only one to know. Nikola put away her handkerchief and composed her face, then she touched his cheek with her own gesture of tenderness. "I've been such a fool all these years, not to know what love waited for me right on my doorstep. Can you forgive me for being so stupid and blind?" she said.

Dan pressed his cheek into her palm. He kissed her hand, then his lips travelled to her wrist. He planted several kisses there and then he drew her over to him, folding her in his big strong arms. "Forgive you? There's nothing to forgive. All I want to do is love you."

They kissed one another and Nikola lay against him, feeling the warmth he emanated from body and heart. She held on to him as if he was a rock which was somehow magically infused with life, a rock of both of strength and tenderness – the strength she clung to, the tenderness she had so long sought for.

They lay together in a silence, not because they had nothing more to say to one another but for what the silent contact gave, a closeness which was more than a clinging together of two bodies in time and space. What it meant, that contact, was a moment of resonance which would be forever endless now; it was Their Moment.

So absorbed where they that they did not see or hear the bedroom door open. Nikola's father, coming to pay a call on his sick friend, popped his head around the door. His eyes widened at the sight of his daughter in the arms of Dan, but not so widely as his smile. Very carefully and quietly, he closed the door again.

Jenevra Klider and her mother were standing by the big potted palm in the Conservatory when Marek came in. For a girl of supposedly eleven, Jenevra was somewhat small. She had a round elfin face which was the setting for two big, long lashed eyes and a bob of very shiny black hair. Her complexion was pale and creamy, like a flower which was never allowed to see the sun. Marek could see how anxious her mother was about her and how the anxiousness communicated itself to the child and showed in the wide frightened look of the little girl's eyes.

"Hello, I'm Matt," Marek said in a friendly voice.

Mrs. Klider came forward, shepherding Jenevra in front of her. "Pleased to meet you. We've heard a lot about you. Do you think you can help my daughter? She has—"

"That's all right," Marek interrupted. Rarely, if ever, did he want to know the names of his patients" diseases, for they were irrelevant to the problem as he saw it. Names meant nothing; they were the labels stuck onto a set of symptoms which said nothing about the sufferer. Marek pointed to a wicker settee in the corner of the Conservatory. It was where he usually took his patients, well away from any other chairs. "I'd like to sit over there with Jenevra, if you don't mind, and if Jenevra doesn't mind."

The little girl was excruciatingly shy. She gave Marek a fleeting glance, like a deer too afraid to investigate a moving bush even when it knew something was waiting for it there. Marek looked at her through the layer of her fear. The fear was something imposed over other more potent things; it was not real. Beneath that layer was another which revealed a powerful will and a strong drive, and underneath that was the child's light burning bright and clear and mighty, like a beautiful flame of the sun. Resonance, Marek felt and thought. He said to Jenevra, "Will you sit with me while your mother stays here? If you want her, then you can always come and get her."

Hesitantly the girl nodded. "Go ahead, dear. Don't be shy," her mother ordered unnecessarily.

Marek sat Jenevra next to him on the settee. Her legs were too short to reach the floor and as they dangled she crossed and re-crossed them nervously.

"When I was your age I used to be shy too. So I know how you feel." Marek said. He grinned at her. "I won't bite you."

Jenevra offered a little smile in return. "I'm not used to strangers," she whispered. "That's okay," Marek told her. "After today we won't be strangers any more, will we?"

"No, I guess not," Jenevra agreed, warming a little to the healer's easiness with herself.

"Your mother brought you to me because you have some problems. Will you tell me what they are?" Marek asked.

Jenevra was so unused to adults asking her about her illness that she started in surprise. Usually it was a case of the grownups discussing her across the top of her head, as if she was some kind of dumb animal which could not speak for itself. "I get sort of tight in the chest a lot. Sometimes I can hardly breathe at all. Then I get scared because I think I'm going to stop breathing and die," she explained quietly.

"When does this happen? I mean, what sorts of things happen to make

240

your breathing difficult?"

Jenevra thought. She glanced guiltily in the direction of her mother. "When Mummy wants me to do things properly and I can't. I make mistakes. Sometimes I'm really dumb, then I get tight. I wish I didn't."

Marek nodded. "What about your father? Does he want you to do things properly?"

"No, Daddy doesn't mind. But because Mummy wants me to, he shows me what to do. Sometimes he even does things for me when she doesn't know."

"And how does that make you feel?" Marek asked.

While she had been talking, Jenevra's feet had remained still. Now she began to fidget again. "I still get tight, but not so much. But I wish Daddy wouldn't do the things because sometimes when I have to do something new … at school … I get all scared and think I won't be able to do it because he's not there to help."

Now Marek truly understood what the false layer of fear was. A demanding mother with too high expectations of an only child and a father who was compassionate but badly mistaken in his idea of a solution to the problem. This little girl felt helpless in her parents" world; it was enough to make her breathless. Marek also realized though that the actual root of the illness was not the parents" fault. As everyone was, the child was her own responsibility. He was not dealing with a brief eleven years, but with lifetimes of emotional strangulation. Well, that would have to be cleared.

"What do you think doing things properly means?" he asked Jenevra.

She gazed up at him. Her elfin face puckered in concentration. "I don't know, The way Mummy wants them done, I suppose."

Marek raised inquiring eyebrows. "Do you really believe that? Somehow I don't think you do."

This was the first time in Jenevra's life that someone had talked to her on a level of intelligence which said to her she was not a child. And he was challenging her, admittedly with a kindly smile. She liked his smile; it said many things to her which, as yet, she did not understand. Suddenly she felt bolder than she had ever felt before. "I just wish I could do things the best I can and that it would be good enough. I just want to enjoy doing things and not have to spoil them by their not being as good as Mummy or Daddy would do them." Now she felt not only bold but fierce too. "I don't

241

think there is a "properly"; at least I'm not certain there is."

"Good for you!" Marek said. He directed Jenevra's attention to the world outside. "Look at all those lovely flowers out there, and the trees. If you went out there and studied every one of them, you'd see something interesting."

"What?"

"Well, every tree, even the ones belonging to the same species, is different from the rest. They all have similarities but no one of them is identical to the other. It's the same with the flowers, and it's the same with everything. Have you ever been to the snow?"

Jenevra nodded.

"I bet you've learned at school that not one snowflake is like another, but they're all snowflakes. So you see, there are so many ways to do or make a thing that nothing in nature is ever done or made exactly the same as another. Do you understand what I'm getting at?"

Jenevra nodded again. "I think so. Even if I do something not as Mummy wants, it's still doing it my way?"

"Yes. And there is something else I think you should realize. Mothers and fathers are just people who are different from each other and from their children, so none of them can do anything exactly alike. When your mother expects you to be exactly like her, she's making a mistake. And when your father tries to help you by doing things for you, so is he. They don't mean anything wrong by it, they're just mistaken."

Marek watched Jenevra think. She had stopped fidgeting and her small face was serious with profound concentration. Marek knew that the parents of this girl would consider his words to be wildly subversive, undermining their position with their daughter; but he knew also that these were the words which would free Jenevra from her prison. It would not be difficult for her to escape, once given this opening key to realization, for her light told him how strong she really was. He glanced over at the mother. She sat by the window with her hands clasped in her lap and, to her credit, she was turned deliberately away. Yet Marek could see the anguish that tormented her; hers was a light much dimmed by so many layers of pain and illusion that it would take much more work for her to get free than anything her daughter would have to do.

Jenevra looked up at him. Her face was full of wonder and light. She

242

was no longer eleven; she looked at him through eyes which spanned the ages; she smiled a secret smile.

"Now I'm going to teach you something very special and important," Marek said. "Will you hold hands with me?"

Jenevra blushed then nodded. "What is it?"

They held hands and Marek felt Jenevra shiver a little. That was okay; often patients did that when they felt the energy of his hands. "I'm going to teach you how to heal your body by yourself." He did not do this very often, only for a very few whom, he knew, would accept and understand.

Jenevra's eyes popped. According to her mother, she had been brought here to be "healed", and here was the healer talking about teaching her how to heal!

The healer told her what she truly was, that she was not just a little girl but was a great and beautiful Light. Her body, he said, was not herself, but was the Earth's and was in her care. Then he showed her where to place her consciousness in relationship to her body. He had her close her eyes and they both went on a journey together to the most wonderful place. And from there, he said, she and he would heal the little body she inhabited, and they did. She could go there anytime, he said, because that was where her Light was. In fact, he said, she should make a point of doing it every night before she went to sleep. When they were finished in the place, a place Jenevra felt she would never want to leave, she opened her eyes and looked at the healer and bit her lip because she thought she might be going to cry.

"I wish I could have stayed there," she whispered to him.

"But you're already there," he explained. "That's where you are; it's your consciousness which is projecting here."

"How did you know all this?" Jenevra asked, feeling so bold and confident now that she could hardly believe it was herself speaking.

"I'll tell you next time we meet. Tomorrow," he said. "I think we should see each other every day for a week at least."

Jenevra felt a thrill she could not explain. She wanted to leap from the chair and go running with joy to her mother, but of course, Mummy would not understand, not yet.

Chapter Four

Trudy Munk had a mind which remembered faces readily. She had always been fascinated by the lives of the rich and famous, mainly because her own had always been so lacking in excitement or glamor. She lived quietly in the village near the Langan Clinic and since she had never married, nor lived anywhere but Upton, nor had done anything but look after a house and parents, just recently deceased, she took her entertainments where she could, from the meager resources to hand. These mainly involved the study of passers-by and any strange faces in Upton, gossip at the village store and an intense perusal of the social pages in glossy magazines. She tended to hoard the magazines, just in case she might like to look at them again sometime, and had stacks of them piled up in her spare room. If Marie had thought she was not paying attention to her sarcastic suggestion about being an East

Coast socialite, then Marie was very much mistaken. The words stimulated in Trudy an idea. "I'm sure I've seen that healer's face before," she told herself. "Maybe it was in something to do with the Society Pages?" When she got home that evening she shut herself in the spare room and started her search. "Yes," she said again, "I've seen that face before, but it was a much younger face."

There were so many magazines that it took her a full two evenings before she found what she searched for, and then it was only a fairly small picture, without good detail, of a serious looking youth of about eighteen at some party or other for the elite teenagers of Brentore. It was not a picture of a single individual, but one of a group of four boys and two girls with their arms around each other, all but that one youth showing their teeth in self assured grins for the camera. "Now why would I have remembered something like that?" Trudy asked herself. Perhaps it was because the youth was the only unsmiling face in the picture. Yet she thought not. She scanned the list of names underneath. From left to right she counted them down and came upon the name of Marek De Ravana.

"My God!" she said out loud. "That's why!"

Several magazines on, she found the reason for her recollection. It was a two page spread on Silene, Baron De Ravana, and the resemblance

244

between that face and the one she had seen today was so striking that she reckoned it could not be just a case of chance similarity.

Excited, Trudy dug out the most recent of her magazines. She remembered only last month reading an article about the Baron. He had always fascinated her, largely because he was so famous and wealthy and clever, but also because she had once dreamed of him as the most handsome man she would like to know, and there had been a dearth of men, handsome or otherwise, in her quiet, uneventful life.

However, this last article showed photos which were much less flattering than they had been fourteen years earlier, and the Baron's face had coarsened and hardened and fleshed out in a way which was no longer very attractive. And he now looked hardly anything like the man of Trudy's acquaintance.

Trudy preferred the earlier version of Silene, and she stared long and hard at it, for it was a version closer to the face at the hospice, the face of the healer, Matt Best.

"They're both De Ravanas, so they must be close relatives," she said aloud again. "But how close?" Too near in age to be father and son, she decided, and she knew for a fact that the Baron had never been married. Brother? Cousin? Nephew? She pondered the options, wishing she knew more about the rest of the De Ravanas, but she did not. She turned back to the small, unclear picture of the boy, searching in the article adjacent to the picture. There was nothing to tell her more, only the one name, Marek De Ravana.

Well, it was enough.

Just wait till I show this to Marie! came her thought of triumph.

The following afternoon Trudy took the two magazines from her bag and showed them one at a time to Marie.

Marie stared at her skeptically then begrudgingly studied the small group photo. "Which one is he supposed to be?" she said uncooperatively.

"Third from the right." Impatient, because she knew Marie was only trying to be difficult, Trudy counted the line of names. "See … Marek De Ravana."

"No!" Marie said. "It's only a similarity. With a picture that small a lot of guys could look like that."

"Then take a look at this and tell me I'm not right." With a flourish,

Trudy presented the second magazine.

Marie studied the spread on the Baron. Almost unwillingly, she shrugged and nodded. "So, yes, they do look a bit alike. But it could be just a coincidence. A lot of people look like someone else without being actually related to them."

"You think so?" For the first time Trudy actually felt a doubt. "I suppose I could be beating up the wrong bush," she admitted. "I mean, why would anyone leave a life like that?"

"Why indeed? I wouldn't," Marie agreed. She studied the two magazines again, as if to dismiss the idea once and for all. Then suddenly she gasped. "Look, Trudy," she said quickly. "We've been so concerned with the faces that we hadn't thought about anything else!" She showed Trudy what she had seen.

"Look at the boy's left hand around the girl's waist ... you can just see a ring there. It's not real clear." She grabbed at the spread of Silene. One of the pictures showed him patting his favorite racehorse. With his left hand he held the horse's halter and the hand curved round just enough to show the glint and design of a magnificent gold ring. "Matt wears one almost exactly the same ... have you seen it?" Marie said.

"How could I not?" Trudy replied. "I was only thinking yesterday how beautiful it was!" The two women exchanged wondering glances.

"Busy, ladies?" came Nikola's voice from the reception desk.

Both women jumped in fright. They had been so absorbed in their speculation that they'd turned their backs on the desk and had not heard her arrive. Seeing them so inattentive made Nikola annoyed, and although she was generally easy with her staff, she didn't like inattention on the job. She noticed the guilt in the gesture as Marie began rolling the magazines into a coil.

"What's so interesting then? Can I see too?" she asked.

Marie thrust the roll of magazines into Trudy's hands. "It's nothing really, not important, just some nonsense. You wouldn't be interested."

Why is she lying to me? Nikola thought instantly. She felt a strange disturbance. "I might be." She held out her hand. "Let me have a look."

She noted the reluctance as Trudy complied. And the expression of nervousness on Marie's face.

And since neither of the women would offer anything else, she had to flip open the pages and scan them herself in order to guess what they might have been looking at.

Then she found it, the most obvious of the evidence, the spread dealing with the Baron. She felt her stomach somersault and a sinking sensation followed. The likeness to Matt which these old pictures carried was undeniable. She leafed through the other magazine without noticing anything else revealing. "What's in this one? I want you to show me what you were looking at in here!" she said, realizing how harsh and irritated her voice sounded all of a sudden.

Both women had paled and Trudy hesitantly turned to the social pages. Without uttering a word, she pointed out the relevant picture. Nikola stared at the boyish face and the name beneath. "Oh, no," she moaned silently.

A nice little piece of detective work, Nikola thought, so it was no use denying anything or pretending she didn't know what it meant. She covered her hand over her eyes for a moment to give herself time to think, then made herself busy as Marie had done, coiling up the magazines convulsively.

Hand pressed at her mouth, Nikola considered the women's faces. Then she decided. "I'll keep these, if you don't mind," she said to Trudy. And even if you do, she added silently to herself.

Then came the necessary lecture. Nikola looked down at her fists clenched around the tightly rolled magazines. She spoke in a voice of exaggerated firmness, though without anger in it, so as to get the attention of the listeners without alienating them, if possible. "We are all friends here, at least I hope we are. I employ you and I also respect you. I have never enquired about your pasts or into your affairs, and I expect the same discretion and respect from you in regard to myself or anyone else that works here or is a patient. We do not gossip here or throw around information about other people's lives; that would be a breach of trust, and I don't wish to employ anyone who does." Nikola paused, staring at the women intently to make sure they were really listening. "I want you to understand this.

Because of some pictures in a magazine, you think you know something about one of us. The truth is you know nothing, and if there is anything to know it is not your business to know it. People have a right to change their lives and to keep their privacy, don't you agree?"

The two women nodded, but their eyes shared a glance, as if each wished to suggest to Nikola that, personally, she was innocent, while it was the other one who was guilty.

Nikola inquired, "Have you shown this to anyone, or spoken of it to

247

anyone else?" And when Trudy and Marie shook their heads, she continued, "Then I advise you not to say anything. Remember what I said. I will not employ gossips, and if I hear of this from any other source, I will know where to look and whom to let go."

The threat was understood, and appreciated, especially by Marie who had been working at the hospice for many years. Nikola saw her cast a sideways glare at Trudy as if she considered the matter to be all Trudy's fault. No doubt there would be a frosty atmosphere at the reception desk for a couple of days.

Nikola turned on her heel and left, taking the magazines with her. Today was one of Matt's working afternoons, so she decided to go upstairs and see Dan and her father about the problem, since she would not interrupt Matt at work.

Dan was no longer bed ridden. In two days he was getting about on sticks, awkwardly it was true, but he was getting there. Bill Langan had taken the revelation of the reason for Dan's fast recovery with less surprise than Nikola had expected, and it was then she realized that Matt and her father shared something she had not been aware of. Her father told her about the journal and with a quick stab of jealousy she wondered why Matt had not shown it to herself. But the jealousy passed as soon as it had come, for she realized that she had not always given Matt the understanding he deserved, and she had her prejudices, had she not? Always, it seemed to her, that she had wanted something of Matt, and had not been content just to let him be. Her father was no such kind of being; he took people as they were and demanded nothing. Ever and always, William Langan had been such an open ended man, and Nikola had never failed to recognize that in him, even when she could not be that way herself. Why could she not be the same? she wondered. Yet the thought did not really bother her all that much. She was what she was, so did it really matter? Besides, she had Dan to fill her heart and mind now, and he had come to be for her the most important thing in her life.

Dan and her father were working together in her own sitting room. William Langan was devoting his hours to helping Dan with physical therapy, as a boost to the healing already underway. They were busy at massage when Nikola burst in through the door. She was on fire with worry and it showed.

"What's wrong with you?" said her father.

Nikola showed them the magazines and explained the facts.

"Do you think it poses a threat?" she asked. "I'm pretty sure Marie won't say anything but I'm not certain about Trudy, she's too new here and I don't know her well enough yet. But I gave them a warning. I said to them that if any of this went any further they would lose their jobs."

"You had better show this to Matt," Dan said. "He has to be aware of the possibilities, and we are all going to keep our eyes wide open from now on, just in case."

"Could there be trouble from this?" Nikola asked Dan. It was not herself she worried about, nor even the hospice. The memory of Matt collapsed on the front step of the clinic in Vargas came back to haunt her and she shuddered. Oh, Matt, I don't want anything like that to happen again! she thought.

"We have to think that there might, if your ladies can't manage to keep their mouths shut," Dan said.

He turned to Bill Langan. "It was a pretty grim business in Vargas, Bill, and De Ravana seems determined enough that he might try the same thing here. We'd best get working, you and I, because I want to get back on my feet as soon as possible. I don't intend to be out of action if there's trouble in the offing."

While they were having their lunch at the table in the little garden in front of the cottage, Marek said to Faran, "My next patient is that little girl I told you about – Jenevra. I'd like you to come with me when I see her."

Faran was surprised. He had never asked her to do this before. "Yes, of course, if you want. But what for? I thought you liked to see patients alone."

"I do. It's not Jenevra I'm meaning for you to see, it's her mother. While I'm with the girl, I'd like you to be with the mother. That lady has a lot of problems of her own, but she's not the sort to ask for help very easily. I think that talking to you might make a difference."

Puzzlement added itself to surprise. Faran said, "What will I say to her? I mean, I'm not trained.

Nikola would be better at that, wouldn't she?"

"If I thought that I would have asked her," Marek said, admonishing gently. "Don't sell yourself short, you've a lot to offer by just being yourself. Don't forget, I'm the one who can see your Light, so I know. Don't worry about what you ought to say, let the mother do the talking and go from there."

249

"All right, if you think I can do it." Secretly Faran was delighted even though she was still unsure. It was as though he had made her his partner in everything now. Now they were truly a team.

"That's it, exactly," he said, reading her clearly. "Faran and Marek, Ozira and Rai-a-ele."

Faran waited with Marek in the grove of the lime colored leaves until they saw the brightly dressed nurse leading the mother and the girl up the path. At the point where the flowerbeds began, the nurse separated the two to escort Jenevra to the grove. Faran took that as her signal to leave and she headed in the direction of the mother. It was something like the same situation as had been with Rezia. Mrs. Klider would have to content herself with a wander amongst the flowers for an hour or so.

After two days of showery rain the gardens were green and aglow. It was as if new life had entered them with the rain, and everything looked fresh and bright. Mrs. Klider, though, was drab in black and brown. A woman with a pall of darkness clinging to her like a shroud.

"Hello, isn't it a nice afternoon?" Faran said sunnily, as she approached from the other side of the flowerbed.

"It's very nice," Mrs. Klider replied, with mild enthusiasm. "I don't usually like the south coast … too hot, but it's pleasant here."

"Where do you come from?" Faran asked.

Mrs. Klider had one disinterested eye on Faran and one very concentrated eye on the grove and her daughter. "We come from Brentore. And you?"

"I live here," Faran replied. "Actually, I'm Matt's wife."

"Oh!" Mrs. Klider scrutinized her with interest now. Her face became suddenly animated and almost friendly. "That's my daughter with your husband now." A glow came into her eyes. "Jenevra is her name. Just look at her, I can hardly believe how well she's come on in only two days. She hasn't had one single breathless spell and she is usually so shy with everyone, including her own relatives. Normally, she would never even say boo to a goose. But look at that!"

Faran turned to watch the grove. The little girl, who according to her mother was so afraid of everyone, had gone from sitting beside Marek to perching on his knee. She even had her small arm around his neck, in a hug. Faran felt a sudden twinge of tenderness, not for the child but for Marek. Momentarily she forgot that she was supposed to be attending to Mrs. Klider, and her mind wandered off into a dream. She imagined another child sitting there on Marek's knee – his own child – a child

250

which was his and hers. What a lovely father he would make, she thought.

With a start she came back to the present. "Matt has that sort of affect on everyone he sees. I guess you could say it's part of his magic." The loving feeling must have been in her voice as she uttered the words, for Mrs. Klider said to her wistfully, "That's the nicest thing I've ever heard a wife say about her husband. You must love him very much."

Faran smiled. "I do." Then, to turn the conversation away from herself, she added, "Did you come here on your own? I mean, is Jenevra's father with you here?"

Mrs. Klider frowned. "Well, he has to work. He has a very important job, you know, in the government."

Faran nodded. "But I'm sure he would have loved to come, if he could have … for the child." "Yes. Georgi really loves Jenevra, I'll give him that, but he was rather skeptical about my bringing her here. He's the conventional sort, you know, he only believes in what the doctors tell him."

"When he sees how his daughter is doing, I'm sure he'll be convinced that it was worthwhile," Faran suggested.

"Yes, he will, won't he?" Mrs. Klider gave Faran a look of triumph. But rather, Faran thought, it was a long distance look at her husband. A look that said: "See, I did know better than you." Which told Faran that the woman was not exactly enamored of Mr. Klider.

The talk subsided for a moment, as it does between new acquaintances. Have I failed? Faran thought. I've barely gotten anything out of her yet. Will Marek be disappointed in me? She was conscious of Mrs. Klider's scrutiny which appeared to shift back and forth between herself and the grove. Then suddenly, Mrs. Klider said from out of the blue, "How did you meet your husband, my dear?"

Faran did a double take. She could hardly say: "In a tower". "Actually I met him quite some years ago, when I was only a girl. He did some wonderful healing on my little brother who was quite ill. Then we met up again after seven years and we fell in love."

"How romantic," Mrs. Klider said, with obvious sincerity. "But you're still only a girl, yet marriage obviously agrees with you. You look so full of happiness and joy; and it's not many that do once their married, not in my experience."

"Are you not happy with your husband?" Faran ventured, hoping she was not going too far, or seeming to pry. Probably all she would get from this was a rebuff, she decided.

However Mrs. Klider surprised her with an honest shake of her head. "Not really, no. I never have been. You see, he wasn't my choice. It just happened, and rather awkwardly." Mrs. Klider lowered her head then lifted it abruptly to gaze into the sky. "Young people today have it so easy. If they don't like each other they leave. If they should have a child by accident then no one really cares. When I was young you had to get married if you made a mistake. I don't love Georgi and he doesn't love me. All we have in common is Jenevra."

Jenevra was only eleven. The mother could have been only about thirty five, she was hardly old.

But Faran thought she must feel old, by the look of her. And by the sound of her voice which was heartsick and weary. Then Faran understood exactly what this woman needed.

"Look at your daughter!" she said, smiling sunnily again. "Whatever was wrong with her health, there isn't much sign of it at the moment!"

Mrs. Klider looked. Jenevra was no longer sitting. Both she and Marek had left the bench and were coming towards the flowers. Jenevra was practically dancing around him. Mrs. Klider bit her lip to hold back tears. "Oh, my," she said.

Quickly Faran touched her hand. "You know, Matt would be happy to talk to you. You don't have to be sick for him to help. Take it from one who knows what he can do; he is a wonderful man."

Mrs. Klider gazed at Faran from moist eyes. "If I do, what about Jenevra? Who will look after her?"

"I will," Faran said. Mrs. Klider nodded.

Marek returned with Mrs. Klider to the bench and Faran was left again to her own devices.

Something told her that Jenevra and she ought to go a little further away, that the child was best out of sight of the mother. "Let's go for a walk" she suggested. "From over there you can just see the sea."

"Matt said you are his wife," Jenevra stated. "Do you have any children?" "No, not yet. Although it would be nice," Faran answered.

The girl followed her, not unwillingly, but she was not so interested in views of the sea. "Matt's nice too, isn't he," Jenevra said. "One day, when I'm grown up, I'd like to marry someone just like him."

The girl has a crush on him, Faran thought, with a smile. "I'm sure you will," she said. "Just look for a man with a good, kind heart, a man who will love you for yourself and you do the same in return."

"Is that what you and Matt do?" "Yes."

252

Faran took Jenevra to see the hospice vegetable garden and Nikola's chickens which provided them all with eggs. On the way she found out many of the things which bothered Jenevra about her life.

Jenevra did not like Brentore, she said, and she did not like school. "Neither did I," Faran told her. "Until I was fourteen I never went to a proper school. Everything I learned till then was from nature and from my father and the other people I met, or from the library we kept at home. Daddy didn't like cities either. He thought they were too false and unkind. But we had to go there eventually, even though we didn't want to."

"Why?"

Faran shrugged. "Daddy didn't like the man he worked for. So we left the place where we were.

We went to Hanna Harbor."

"My daddy doesn't like the man he works for either, but he still works for him," Jenevra said. "Maybe he should leave too, like your daddy did."

"Maybe," Faran said.

After Jenevra and Mrs. Klider had returned to Tempah Springs on the bus, Marek still had other people to see, so Faran wandered back to the cottage. She had work of her own to do there, of the housekeeping kind, which she didn't mind doing usually, yet somehow she could not put her mind to the tasks now. All she could think of was the child, or rather the notion of "a child", but it was too soon to be thinking of that, wasn't it? She would like to have a child though, she realized – Marek's child and hers. Yet could they afford to involve another while the world was so uncertain? Ever present in her mind was the knowledge that Marek was still hunted, so was it fair to bring a child into such a situation? Thinking that then, she decided not to dwell on the subject any longer and cast it from her mind. She didn't really need a child to make their life complete, for it was as it was. As Ozira said, their moment was eternal and their moment was NOW. Whatever else there needed to be would manifest, so she did not have to worry and plan.

Chapter Five

By four thirty Marek was done and he arrived back at the cottage ten minutes later. "I saw Nikola a few minutes ago," he said. "Something is really bothering her. She said she wants to come by this afternoon and Bill's coming with her."

"I wonder what it is?" Faran said.

Half an hour later Nikola and Bill Langan knocked on the cottage door. Faran let them in. "Hello, gorgeous," Bill Langan said, with a roguish smile. He had taken a shine to Faran and liked to tease her.

Nikola, though, looked very serious. "Where is Matt?" she asked. Marek came down the stairs as she said it. "What's wrong, Nik?"

Without either explanation or delay, Nikola showed him the pictures in the magazine. Marek stared down at Silene, a Silene of years ago with all his glories around him. Marek even remembered the racehorse. It had been a nervous, oversensitive creature which Marek had felt sorry for even then.

Then he studied the photo of himself. Great Heavens, how unhappy I looked in those days, he thought. No wonder Marielle saw it easily. The boy's face was so tense and strained and sad; it was a face he did not recognize any more; it was like it belonged to someone else. He said nothing and handed the magazines back to Nikola, waiting for her explanation.

"The new girl at reception, she must have thought she recognized you. She dug these out from somewhere. Only she and Marie have seen them, as far as I know. I warned them to keep quiet, or else," Nikola stated.

Marek sighed. "It was bound to happen one day, I guess."

His lack of agitation was an enigma to Nikola. "Doesn't it worry you?" she asked passionately. He did not answer the question. "Do you want me to leave the hospice?" he said instead.

Nikola was astounded. "Leave? No! Of course I don't want you to leave! But I don't want anything to happen to you, not like in Vargas!" She stared at Marek then at Faran. "It's not the hospice I'm thinking about, it's you!"

Marek nodded. "I'm sorry, Nik, not to seem upset, but I decided that when I came back to Telaia I wouldn't run again, no matter what. However I won't stay here if you think it will put the hospice and yourself in danger."

Nikola was nearly in tears. "No, Matt, you mustn't leave. You're in danger wherever you go.

Besides, Dan says he wants to stick by you and protect you, and you know he will. But if anything should threaten we ought to have some kind of plan." Nikola glanced at her heretofore silent father. "Dad has lots of connections. He can see that you go somewhere safe, if need be."

Bill Langan merely nodded. "Whatever you want, my boy, I'll do. But first we ought to make some decisions about those two books of yours. Are they ready yet for publication?"

Nikola obviously did not consider the subject of books to be so important at such a time. "Oh, Dad!

Not now!" she said in frustration.

But Marek nodded. "Yes, Sir, they are. You can have them whenever you want."

"Well I'll get them copied for you, then you can keep the originals. I have a publisher friend who I know will oblige me. I've already talked to him about it and he's interested. But I think it would be best if we rewrite the journal a bit and edit out the names, your brother's especially. Things like personal and derogatory references to a man with your brother's clout will only scare a publisher off.

Besides, it's the other stuff which is the most vital—"

Nikola interrupted; she was very annoyed. "Excuse me, Dad, but is this necessary now? Don't we have more important things on our minds?"

"Everything's important," said her father.

Marek could see that beneath the layer of Nikola's frustration was the fear she really felt. He did not want that fear to communicate itself to Faran, he thought. He knew that Nikola was only remembering the horror of Vargas which seemed to have repeated itself recently through Dan. It was all this which frightened her, nothing more. So he put his arm around her shoulders and led her outside. "Nik, dear, don't be afraid," he said quietly. "What Silene tried in Vargas, he won't try here. Believe me, I know him, I know how he thinks and operates. The bounty hunter was all very well for Arpay, but he'd be an embarrassment in Telaia. And I know for a fact that Silene has never used him here. Whatever happens, happens; you must not let your imagination terrify you, please."

"Are you one hundred percent certain of that?" Nikola asked, for she did not fell very reassured. "No. To be honest with you, I'm not absolutely certain. Nothing is ever so cut and dried. But it's time we all had a little faith in the universe, don't you agree? If we keep on running, or letting fear control us, then it's people like Silene who win ultimately."

Reluctantly Nikola acquiesced. "I'm just glad Dan is on the mend. I always feel a whole lot safer with him around."

When the Langans had returned to the hospice, Marek saw that Faran had grown very quiet and sombre. She also looked rather pale, as if she might even be feeling ill. Damn! I was too slow, Marek thought. Nikola has already gotten to her. "Sweetheart, are you all right?" he asked, coming over to take her in his arms.

"No, I'm not all right," Faran said to him. "Actually I feel a bit strange; my head is buzzing." Abruptly she closed her eyes and swayed.

Hastily Marek helped her to the settee. "Oh, love, did Nikola frighten you?"

Faran opened her eyes. There were tears in them. Marek felt her clammy hands as the sweat poured off them. Her forehead was damp and her skin cold. Marek made her lean forward and breathe as steadily as she could manage. In a few seconds she was right again, but her eyes still held the tears. "I don't know how it happened. I was listening to Nikola and I knew how upset she was, then suddenly it was as if I was seeing you through her eyes, as if I had gone to Vargas and seen what she'd seen. Then I felt the same fear and it made me come over all strange."

Marek nodded, understanding. "But you must realize that it was her fear and not yours."

"I know what it was," Faran asserted. "But I still can't help worrying about you. Will there be a problem?"

"Can you handle the truth?" Marek was not sure she could at this time. But Faran nodded resolutely. "Yes."

"Then, something will happen, although just when, I can't say. I've felt for a long while that there might be a confrontation. Now I'm sure of it. But it won't be because of a couple of magazines."

Faran stared up at him, however she said nothing.

"It's the Kliders. Jenevra's father works for Silene. I thought I recognized the name, but I didn't think much about it because there could be any number of Kliders in Brentore. But some things Jenevra said about her father told me that he was the Klider I knew once."

"You knew Mr. Klider?"

"I didn't know him very well, just to nod to."

"And he works for Silene? Mrs. Klider told me that her husband had a job in the government, but I never thought ..." Faran said. "Does it mean though that anything will get back to Silene? If Mr. Klider only works there why would he say anything in particular about you to anyone?"

"Klider doesn't just have a job in the government, although I would guess that his wife knows nothing but that. Klider actually does other things, especially for Silene. He was one of the men who put me in the tower."

"Oh, Marek!" Faran's hand flew to her mouth. "What are you going to do? Will you still see Jenevra and Mrs. Klider after this?"

"Of course I will," Marek said. "It's not their fault, after all."

For the rest of the week the Kliders shared their time with Marek. Jenevra's health improved vastly and the mother's own manner warmed considerably as the pall of sadness and resentment lifted off her as though it was a fog rising and dispersing in the heat of the sun. When the week was up and Mrs. Klider came to say goodbye she asked to see Faran as well. All the stiffness has gone out of her, Faran observed. It was a very pleasant woman now who gave Faran a hesitant kiss on the cheek. "We've had the best time here," Mrs. Klider said. "It was better than a holiday, and I do believe that Jenevra would rather stay here than go back to Brentore. Nevertheless, we must go back. I've promised her, though, that we will come again, if only for a visit."

Faran did not know what to say. On the one hand she was glad for the Kliders, but on the other hand she could think only of the husband who had put Marek in the tower.

Then the Kliders were gone and life seemed to settle down again. Until a few days later when Nikola stopped Faran in the garden and gave her a letter.

"I was just on my way to the cottage, to give this to you. It came with the post this morning."

"A letter for me?" Faran said. The postmark was Hanna Harbor, which usually meant Young Will, but this time the sender's name on the envelope was Hanna College itself. This is something about Young Will, she thought, worrying immediately. Her hands trembled as she tore it open.

"Oh, no!" she said as she read.

"Bad news?" Nikola asked, with concern.

Faran looked up from the letter. "It's my brother; he's run away from school and they have no idea where he's gone. The Head Teacher says here that my uncle and aunt wanted to alert the police to look for him, but that he had to point out to them that as Will is now sixteen he is legally entitled to leave school, so it's not really a police matter. He suggests instead that Will may be on his way to me, and that if he arrives here I should let them know and try to persuade him to go back."

"Oh dear, what a worry," Nikola said. "Do you think the teacher is right?"

"I hope so. Will has nowhere else he can go, or no one else to turn to. I knew he was unhappy at school but I didn't expect he'd run like this. Oh, Nikola, what shall I do? Where could he be?"

"Hopefully, on his way here," Nikola said comfortingly. "And he is sixteen. He's not a child."

Faran agreed, but she was still worried. "He's a big boy, he's looks older than he is, but he's still only a baby when it comes to getting about on his own. It's that which worries me ... if he's wandering about the countryside on his own, he could get into trouble because people will think he's not such a kid."

Nikola took Faran by the arm. "You'll have to tell Matt later, but at the moment there's something else we can do. We'll go and see Dan, he'll know how to approach this, I'm sure. He used to be a policeman so he'll know what to do."

Dan had recovered full use of his legs by now and was more or less his own self again. Technically, he was still convalescent, or that was how Nikola would have it, at least. Personally, he did not agree, so he had made himself a workout space in the sitting room upstairs in the main house in order to get back to full strength and to prove Nikola wrong. Bill Langan had fetched him some weights and gym equipment from Tempah Springs and these he used every day, with an almost religious devotion and zeal. The good Doctor himself was not there at the moment, having taken copies of Marek's books to his publisher friend, as he had promised he would.

Dan had on loose pants and a sleeveless, singlet top; his muscles bulged out from under the shoulder straps. To Nikola he was always a glorious and comforting sight, considering what she worried about daily. To Faran too, as it turned out.

"Let me see the letter," Dan said, wiping the sweat from his neck and hands with a towel. Faran gave it to him. Dan read then thought for a while. "You and your brother have a good relationship?" he asked Faran finally.

"Yes. I'm all he has and he knows I love him. We've always been very close."

"And he's never mentioned to you anything about someone he might care for in Hanna Harbor? A girl, maybe?"

Faran hadn't thought of the possibility of romance. "I don't believe he knows any, at least he's never said anything. And he's only sixteen!"

Dan raised one shoulder in a quizzical gesture. "Youngsters feeling their oats get up to all kinds of things we might not approve of. But I bow to your better knowledge of the boy and most likely you are the destination. However, this letter was posted yesterday and he'd already been gone two days before that. Three days is a long time to get from Hanna Harbor to here, so we have to assume that if he's headed here then he's not riding comfortably in a bus. Does he have any regular source of cash?"

"Only his pocket money. The families direct it to the school and they dole it out, so that none of the boys has more than the other and not enough to get into too much mischief with. I'm afraid it would be very little, unless he's been deliberately saving it up."

"To do this, do you mean?" Dan said.

Faran shrugged helplessly. "I just don't know. He wanted to leave the school and he asked me to get him out, but that was last Spring ... before he turned sixteen, so I couldn't do anything legally. But I wrote to him after and told him that as soon as he had his birthday I'd help him. Marek and I had already planned to do it. I was going to write to the school and ask for his release. I don't understand it ... Will knew all this, he had only to wait a little while, so why didn't he? There was no need to run away."

"No need that we know about," Dan mused. "When was his sixteenth birthday?" "Four days ago."

Dan raised puzzled eyebrows. "Have you sent your request to the school already? Could there have been some trouble about that?"

Faran shook her head. "I just finished writing it last night. It hasn't even gone off yet."

Meditatively Dan rubbed at the stubble on his chin. He said to Faran, "If you have a recent picture of your brother, I'd like to see it. A good, clear one that makes him easily identifiable. How tall is he?"

"He's big for his age," Faran said. "Last time I saw him he was nearly as tall as Marek, but he's heading towards a bigger build. He takes after our father who was almost as big as you are, Dan, and he told me at the school that he was doing weights, or something like that."

"Okay," Dan said. "Will you go and find that picture now? I want to get started on this right away." "What are you going to do, Dan?" Nikola asked after Faran had left.

Dan pulled on a cotton sweater over his singlet top. "Well, first I'm going to make a few calls … to people I know between here and Hanna Harbor, then I'm going to take a shower. Then, if it's all right with you, Nik, I'm going to borrow your car and look for the boy myself."

Nikola balked at this. "Do you think you're well enough to be running around like that? I don't know what Dad will say."

"If he was here, Bill would probably come with me. And I won't be running around, I'll be driving, that is if you let me have the car keys. Or are you going to pull rank on me and play the big bossy doctor again?"

"No, Dan, I wouldn't do that," Nikola said, sighing philosophically.

Faran hurried back to the cottage and found the most recent picture she had of Young Will. It was a school photo, taken the year before, so it was a good, clear likeness and had the benefit of being large. The boy looked out at her from blue eyes and a pink cheeked, fresh faced smile. His golden brown hair was cropped close in the obligatory school fashion, but Faran knew how readily it curled if allowed to. She supposed he would look similar to this now, as long as he'd had a haircut recently. The photo had Love to Faran, from Will written on the back in the boy's loose, scrawling hand.

It was then that Faran wondered for the first time how the school had discovered her address. It was not registered anywhere and her aunt and uncle did not know where she lived. Only Will knew that and she had asked him never to tell anybody or show them his letters addressed to herself, and preferably to destroy hers once he'd read them. When she had told him why the secrecy her brother had been surprised, but he had accepted the reason without much comment. As if, to him, anonymity was a natural fact, as if it was a part of his nature also to desire it.

The only explanation she could think of then was that, somehow, the Head Teacher or someone had managed to see one of her letters to Will, or one of his to her before he had sent it. This thought disturbed her greatly; what it might mean then was that someone was monitoring Young Will's mail. I must tell that to Dan, she decided, without really knowing why it was important. It just seemed to her that it was.

There was a sound below and it was Marek coming up the stairs two at a time. He looked cheerful and unruffled, glad to see her, so it was obvious he hadn't heard. But immediately he took in her worried face he came to her. Faran showed him the letter and he read it with downcast eyes and a frown.

"Why did he run?" Why?" he said.

"I don't know. But Dan is going to help. He didn't say so while I was there, but I think he's going out to look for him."

Marek nodded. "That would be Dan. Let's take him the picture then. Do you want to go with him?" Faran started. "Would it be okay if I did? You wouldn't mind?"

"No. Will's too important. But Dan might not want you to, we'll have to wait and see."

As it turned out, Dan did not want Faran to go with him, especially after she had told him of her suspicions surrounding her brother's mail. He seemed very thoughtful after that but he did not say anything. "I'll keep in touch regularly," he promised. "As soon as I know anything I'll let you know too."

Faran had to be content with that. Even so, she and Nikola shared a shrug about the stubbornness of males. "Come and have some tea," Nikola suggested to Faran. "You look like you could use it. Do you want any, Matt?"

Marek shook his head. "I have to get back to work, and I want to talk to Dan for a minute first."

Marek went into the bedroom where Dan was throwing a few clothes into a bag. "I don't know how long this will take," Dan said. "If we're very lucky the boy could just turn up here by tonight and you'd have to let me know. Or it might take a while." Into his coat pocket, though, he slipped something else. It was a pistol. "Don't look at me like that, and don't you go saying anything to the women," he ordered Marek. "I saw it on your face the minute Faran said about the boy's mail. You know it and I know it…most likely the boy is in some kind of trouble." "Maybe he is," Marek affirmed. "But a gun, Dan?"

Dan shook his head. "You of all people should know what trouble the boy could be in. After all, he is, in a roundabout way, connected with you, so we have to expect anything. The gun is a precaution, nothing else."

Marek had to agree. The brutal fact, as Dan had stated it, honestly and without emotion, was that Marek, himself, was always potential trouble, and it had been that way for over seven years.

"There might be something I can do to help you find him, Dan," Marek offered. "Oh? What's that?"

"It's difficult to explain. I'll just do it and let you know if it was successful. When are you going to get in contact? Tonight?"

The expression on Dan's face said that he didn't like mystery, but he shrugged. "I'm going straight to the Springs, to see someone I know, and I'll look around there. If I don't get anywhere there I'll head off east. But if you want to get in contact with me at the Springs, I'd better give you a number. That way we won't miss each other because I'll check in with my friend before I leave." Dan found a scrap of paper and a pen on the bedside table and he scribbled a name and number and handed it to Marek. "Okay?"

"Thanks and good luck." Marek turned to go.

"Just one more thing before you go," Dan said hurriedly. "You know that bounty hunter in Vargas, what does he look like? Describe him to me."

"You don't think he'd be involved in this, surely?" Marek asked.

"No, not this. Nikola told me you said that the Baron never used him in Telaia, but that you weren't one hundred percent sure. I'd just like to know what he looks like, seeing as I'm going to be travelling. One never knows and I like to be prepared for everything."

Marek could never forget that evening in Vargas, and the face which had stared down at him so scornfully was imprinted on his memory forever. "All right. The Vorken, that's the title he goes by, I don't know if he's got another name. He's about forty, I'd say. He's totally bald and his two front teeth are gold. He's dark complexioned, I think he's Arpayan, he has that accent and the features, and he's average height, light build, rather thin and wiry. And he walks strangely, sort of slides sideways when he moves. Oh, and this other thing you would not miss: for some strange reason he has only one eyebrow, as if the other one was torn away; there's just a scar there where it ought to be. And he's very dangerous."

"Good description," Dan commented. "But I already figured out the dangerous part myself," he added, with an ironic look at Marek.

Chapter Six

Will Crafter's first indication that something insidious and unpleasant was happening in his young life was the suspicion that somebody, he didn't know who, was tampering with his mail. The last letter he had received from Faran was bent and crumpled and scuffed, as if it had been stepped on accidentally by the postman, but this did not hide the subtle misalignment of the envelope flap. It was as if someone had opened the letter, read it and re-sealed it clumsily and had tried to disguise the fact by making the whole thing look damaged. Well, that was the theory of Will's room mate, Andrew, who had an obsession with mystery and intrigue and fancied himself something of a detective.

What Andrew did not know though was that Will had a secret. Since seeing him in the Spring, Faran had told him in her first letter after that of the reason for the Crafters" flight from the Towers. It was only fair that he should know, now that he was old enough, she said, and she told him also the identity of the man in the tower and that she now lived with this man. Will had been shocked at first, then he had cast his mind back to those days long ago. He remembered little of the man himself, but something he had not forgotten was the power and gentleness of the man's touch and the kindly light in his eyes. He knew he had been very sick and the man had healed him somehow, so how could he think badly of someone like that? He could not. In Faran's second letter she told him of how she loved the healer, and Will was not too young any more to understand something like that.

Then Will had become aware that he was being watched. Actually, he had been conscious of eyes upon him before, however it had meant nothing much until after Faran's pertinent letters. Then he began to take notice and saw that everywhere he went certain faces appeared in the crowd, and the feeling of being constantly observed became almost too great to bear.

What caused him, ultimately, to run, however, was something more. At first he had believed himself safe at school, protected at least by the stern walls of rule and authority. Then one afternoon he had been passing by the Head Teacher's office – as it happened, he was in a spot of trouble again and had to report to the detention room for punishment – and he had heard through the half open door, his own name, or that of William

Bolton, as he was called at school, spoken by a strange voice.

Instead of going to detention, Will decided to see who had spoken his name. He hid down the hall a way, in an alcove which led to the nurse's office, and watched and waited.

Three men came out through the Head Teacher's door: the Head himself and two men in dark suits and dark glasses to match. Will had seen those men before, wandering behind him in the street. When the Head and the men shook hands, Will knew for sure that it was time to go.

He felt a tremor of fear as he headed back to his room. There was no way he was going into detention, where other eyes could watch him at their leisure. He needed the time to plan his escape, for escape was how he thought of it now.

The room he shared with Andrew was empty. Andrew would be at orchestra practice, where Will should have been himself except for the detention. Will noted, with a sneer, how common it was for a teacher to stick a detention on a boy when he had after hours activities to attend. Almost as if the teachers themselves liked nothing better than to mess up the arrangements of another teacher. They were a spiteful lot, Will thought.

Quickly he pulled his large sport bag from the wardrobe and cleared it of everything except his running shoes. Then he pushed the sport gear under the bed. He dug out all his underwear and socks and stuffed them in the bag, and his set of casual clothes he had for trips away. His other plain clothes: long track pants, t-shirt and a jacket, he folded and put under his pillow for later. The sport bag had the school crest sewn on the side. Will fished his penknife from his pocket and patiently picked at the stitches. He would wear nothing or take nothing which marked him as belonging to the school, he decided, then he would not be so easily identifiable.

From the drawer by his bed he took his beloved flute in its leather case. It would make heavier carrying, but he was determined not to leave it behind. It was the only thing he had which made him feel an individual in this school of sameness and conformity. It was like a part of himself, really.

Andrew would be back soon so he had to hurry and get done. Into the bag as well went a water bottle which he filled from the tap at the sink, and his torch. He wished he had time to get new batteries but he didn't see how he could manage it now. Then he counted out his cash. There wasn't much, not enough for a fare on the bus all the way to Tempah

Springs and he knew how much it cost because he'd contemplated the trip several times. Then he realized how foolish it would be to take something as obvious as the bus, especially when he was the object of someone's interest. I'll just have to get there by other means, he decided. He felt a thrill of excitement then – he was a boy after all – and in spite of the circumstance this seemed almost an adventure.

The bag went under the bed with everything else and Will settled down with the intention of appearing to study whilst he really went over his plans in his mind. This was the study hour before dinner and the boys were expected to stick at their books in their rooms until the dinner bell rang. I'll go into the kitchen after dinner and see if I can get the cook to give me some extra, Will thought. The cook was okay, a nice motherly woman who didn't mind sneaking extra to the boys who wanted it, although she was not supposed to. Then Will took out his Atlas and found the map of Telaia's south coast area. It wasn't as good as having a road map, but it would have to do. He studied it for a minute then tore out the page and thrust it under his pillow with his clothes.

Andrew returned late, and the atmosphere about him smelled richly of cigarettes. "Smoking practice." Andrew grinned and went to wash the smell away at the sink. He had offered Will cigarettes once and Will had tried them, but he hadn't liked smoking because it made him cough, and he couldn't play the flute if he coughed.

Around midnight, while everyone else slept, Will crept down the back stairs of the dorm and left Hanna College forever. He didn't even look back, having nothing about the place which he wanted to remember.

It took Will an hour to walk out of Hanna Harbor, to a place where the transport trucks left for the north and west. Will hoped that by hanging around the truck stop, he could cadge a ride as far west as possible, so that he could get to Tempah Springs almost as quickly as he would on a bus. Besides, busses did not run in the middle of the night, whereas trucks did.

In half an hour, after several refusals, he found a driver willing to let him ride. But the ride was only good for two and a half hours because the truck was turning off to go north after that. "That'll do, thanks," Will said cheerily, as he accepted. Better two and a half hours in the right direction than nothing at all.

The driver was not too concerned to know about Will. Clearly, he thought Will was older than he was and it didn't matter to him that a young man needed a ride. Will tried to sound as mature as possible

266

because he realized that it might have been a different story had the driver known he was ferrying a runaway schoolboy. For the duration of the journey they talked about general things, like sport and fishing, such as were the driver's interests mostly.

When they reached the turn off point, the driver said, "Keep straight on this road, don't veer off, and you'll be okay. Hope your torch is a good one. Make sure you stay away from the shoulder of the road while it's dark, we get some speeders along here."

Will thanked him again and waved goodbye in a cavalier fashion, but, in truth, he was somewhat daunted by the highway in the dark. His torch was fine at the moment but he wasn't sure how long the batteries would last and he didn't have any spare.

Dawn was at least an hour and a half away and it was a great struggle to negotiate the rough roadside verge. There were no concessions to walkers on these open highways, no footpaths as in the town. And about only half an hour had passed when Will noticed his torch beginning to flicker. At the same time the road came to a fork with a signpost so dim and flaking that he could not read it in his torch's feeble light. "Don't veer off," the driver had said, but how was he to tell at a fork which was the right road? Discouraged and afraid of choosing the wrong direction, he decided to wait for the dawn when he could look at his map in good light. He chose a fallen log in some bush near the sign and sat down.

When it did come, the sun jumped up in a flash, like a person leaping out of bed. Instantly it was bright and already hot. Will took off his jacket and stowed it in his bag. He sipped a little water and unfolded the atlas page. "Left fork," he said, and sighed with relief. He felt very sure that had he chosen in the dark, he would have taken the right. He got up eagerly. Now that he had light, it seemed that the adventure had really begun!

The thrill of the journey was beginning to wear off as Will grew wearier and wearier. For two hours he had walked without anyone stopping to give him a ride and he was very hot and certainly hungry. He had food, if you could call four stale bread rolls and a piece of cold meat pie that, but he didn't want to eat it until he was really desperate, in case there was nowhere to buy more on the way. When he came to a sign indicating a small town to his left he looked at his map. The town was a seaside one and it did not seem far away. The map said that there were no more stops along the highway until the major town of Bredale, so he made the momentous decision to pause in his westward journey and head south temporarily. The journey then became mostly downhill, fine when he was so weary, but the thought of coming back depressed him. But he had no choice, he knew. It was go down this road and find somewhere to rest and eat, or pass out on the main road from hunger and heat exhaustion.

The little town sat at the very bottom of the hill, in an estuary of sand dunes and sea grasses. It had a small shopping center and the houses were clustered mainly about the flat areas, although there were some on the hill. It seemed like it was a town inhabited mostly by old people, or so they appeared to Will. A retirees town, probably, but Will did not know much about that. Between the shops and the sand dunes was a park filled with leafy trees. Will wandered into the park and found a comfortable dip in the sandy grass. He sat in the shade and ate his stale fare, planning to buy something else for later. This is not so bad, he told himself. I'll just rest here for a while.

After he had eaten he lay back in the grass and gazed up at the blue sky through the green leaves. It was very pleasant there and he did not even notice when he closed his eyes. Then, half aware that some time had elapsed, he opened them, and found himself staring into the face of a man who looked down upon him with interest.

Will started. It was a policeman! He fought the urge to leap up and run. Instead he nodded and said, "Good morning," as coolly as he could.

"Morning? It's gone noon. I haven't seen you around here before and this park isn't a hotel," the policeman said.

Will looked at his watch. He had slept for over three hours! "I'm sorry," he said deferentially, and jumped up quickly. "I was so relaxed I just dropped off for a minute. It's rather warm."

"Hmm." The policeman eyed him. "Just passing through?"

Will nodded. "Yes. I'm on my way to Hanna Harbor," he lied. "I came down here to see the sea and get something to eat."

The policeman watched him all the way to the shops, following at a distance then losing interest once Will began back along the road. Will was rather depressed by his stay in the park. He hadn't meant to waste so many hours, however he understood that he must have needed the sleep or it wouldn't have happened. I just hope I can make it to Bredale before dark, he thought.

However, on the highway he got lucky for once and a farmer picked him up in his smelly truck and took him almost all the way to the town. Then he had only to walk the distance of some outer suburbs and he was there, in Bredale, the only other large settlement between Hanna Harbor and Tempah Springs.

Bredale was not a very salubrious place. Being somewhat inland, it had none of the charm of a seaside town and none of the interest of a place like Hanna Harbor. In fact it was more a collection of flat, unprosperous looking suburbs, mixed together with dirty industrial areas and a very dull merchant district. Will searched for ages before he found evidence of the kind of hostel he knew existed in every town along the southern strip. It was the sort of place where hikers stayed. It charged very little for the basics of a bed and a shower, and this one, in particular, was not very well run. It was dirty and, to Will, who was used to far better, seedy and rather nerve wrecking to stay in. He slept badly that night, fully dressed and with his money in his pants pocket. His bag he pushed to the furthest reaches underneath the bed, for he worried mainly about the security of his flute, it being the only worthwhile thing he possessed.

But Bredale proved entirely uneventful, the dullest place on Earth, Will decided. It was also difficult to get a lift from, and after finding a place for a very brief and cheap breakfast, he gave up trying and began the long walk again. He walked for three hours before he had any sort of ride and then it was only for another hour. Part of the reason for this was that he distrusted rides in a car rather than a commercial truck. He had read enough in the past about mad kidnappers or perverts who liked to pick up hikers, but he was also wary of other things, like the possibility of men in dark suits cruising the highways in search of their quarry.

But he saw no sign of men like that and had so few rides that day that he walked until he could walk no more. Even though, by sunset, he guessed that Tempah Springs could not be too far away, he gave in to the overwhelming weariness and finding a haystack in a field, lay down underneath its minimal shelter and slept until the dawn and the dew and the lowing of cattle woke him.

Chapter Seven

Georgi Klider's main dilemma of the morning was to decide what to do about the information he had received the night before. It was a new experience for Klider, to make a decision about anything not to do with his personal life, for he had always been the consummate employee, objective, disassociated and obedient. And chiefly obedient; never before in his working life had he ever considered crossing the rules or say so of his employer.

Yet, in a way, this was a personal thing too. Had not Millicent, his wife, come home on fire with enthusiasm about the healer in Tempah Springs? Had not Jenevra astonished him with her newly found energy and confidence? Had not his daughter, the one beloved thing in his entire life, found healing so far away from home? He could not deny that this was all true. Neither could he deny how happy it made him feel. Why, even Millicent had softened toward him, and that he could hardly credit.

Then to learn that Tempah Springs was were the Crafter girl had gone to, the one who so interested the Baron. Well, that was a coincidence, was it not? Or so he had determined, which was natural enough to do without further logical connection.

The girl had made her way there from Minerva, then had gone further, to a hospice called the Langan Clinic. How strange, how synchronicitous, he thought, that my wife and child should be at the very same place as this girl I am supposed to find!

When a copy of the girl's letter to her brother in Hanna Harbor had appeared on his desk, he read with interest some of the details in it. But chiefly he read the name Marek, and that was the most interesting thing of all. So that is where he is, Klider thought. Marek was not a common name and the association with the girl of the Towers was too coincidental to be dismissed without checking further.

Klider made a time with the Baron's secretary to see him that afternoon; however, the Baron was called away, so Klider went home with his mission only partly complete. As usual, he never took his work home, at least not the secretive part of it. Millicent had made the three of them a wonderful meal, a thing she did not usually relish doing, and after Jenevra had gone to bed the two of them sat in a peaceful silence on the veranda of their spacious home and sipped their coffee.

"I'd like to take Jenevra back to the clinic in a couple of months," Millicent said.

Klider felt a niggling of fear. "Why? Is she getting unwell again? I didn't think she was, she seems so bright and I haven't once heard her cough or wheeze since she came back."

"No, there's nothing wrong," Millicent assured. "It's just that she loved it there so much that I thought the treat would do her good. And I did promise her."

"It must be a really nice spot," Klider remarked, thinking to himself that other people seemed to like it too. "What's the attraction?"

Millicent smiled. "The healer, Matt Best. I think Jenevra is sweet on him. But they're all very nice there actually, they make you feel welcome."

"Jenevra is too young to be thinking like that," Klider said critically.

Millicent laughed. "Of course she is! But Georgi, little girls do have their crushes, you know. And they're all perfectly harmless and perfectly delightful."

"Maybe I should come too. I've an inkling I ought to see such a chap as can turn my little girl's head. I don't think I fancy that idea," Klider retorted, not to be sidelined so easily. For the truth was that he felt a trifle jealous.

"Georgi!" Millicent laughed again. "Don't be so serious. If you met the healer you'd know why she likes him. He's really just a very kind man who knows how to listen and how to help."

And I don't? Klider thought grumpily. "What's he look like, this healer chap, anyway?"

"Oh, he's dark haired and tall and he's rather better looking and younger than you," Millicent said pointedly, with a smirking smile. She may have changed somewhat, but she still enjoyed taking a cruel poke at her husband now and then. "It's funny too, it was something I couldn't help but notice, but he has a ring which is a lot like the Baron's. Every bit as expensive and as beautiful. And you know, he looks a bit like the Baron too; isn't that odd?"

Klider straightened suddenly in his chair. "How old did you say this Matt Best was?"

"I didn't." Millicent got up to take their empty cups inside. "About thirty or so, that's my guess, at least. Do you want any more coffee?"

Klider didn't really want more coffee, but he said yes, just to get rid of his wife for a while. He had to think. So, the Crafter girl had made her

271

way to the hospice, there to take up with someone she called Marek in her letter. That had created suspicion enough in Klider's mind to justify further investigation. And now here he was being given, by his own wife, proof positive and the final piece of the puzzle! The healer, Matt Best wears a ring like the Lord Silene! Only one other person in Telaia had a ring like that, Marek De Ravana!

It was difficult to reconcile the two images. Klider remembered the young, spoilt brother to whom the Baron had appeared so ardently devoted. And then their spectacular falling out. He had never understood what caused the breach between the brothers, but then the likes of Klider were not privy to the personal lives of the great, were they. Neither did he understand why the Baron searched so desperately after all these years. Klider had never detected a sign from the Baron that he had softened his view towards his sibling, however the Baron was far from an open book and never showed his true intentions to anyone. Could it be then that His Lordship secretly missed his brother and wanted him back? That his feelings had reverted to the days before the trouble? Klider shook his head in denial. The Baron with feelings? No, it was not even a possibility.

So here was Georgi Klider with a dilemma such as he had never experienced before. There was a conflict inside him and it had to do with loyalties. On one hand, there was the healer who had done so much good for Jenevra, and on the other hand, there was a wanted man who had to be turned in. It was true that Marek De Ravana was not wanted by the law of the land for any wrong doing, but, as Georgi Klider knew only too well, there was a power which operated beyond such trivial things as the law, and that power was the one he owed his livelihood to.

Klider rang through to Silene's private secretary. "The Baron isn't here. He's had to go to a meeting," the secretary said.

"When will he be back?" Klider asked.

"Not for a couple of days. The meeting's at Stretton ... some bigwigs from overseas. But he asked me to take any messages from you and pass them on, but only if they're important. Do you have anything in particular?"

Klider sighed convulsively. Suddenly it felt to him that he was being given a reprieve. "No, nothing that important," he replied.

When he had left Dan, Marek ran down to the garden to his next patient. Then he had two more to see after that, so he put Faran's brother out of his mind temporarily and concentrated on the tasks in hand. Only when these were done did he take the moment to relax and turn his thoughts to Young Will.

To accomplish what he wished to do he had to have peace and no disturbance, so instead of heading for the cottage, he took the short cut across the road and down to the cliffs. It was a beautiful day, clear and very warm, and because of a land breeze the sea was still and quiet, as the largest mill pond in the world. It suited Marek, that calm, quiet, vast expanse of water; it became like a mirror to his mind, and he cast himself adrift on it, like a slowly moving sailboat.

He did not want what he was about to do to open himself to anything untoward, so he spread his Light around him like a shield, extending it far and wide. He knew, though, that an operation of this kind would not go undetected, however he did not worry about that. Instead, he used his memory of the picture of Young Will which Faran had given Dan and matched the image of that face to the feeling he'd had from the boy so many years before.

For a while he merely drifted within the projected image, until he came at last upon the boy. Will was not all right; there was something physically wrong and he was experiencing fear. "Of what?" Marek asked. "Of the Dragons!" Will cried. "They're coming after me!" "No they won't. Turn your gaze away, they have no power over you," Marek said. He saw where Will hid. It was in something like a crypt, for the walls were old, of yellowed stone and water-stained, as if this was a place which had once been flooded. There was a hole near the center of the floor. It was very dark and appeared deep. Perhaps it was a well. Marek placed the Light around the boy. It was all he could do for now.

Chapter Eight

Will stood up, stretched stiff limbs, then relieved himself in the haystack. He decided that even though it was just light he might as well get moving again, since he had run out of food and had very little water left. There was nothing here for him except the prickly hay, some curious cows and one interested white horse, and he was sure ... well, he hoped, that Tempah Springs was not too far away. Avoiding the cows and horse, he crossed the field to the verge. The road was quiet; nobody else was awake yet. He did not mind that though, for in spite of his hunger he was feeling quite refreshed. He had walked only a little way, perhaps for no more than five minutes, when the road turned a corner under a hill and came out onto a plain. At the end of the plain, which was filled with fields of a high growing plant with purple flowers, and no further than a walk of about an hour, were other, higher hills, and rambling in between and over them, like a many-armed creature glowing golden in the morning light, was a town. Tempah Springs, Will knew. For geography lessons had said that it was an old, old town built from a special white-gold stone, from which the springs flowed hot and energetic and full of the minerals which made aching bodies feel well again.

Will stared at the town. It was incredible to him that he had spent the night in an uncomfortable field when, right around the corner was the very place he wanted!

The sight of Tempah Springs spurred him on, and he was beginning to feel very pleased with himself when a car sped by him on the road, then slowed, stopped and began to back towards him.

Will had not gestured for a lift ... not thinking he needed one. He stopped too, trying to decide what to do, but before he could even get off the verge, the car was upon him. The car door opened and someone beckoned. "Get in," a voice ordered. "We've had quite a time looking for you."

Will did not wait. He turned and ran. Down into the roadside ditch and towards the field, he stumbled and ran. But the man who gave chase was wiry and athletic and unhampered by any bag. He kept up the pace and was closely followed by a second man. The two men pursued Will even when he climbed through the wire fence, and the crop of purple flowers was trampled into a flattened trail as they pushed through it. Will did his best to outrun them but he could not see where he ought to go. The field was huge and open and, but for the flowers, it was empty.

But he ran on, knowing that at least his youth gave him some advantage. Then suddenly there was the sharp sound of a gun. Crack! The noise exploded around his ears and he felt something hit him in the back. He stumbled, conscious of the sting, but aware that it was not a savage wound. Still moving, he tried to discover what had hit him, reaching around with his hand to feel, but all of a sudden his hand would not work and his legs went all rubbery under him.

"Little ferret, now we've got you," said the man who leaned above him. Will could not see the man's eyes because they were behind dark glasses, but he had a face like a horse that was steadily becoming more and more distorted. "No!" Will said fiercely, then the face seemed to dissolve in front of him and only darkness followed.

Will came to in the back of the car. He was rolled in a blanket and he saw that his bag was on the floor beside him. He felt groggy and slightly drunk, as if he had been too long at a party, but he was not in a party mood. There was an ache in his back where the tranquillizer dart had stuck; he guessed it was that sort of thing used to capture wild animals with. And when he tried to move, he seemed to have limbs of lead, and every joint in his body felt stiff and sore. The car, though, was stationary, and Will wondered where he was. He could not see any heads above him and realized he was alone. "Well, I'll just have to get out," he said to himself, when he saw the shadow of a man at the window. The man had his back to him but it was obvious he was standing guard.

Where were they parked? Trying not to reveal that he was awake, Will peered up through the top of the front window. He could just make out roofs of red tile shining against a blue, blue sky. Those roofs he recognized, for not long ago he had been gazing at them from across the plain. Will was amazed. The men had brought him to Tempah Springs!

He shut his eyes quickly then, because the man was opening the car door. "Still out of it, is he?" He heard a voice say. "Looks like it," another voice replied. "Good thing. We don't want him knowing where he is." Then rough hands grabbed him and dragged him from the car. Will let himself relax and his head loll. He didn't want them knowing anything either.

He was put somewhere alone in a darkened room, in a bed which was actually quite comfortable. But he certainly didn't intend to sleep and knew that the men would be checking on him soon. He used the time to focus on everything about him. From outside he could hear street noises, the usual kinds, so he was in a populous area of the town. As his eyes adjusted to the dark, he made out rich furniture and walls covered in some sort of decorative drapery. There was only one small window, and that was heavily shrouded by a thick curtain, no doubt to keep out the daylight and stop Will from waking up too soon.

Carefully and quietly, so that the bed wouldn't creak and give him away, Will sat up. However, immediately, his head swam and he thought he was going to be sick. Not willing to lie down again, he struggled with the feeling until he felt he had mastered it, then he climbed from the high bed and tip- toed to the window. He pulled the drapes aside, only to find that the window was firmly shuttered from outside, and that the window itself was locked down. All he could see of the day was the thin line of light which bled through the shutter cracks. No way out there. Will turned in despair and looked at the closed door. How was he going to get away?

Suddenly the door opened, and seeing Will on his feet, the man who had entered shouted out. Will made a desperate rush at him, not really believing he would escape, but determined to show that he was not just going to accept what they were doing to him. He was stopped by a hard fist which took him on the side of the head, making his ears ring, then another in the stomach, which doubled him over, taking his breath away. The man was about to hit him again when he was forced away by another. It was the horse-faced man, tugging at Will and dragging him back to the bed while he struggled, and saying to the other man, "There's no need for that, he's just a kid."

"A bloody big one," the other man complained. "He's stronger than you think." "Maybe, but that doesn't mean we have to hurt him."

"Patsy won't like it," the other one said sulkily. He glared down at Will who was still fighting the pain of abruptly bruised ribs and short breath. "How's Patsy going to handle a kid like that?"

"Shut up!" the horse-faced man ordered. "I can do something about that." He gazed thoughtfully down at Will, then smiled, showing yellow horse teeth. "Behave yourself, kid, and I promise no one will hurt you again."

Will stared back fiercely, but he was having a battle to hold in tears of frustration and fear. "Why are you doing this?" he said through panting breaths.

The man did not answer. Instead, he took from his pocket a set of

276

handcuffs. "No!" Will yelled, but the two men held him down and Horse Face locked a cuff around Will's wrist and the other around the metal bed rail. Then they simply left the room, pulling the door behind them and plunging Will into near darkness once again.

Will lay in the bed and tried not to cry. Occasionally, he tugged viciously at the handcuffs, but since that did nothing but hurt his wrist he soon gave it up. Through the door, which had not been shut properly, he heard the voices of the two men joined by another voice. It was a feminine sounding voice which whined constantly and from what was said, Will gathered that this place was the third person's house and that the other two were planning to leave.

There was a bit of an argument going on. Patsy, the house's owner, did not like being left with a prisoner, especially when it was a troublesome boy. "I'll give you something to keep him quiet," said the voice of Horse Face. Will wondered what that meant, since Horse Face had seemed determined not to do his prisoner any more physical damage, at least.

Then the house went deathly quiet, as if everybody had gone. Will wondered how long he would be left there on his own. What if he wanted to go to the lavatory? Would he just have to do it in the bed, like a baby? Yet he didn't feel as if that would be a problem for a while. In fact he was feeling curiously dehydrated. His mouth was very dry and his face was hot, and when he moved in the bed, the aching place in his back stabbed with pain and felt very tender. He shifted to ease the pressure and to reach and test for what might be wrong. When, awkwardly, he touched the place, he almost gave a yell. The point in his back where the dart had entered felt swollen and hot, like the sting of a giant bee.

No one bothered with him for nearly an hour. It was lucky he still had his watch with the light in it, he told himself. He looked at it in the feeble gloom; nine in the morning. It was hard to believe that so much had happened in so short a time. He wondered why he did not feel hungry, since he hadn't eaten now for nearly twenty hours. But the fact was that merely the thought of food made him feel nauseous.

The door opened at last and a man came through, switching on the light as he came. It wasn't a very bright light but it dazzled Will for a moment. "Can this be Patsy?" Will wondered when he could see properly. By the voice and the name he had thought the third person was surely a woman, but perhaps it wasn't so. Then Will guessed. Patsy was a derogatory name for a man who was … well, less than masculine. Will wondered if the other men called him Patsy to his face or just behind his back. Either way, it wasn't very nice.

Will stared up at "Patsy". He was clearly a delicate being with the narrow shoulders and the fine bones of a man who had not developed past the slenderness of a boy. He had a thin face and a beaky nose, which he held high, as if he was sniffing at something unpleasant. He was older than the other two, and much more elegantly dressed. In his two expressive, ring-decorated hands he held a tray, upon which was a bowl of soup and a carafe of water and a glass.

The smell of the food revolted Will, yet the water now drew him powerfully, for his mouth was burning dry. Then he remembered Horse Face's words … I'll give you something to keep him quiet … Will shook his head at the offering. "Take it away, I feel sick, I feel sick."

"Patsy's" face blanched. "Oh, no, not in the bed! Not in my bed!" he gasped.

Will listened to the polished, precious tones and heard the horror in them. Here was a man who would not tolerate anything which might mess up his elegant home. "I want to be sick, I want to be sick," Will moaned then, taking the advantage, but it was close to the truth anyway.

A delicate, chilly hand descended on his forehead. "Patsy" gasped again and ran outside. Then he returned with a bucket which he shoved under Will's nose. "Don't make a mess on the bed," he said anxiously, and he ran outside once more. Obviously, the sight of someone throwing up was not something his refined senses could endure.

Will sat up and vomited, on cue. Not difficult under the circumstances. But this was no good, he realized when he felt better. Just throwing up was not going to get him out of the handcuffs or the bed. He called out to "Patsy". "Help, please … I want to go to the lavatory! I have to go to the lavatory, NOW!"

"Ooh!" "Patsy" dashed in the door. "Don't do anything yet, please! Don't mess up my lovely sheets!" He fumbled with the handcuff key. His face was white and terrified. If it had not have been so serious at the time and he did not feel so ill, Will would have laughed.

The lavatory was down the hall. "Patsy" hurried him along and bundled him inside. Will leaned against the wall of the tiny room and thought. It was fortunate that "Patsy" had made the mistake of uncuffing him rather than merely loosing the cuff from the bed rail, but now he had to get the man back near those cuffs, and they would change places. But how was he going to manage it?

He flushed the toilet and staggered out. What surprised him most was that the staggering, whilst exaggerated, was not pretence. He really did feel terrible, though not as terrible as "Patsy" would believe. He almost fell, so that "Patsy" had to support him all the way back to the bedroom. As he did, "Patsy" muttered constantly. "They didn't tell me he was sick. They didn't say that. I wouldn't have agreed if I knew that."

Near to the bed Will pretended to faint. When "Patsy" reached to catch him, Will shoved the man on the bed and used his greater weight to hold him down while he fixed the cuff on the man's wrist. It wasn't easy because "Patsy" struggled and shouted, but finally the cuff clicked. The key was on the bedside table. Will pocketed it. His bag was on a chair nearby. He checked through it to see if everything was there, then he left the wailing man behind.

In the kitchen he drank quickly from the tap, guzzling down water as if it was liquid gold. He filled up his drink bottle, but he decided to leave food alone. For two reasons actually: he didn't know what might be drugged and he had no appetite at all. That was the fever, he told himself. It always left you that way. The last thing he did was to rip the phone from the wall and hide it in a drawer, just in case. He had no idea where he was going to go, or what he could do in his condition. All he wanted at present was to get away from the house, as far away as possible.

Outside, the world was a glare of gold and white which hurt his eyes. The house had its own courtyard, which explained how the men could have gotten Will inside without anyone observing the operation. Will peered cautiously around the metal gate and saw nothing but an empty, hilly street.

Which way? he thought. Who cares, as long as I'm out of here, he decided. He took the downward route, since it was easier on his aching legs and unsteady gait. By now he was beginning to understand just how truly ill he was. He wondered what had caused the illness. Was it the tranquillizer dart?

"How far am I going to get?" he asked himself. Tempah Springs was a hilly town; it was taking a lot out of him already. He knew that to reach the Langan Clinic he'd have to walk somehow because he had no more money for a bus. Faran had said the clinic was a forty minute ride away. To Will, now, forty minutes seemed like forty hours. "It might as well be," he muttered feverishly and aloud. "I'm not going to make it, am I."

He seemed to be moving away from the inhabited area of town, for less and less people appeared in the road. He didn't mind that because a lot of them had stared at him curiously, attracted by his staggering walk. But no one had actually stopped him to ask if he was all right or anything, probably thinking he was just one more hopeless youth on drugs, or something like that. Gradually, as he walked, his eyes were blurring. The buildings at either side of the road had begun to take on fantastic and unusual facades; they were all moving slightly, as if swaying in a wind. He was so hot, his face and back felt to be on fire, and the sun burned his head from above. What he wanted now, most of all, was shade and a safe place to rest.

He came to a place where the street ended in a cul-de-sac and the buildings took on a tumble-down appearance. A yellow stone wall, crumbling and moldy looking, meandered off into a grove of dark, leafy trees. Will followed the wall, as if it was a path to lead him to somewhere cool. Indeed, the trees looked inviting and there was grass to lay on.

In the center of the grove was an old, old ruin of a building. It was so ancient that trees even grew from its walls, and these trees were not saplings but were fully mature specimens. Will wandered this ruin for a while without knowing what he wandered for. By now, he had lost the power of logical thought and decision; he was in a very great fever and had ceased to comprehend where he was or why.

Without conscious motivation, he descended an old worn stair. It wound down into a gloomy passage which was half underground. The passage led off in three different directions. Will did not choose; he was beyond that now. He followed the one to hand and pretty soon he had lost his way in a subterranean cavern of damp yellow stone arches and blank walls.

But it was cool, oh, so cool, in here. Will dropped onto the broken, flagged floor. Now he could rest. There was some moss growing like a cool green cushion over a hump of earth. He lay his head down on it and slept.

How long Will had slept, he did not know. Dazed, he studied his watch, but in his fever he could not make sense of the dial. He turned his wrist this way and that, trying to decide the time. Was it two thirty or three thirty, or eight o"clock or nine? He didn't know. He was conscious, though, of a great thirst, so he fumbled open his bottle and drank. Then he dropped off into unconsciousness again, this time dreaming about men with faces like horses, in cars. The horse faces leered at him and became something more horrible. What were they? In his dream Will cried aloud.

Dragons! Fiery, scaly monsters with breath so hot and foul that they scorched his own face. Terrified, Will tossed around on the stones, crying and moaning. "Turn your gaze away," someone said. "They can't hurt you. They have no power over you." Will obeyed the voice, which seemed to come from inside his own head.

However the Dragons still hung around, trying to get his attention and burning his back with their fire and making it hurt. It was along time that he lay like this, far longer than he knew, and above him, on the streets of Tempah Springs, citizens had passed a whole day and were making for their homes, in readiness for the evening meal.

Chapter Nine

Dan Coel drove into Tempah Springs at five minutes after twelve in the afternoon. His first act was to go and see his friend, Micah, who was still the oldest surviving cop in the town. Micah was one of a rare breed, an honest man in a largely dishonest business; however, Tempah Springs was not exactly a center of organized corruption, so it was not so difficult to be straight there. Dan showed him the boy's picture but Micah had seen nothing out of the ordinary for many days. As far as he knew the boy had never been in Tempah Springs.

Dan's next move was to visit the bus station and every cafe and eating place. In fact, he toured every public place there was, even the spa and the hot springs themselves, just to show the picture and discover if anyone had seen the boy at all. He walked the streets, thrusting the face of Will Crafter at every passer by, but all he came up with was a shake of the head and a disinterested rush onwards. People were not much concerned with a missing boy; they had their own problems.

By late afternoon, Dan decided he was getting nowhere. Time to move on, he thought. But first he had to go back to the police station, to check in with Micah.

"I'm glad you're back," Micah said. "You had a call earlier, from someone named Matt. He's asked you to ring as soon as possible."

"When was this?" Dan asked.

"A few hours back. It sounded to me that he was anxious to get in touch, but he didn't leave any kind of a message, just for you to get back to him."

Dan dialed Nikola's private extension at the Clinic and it was Nikola who answered. "I'll just get him. He and Faran have been sticking by here in case you called."

Marek came on the line. "Dan, don't leave the Springs, I'm sure Will is there. Don't ask me how I know, just believe me. He's hiding somewhere and he's very much scared. It's a place which seems quite old to me ... underground ... like a crypt or something. It's very damp and cool, and I think there's a well. Some sort of ruin is what I see."

"Hold on," Dan said. He turned to Micah. "You know any place like a crypt? Somewhere with a well? Somewhere old and ruined?"

Micah nodded. "The old abbey. It's a total ruin. It used to be the major site of the springs, in the days when religion had control of the town. There is a well. It was the first place where the waters were discovered to be special. People used to come from everywhere just to drink the water, then religion got hold of it and they built an abbey over the top, so they could control all the comings and goings."

'Right," Dan said. He told Marek what Micah said. "I'll go look there, then I'll let you know."

It doesn't seem fair and it doesn't make sense, Dan thought, that people like Matt can just know where someone might be when I have to slog around a whole town, looking in every nook and cranny. Still, not a lot about Matt made sense to Dan, even while, if asked, he would always back him up in anything now.

Following Micah's directions, he drove down the right road until he came upon the relic of the abbey. He parked the car in the cul-de-sac, then entered the little grove where he found the stairs leading down ... into the very earth, or so it seemed. Staring down at the ruined steps, he felt his skin crawl. The place gave him the creeps. But he went down anyway, and at the same junction where Will had stood he paused to consider the ways. Then he heard the sound. It was a sort of muffled sobbing, like the anguished noises of some mourning ghost. The sound sent a shiver up and down his spine, but he pressed on regardless in the direction from which it seemed to come.

Then there, so suddenly and unexpectedly and unmistakably, was the boy. He was huddled on the stones, against a mound of fallen rubble. He did not see Dan at first. He clutched at a grubby sport bag, convulsively, as if it was his lifeline to an ordinary world amidst this other morbid one of shades.

"Will," Dan said softly, so as not to frighten him.

But frighten him he did, for Will was in no state to be anything else but terrified by now. Will stared up at him, then he groaned and scrambled to his feet. "No! No!" he shouted hoarsely and went to run.

Dan caught him as he stumbled. The boy was all in, Dan realized, yet how he fought. They struggled together, Will fighting like a wounded young lion, his eyes wild and his exclamations incoherent. Dan hung on. The boy was strong, stronger even because of fear. "Will ... Will." Dan tried to soothe as he kept his grip on the struggling, thrashing arms.

"I'm a friend, Will. Listen to me. I won't hurt you, I'm a friend!" Dan

283

locked one arm around the boy and with his free hand managed to work the photo of Will from his coat pocket. He thrust it under the boy's grimacing face. "Look. Faran's picture. She gave it to me so I could find you!" He turned it over. "See … what you wrote yourself."

Will paused in his struggle. "Faran," he said weakly, but then he shook his head. He began to try to fight again but he was obviously nearing exhaustion.

Dan held on. "Will, boy, trust me, son, I'm your friend. I'm Faran's friend. I'm here to take you home," he exhorted.

It was the end, the struggle was over for Will now. Even if he wanted to he could not win against this big strong man, his mind told him dimly. Was this man truly a friend, or was it just another trick? He collapsed against Dan's chest and began to cry. He didn't want to cry, he didn't want to sound like a big baby, but there was nothing he could do to stop the tears now. "I want to go home," he whimpered. "I want to go home."

"It's all right, son … it's all right." Dan soothed, holding the boy tenderly against him. Will had gone limp and his bare arms felt like ice to Dan. Yet Dan could also feel the fever and sickness in him. When, finally, he got him to the car he had to haul him bodily into the back seat. "My flute," Will said faintly.

Flute? Dan did not understand, but Will gestured frantically at the bag. Dan tossed it in beside him and Will grabbed it up and clutched it to his chest.

"Forty minutes, and you're home for good," Dan assured him. "Just lie still and rest and I'll have you with your sister in no time at all."

Restlessly Nikola paced the sitting room floor, one turn for the carpet by the door, then behind the couch and over to the window. She tried not to look at Marek or Faran, not to bother them in any way. The two of them seemed almost as one identity to her as they sat together and Marek held his arms around his worrying wife. Nikola had never observed their intimacy at such close hand before and to do so now made her feel like an intruder in her own house. "Oh, why hasn't Dan called?" she fretted under her breath. "It's been over an hour and a half since he and Matt spoke, so why hasn't he let us know what's going on?"

As if in answer, the sound of a car drawing up outside took Nikola back to the window. She peered down onto the drive. It was her car and Dan was already climbing out. She could see no sign of anyone else though. "Dan's here," she said.

They all hurried downstairs. Dan had the car's rear door open by now and he was half inside with his back to them. He was trying to help someone out but he was not getting much cooperation.

Marek ran forward with the women close behind. "Let me help," he said to Dan. The two of them prised Will from the car and he hung between them on rubbery legs. "Faran," he murmured weakly as his sister rushed forward to hug him.

When she threw her arms around him and pressed him close, Will drew back and let out a yelp of pain. "He's hurt!" Faran gasped. She looked into his red, burning eyes. "And sick!"

"He sure is. There's something wrong with his back," Dan said. "I didn't take the time to find out what or why; I just wanted to get him here as quickly as possible."

"Upstairs with him," Nikola ordered. "NOW!"

Once upstairs, they eased Will onto Dan's former bed and Nikola stripped off his shirt. There was a collective gasp as they all saw the angry red swelling and the mark at the center surrounded by a purplish bruise. "Oh, Will!" Faran cried. "What is it?" she said to Nikola.

"Some kind of puncture wound, by the look of it. And it's infected. That's the reason for him being so ill, I'd say, at least at this stage," Nikola said. "Matt, will you help me? We'll need some very hot water and some gauze, and I must fetch my bag."

Nikola took Will's temperature. She held the boy's hot face in her hand and looked into his eyes. It seemed that he was almost in a trance. "Can you pay attention?" she asked him. "Can you tell me how you got this? Tell me what made that hole?"

Will looked at her vaguely for a moment then he nodded slowly. "A man shot me ..." He paused and searched for Faran with his eyes. "Faran, they were watching me at school, for ages, some men. I got scared, so I ran away."

"Oh, Will—" Faran began.

Nikola interrupted. "Don't let's worry about that now. That's not a bullet hole. What did the man shoot you with, Will?"

His eyes wandered back to Nikola's face. He was still trying to work out who she was. "With a dart; you know, those tranquillizing things, like for wild animals. They chased me but they couldn't catch me, so they did that. Then they took me to Tempah Springs in their car."

Marek returned with a bowl of hot water, tape and gauze and some towels. "Okay," Nikola said to Will. "Now I have to fix your back. Lay down on your stomach first, there's a good boy, and we'll see to that wound. Then I have to give you a couple of shots and check out the rest of you. After that you can have a nice rest."

"What men could the boy have been talking about?" Nikola asked Dan later. Marek and Faran were with Will in the other room. Nikola had just made Dan tea and toast. She could see how exhausted he was. After all, it was not very long ago that he was stuck in the same bed, an invalid himself.

"Some very unpleasant ones, that's for sure," Dan said, frowning. "To do that to a boy they'd have to be low types. So that makes me figure government men, the kind Matt's brother employs."

Nikola was horrified. "Do you think it's because of Matt? I mean, were they watching Will because he was connected with him all those years ago? It doesn't seem possible!"

"Maybe," Dan said. "Maybe not. It's hard to tell. What I can't understand though is why they went after him once he ran. What did they want from him?"

The same questions were being asked in Marek's mind, but he did not want to bother either Faran or Will now. Instead, he sat on the edge of the bed with Faran. Will was not sleeping yet and Faran had been bathing his face with cool water and gradually feeding him liquid through a straw, for he needed it badly.

Marek looked down at Will and smiled. "We have to stop meeting like this. Do you remember me?"

Will nodded. "You're the man from the tower. And you made the Dragons go away."

Marek ignored Faran's questioning stare. He said to Will, "No, you did that all by yourself. But I think we ought to make sure they can't come back, because they'd like to and they know your body is ailing at the moment." Marek lay his hands on the boy's forehead and chest, much as he had done seven years before. "There," he said, after a while. "You'll rest much better now."

Will seemed more relaxed after this, yet he was clearly still disturbed and he would not close his eyes until he'd told Faran something. "What's the matter, love?" Faran asked. "You have nothing to worry about any more. You're safe here."

"I know," Will said. "I'm just sorry, that's all. I wanted to get you a birthday present and I'd saved up as much money as I could, but then I went and spent it all, trying to get here."

Faran's twenty second birthday was not long away. She bent and kissed her brother on the cheek. "Willie, love, just having you safe here is the best present in all the world."

The next morning Will was much better and he was able to sit up in bed and relate his experiences coherently and in detail, starting with the school and ending with his escape from the house in Tempah Springs. By turns, all four of his listeners were worried, upset and then angry that such treatment should be handed out to an innocent boy, but, even so, they all laughed when Will told them of "Patsy", describing him with an unexpected burst of humor and mimicking his precious speech. "What an odd character to be involved with those other types," Nikola remarked. "I wonder what hold they have over him?"

"I don't think you would really want to know that, Nik," Dan said, with a wink at Will. He was coming very quickly to like this bright, courageous boy, just the sort of boy he would have wished for as a son, he thought wistfully.

"I've been giving this situation some thought since last evening," Dan remarked, addressing them all, "And I believe that we have to assume this has everything to do with what happened seven years ago at the Towers. There could be no other reason for the interest in Will otherwise. Faran wondered how the school knew where to find her and Will has confirmed that at least one of her letters to him had been opened before he received it, so it's logical to assume that whoever is doing this is interested in both of them, and the only reason could be because of their connection with the Towers."

Dan regarded the sister and brother thoughtfully. "My guess is that they have been keeping track of you for a long while now. When you left Minerva, Faran, they lost sight and so they started to spy on Will more closely to find you again, which they've done now. Last night I couldn't work out why they chased after Will, but now I think I understand. They must have guessed that Will suspected something and decided that they didn't want him running off and letting you know, Faran."

"But I don't understand," Faran said. "How did they find us in Hanna Harbor? We changed our name and everything."

Now, for the first time, Marek decided to speak up. It was not something he wanted to mention but he knew that it would come out eventually as Dan delved deeper into the past. "To adopt Will, your

287

uncle had to register his correct name with the authorities. That's how they found you." Marek did not mention the other thing, however: the suspicion which had bothered him from as long ago as when Faran told him about her father. That in his desire to take the children from their father, the uncle had "Shopped" Will Crafter Senior to Silene's operatives long before, and that perhaps Will Crafter's "accident" was not an accident at all.

Marek turned his eyes away from Faran's and Will's shocked faces. Thinking the rest, he did not want to look them in the eye and have them see that there was more. It was not guilt which made him feel pained at the moment, but sadness. The world was a sorry place, was it not, when selfishness and greed over-ruled all common decency and caring? Had this been other years, long ago, or other lives, he might have been tempted to torture himself with the belief that he might have been indirectly responsible for another man's death, and it was accusations like this which the Dragons loved to have the human ego indulge in. But other people's lives were their own and what befell them was part of their experience. All that counted was intent, and it had never been his intention to hurt another being, nor to cause anyone pain and loss. That was Silene's intent though, and, through their greed, the intent of men like Faran's uncle.

Even so, I did make a mistake seven years ago, Marek thought then. I was wrong to believe that Silene would not bother with the Caretaker of the Towers after I had gone. I thought he'd consider the man a dupe and not worth worrying about, even if he didn't buy his story. I was wrong to think that; I underestimated Silene. I didn't know he would go so far to cover himself in regard to the Towers.

Turned from Faran and Will, he caught Nikola's gaze upon him. She had an expression of curiosity and concern on her face, as if she had perceived the pain which he hid from others and was about to ask him what was wrong. He gave her a slight shake of his head and a frowning look which asked her not to speak, and she seemed to comprehend and, thankfully, to agree.

After a few more days, Will was his old self again. It was decided that he should stay living in the main house, in the set of rooms where he was already, since the cottage where Faran lived with Marek was much too small for three. "Besides, you can't go barging in on a couple of lovebirds like them," Dan said, grinning at him. He showed Will his set of weights and offered to help him keep to his training. Then he regaled him with stories of his days in the police force and the times in Vargas. He told Will of his own adventures with ruffians and they compared notes and scars. Then Will confessed all his wrong doings and scrapes at school, at which Dan only laughed. He showed Dan and Nikola his flute and played them some of his best pieces, and they sat and listened like indulgent parents. All in all, he was rather happy living in the house with them, and with Faran and Marek just nearby, it was like having a real family again, he decided, and a bigger one than ever before, at that.

Faran was surprised by her brother's instant and unquestioned acceptance into Nikola's house. She had realized right away that Dan liked Will a great deal, but Nikola was the real astonishment. For the first time ever she saw a warmth in Nikola which she hadn't known was there. When she spoke of Will, Nikola's face colored with pleasure. "He truly is the loveliest boy, so charming and open and friendly. I'm so glad he didn't let that snobby school ruin him." It was as if Nikola had fallen under some spell cast unconsciously by Will, and that she knew it too and didn't mind one bit. So, you could be wrong about people all the time, Faran told herself, and that means you shouldn't judge them one way or another.

Only one thing bothered Faran about what had happened to Will, and why, but she could not tell anyone but Marek. She did so the very same day that Will told his story of his flight from school. After they had left Will in the care of Nikola and Dan, she and Marek went back to the cottage for breakfast and a shower and a rest, since they had sat up all night to watch over Will. The need to confess was pressing hard at Faran but she waited until Marek was in the shower before doing it, for she thought he might be upset with her when he heard.

She made her way through the steam to him, like an explorer who didn't really want to find what she was supposed to be searching for. She stood barefoot on the tiles and hung by the shower door.

"Marek."

He hadn't heard her come in. "Hey! You're coming to join me?" he asked enthusiastically.

"I have to tell you something."

Marek poked his head from the shower and saw how the seriousness of her face matched the tone of her voice.

"I did something wrong. In my letters to Will I called you Marek, not Matt, as I should have. If they've been read, then."

Marek did not let her finish. He reached out and put his fingers over her lips. "Don't do that to yourself, Sweetheart. Don't go saying 'I should have'. And, in any case, you're forgetting Mrs. Klider. Remember, I told you before, the thing is already underway. Nothing you did or did not do is going to make any difference."

Marek's fingers travelled across Faran's cheek and as he lifted her face to look at him, he smiled. "Trust, Sweet, that's all you need, to know that everything will turn out right."

Faran brushed a soap bubble from her hair. "I know … I know what you're saying, but even so I'm just a little bit afraid," she admitted. " I know I shouldn't be but I can't help it. Look what they did to Will; I'm afraid of what they'll try to do to you."

Chapter Ten

When the message came to him about the Crafter boy, Klider was extremely annoyed. In detail it revealed to him just how incompetent the Hanna Harbor agents really were. "Ham-fisted fools! Half- assed morons!" Klider cursed. Not only had the idiots gone off after the boy on their own, without any authority from above, but they'd bungled even that attempt, and who knew now where Will Crafter was or whom he had talked to?

With the stroke of a pen, Klider had those agents recalled; they wouldn't work in the field for a long time after this. But that did not solve the problem of the boy, and how to keep the Baron from finding out was Klider's real concern.

But, of course, he should have known better, because nothing remained a secret from De Ravana for long. A day later Klider had a call from his boss's office and found himself carpeted, and afraid, in front of a furious man.

"Explain," was all the Baron said, in an even, unemotional tone, but his eyes glittered dangerously.

Klider tried, yet he knew that nothing he said would be good enough. Only one thing could save him, he realized, and that would be to tell the Baron about his brother, then all the rest would mean nothing.

"Sir, I have reason to believe that the boy was running to his sister, and that she knows where your brother is. We have the copy of a letter … from her to the boy … which mentions the name Marek."

The Baron leaned forward in his chair. "Where is the girl?"

"Near Tempah Springs, Sir. At a place called the Langan Clinic. She works there, apparently, and lives there too, with someone she calls Marek."

Klider saw how the Baron's face hardened. His eyes had thinned to a strange, almost impossibly narrow degree, so that he appeared entirely inward looking and concentrated upon a world which Klider could not and did not want to reach. As he observed that strange, almost reptilian expression, Klider was more afraid than he had ever been in his life, and the fear – who or what it was for, he did not know – made him hold his tongue on the rest of what he had been about to say. How this fear caused in him a curious temerity, making him able to withhold information from the Baron at his own peril, he could not understand afterward … but the upshot of this was that Klider neglected to mention the damning proof of the ring, and so the Baron was made to assume that the brother he sought was only "possibly" living at the Langan Clinic, but not "actually".

"So, we may be near," the Baron said, almost under his breath. Yet Klider heard the words and the horrible menace in them. The Baron's eyes fixed themselves upon him then, boring into him like the points of two red hot needles. "I want you to go to this place and take with you only the most reliable of men. Only those whom you have often employed before. And, as always, we will buy their silence with more than cash," he said to Klider.

Such men as the Baron referred to were the sorts of men who could ill afford to cross him in any way. They were all men with "pasts", to whom the Baron had given immunity in exchange for any onerous duty. Continued immunity depended upon unswerving loyalty and absolute silence, and that would be pointed out again, and it did not hurt if the job was to be sweetened with an extra reward. Ostensibly, they did not work for the Baron but were employed and ordered about by Klider himself. Rarely, if ever, did any of them meet with the Baron, even while they guessed where all the blessings flowed from ultimately.

"What do you want us to do, Sir?" Klider asked. He was filled with a sudden resurgence of the fear, which, he recognized this time, was not for himself but for the healer. He wished to himself that he could escape from the mess he was in. What would Millicent say if she ever found out? And Jenevra? It didn't bear thinking about.

"If it is my brother, I want him brought back here to me, of course. No arguments, no delays." "Sir … he may object. How shall we handle it then?"

"Are you stupid, man? Do you ever listen? I said, no arguments and no delays. What that indicates is that you just do it, by whatever means are necessary. All I require of you is that you succeed. If he objects or refuses, then you bring him here by warrant and by force. I will issue you with the appropriate papers, however I do not expect any public notice over this, so you will have to do it with the utmost discretion."

"That means a "Snatch" then, Sir, if necessary," Klider said, feeling suddenly sick to his stomach. The Baron dipped his head in a reply which was also a dismissal.

"Crudely expressed, but essentially correct … yes."

"I think I'll come with you this morning." Faran said to Marek. "I want to go to see Will and invite him to lunch with us."

"That'll be nice." Marek buttoned his shirt and tucked it in. "It's great to see how well he's getting on with Nikola and Dan. They don't seem to mind having him there, do they."

"I believe they like it. Nikola was talking to me about Will finishing his studies. I said that Will wouldn't want to go away to any school, but Nikola said she didn't mean that … that Will could finish school by correspondence so he could stay with them there." Faran laughed. "I listen to Nikola and she sounds to me just like a regular parent. Do you think she is feeling that way?"

Marek nodded. "Could be that she's enjoying the feeling too," he said. "That lady has spent a whole lot of years devoting herself to helping other people, but she's always managed to keep her "Self" out of the picture. She's never given much time to her own feelings and now she's finding out what a joy real feeling can be. What with Dan and now Will, I'd say that she's making up for lost time."

After breakfast they walked to the hospice, Marek to his first patient and Faran to the house to see Will. But when Faran got there she found Will ready to race away. He was going with Dan and Bill Langan down to the mooring to see the Rhona and he was excited. "Nikola said I could take a trip on the boat sometime!" he told Faran eagerly. "But we're going to have lunch on the boat today."

I suppose lunch at my house can hardly compete with that, Faran thought wryly, so she invited him to dinner instead, then watched him run off to the car with Dan and the Doctor. She went downstairs and into the kitchen, for she wanted to get some supplies from the hospice store.

Getting everything together took some time and she had to load the things into a box, then found that the box was too heavy to carry so she had to spread the load over two instead. I'll wait for Marek to finish his first patient, she decided. Then he can help me take this back before his next one is due.

Faran knew that, this morning, Marek was going to come to the main house to see one of Nikola's people, an old lady whom Nikola felt was needing more of comfort than anything else, and Marek was rather good at providing that.

Faran wandered towards the reception hall and met Nikola going the same way. "Did you catch Will before he went out?" Nikola asked.

"I did. And I invited him to dinner tonight," Faran answered.

At reception Nikola handed in some forms to Marie and collected three others. "We're very busy this morning," she said. "We—" The sound of cars crunched on the gravel outside, and through the wide open door she and Faran and Marie saw two cars with darkened windows pull up in front. The cars seemed almost like hearses, they were so long and black and official looking.

"What on earth?" said Nikola, as seven men, in suits as dark and official as the cars, got out. Two of the men waited by the cars, two placed themselves at the bottom of the steps outside and three came up the steps and into the house. Faran moved to Nikola's side. "Nik ... I don't like the look of this," she whispered nervously.

One of the men was a very small, twisted looking creature, yet he was the one in charge. The two other men stationed themselves like identical bookends in a position three paces behind him. He came forward to the desk and stared at the women, as if they were the intruders into his world and not the other way around.

"Direct me to the owner of this establishment," he ordered curtly.

Nikola glowered at him and her words were just as terse. "You're looking at her. Who are you and what do you want here?"

The little man did not reply immediately. Instead he stared at Faran and smiled, a not very reassuring smile to the minds of the women present.

"Well, Miss Crafter, at last we meet," he said.

Oh God, I wish Dan was here, Nikola thought then, and she moved herself in between Faran and the man, as if by this she could protect the girl somehow. "I asked who you were and what you want," she demanded fiercely.

Again, the little man all but ignored her question, saying to her but keeping his eyes on Faran as he did, "Miss Crafter knows, doesn't she. And I figure she knows who it is I want."

"See here—" Nikola began.

"Be quiet!" the little man ordered, and as if to add force or even a threat to his words the other two men spread themselves wider in the room. Behind the reception desk Marie made a frightened noise as one of the men approached her side.

"Miss Crafter, you will tell me now if you know the man called Marek

294

De Ravana," said the man in charge. He held up a wad of folded paper and waved it in the air. "I have here a warrant for his arrest, and we suspect he is here. You will be so kind as to direct me to him, please."

Marie squawked and Nikola bristled; but Faran stood speechless, whether in fear or by intent, no one else could have known but she.

To Georgi Klider, the Crafter girl came as a surprise. Of course he had known from his files what to look for, as the photo they had of her was only from the year before. It was a blown up thing, taken with a telephoto, yet it was clear enough, and it showed a pretty girl of rather delicate appearance with very beautiful hair. Then, unknowingly, Millicent had added some personality to the picture, so that Klider believed he had captured the girl in his mind, at least. But now to see her, to stand in her aura, so to speak, he was dumbfounded by the effect her presence had on him. He could not explain it to himself when he felt the overwhelming wave of sorrow and regret as he spoke the harsh official words – they were not the words he wished to say – but this sudden complication of feelings with duty made the words come out in an even more insinuating way than he intended. The more he wavered inside himself, the more frightened he was becoming, and the harder his outside manner. It was something he was having great difficulty dealing with and he did not know what he was going to do. He felt a great sickness rising up in his belly, but because of the men with him he had to remain hard and unaffected, or to appear that way, at least.

"Miss Crafter, I am speaking to you," he said mercilessly, although his bent heart quailed. "Leave her alone!"

The voice, strident and angry in tone, came from behind, and Klider turned to see the very one he wanted standing at the open door with the Baron's men crowding the space behind. The men had been ordered by Klider not to touch their prey unless absolutely necessary. He had explained to them the Baron's desire to have the brother brought back to Brentore without any publicity or any trouble, and had added the codicil himself that not a hair of the prisoner's head should be hurt.

"Marek De Ravana?" Klider said, as if he was really asking and not stating the obvious.

"No, he's not!" Nikola exclaimed, darting towards Klider suddenly. "You've got the wrong man!

He's Matt Best, and we can prove it. And who are you, anyway?"

Klider recoiled from her fire, but he felt the wavering grow more urgent. "Ma"am, you had better be quiet!" he barked, growing increasingly irritated. He directed his gaze at Marek. "Matt Best, is it? Well, I want to see some I.D. Everything you have."

"I don't have that kind of thing on me, I'll have to get it," Marek said.

'Right, so you shall," Klider said. He motioned to three of the men outside. "You, you and you, accompany Mister Best, and I will go too. The rest of you will stay here and keep an eye on the ladies, to make sure they don't do anything foolish."

Faran started forward. "I want to come, please!"

Klider glanced for a moment into the living light of her eyes. He saw in them the desperate love for the man at the door and remembered Jenevra. He shook his head. "No. You stay here," he said, with the harshness all gone from his heart and voice together.

Marek said, simply, "This way," and the four men followed him.

Marek walked quickly ahead, conscious of the men at his back and more acutely conscious of Klider slithering along behind. And conscious, too, of how confused he was at the moment. What was Klider up to? he wondered. He knew Klider and Klider knew him, yet here was the man playing out some sort of game in which he wanted to see papers of I.D.? It didn't make sense. Klider needed no I.D. to mark his quarry, for how many times had they met in the past? A dozen times, maybe more, though not to speak beyond a few civilities. And then there was the business of the tower, of which Klider was in charge. That is why Silene sent Klider in particular, Marek decided. Silene trusts him, and he knows without a doubt who I am.

At the cottage Klider ordered all the men to stay on watch outside while he went indoors with Marek. Anxious to find out what was really occurring, Marek ran upstairs to fetch his bogus papers. He was glad that the books of Ozira were still temporarily in Bill Langan's hands and that Bill had been slow in returning them. If the Baron's men decided to search the cottage, they would not uncover anything worth finding there.

Marek came back downstairs to see Klider slumped into a chair, looking like a weary, defeated man. Yet when Klider glanced up at him, his eyes were over bright in his gnomish face. He scanned the papers, seemingly without much interest, and sighed. He said, "I have decided. I want you to come outside while I show these papers to the others. I'm going to tell them you are not Marek De Ravana, and that's how I shall report to the Baron. I will say that whilst the man called Matt Best bears a similarity to Marek De Ravana, he is not the one we seek." Klider's over bright eyes rested on Marek's left hand. "I'd get rid of that damned ring, if I were you. I can't think why you didn't do it years ago."

Marek stared at him in wonder. "I can't get it off, that's why."

"Then turn it round on your finger, hide the setting and the stone, for now at least. I don't want my men seeing any more than they have already."

Marek did as Klider ordered, twisting the tight ring until it showed only as a band. "Why?" he asked, but he was not speaking of the ring.

On Klider's face was a resigned half smile. "One word is all I'll give you. One word: Jenevra."

They left the house and Klider told the men in not uncertain terms that they had followed a false trail. The men shared a glance between them, and Marek saw for himself the questions on their faces. But since they were actually in Klider's employ and not directly in the Baron's, they bowed to his words, accepting. Then they simply left, whilst Marek stood and watched them go, and uncertain about what would happen next. Would Silene believe Klider? Marek could not help but doubt it. And, even if he did, what would that mean? Just that the confrontation was to be postponed, nothing more.

This waiting is hell, thought Nikola. With Faran so unnaturally silent and still and Marie practically whimpering in a corner, and the men eyeing the three of them with tasteless, insulting gazes, she felt angry and frightened all at the same time. If only Dan was here, he'd know what to do, she told herself, then immediately was glad that he was not, in case he caused an upset and got himself hurt in the process.

But what of Matt? Or Marek, as she had begun to think of him again? What would they do to him? Other people had started to come, in the normal course of their day, from the halls to reception and

Nikola had to warn them off, telling them to go elsewhere for a while without saying why. Nurses with patients, staring at Nikola's agitated face with puzzled, curious expressions. Nikola wondered what rumors must be flying around the hospice even now as everyone noticed the strange parked cars and the even stranger men outside.

Then suddenly the waiting was over. The little man appeared with the three others and came indoors. He ordered the other men to leave the lobby and said, to Faran mainly. "Mr. Best is not the one we want. Good day." Then he turned and hobbled away.

"What!" Nikola swung around and stared at Faran. Faran looked stunned but she didn't say a word.

Instead she followed the men out the door and stood at the top of the steps with her hands pressed over her mouth, and watched until the cars had left the hospice grounds. She seemed not to notice that Nikola had joined her.

"But where is Matt?" Nikola said, reverting to old habits now that the tension was nearly over. "There he is!"

Faran darted away, for she could see Marek coming along the far path at a good pace. As she ran she found herself starting to cry, tears which would not subside until she had him safely in her arms again. When she reached him she practically threw herself upon him.

They held on to each other, as if letting go was the real crime of the day. "What happened?" Faran asked when she was capable of speech.

"That was Klider."

"Klider! So he really knows?"

"Yes. But he let me off, for one reason only."

Faran nodded, not having to guess, as she understood. "Jenevra."

Chapter Eleven

The trip back to Brentore, first by land then, more speedily, by air, felt for Georgi Klider much longer than the prescribed four hours. It was as if he lived a lifetime in that four hours, as the very feeling of being alive became for him more intense and realized than at any other time in his forty two years. A huge leap in consciousness seemed to have occurred inside him, or was it that a key had somehow fallen into his hands and that, taking it up, he was now looking for the door it opened? Like a man wandering a maze and finding a signpost which pointed vaguely towards the way out, he was still searching, still following a dimly felt direction, but not as yet seeing the parting in the wall.

He was about to lie to the Baron De Ravana, and that fact was, in itself, momentous. To play such a game with Silene De Ravana meant to dance with the devil himself, Klider knew. It was a dance of death.

At Brentore airport Klider farewelled the men with a warning. They were to keep absolute silence about the day's proceedings, or else. As the Baron always said, it did not do to let men forget either their obligations or the punishment due if they did not honor them. In this case Klider was only too happy to parrot the Baron and conform, for he did not want the chance of a wayward word getting back to his employer. Some of the men had shown by their faces that they thought Klider had made an error of judgement in not detaining the man at the hospice.

At three in the afternoon, the Baron was usually in his office, unless he had a meeting somewhere. Klider made his way directly there. He was somewhat surprised by the calmness of his state of mind, considering what he was about to do. The thought of a lie was not new to him – after all, he lived in a world of lies – but the one he was about to lie to was almost as a god to him. A wrathful, terrifying god, if his subjects failed to please, it was true. An unkind, loveless god, full of sarcasm and cruel wit. A demon-god, perhaps, whom Klider did not love, but hated. But a god, nevertheless.

"Well?"

The Baron seemed almost to be waiting for him.
"I'm sorry, Sir, but although the healer, Matt Best, bears a striking

similarity to the one you seek, he is not that one. I found all his papers in order, and since you sent me specifically to identify him, I can say that he is not Marek De Ravana," Klider said, with as straight a gaze at the Baron as he was capable of making.

The Baron slid back in his chair, rested his elbows on the arms and his chin on his elegant, interlaced fingers. Then pointing his two forefingers in the shape of a steeple, he began to tap them meditatively against pursed lips, over and over, while he stared at Klider.

The way he did this was more than Klider could bear, yet bear it he had to. The silent tapping, the cold, penetrating stare, the obviousness of inward calculation and the prescience it suggested, was laid before Klider in a way that made him certain that the Baron did it on purpose, to intimidate him and, perhaps, to expose and break the lie. The Baron knows I'm not telling the truth, Klider thought desperately. He knows.

Abruptly the tapping ceased but the Baron did not move or shift position. "Healer, you say? Is this what Best does?"

Klider tried to swallow his fear, but it remained at his throat, like a coil of knotted rope. A hangman's knot, maybe. A former perception, experienced at an earlier interview with the Baron, became suddenly a sure understanding. The Baron had nothing but evil intent towards his brother. Perhaps he even wanted to kill him. Klider found that the knot in his throat had loosened. "Yes, Sir," he managed to answer.

"You also said that the Crafter girl called someone at the hospice Marek."

"Yes, Sir. The man she lives with. But that is another man, Sir. The name is just a coincidence." Klider shivered. On fearful impulse he had just told the most preposterous lie of all, one which could easily be uncovered. What the hell am I going to do now? he wondered.

The Baron moved his hands from his chin to the desk, where, worryingly for Klider, he began to tap his fingers once again. Then, suddenly, he sat forward. "All right, you can go now," he said dismissively.

Klider fled, relieved to be freed from that relentless gaze. But even as he fled, the thoughts spun round and round in his head. Too soon ... too soon ... he released me too soon. He had another fearful impulse now, and that was to run. Run. Run. Run as far away, and as quickly as possible.

Where would he go? Klider considered his options. There weren't many and one of them was not to go home. Home would be the first place they would come for him, he realized. He thought weakly of Jenevra and was tempted to ignore good sense and go home anyway, then he thought again. He must not bring his child into this, not ever. Even if that meant simply waiting for the blow to fall, at least he could let it fall far away from her.

Taking the back stairs of the offices, Klider left the building. He also left his car behind, for he wanted no one following him so soon in the game. Instead, he caught a bus and mingled in with the common herd. He did not know how long it would be before the Baron made his decision.

He had to make a decision of his own, he thought. Was he to run like a criminal, forced to hide for the rest of his life from the Baron? A lie wouldn't seem much of a reason to be persistently pursued, but for the Baron it was enough, and when he wanted something badly enough the Baron never gave up.

Getting off the bus somewhere downtown, Klider found himself walking aimlessly at first; then, as an idea formed in his mind, he made his way to a district where he knew he could buy anything with no questions asked. What he wanted was a weapon of some sort. For protection. He had a great deal of cash on him, always carrying a slush fund on days like today, in case he had to pay off anyone or dole out bribes to get a job done right. He found what he sought for in a moth-eaten pawn shop – he wasn't so stupid that he would go to a gun store where every purchase was supposed to be registered. Besides, a gun wasn't what he chose to use, for the chief reason that he had never learned to handle firearms and had rather a horror of them.

Outside the pawn shop Klider examined his purchase. It was a hunting knife, of the long and very sharp variety, with an ornamental handle of silver and bone. The pawnbroker had kept it whetted and in a locked glass case along with diamond rings and watches and a set of crystal dishes, as if on prime display and ready for an eager customer. The knife was fearful enough if one raised it in self defense, but self defense was not the only thing on Klider's mind any more. Over and above everything else he thought about was an image of his wife and child. Millicent and Jenevra. What would happen to them if he became a fugitive from the Baron's anger? How could he protect them from the spiteful wrath of a man like that?

And he thought also of the healer, the brother. That young man whom he had once taken pleasure in throwing into a tower, what did he do now but give help and healing to others? Klider shook his head. How could he let such a man fall into the hands of evil?

While Klider took the advice of his own fear and was already on the run, Silene De Ravana considered his own next move. Of course he had not really believed the lies just told to him so blatantly, but what he couldn't figure was why they had been told. Klider had never been one to lie and had always been loyal, one of the very few whom Silene had seen fit to trust and who had always done his duty to the letter. Failing to understand the why of it, Silene acted on the fact. He would have Klider arrested and detained, perhaps even before he had left the office.

But Klider was not in his office, although his car was still in the underground garage. It took some time after that for Silene to have the building searched and to comprehend then that the little man had absconded. A check at the man's home proved that he had not yet been there, so Silene had a watch posted. His chief suspicion was that Klider had bolted in the fear of being found out; for Silene knew that his employees were very much afraid of his wrath.

Silene thought about Marek then. Klider's unconscious slip in using the word "healer" had been the revelation to Silene that Matt Best was truly his brother. Of course, Klider could not know of the brothers' discourse of years ago, when Marek had expressed his wish to heal the ills of mankind.

How Silene had scoffed at that, yet Marek had persisted in the dream. "But some dreams must come to an end, brother dear," Silene whispered under his breath. "You will not escape me this time."

Would Marek run? Silene wondered. Only if Klider alerted him, he decided. Perhaps he had done a deal with the little dwarf man. Was it possible? Something in that did not sound right. But what other explanation was there?

In case Klider had already contacted his brother and warned him, Silene got an agent from Tempah Springs to make speedy and discreet enquiries about the presence of Matt Best at the clinic. By five thirty in the evening, the agent called him back, saying that she had masqueraded as an intending patient and that she'd made an appointment for the afternoon of the next day. The receptionist had been quite open, she asserted, even pointing out Best to her in the garden, so it was clear that he had not run or was not intending to.

To make sure that Klider would be unable to contact Marek easily or quickly in the future, Silene sent a directive to the phone company. Close down the lines of communication to the Langan Clinic until otherwise ordered. After that he had the search for Georgi Klider stepped up to a cracking pace. "We'll get you, Klider, you little turd," he said to himself with a bitter smile. And then, since he could do nothing more that night, he called up his chauffeur, put on his coat, and went home.

Silene De Ravana had three homes in the environs of Brentore. One was a spacious apartment not far from government center, which he used when he was very busy. The second was a retreat on the lake, an establishment of modernity as big as a country club, where he stayed on weekends and entertained. And the third, but certainly not the least of them, was a city mansion of great stone arches and columns and brooding cloisters all surrounded by a high stone wall, with metal work gates fronting onto the avenue. This last was the ancestral palace of the De Ravanas and it was Silene's birthright as Baron and his sole property, to the exclusion of the rest of the greedy, grasping family who resented him fiercely and would have stolen it back if only they could. Here, he had been born and had grown into manhood along with the noisy, petulant brood of females who were his sisters.

Here, he had, at fifteen, discovered a newly born rival in the only other living son, Marek, and two years later had to watch and listen as his father, the current Baron De Ravana, enthused about the newcomer, speaking also as if it was this child, instead of Silene, who ought to bear the title of His Lordship. Here, then, at this time had Silene first conceived the notion of secret murder, which later on, some ten years later in fact, he had successfully carried out.

Thus had the old Baron died and Silene had taken his place at twenty seven.

The boy, the child Marek, had not been the direct subject of any displeasure for Silene, however.

Once he was Baron, Silene found it in himself to be generous. And the truth was that he coveted a special relationship with his young, child brother. All the better to keep an eye on such a one, he had decided. And "Chameleon Eyes", as the old father had named the boy, was a coup worth hanging onto.

To mold the child into a likeness of the man he most admired – himself. That was Silene's aim. And he had almost done it. A puppet child, a living replica worthy of succession. Well, he had nearly got there, hadn't he?

How it had cut him later, when Marek turned away. Cut him deeper than he was prepared to admit at the time. He had thought about it since and had faced the reason almost without flinching. Almost. The truth was he had really loved that boy, but love was an impulse which you had to filter through other things. Pure and straight on, love was an impossible force to manage and a very great distraction from other important aims. Silene had, on occasion, offered his own peculiar brand of love to those who attracted him: youths he thought beautiful, whom, he hoped, would admire him in return; but nothing had ever come of it. Affection, he could not give it, he did not know how. Rather, his moments of love afflicted him with a sort of painful, burning intensity inside, which he was unable to translate into outward expression, and which, consequently, he was forced to deny. Marek had been the only constant of real feeling in his life, not as an object of any unnatural affection, he told himself, but the intensity was there. To understand the intensity, and to deal with it, he had colored it with the desire to order and control in the most intimate of ways. That his brother should pattern him in his inmost self; that Marek's very psyche should belong only to Silene.

Although he had been staying in his apartment for the last few nights, Silene decided that he would rather spend this night in the ancestral home. He directed his chauffeur to take him there, not noticing that behind his car there followed another persistent vehicle which overtook when his chauffeur did and turned off at every same corner.

Klider had fixed on the idea of hiring a cheap car at the same time which he had formed his plan in full. The car he chose was of the rent-a-bomb type, from a dealer who looked at the wad of bank notes more carefully and eagerly than at Klider's licence to drive. He drove it to a lane way opposite the office and waited until he saw the Baron's chauffeur arrive. Then he simply followed. He had thought that the Baron would go to his apartment, and the thought of that had daunted him somewhat. Guarded by a militant Concierge, and with security cameras everywhere, a modern apartment building was much too difficult to get into. But an old, rambling palace, even one with guards, that was another matter.

Klider had been to the palace a few times before, and it was enough for him to know that the big front gates were not the best or only way in.

At the side, which abutted onto lesser streets, was a tradesman's entrance, and Klider, being classed on the same lowly level by the obsequious servants, had been obliged to use it previously. The man at the door there knew him well enough to let him in, no questions asked, for that was how the Baron had Klider's comings and goings arranged. Klider's only hope this time was that the Baron was not wary enough to realize just what might occur, and that he would not have warned his servants of a possibly unwelcome intrusion.

At the gate Klider boldly rang the rusty bell. The gateman opened it and with a nod, let him in. "No need to announce me, I'm expected," Klider said with a secretive, conspiratorial gesture of his head, and the gateman assented. Nothing out of the ordinary, as far as he was concerned. It was a tremendous punt, Klider thought, but a risk worth taking. For what else was there but this? What else for Georgi Klider but to take the ultimate way out?

He had never before found the way to the Baron's private rooms, although he knew they were on the second floor. But it was not too hard to vanish into the huge, rambling halls, there to explore in a largely unpopulated wasteland of luxury, to flit between the vile old furniture and cavernous folds of drapery, a small, twisted shadow amongst the darkened shadows of the centuries.

At nine thirty, after a long, slow dinner alone, Silene retired early to his private chamber. It was a room in which he always disdained the appurtenances of modern life. Where he might have chosen to switch on an electric light, he did not, and preferred instead the more mellow glow of candles or an illuminated lantern with the scent of fossil fuel and incense, reminding him of the mystic darkness of ritual and ceremony. So much of Silene remained essentially an ancient spirit that, sometimes, the harshness of the modern world was to him a discordant note, and a thing to be discarded for older, more primal experiences. For this reason he liked better the marmoreal antiquity of the family home, especially at times like this, when he felt the dark, black-blood force of the Dragons moving in him.

Amidst a world of overworked brocade and heavy velvet, Silene could experience outwardly the same sort of rich unctuousness as his soul inhabited continually. His bed was draped in the old fashion, curtained and coroneted like an emperor's tent. The carpeting on the floor was soft and nearly ankle height in richness. Cherubs sported in the shadows of the ceiling and the walls were littered with mythological lovers and the battles of the mighty, rimmed and framed with gold.

But for the ill lit passion of the walls, stillness filled this room. A silent quality due more in fact to the dampening power of so many layers of luxury than any sort of peace, spiritual or otherwise. It was this dampening effect and the general, overall darkness which allowed Klider to move in undetected while the Baron undressed slowly.

Only at the very last minute, as Silene glanced sideways at his own pale nakedness in a long mirror, did he comprehend that he was not alone. Then it was over in a flash as Klider, who, although only a little man, had just the right height and enough power in his stunted body to place the hunting knife where it would do the most damage, lunged. The knife embedded itself deep in Silene's flesh, under ribs and thrusting up to tickle his heart, and Klider left it there, like one more silvery decoration in this over decorated room.

The Baron took slightly more than a few seconds to die, but Klider did not wait to see the final breath. He had done his bit for freedom, he decided, and now it was time to leave. He could not head for home, he knew, but that didn't matter. He had come to his own end anyway, and there was nowhere else to go.

Chapter Twelve

Faran had invited Will to dinner, however, after such a stressful morning, she decided to have the two Langans and Dan there also. It gave her something to, to have to plan a larger, more impressive meal for six, and she needed the distraction. Marek was okay, he had work to keep him occupied, but she had nothing but worry on her mind.

Faran didn't want to worry, but as Marek had pointed out, the little man, Klider, might not be able to convince Silene, and even if he did so, that would not stop the search. So they were not clear and free, not yet.

Will, the Langans and Dan arrived for dinner at seven thirty, and it was all over by nine. But they stayed on, no doubt anxious enough themselves and keen to discuss the situation and to feel a solidarity of spirit. However, since there was really little to determine and Nikola would not hear of anything to do with Marek's leaving the hospice because of the trouble his presence had caused, the intense talk died early and they were left with more personable matters, such as Will's future. He didn't know what he wanted to do as yet, he stated. What he did want, though, was to keep on playing the flute and be having a good time. There was laughter at that and the tension relieved somewhat.

Marek listened with quiet pleasure to the more relaxed babble around him. He didn't feel much like talking himself, but that was okay, for no one seemed either to notice or to think that it mattered. His pleasure extended to watching Will and Faran together. Their fondness for each other was sweet to observe and endearing to see. Sister and brother: theirs was the kind of family feeling he would have liked in his own young life.

Marek found himself smiling abstractly. Then, suddenly, without warning, he could scarcely breathe. "Excuse me a moment," he gasped, and bolted for the front door. He flung it open and plunged into the darkness of the garden.

What Marek wanted most was air, and release from the sudden pain which felt like a heart wound.

What he had heard, which so dimmed all the other sounds around him, was a cry. A cry that he had never expected to hear but to which he felt an instant response.

Of course, seeing Marek come over strangely and dash so suddenly outside, the others immediately ran after him. When they found him in the shadows under the trees he was bent over double with his hands cupped over his nose and mouth, trying to forestall the threat of hyperventilation. But to the others it did not look like that, especially by the poor light in the garden, and they thought that he was having some kind of attack.

He tried to reassure them, but there were too many opinionated doctors in such a small crowd and they hustled him inside. They sat him on the couch and gathered speculatively around him, which was exactly what he didn't want at the moment.

"Are you ill? Are you in trouble?"

Bill Langan and Nikola both wanted to examine him. Marek waved them away as politely as he could. "No." He could see Faran struggling to hold her peace, but her face told him she was losing the battle. "I'm okay," Marek said. "I'm not the one in trouble. It's my brother who is in trouble."

His words, the statement of fact coming from his lips so naturally and so full of feeling, stunned Marek, but from the others came only a surprised, rather shocked silence. Marek could feel that there were tears in his eyes, too, although he wasn't sure why they were there. The silence had become awkward, as it is when people don't know what to say or how to react. "Well, if you really are okay, I think we had better be going home," Bill Langan said tactfully.

Marek thanked him with a glance. "All I want to do now is go to bed. It's been a long day."

Faran followed Marek upstairs. She had been too stunned herself to say anything so far. To hear him speak the word "brother" in that way, when she knew for a fact that he hadn't called Silene that for years and years, this troubled and puzzled her beyond her present measure of understanding. Not until they were both in bed did she venture to question him, not sure if he wanted questions, even from her.

But Marek had never excluded her from his thoughts or feelings and he did not do it now. He stretched back against the pillows and stared at the softly lit ceiling, as if trying to find explanations in the mellow shadows. "Something has happened to Silene," he said. "I don't know what, but what I do know is that he appealed to me, and that something in me answered the appeal."

"Appealed to you for what?" Faran asked.

Marek turned his face towards her and she saw upon his half lit features an expression of wonder mingled with pain. "For help. All he wanted of me was help."

"I don't know what that could mean," Faran said. She rose on one elbow and gently caressed his cheek and hair. She felt that he needed some kind of comfort, but she had no idea what it was for.

"I don't know either, not yet," Marek said. "But I feel so awfully tired all of a sudden." "So you ought to sleep, not talk." Faran bent and kissed him then she put out the light.

Whether it was five minutes or an hour, or several hours after he had gone to sleep, Marek did not know, but he woke suddenly, with a start, fully alert. Silene was there. Silene was in the room with him, now, and the room was lit with pale moonlight.

Marek sat up.

Silene hovered at the end of the bed. He was rather older than Marek remembered, seeming as worn and tired as an elderly man, although he was only forty seven. The way he had of looking at Marek, though, that had not changed. There was a sort of half smile on his lips and a shadow of irony in his eyes, eyes which darkened now as they looked at Marek then abruptly turned to fire.

"Well, Brother, so this is it," Silene said.

"What is … it?" Marek asked, not understanding.

Silene appeared surprised. "Do you not know? I would have thought you did, a magician such as yourself. Did I not say once that you would become a greater magician than I?"

"I rejected sorcery, you know that," Marek replied.

"And yet you work your magic all the same," Silene said with even more irony in his smile. He moved closer to Marek's side of the bed. "OZIRA," he intoned. "Ozira, you have defeated me. The Ravana which I am bows to all that Ozira is, and my days in the great world are surely at an end. Can we not now be true brothers?"

Marek felt himself breaking into a cold sweat. Was this a trick of Silene's? "The Ravana?"

Silene bent his head in assent; but with what kind of attitude, Marek could not tell. "As you are Ozira, I have always been Ravana. Our father was never That. Look closely into my eyes, Ozira, and see that mirror of yourself which you say you have rejected."

The truth was beginning to dawn in Marek's mind. His body shivered with the realization. "But that mirror is false," he said. "An illusion."

"As the fire in my eyes became false once you answered my appeal," Silene affirmed. His eyes had softened, turned to light instead of darkness or fire. He moved away again and seemed to be fading into the line of moonlight which streamed in through the bedroom window. "Goodbye, Brother," he said, and the now broadened smile of irony turned into a laugh which faded with him.

Marek extended his left hand and on his finger the ring stone flashed like the moonlight. Silene turned once more and laughed again, repeating the word "Brother" like an answering flash in the dark.

"Brother," Marek said, in return.

Even in her sleep, Faran knew that something odd had occurred. She woke and rolled over in the bed and saw Marek sitting up, staring at nothing. She touched his hand but he did not move. Faran started. Marek's hand was icy cold. She ran her fingers the length of his arm and shoulder and found the same. Worried now, she kneeled up beside him and touched his brow. Sweat beaded his forehead and face and had run down his neck and chest. But still he did not move.

"Love, wake up," she murmured, stroking his arm gently, thinking he was in the grip of some nightmare.

"I'm not asleep."

His voice startled her so that she jumped. "But you're freezing!" She dragged the top bed cover up over him, covering his shoulders and back and wrapping it round. She pulled him down into the bed and curled her arms around him. Through the coverings she could feel his heart thumping hard in his chest. "What's the matter?"

Marek sighed and turned in the bed. His voice sounded hoarse and strained. "Faran ... Silene is dead."

Faran was not sure who it was that shivered most now, herself or him. "How do you know?" "He was here. He said goodbye. He said I had defeated him. He called me Ozira."

Faran did not disbelieve him; even so her eyes grew wide in the dark. "He-he didn't try to harm you?" she asked, feeling nevertheless that the question was rather a stupid one.

Marek shook his head. "He didn't want to."

The moonlight shifted in the room as a breeze moved branches and leaves outside. It was only because of the shifting light that Faran was able to see there were tears in Marek's eyes. Tears for his brother ... is that what they were? She did not like to ask. Instead she took him in her arms and held his cold cheek to her own, warmer one. She murmured against his face, softly, lovingly, words which said that she loved him and which were mainly meant to soothe.

Marek lay in her arms, growing warmer and more relaxed by the minute, then, very simply, he went to sleep. Faran took a while to relax, however, for she could not get the exultant realization from out of her mind that now, finally, Marek was free.

Chapter Thirteen

Nikola woke and stretched. Then, in sudden panic, she reached for the clock to look at the time. It was seven thirty, already half an hour later than she was supposed to rise. She glanced over at Dan, thinking to herself that it still felt strange to have him in her bed, although she would not want it any other way. She studied him with tenderness as he lay on his back and snored. The snoring she could do without. But Dan? Never again! Gently, Nikola pushed him, not so much to wake him as to roll him onto his side. There was no reason for him to get up if he was tired, but she had to.

Yet her push woke him. "Is it late, Nik?" he muttered sleepily. "Isn't this supposed to be your day off?"

Seriously ill people do not have days off, Nikola thought. At the hospice one was always on duty, and if not, at least on call. Only Matt had the privilege of time away, which, assiduously, he had always protected. Somehow, Nikola wished she could find that same balance, but it was the problem of being the employer and not the employed. Well, she thought, I chose this way of life, so I'm stuck with it.

"Got to get up," she said. "Breakfast will have to be rather rushed this morning."

At breakfast the newspapers had not yet arrived so Nikola began rather hurriedly on her cereal, toast and tea. Dan wandered in some ten minutes later, still yawning. "I saw Marie from the window, running up the drive. She seemed rather agitated," he commented.

As if manifesting on cue, Marie was suddenly at the door. Which was unusual, since the staff rarely intruded to the first floor. Leaving Nikola her privacy the minute she went upstairs was a golden rule which was generally observed, except for emergencies of course.

"I'm sorry to disturb you," Marie said breathlessly. "I brought the papers with me. Just wait till you see what's on every front page!"

She threw three different newspapers down on the breakfast table. Emblazoned across each one, the headline banners were almost identical:

"BARON SLAIN – KILLER TAKES OWN LIFE!" "SILENE DE RAVANA DIES BY MANIAC'S HAND!" "THE BARON IS DEAD! MURDERER SUICIDES LATER!"

Nikola grabbed one paper and Dan another. Each of them read stories so similar in content that only a word differed here and there.

"The Baron De Ravana was murdered last night by one of his own employees. The killer, whose name is yet to be released, later took his own life by driving his car off a high embankment overlooking a major road works in the hills district, plunging the car into a deep ravine. Police were able to identify the killer by fingerprints found on the murder weapon, a hunting knife which was left in the victim's body, and information provided by another employee. The Baron is believed to have died from the abrupt severing of the abdominal aorta, but more information will be released at a later date."

The story continued with details of the Baron's life, irrelevant to the moment, perhaps, but full of meaty morsels for the voyeuristic reader. The next three pages were devoted to more and more of Silene and not the least being an eloquent piece of hysteria regarding the security of important leaders. It was as though an alien from a distant planet had suddenly swooped from outer space and cut down one of the most beloved members of society, and not that a little man with a taste for freedom from tyranny had taken the only way out he could understand.

Nikola and Dan read in breathless silence, and having forgotten that Marie still stood there, until she intruded again and picked up the third paper, saying, "There's an extra piece in this one. It says that the Baron is reputed to have left his entire fortune solely to his brother, even though the brother, Marek De Ravana, went missing over seven years ago and hasn't been seen since. "The Baron," it says, "was always assured that his brother was alive and so never changed his Will. However, the De Ravana family, which comprises of four sisters and their spouses and dependents, will surely contest the Will if the missing brother cannot be found. A search is already underway for Marek De Ravana until he is either found or it is decided irrevocably that he is dead. Of course, if he is alive, Marek De Ravana automatically inherits the rank of Baron, being the only other direct male heir to the title."

"Great Heavens!" Nikola said, taking the paper from Marie and reading for herself. "What on earth is Matt going to do about this?"

"So Matt is Marek De Ravana; it wasn't a mistake," Marie said with a hint of crowing satisfaction in her voice. Clearly, in the earlier matter of the magazines, she felt vindicated now.

"There's no use pretending any more, I guess," Nikola replied. But she fixed a glare on Marie. "Even so, you're not to go gossiping about this! We don't know what Matt will want to do, and it's really none of our business. What I said about letting gossips go still stands, remember. And I mean it, Marie, now more than ever!"

Marie grimaced then shrugged. "Well, my job's worth more to me than a good chin wag, so I'll keep my peace. I kept quiet about yesterday when you asked, didn't I? But it won't be easy, not when Trudy turns up this afternoon."

"Easy enough if you keep in mind what I said," Nikola assured.

Marie turned to go." I had better be getting to work." She paused to recollect something else. "Before I go, I meant to tell you this last night, but we seem to be having some trouble with the phones, so I called up the phone company from home. They'll send someone out today, but until then we're out of touch with the world, I'm afraid."

As soon as Marie had left, Nikola said to Dan, 'Remember what happened last night? How Matt went all strange and said that about his brother? It's rather spooky, isn't it?"

"Spooky is one word for it, I guess, yeah," Dan agreed. "He won't have seen the papers yet though; between them, he and Faran don't seem to bother with the news of the world much. I think we'd better get over there with this, don't you?"

"Yes. But not before nine," Nikola said. "It's his day off today and I don't think he'd appreciate an early intrusion." She rose and went to test the phone. She frowned. "Dead. I wonder why? I want to make sure the phone company does its bit as early as possible, so I'll go down to the village to ring as soon as we're finished up here."

Dan gulped down his tea. "I'll go with you. But before we do, we ought to show Bill the papers if he hasn't seen them already."

"Yes," Nikola agreed. "And the boy, too."

Waking up earlier than she wanted to, Faran opened her eyes and found that Marek was already awake. He was just laying there, staring at the ceiling, as if his thoughts were far away. Faran wondered how well he'd slept. After all that had happened last night, she hadn't fared too well herself, being tormented by dreams which had evaporated like phantoms the minute she awoke.

"Hello, are you okay?" she asked, prompting him to return.

He looked at her and smiled, reassuring her immediately that at least he was not distant in his heart. "Yes. A bit washed out, that's all. I was thinking about Silene."

"Is he really dead?"

"Yes. I know it. But something tells me he's not finished with me yet."

Faran felt a renewed sense of disturbance. "Not finished? What do you mean?"

"I mean … I know what last night was about … that on his death Silene came to a point of reconciliation and acceptance with me. And I'm glad for him … and glad for me. But there are things he's left behind which he can't control any more … things he set into motion while he was still determined to do whatever it was he'd wanted to do."

"What things?"

"That's just it, I don't know." Marek said. "And since I don't know, I'm not going to worry about it." He shrugged philosophically and rolled towards her in the bed, with another smile playing on his lips. A loving smile which filled his violet colored eyes with a beautiful light. "Life isn't meant to be so sombre and full of care, is it." He reached for her. "No point worrying about shadows when the light is all around you."

"We had better be getting up, I suppose," Faran said reluctantly. It was eight thirty. Marek made a disgruntled face. "Why?"

"Because it's a beautiful day, and your day off. And it's my birthday, remember. We could go out somewhere and enjoy ourselves."

"That's true." Marek kissed her. "Happy Birthday, Sweetheart. But I didn't forget. I've got something planned for today."

"You have? What is it?" Faran asked eagerly. "No. You have to wait," Marek teased.

They rose and showered and dressed, but before they had even sat down to breakfast there was a knock at the front door. Marek made a noise which sounded something like exasperation and went to open it. On the steps stood Nikola and Dan, Bill Langan and Will. They had newspapers in their hands and concerned expressions on their faces.

"We thought you ought to see this. We tried not to come too early," Nikola said apologetically.

Marek invited them in and took the papers. He studied the headlines in a way that made the others start, for he did not seem at all that ruffled by the news. "Who killed him?" he asked.

"It doesn't say as yet," Dan said. "But you don't seem very surprised. Does that have something to do with last night?"

Marek nodded. He called to Faran and she came from the kitchen,

315

wiping her hands on a towel. When she saw the headlines she frowned and bit her lip, but in the eyes of the visitors the effect of her reaction was the same as Marek's.

"Neither of you do," Nikola said, staring at them both.

"I knew he had died, last night. But not how." Marek explained. Yet he kept his mouth closed on any further revelations. People just would not understand, he knew.

Then Dan pointed out the article relating to Silene's Will and the issue of succession. Marek read this with more disturbance on his face and when he was finished he handed it to Faran. "I knew he wasn't done with me," he said to her grimly, 'and this is what I meant."

The others did not know what he was talking about. Marek tried to explain, at least briefly. "Everyone will be looking for me now and it won't be long before I'm found. I don't want any of what he's left to me. None of it. I just want to be left alone."

Nikola had been watching Marek's face as he read, and, on hearing these words, there was something she could not understand. So she said, "But, Matt ... Marek ... legally you are the Baron now. Everything that ever was his will be yours. Just think what good you could do with that! The name, the position, all that money ... why, you could do so much good in the world! You could undo all the harm he has caused. You could help—"

"Nikola!" It was Bill Langan who called a halt to her earnest persuasion, for where she had not read the thoughts of Ozira and did not know the inner workings of the mind before her, he had and did. Bill rested a hand on her arm, kindly but firmly. "Nikola, don't. Let it go, will you? Give the fellow a chance to think."

As if she had come back to herself after an absence of mind, Nikola looked suddenly surprised. "Oh, of course. I am sorry, Matt, I didn't mean to badger you. I just ..." She laughed a little, embarrassed by her own display of eagerness. "It doesn't matter. We'd better go. Let you two get on with it."

Faran pushed between the long coastal grass, feeling it brush against her bare legs with a touch which was not quite rough nor soft. With her free hand she swept her hair from her eyes as she and Marek turned from having the wind in their faces to having it at their backs.

"Just down this way," Marek said. He held her other hand in a strong, warm grip and they descended what was no more than a precarious, narrow goat track, into a ravine and, thankfully, out of the energetic wind. As they descended, the tussocky grasses gave way to ferns which grew taller and more luxuriant the deeper they went. At the bottom of the ravine the ferns reached to greater than man height, spreading like lacy umbrellas above them and creating a world of emerald and golden light. There they paused for a moment to catch their breath and to capture the sights and the sounds and the scents.

"It amazes me that I haven't brought you here before," Marek stated. He began to lead her again, slowly and leisurely now, along a path of rich brown earth and leaf litter. Central to the 'V"-shaped cut of the ravine was a small, fast running stream edged by the natural flagging of flat, grey stones which looked as if they had been deliberately lined up by a giant hand, and further up they formed a rough crossing from one side of the stream to the other. The stream would run down between the headlands of the cliffs and into the sea, Faran realized, for this haven of warmth and wild luxury was tucked behind their high ramparts. Like so many places in this area west of Tempah Springs, this place was rarely visited. As if the more obvious attractions of the Springs told the tourists: "Go no further than us. We're the best there is."

In the deepest part of the ravine, after they had crossed the little causeway of stones, they came to rock walled space like a small grotto. All around was a lemony scent of flowers and Faran saw that the flowers which gave off the scent were white and very tiny flowers indeed, and that the bees loved them. With all the formality of someone showing off to a visitor the best room in the house, Marek led her to a smooth rock, there to sit with him. The rock was covered in golden lichens and soft green mosses.

"I found this the summer after I came to the hospice," Marek said. "Last summer – somehow that seems such a long time ago." He curved his arm around her waist. "These months with you have been so wonderful and intense that I've lived a lifetime in them. I feel as though I need no other."

Faran understood. For her, the time between the Towers and the hospice had seemed like only waiting – waiting for him.

He had brought her here for her birthday. "I have nothing to give you but this," he said apologetically.

"It's a beautiful gift. It's a beautiful place." Faran reached for his hair, brushing it lightly. Her hand travelled to his face, turning it toward her. She touched his mouth with hers. "But you are really my gift, you and the

317

Light – all I ever want," she said softly against his lips.

Marek opened his mouth to hers. Her kiss was so warm and sweet. If there was nothing in the world but that, it would do him nicely. He pulled her down from the rock onto the soft, leaf covered earth, and made love to her.

Hand in hand, they strolled the length of the ravine. Further along there was a strange sight and Marek wanted to show it to Faran. It was an old weathered rock in the shape of a huge fish, like a dolphin arching into the sea, or a great whale in a dive. In vertical rows all along its breadth were carved strings of tiny, interlacing cup marks, looking like links in a chain. Where the circles interlinked, in the shape they formed, were bored long holes, one in each, at the center, the whole thing reminding the onlooker of a series of cat's eyes.

"How old is this?" Faran wondered.

"I don't know, but it appears ancient, doesn't it," Marek said. "I wonder who did it … and why?" "Maybe this was some kind of old ceremonial place, where people prayed to old gods or spirits," Faran suggested.

"Maybe." The thought of ancient ceremonies and the like brought Marek unwillingly to the subject he had been avoiding all day. He knew Faran was aware of his avoidance, although she hadn't said anything, preferring to let him deal with his conflict without her interference. Unlike Nikola, he thought, who was all too ready to drive him in certain directions for reasons which, to her, seemed only logical and right.

He could not hold onto it any longer; he had to speak.

"Faran," he said, almost idly. "About Silene's Will and everything … I don't want any of it."

Faran turned from running her fingers along the carved lines of the rock. "I know that and I don't want you doing anything you're unhappy about. But won't you have to do something? I mean, let them know that you're alive, so that you can formally give up your claim and then they'll leave you alone?"

Marek thought a moment. "Yes, I guess that's what will have to be done, if I'm to have any peace in the future. But I don't want to go to Brentore; I have no interest in going anywhere near the family."

"Were they so terrible?" Faran asked, wonderingly.

Marek grimaced. "I've about as much affection for the lot of them as you do for your aunt and uncle.

Does that explain it?" "Perfectly."

318

"So I guess I'll have to make some arrangement, get the lawyers to come here, if Nikola doesn't mind."

"Nikola … yes." Faran looked speculative. She said, "Nikola seems to be of the opinion that you ought to use Silene's great fortune for the world, be a benefactor, or something."

Hells Bells! Surely Faran doesn't believe this too? Marek thought. He said in reply, "Nikola means well, but she thinks from only a certain perspective. It's true, you can do a lot with money and power, but it isn't what this Earth really needs. If I was to sink myself back into that then I wouldn't be able to do the other thing." Marek paused, not to gather more thoughts but to stop his hands from trembling.

For a while this morning he had felt the temptation of money and power. Those insidious words and promises of Silene:"The whole world, Brother. I can give you the whole world." Such a gift, such an offer as that had once made him only nauseous, now it was being presented even more insidiously, in a slightly different way. A redecorated, prettified gift in the guise of "doing good"; but, underneath the wrapping it was still the same. No, he had chosen to step away from all that, not to turn his back on the world of humankind, but on the illusion which so many of them believed in. He had turned to the Earth and Its consciousness, and to the Light in himself and other men and women, and you did not need a great fortune for that.

Faran must have been reading the look on his face, or had seen the trembling of his hands, for she said, smiling at him sympathetically, "Daddy used to say this about the way of the world, that it would never change because of anything he did to it. I think he was referring to the way people think they can change things by operating inside the systems, like joining political parties and organizations or being a bigwig in the city council, like my Uncle Josh. He said that if you jumped into a mud puddle, then you were bound to get dirty. He said it was better to keep yourself clean; it did more good to those around you and, in the long run, to the world outside."

"Your father was a wise man. He should have known my mother; they would have got on well together," Marek said, smiling back. He knew she understood and that she shared his vision as her own.

"How could I not support you in what you want to do?" Faran said, as though she had read his mind. She chastised him gently. "I live with you, I dream your dreams, I share them in my heart. I know what the words of Ozira mean. I know how important it is for you not to get caught up again in that illusory world." She came to him, flinging her arms around his neck. "Marek, I am a part of you. I am not separate from you, not in my mind anyway."

He caught her round the waist, lifted her and held her close against him. "Not in my mind either," he said.

When they arrived back at the cottage Will was waiting for them. "Nikola asked me to bring this," he said. He handed them the evening paper. "More about your brother and who killed him. Nikola seems to know the name of the murderer. She also seems to be rather put out about something, but I don't know what."

At the sight of the murderer's name Marek closed his eyes and sighed. He had suspected as much although he'd hoped it wasn't true. Poor Mrs. Klider, poor Jenevra. He showed the paper to Faran. She read the words and whispered, "Oh, no."

It did not take Marek long to decide what to do. All his resolve never to see Brentore again vanished along with that name in the paper. After Will had gone he told Faran. "I have to go there now. I can't leave the Kliders dangling in this mess alone, so I might as well get everything over at once."

"Will you even see your family?" Faran asked.

"Only if it's absolutely necessary. But mainly I have to help Jenevra and her mother in some way." He held up the paper, thick with extra pages filled with eulogies for Silene. From the flowery prose and the paragraphs of righteous indignation, one would have thought Silene was a butchered god or a martyred hero instead of an impossibly rich and powerful, dead bureaucrat whom many people hated and feared, and, most likely, may have wished dead themselves. "Look at this twaddle. And every second line condemning Georgi Klider for the worst crime of the century. What sort of a life will Jenevra and her mother have in Brentore now?"

"I agree," Faran said. "But you're not going to do this alone ... I'm coming with you." "Well, I didn't think you wouldn't," Marek replied.

Chapter Fourteen

The journey to Brentore had to be thought out carefully before it was made. By now, everyone in the hospice knew that Marek De Ravana was alive and where he was. Not only that but the evening papers had also carried a large and very clear photo of Marek taken when he was about twenty two. Although the photo was ten years old and Marek had lost the more boyish look of those days, he had not changed all that much. As he remembered it, the photo was the best result of a portrait session, agreed to by himself only under duress and at Silene's insistence. Almost every other photo turned out terribly, showing quite clearly Marek's unwillingness to participate, and both the photographer and the watching Silene had been seething with frustration. It was only after Silene grumpily left the studio that Marek was able to relax, and the alert photographer perceived why. After talking to Marek for some while, he cunningly pulled off a few quick, casual shots, taken before Marek realized and which were totally unposed, and the result was several less formal but more natural pictures. The best of them was even quite personable and revealed some character and intensity of feeling, and Silene enthused when he saw it. It then became his personal property.

Silene had the photo hung on the wall in the sitting room of his city apartment, or that was where it was the last time Marek saw it. So the newspaper people must have procured it somehow, possibly by dishonest means or perhaps Silene's lawyers had allowed it.

Marek was not very pleased to see his face spread across page two of the paper, and, as Dan pointed out, anyone who had ever met him as Matt Best was going to make all the right guesses now. Already, the little village near the hospice was buzzing with the news and in Tempah Springs it was probably the same. Already, once the phone lines were working again at the hospice, Faran had received a prying call from Jan in Minerva, asking her if she had known who Matt Best really was. To which Faran had replied with rather bad grace that it didn't matter to her one way or another if Matt was Marek or Marek was Matt, and hung up.

It was Nikola's opinion, and the others agreed, that it would be a wise move to get in quickly and contact the lawyers before any of the gossip mongers did. "I'll do it for you, and through my cousin," Bill Langan offered. "Better an intermediary than doing it yourself." He had personal knowledge of the ways and means of lawyers since his cousin was a retired big business lawyer who lived in Brentore. Both he and Dan said they would come to Brentore too, Bill to liaise with his cousin, Charles, and Dan for reasons he did not disclose at first. Marek smiled to himself. He knew that Dan felt he still needed protecting and as Dan said, unless the lawyers were particularly discreet, their time in Brentore could be very difficult. "Once the media finds out you're there, you'll need a mountain like me in between you and them," Dan admitted then.

Just before they were ready to leave early the next day, Nikola came to see Marek. She looked him up and down, studying in a rather critical way his thin shirt and well worn trousers, topped with the jacket she'd bought him in the Springs over a year ago, which, she decided then, was the only redeeming feature about his attire. And his hair was too long, she thought. All in all, he needed a good brush up, and a proper suit would be an improvement, too.

"You don't have any decent clothes," she said in a rather querulous way that made Marek wonder about her present state of mind and think back to what Will had said about Nikola seeming "put out".

"I get the feeling you're annoyed with me for some reason," he said.

Nikola frowned. "I just wish you'd told me about the Kliders when they were here, that you knew the husband like that."

Marek shrugged. "What difference would it have made?" "I just would have liked to know, that's all."

"I don't see why. Your knowing wouldn't have changed anything," Marek said. He looked at Nikola squarely. "I know what sort of person you are, Nikola. You care about people. Whoever the Kliders were, you wouldn't have treated them any differently. They came here solely for help and they received it. Mrs. Klider told me how impressed she was by your kindness, and by the hospice, too. I think she would even have liked to offer to help you in some way; she intimated something of the sort just before she left."

At that, Nikola blushed. "Okay, you're right, I suppose. You always are." She smiled slightly, but it was not the sort of smile which revealed a proper acceptance. Something else bothered her, Marek was sure.

He touched her hand and felt the sudden grasp of her fingers at his. "Nik, what's wrong?"

"I don't know. I feel uneasy, somehow, about you going away. Before, I thought how wonderful it would be if you chose to be the Baron and use all that money for good, then I realized that if you did that, it would mean you'd be leaving here. I-I didn't think I could bear not hardly seeing you again."

This hesitant confession of such obvious affection touched Marek to the core. "But, Nik, I'm not choosing that, you know I'm not."

"Maybe not now, not while you're here. But what happens when you get to Brentore?" Nikola stared up at the ceiling, as if to hide a look of shame. "I'm being selfish, I know. I'm afraid you'll change your mind and you won't come back."

"I'll come back," Marek assured her. Believe me, I will come back." He felt very tender towards her. Knowing how, in the past, she had taken great risks of her own to bring him to Telaia and to shelter him in her home, where she had virtually fed him and clothed him – these were not small things to be ignored – but knowing also that she had never truly understood his purpose, he thought that, now, it was the right time. "While I'm gone you can read my books. Bill still has them but I'll ask him to give them to you. Once you read those then you'll understand why I will return."

Nikola looked both relieved and pleased. "You will? That would be wonderful!"

To reach Brentore without Marek being spotted and identified, it was decided that the four would go in Bill Langan's spacious car. It meant a journey of two whole days, staying two nights over in inconspicuous hotels. Having to smuggle Marek into the room each night and out again in the morning became a source of perverse amusement for them all. Before and after the pompous State Funeral, which Marek was very glad to have avoided, the newspapers were constantly full of Silene, more and more of them delving into every known aspect of his life. But they never succeeded in touching the real Silene, Marek observed. Had they done so, though, he doubted if any of the facts uncovered would be believed, for the illusory world had a way of defending itself from attack, and that defense came in the form of both a deliberate and unconscious blindness to the truth, a blindness to which so many religiously adhered.

On the morning of the third day they arrived in Brentore. Faran, who had never been to the capital, stared from the car at the towering pinnacles of steel and glass, at the ornate facades of government. Silene's lawyers had offices in an older district, which was a world of crusty looking elegance decorated with smog blackened gargoyles. However Marek told her that much of the area's real history had been demolished and replaced by imitations in flagged concrete, so it was hard to tell if what she was looking at was genuine or faux. Marek's family home, to which he did not particularly want to go, was in the more authentic district, a place of wide avenues and heavy foliaged trees where the great carriages pulled by teams of plumed horses had once paraded for the pleasure of an older ruling class.

Bill's cousin, Charles Parbara, had already made them an appointment with Mixen, Mixen and Glubster, the venerable and ancient firm which Silene had appointed as his Executor. When they passed through the cool, marble lined lobby and outer offices they were met with questioning and interested gazes from the staff, for it appeared that they were expected only by the elder Mixen himself. The old man, Mixen, appearing almost as bent and wrinkled as the gargoyles on the facades outside, ushered them inside his office, with a squint and a sniff that said that he was used to these kind of awkward matters and that they held no mystery or problem for him. Once in this office, a chamber of panelled oak and gilded, upholstered period chairs, and almost as spacious as all the rooms outside put together, they were met by another, a straighter, more youthful version of the old man. Mixen the Younger, apparently.

Old Mixen hobbled to his desk. "We have already had two other claimants so far."

"And they both turned out to be impostors, although they were reasonably similar to the photo," chimed in the Younger.

"So what makes you think we won't find you out, if you're the same?" the elder one continued. It was as if they spoke as one man, each taking his turn from the comments of the one proceeding. Faran thought them very strange. She wondered where on earth Glubster could be, if he existed at all.

The old man peered at Marek through screwed up, watery eyes. "You look close enough, in fact you're the closest one yet. What proof do you have of who you say you are?"

Marek sighed. He hadn't thought of spurious Marek De Ravanas appearing on the scene to collect the big rewards. He held up his left hand. "Nothing but this, I suppose, and my own say so. And you can ask me any questions you like and I'll answer them."

"Oh, we intend to ask questions, although it may not be necessary at all," Mixen, the Younger said curiously. Whatever he meant by that, neither Marek or the others could comprehend. The two men then studied the ring on Marek's finger with interest and seemed genuinely impressed, but not entirely convinced. "How long have you worn that? It doesn't seem as if it would come off all that easily," Old Mixen commented.

"It doesn't come off, it's too tight. Silene gave it to me when I was sixteen," Marek said.

"So you say." The elder Mixen smiled a secretive, self satisfied smile that said he had other cards to play.

"Well, the way we sorted out the other two, and saw them off with threats of prosecution, that we would have followed up had they not left town …" he grinned toothily at Marek and the others, as though saying to them all that they had better think twice about wrangling with such formidable beings as Mixen and Mixen … "was to have them formally identified by members of the family. They are here, waiting in the next room, so if you are not prepared for that, you had better leave now."

His coup played, the old man waved the younger one to an adjoining door. He stared at Marek, challenging him from his watery eyes, and since Marek did not budge, he motioned his partner to open the door. He waved a hand at Marek. "If you would oblige, young man; in here, please," and followed behind Marek on rickety legs.

For the third time since Silene's death, the four De Ravana sisters, always accompanied by the husbands who clung like ivy to their stout walls, had found themselves summoned to the lawyers" chambers to identify a so called claimant to their fortune, or so they termed it privately amongst themselves. They were beginning to be fed up with this procedure and, to tell the truth, not one of them wanted to believe there was a Marek any more. They hoped he was dead, they wished it, they would have even arranged it if it could be arranged. All of them had hated Silene, resenting him for never inviting them to their former home, jealous of his enormous wealth, angry over his pointed exclusiveness. If they hated Silene, they disliked the idea of his heir even more. They knew that, once no heir came forward, then they would be entitled to a four way split as their share, and that share was very great.

The four sisters were, in descent of age, Camille, Carolin, Angelique and Katrin. Of the four, Angelique had the most to lose if the next Marek De Ravana turned out to be the genuine article. She had been the first of the sisters to bear a son, and, baring any other claimant, that son would inherit the title of Baron. So the thought of another Marek clone did not please her at all, and she was determined to repudiate every one.

When the door to the outer office opened, however, and Marek walked through, not one of the sisters could deny to herself that this was surely he. The he whom they had wished never to see again. The he who

325

was to be the destroyer of their dreams.

There was a collective start when they saw him, from the hovering husbands too. And then, up close, they observed the ring, identical in every way to Silene's, and their eight pairs of eyes followed that lead and looked into Marek's eyes for the sign which would tell them that they could hope no longer. And Marek, who had also been observing them through the veils of unleashed memories and strained feeling, obliged them without conscious intent as his eyes changed color from blue-green to cold grey.

Of the four sisters, Angelique had the quickest intelligence. Her adept thinking powers and a persistent respect for common sense had made her into an adaptable woman, quick to seize for herself the best out of any situation and hold onto it. She saw now that denial was impossible and that there was only one way to salvage a disastrous future. Her hope was that Marek still retained those aspects of his personality which, in the past, had made him easier to reach and appeal to than was his older brother. He had never been a cold, callous boy, as was Silene, never with that touch of cruelty which Silene possessed. He would be amenable, she told herself. Angelique thrust herself to the fore, coming up to Marek with a smile. She grasped his hands and said, in a voice as thickly sweet as golden syrup, "Marek, you naughty boy, where have you been all these years?"

Marek did not answer the ridiculous question. "Hello, Ange," he said, using the family short name, which Angelique had long ago made the rest of them stop using because she did not consider it suitable for a matron of dignified years. Marek, of course, didn't know that, as he didn't know so much about his family any more. He gazed upon the others who began to gather round. They were a substantial bunch, he thought, looking solid and well fed. Only the greed in their eyes told him that they were actually hungry. They were hungry indeed for anything they could get.

Then the noises and false gestures of welcome. Outwardly the family acted as if they were pleased to see him. Inwardly they were fuming with anger and disappointment, Marek knew. He felt the hostility there, their thoughts flinging at him, like knives.

After having addressed him derogatorily as "young man', the old Mixen now bowed and scraped and called him "Sir", and the younger one mimicked the elder. They all repaired to the outer chamber and the family stared with blatant curiosity at Faran, Bill, Dan and Charles, as if they were inmates of the city zoo whom Marek had brought along for the

326

ride.

Feeling strangely apart from the whole situation, Marek made all the appropriate introductions. Then he said, that before anything else was done he wished to speak. The family appeared subdued at this, as if the rebuff they had all secretly feared was about to occur. They shrugged and glanced at one another, while hope died in their eyes.

"I have two things to say and it won't take long," Marek said. "The first is that the reason I've come here to Brentore is to establish the facts that Marek De Ravana is not dead, and that I am he. I've come here to establish this legally, for your sake and mine, so that we can all get on with our lives without any more speculation."

The family – sisters and their husbands – stared at Marek with expressions of incomprehension on their stout faces. What the hell is he talking about? they all thought silently.

"Once I've done that," Marek continued, "I intend to go back to where I came from. I never wanted anything from Silene or the rest of you, and I don't want it now."

Jaws dropped open in utter surprise, ten of them, counting the lawyers" as well. "Excuse me, Sir," Mixen said breathily. "Are you saying that you wish to renounce your inheritance?" He whispered the word 'Renounce" as if it was some foreign utterance he could barely understand, much less believe, and as if he might choke on the word if he spoke it louder.

"I am," Marek affirmed. "How it is to be done I will leave up to you, but I want it done, as quickly and with as little fuss as possible."

"Well, yes, Sir, if that's truly what you want. I can have the appropriate papers drawn up. You will have to sign … witnesses … everything … a day to get them prepared … tomorrow afternoon."

"That's fine. But no longer."

The family members seemed collectively struck dumb. It was beyond their expectations that one so gifted should suddenly give all his gifts away. Yet as their brains unfroze, and in particular, Angelique's, the issue of the title was remembered. It flowed as an invisible stream from one to the other, lit from one brain and firing the rest, until it seated itself in the mind of the Mixens.

"Er, Sir, if I may also remind you: there is still the title," old Mixen said hesitantly. "A separate issue, as you know. Legally, you are the Baron now. Surely you do not intend to give that away too?"

"I do."

"Y-yes Sir. Whatever you say." Mixen sounded shaken. "Then we shall add that to the list of papers you'll need to sign; it has to be done formally."

"Whatever." Marek continued, "Now, there is just one thing upon which all of this hangs. When my mother died she left all of her jewelry to me, and because I didn't have a present use for it, Silene had it stored. I want to know what happened to it and I want it, since it's legally mine."

Mixen waved his hands helplessly. "We were not her lawyers, but the family ..." The little old man cast questioning glances at the sisters. "My Ladies, you must know the answer to that?"

Together, Camille, Carolin, Angelique and Katrin all shrugged their matronly shoulders. Camille said, "Well ... after you disappeared we divided it up. I've got some and the others have the rest. I don't wear it, it's in our bank vault. If you want it back, Marek, then you're welcome to it." The other sisters nodded, as if to say that it was all redundant stuff in any case and they didn't really like it, and what kind of a fool had their brother become, anyway, that he would trade a Baron's position and fortune for a few bits of diamond and pearl?

"And then there's the Collection," Marek added. "That is one little bit of heritage I would like to take with me."

The women stared at him. "You want that too?" Camille said.

Marek nodded.

"But you can't!" Angelique moaned.

"I believe I can," Marek said. "Until I sign anything I am still the Baron." He glanced towards Mixen the Elder. "Is that not correct, Sir?"

"Yes, that is correct, now that you have been formally identified by your family, in front of witnesses; you are the Baron De Ravana."

"Then, as the Baron, I claim the Baron's traditional right to the Collection." He fixed his sisters with a steady gaze. He said to them, "Look at it this way: you can get rid of me so easily just by giving me what I have asked for. It isn't very much, not weighed up against the rest, is it? Besides, it's not really yours to withhold."

The sisters shrugged again. They looked at each other and nodded, all except Angelique, who sulked and sighed.

"All right," Camille said on behalf of them all.

"Good," Marek said. "Just have it here tomorrow then, with Mother's things, and then I will sign. If not, well…"

328

"What was that last all about?" Faran asked Marek as they left Mixen's chamber for the outer offices. Faran had not known that he was going to attempt to bargain or make deals of any kind with his family. Such acts as that were not in character for him, she thought.

Marek shook his head, as if to silence her questioning, and they passed through a gaggle of interested clerks, who by now had seen this latest Marek De Ravana not being roughly shown the door, and had therefore drawn the only conclusion they could.

When they were safely in Bill Langan's car again, Marek told her quietly. "My mother was the only person who meant anything to me. She left me her jewels because she knew I'd value them. She's the only one I want to remember from that time, and they don't care about her, or her things. They'll gladly give a little away for the lot they're going to get between them."

"What is the Collection?" Faran wanted to know, but Marek would not elaborate. "I'll tell you later," he said.

Before they drove away, Bill Langan said from the driver's seat, "Marek, you mentioned wanting to go somewhere else before we head back to Charles" house."

Marek leaned forward and handed him an address penned on the back of one of Nikola's cards. "Yes, if you don't mind. That's the address, but I don't recognize the name of the area."

Bill handed the card to Charles who was sitting next to him. "You know this place?"

Charles nodded. "It's in the Heights, but one of the new suburbs further out. It's very classy and expensive, but a bit too nouveau for my taste. You know how to get to the Heights, don't you, Bill?"

"I do."

"Then I can direct you once you reach Willow Bend. Pepper Grove is not that much further on. I always think it's ironic how land developers strip an area of most of it's lovely trees, then go on to name the suburbs after them. Like a sick joke," Charles commented. He twisted towards the back seat. "May I ask who it is you're going to see, or is that none of my business?" At their first meeting he had given Marek a rather cool, though certainly polite, reception, and had only invited him to stay in his house because of his friendship with Bill Langan. But when he heard of Marek's intentions towards the Baron's fortune, he warmed considerably,

329

although he never said why. It was only Bill who told Marek later that there was no love lost between the Baron De Ravana and Charles Parbara, due to some confrontation in the past.

"That's okay," Marek said. "I want to see Mrs. Klider and her daughter."

Charles twisted further, to stare incredulously at Marek. "You know the family of the murderer? Do you think that going to see them is a wise thing to do?"

"I don't understand what you mean about "wise", but it is necessary," Marek stated definitely. "And I hope you three don't mind waiting in the car while Faran and I see them."

"They might not be there," Charles said. "I believe the press gave them quite a time of it for a while. It's only a good thing that the chap topped himself, instead of letting this thing go on and on, otherwise there would still be reporters outside their house."

At Charles" direction, Bill soon found Pepper Grove and the street where the Kliders lived. The house was large, built of raw pink brick with a high wall and locked wrought iron gates to surround and protect, and the garden inside, which they could see through the gates, looked newly planted.

There was a security guard at the gate and when Marek got out of the car, the guard said to him curtly, "If you are reporters, you might as well make tracks. Mrs. Klider don't want any of you snooping around here."

"We're not reporters," Marek said. "I'd like to see Mrs. Klider. Could you ring through and tell her that Matt and Faran are here and would like to come in?"

The guard shrugged. "Okay. But what about them other three?"

"They'll wait in the car. It's just my wife and myself that want to see her."

The guard rang through to the house and after a few seconds he nodded at Marek and opened the gate. Marek and Faran passed through and began the walk up the wide pink gravel drive to the Klider's front door.

Chapter Fifteen

The foyer of the Klider house was the sunny entrance into a sitting room of rattan and colored print upholstery. In one corner stood a huge vase filled with pale papery flowers. In the opposite corner a fireplace with a shining copper hood, out of use in the summertime but a charming necessity in the colder months. Rugs of fleece covered the floor tiles in the appropriate places. The house looked like something out of a home decorator magazine.

Mrs Klider arrived only after the maid who had opened the door had left. It appeared to Marek and Faran that she had been struggling with some emotion and at last had been able to get herself together, enough for this interview, at least. Her face was pale and strained and her eyes were lined and tired looking. She pushed a stray wisp of hair from her cheek.

"Fancy, you coming here," she said to them both. "After what Georgi did I never would have expected this."

Of course, from the moment she had seen the old photo of Marek in the papers she had realized who Matt Best was, but although astonished, she was too stunned by all that had happened to respond in any other way than to banish the issue of Matt and the hospice into the furthest corner of her mind. Yet there was still Jenevra, and she had seen the papers too and was old enough to come to some conclusions of her own. "Is Matt the Baron's brother?" Jenevra had said. "Will he be angry with us now?"

Marek had not been sure how he was going to handle this meeting, but seeing Mrs. Klider's guilty expression he knew that he had to allay the guilt first, before they could go on to anything else.

"Mrs. Klider, your husband did what half this city wanted to do. The Baron may have been my brother, but he was not a good or kind man. He was guilty of many crimes against others, although none of them would ever have been provable by law. I hadn't seen him in over seven years, and that was by my own choice. The truth is that I had to protect myself from him, which is why I changed my name to Matt Best."

Astonishment mingled with weary relief and overcame Mrs. Klider's face. "Protect yourself? Why, what did he want to do to you?"

"Kill me," Marek said. "He wanted me out of the way because I knew too much about all of his dishonest affairs."

Mrs Klider covered her face with her hands. "My goodness! Did

Georgi know this?"

"Yes, he did, at least to the extent that he knew the Baron wanted me found. I don't think he would have known about the killing though; Silene would never have made something like that public, not to anyone."

"Oh, dear …"

Mrs. Klider looked as if she might faint, so Marek helped her to a couch.

"Would you like some water? Shall I find the maid?" Faran asked. But Mrs. Klider shook her head.

"No, I'll be all right in a moment." She gazed up at them from tear filled eyes. "It's been very difficult. But I am upset now because I remember that I told Georgi about you … about your ring. I think he must have known who you were because of that."

"Yes." Marek sat down beside her. "He knew. And he came to see me at the hospice. He was supposed to bring me back to the Baron, but instead he said that he would tell Silene that Matt Best was not his brother. So you can see, he had decided to lie to the Baron in order to protect me."

"Oh!" Mrs. Klider said. "When was this?"

"On the morning of the day he … killed Silene." Marek took her hand in his. Her skin felt cold and clammy. "I think he must have guessed what Silene meant to do, and realized that the lie would be uncovered eventually. I believe that your husband chose the only way he could think of, to save me from my brother and to rid the world of a man he believed was evil. I think Georgi didn't see any other way out of it at all."

Mrs. Klider bent her head, biting back new tears. "I-I don't feel so bad now that you've told me this … but it's been so hard on us. The papers, and the police tried to suggest all kinds of motives, until they settled on saying that Georgi had been mixed up in some sort of criminal business and the Baron had found him out and was about to have him arrested. Apparently the Baron had a dossier on him …" Mrs Klider's words failed her and she hung her head. Then she lifted her eyes to Marek, and to Faran. "I just wish … it-it's Jenevra … so difficult for her to … understand …" she said haltingly.

"Where is Jenevra? Is she here?" Faran asked.

Mrs. Klider's gaze travelled wistfully to the rear of the house. "Yes, she's out the back … in her playhouse, probably. She's been spending a lot of time there; it's too small for most adults to get inside, except that Georgi used to fit …" Her eyes began to water again and she wiped them

332

quickly.

"Do you think I could go and see her?" Marek asked.

Mrs. Klider nodded, then showed him the way. "I didn't tell her you were here," she said.

"That's okay," Marek said gently. "While I'm with her Faran will stay with you. She has something to talk to you about, an idea which we had and thought you might like to consider."

The backyard was acre wide and filled with new garden and landscaped paths. There was also an old pepper tree of huge dimensions, surrounded by low bushes and flowerbeds. It was obviously one of those which the developers had left intact, and it formed the centerpiece of the garden. Suspended from one of its low heavy branches there was a swing and under the leafy shelter, on the near side, was the little playhouse Jenevra's mother had spoken of.

Jenevra was not in sight, so Marek assumed she must be inside the little house. Clearly, he could not even fit in the door, so instead he sat on the swing and began to rock to and fro. He called to her softly, "Jenevra, are you there? It's Matt. I've come to see you."

He heard a sound like a scuffle and Jenevra appeared at the door. Her eyes were huge and dark as she looked at him, and filled with pained surprise. At first she seemed about to run to him, then she checked herself. "But Matt isn't your name really, is it. It's Marek," she said from the door.

"That's true," Marek said. "But that doesn't change anything, does it? I'm still the same person I was at the hospice."

Jenevra did not move. "Mummy says you'll be the Baron now. So you can't be the same."

Marek felt her pain as if it was his own. "I'm not the Baron, I'll never be the Baron, because I don't want to be. All I want to be is what I am, and you know as well as I do what that is." He held out his hand. "Jen, come here."

But Jenevra bit her lip and stayed where she was. "Daddy killed your brother. People say that my Daddy was a bad man because he did that."

Marek shook his head sadly. "My brother was the bad man, not your daddy. I've already told your mother about it, but I'll tell you now. My brother, the Baron, wanted to hurt me, but your daddy tried to stop him. He did it in the only way he knew, because the Baron was so strong that nothing else could have stopped him. Your daddy was a brave man who only tried to help."

Jenevra's bottom lip trembled. She left the sanctuary of the door and took a step closer to him. "Is that really true?"

"Yes, it's really true. You know I would never lie to you, don't you?" Marek said.

She took another step, and the tears were running down her face. "I loved my daddy," she sobbed, and closed the distance between them in one swift movement.

She rushed into Marek's arms and he pulled her onto his knee. He rocked the swing gently and held her tight until the sobs subsided. Finally she looked up at him. "I love you too, but when I saw your picture in the paper I thought you might be mad at us because of Daddy."

"And now you know that I'm not," Marek said. "That's why I had to come here, because I was worried about you and your mother, and because I missed seeing you. I didn't like the thought of your being alone here."

"Mummy doesn't like it here any more, she told me. She thinks we ought to go away somewhere," Jenevra said.

Marek nodded. "Would you like that?"

"Yes." Jenevra placed her little hand over his and touched his ring thoughtfully with her finger. "Is that why you changed your name to Matt Best so your brother wouldn't know where you were?"

"Yes."

"Why did he want to hurt you?"

"Because I wouldn't do what he wanted." "What was that?"

"For me to be exactly like him. To do everything like he did, and a lot of it wasn't very nice. But I wanted to be myself, and not do wrong things. I wanted to do what I actually do at the clinic now."

"And he got mad at you, so you had to run away," Jenevra said. "Yes."

"Before I met you, I used to think of running away when I got old enough, but only from Mummy, not Daddy," Jenevra confessed. "But now it's so much better at home. Mummy used to get mad with me but she doesn't much now, but I don't think she'd ever get as mad at me as your brother was at you."

"No," Marek said wistfully as he stared across Jenevra's head at the wide garden. He felt a certain sadness then, thinking of Silene. "Your mother still loves you even if she's annoyed with you. Being annoyed just makes her forget the fact sometimes, that's all."

"Did you come by yourself, or is your wife here too?" Jenevra asked. "Faran is here. She's inside, with your mother."

Jenevra slipped from his knee and wiped her face on the edge of her shirt. "Let's go in then." Suddenly grown up and formal, Jenevra took his hand. "She's pretty, your wife is. I'd like to see her again."

Charles Parbara's house was like the Kliders" house, expensive goods; but, as he said, he did not like "nouveau". His house had the gracious dignity and ambience of another era. It was old but well maintained and the gardens were luxuriant and overgrown, in spite of the fact that he employed a gardener. It was a big house, built to suit a large family, and since all the children had grown up and left, there was plenty of space for guests.

Marek and Faran waited until after dinner and they were alone in their room before they discussed Jenevra and Mrs. Klider. Their ears were burning too, as they felt themselves to be the topic of others" conversation, from the Kliders, to Charles Parbara and his wife, and Bill and Dan, right down to the astonished staff of the Parbara household.

"Weren't you impressed how Jenevra behaved when we invited her to come back to the hospice with us while her mother sorted everything out?" Faran asked Marek.

Marek threw himself down on one of the two beds, pulled off his shoes and put his feet up. To him, it seemed to have been a very long day, and he was tired. He smiled lazily, thinking of the Light which was Jenevra, how Its power could suddenly overtake her child's form and transform her into a living prescience of the lovely woman she would become. He had seen it then, at the moment of Faran's invitation, the helpless, needing child retreating before the sensitive, thinking adult. "Thank you," she had said, drawing herself up to full height after casting a brief, longing look at himself. "But Mummy would be alone then, and I don't think she should be. I want to be here, for her." How Mrs. Klider had seemed then! Marek thought. Touched to the point of tearfulness, but most of all surprised. "I was impressed," he said to Faran. "But not nearly as much as Jen's mother was. For too long she has underestimated that girl. It's about time she saw her true worth and her strength, and stopped thinking of her and treating her as if she was a baby."

"True," Faran said. She started to undress, laying blouse and skirt over a nearby chair. "When I was twelve … and Jenevra's nearly that … I thought of myself as very grown up, and Daddy always treated me as if I was … you know, respecting my ideas and opinions. But then, there had never been much time for babying me, what with Young Will losing his mother so early on. I felt like a mother myself because I had to look after him so constantly."

Marek watched her undress, feeling desire rise in him. But he dampened it down, not only because they were guests in someone's house but because he was actually wearier than he had realized.

However he studied the various beauties of her form, caressing her with his eyes, until she found the nightdress she was looking for.

"And you would have been a good little mother too, I should imagine. I remember how passionate you were about helping Young Will get better. I almost believed you would try to hack the chains off me, you were so fired up."

In nightdress and bare feet she came to him. "That wasn't the only reason I wanted those chains off you." She started to undo his shirt buttons. "Aren't you going to bed? You look all done in. Am I going to have to undress you and tuck you in, as if you were Young Will?"

Marek grabbed her hand and kissed it. "Better not or I might not be able to behave myself," he said.

She whacked him over the head with a gentle hand. "What rubbish! Look at you! The minute you lie down you'll be asleep, you're so worn out!"

They had separate beds, and Faran lay in hers and watched Marek fall asleep as quickly as she had predicted, before she had even switched out the light. It was true, he was exhausted, she thought, but not because of any physical exertion. She realized now that this day had been a strain for him, even though he hadn't shown it or expressed it, not even to her. The meeting with his family – oh hell, they were an awful lot! – must have brought forth memories he did not enjoy. And what was this obsession with his mother's things? Obsession? It did seem like that to her, although she had listened to his explanations and they sounded reasonable enough. But to hinge the signing of the papers on the delivery of a few jewels, that Faran could not understand.

And this Collection … what was that? He had not told her as he said he would. "Oh well, I'll understand when tomorrow comes," she said softly to herself, because she had never known Marek to do incomprehensible things or to be the victim of unconscious, uncontrollable desires, for those were the icons of a darkness he had banished long ago.

For the second excursion to the lawyers" office they travelled not in Bill Langan's leisurely car but in Charles" smaller but sportier vehicle. Charles had an inkling, he said, that this day they were going to need to be quick off the mark, because he sensed that the media was not far away and that, consequently, they might have to make a fast escape.

"What, do you think the lawyers would alert them?" Dan asked from the back seat where he was squashed in beside Faran and Marek. "Or one of the office staff? They looked like a nosy bunch to me."

"Maybe. But I've a suspicion it's more likely to be one of the family, or the whole lot of them. You have to realize that this is a coup for them and that they're going to want the world to know. After all, they want to be seen getting hold of the estate by legitimate means, instead of by all the wrangling that might have taken place if they had to fight with Marek over it or had to wait to prove that he was dead," Charles explained.

"So, I'm doing them a favor," Marek said with a wry smile. "I can't think that all that money is going to make them any happier, though. They've more than enough already, they always have had, but it's never changed anything."

Pulling into a reserved place in front of the lawyers" chambers, they saw that Charles" expectations had been true. Further down the street were the vehicles and high topped vans of the media already in wait. "Get out quickly," Charles advised. "Maybe we can get you inside before they realize you're here."

Everyone piled out, leaving Marek until last. They started for the stairs, then a shout went up. "Hurry!" Charles urged, and they had to run.

Once they were inside it was the office staff who cooperatively blocked the way behind them, forcing the frustrated media to stay outside. Dan glanced over his shoulder to see a clerk slide a heavy bolt across the oaken panels of the door. Clearly, this had either been planned or expected and no one was going in or out until everything was done. His mind shifted to afterward and how he was going to protect his friends, and with that thought he found his fists clenching suggestively. He did not like the media, not one bit.

Instead of being shown into Mixen's office again, they were ushered into an even larger room. It was a sort of boardroom cum legal library and the walls were lined from floor to ceiling with extremely dull looking books. It was both a meeting area and a place for study and research, for its centerpiece was a great long table of polished wood with a mirror shine. There were thirteen chairs at this table, ten on one long side facing a single chair on the other, and a chair at each end. The ten chairs were already filled by Marek's sisters and their husbands, and two men who were obviously their legal representatives. For Faran, Bill, Dan and Charles there had been placed around the perimeter of the room, a number of armchairs, as a courtesy, which, however, effectively removed them from the central action.

The Mixens were also there, waiting each at his own end of the table, with his own sheaf of documents in front of him. They looked like a pair of dusty bookends to Faran, and she thought, entirely irrelevantly, Where, oh, where is Glubster?

But the Mixens stood up quickly when Marek and the others entered and they both came forward and shook Marek's hand and bowed to Faran and nodded politely to the three men. Faran was surprised by this new show of respect and deference, which said to her that they did not necessarily regard Marek in any derogatory way. How did they see him? she wondered. A man who was about to reject a fortune, was he interesting to them? Was he an eccentric, slightly mad though harmless?

Certainly it was an extraordinary moment in their experience, the first act of a kind which they had never witnessed before. But it was all speculation, wasn't it, and Faran knew that Marek cared not for what the lawyers thought, nor anyone else for that matter.

From her chair, Faran had a view of all the relatives" faces. They had made no attempt to stand, although their lawyers did. The sisters had offered not a single greeting to Marek beyond a flicker of recognition and a slight nod. Faran thought she saw only contempt on their faces for their brother, as though they considered him a fool to be surrendering, so easily and voluntarily, the riches and power of a virtual kingdom. She felt offended by that momentarily, for Marek's sake.

"Well, I didn't expect any more of such relatives," Faran told herself. That they should be cool and ungrateful was not a surprise, when they believed they were only getting their entitlement.

She switched her gaze to Marek now, curious about how he would take such rudeness from his sisters and their spouses. And received another surprise. She stared at the change which seemed to have come over him. "Where is my Marek?" she asked silently.

As the younger Mixen showed him to the single isolated chair, Marek nodded curtly and sat with a cold dignity which bordered on the imperious. Faran tried to see his face, although it became slightly turned from her view, yet her impression was that it was entirely expressionless. So used was she to Marek's customary warmth and gentle affability and the kindly modesty which characterized his everyday and his working self, that to see him now, so hard and unmoved, disturbed her greatly. She clenched her hands and forced them to stay still in her lap. She was not happy or comfortable.

Slowly, Marek read the first batch of papers brought to him. With careful deliberation he put each paper aside as it was read and when he was done with them all he signalled to the elder Mixen. "Mr. Parbara shall read these for me also. Give them to him, please." Faran listened in awe and more disturbance. He sounded to her just as he had sounded that one time in the tower, when he had asked her to send her father to him, lordly and in control. Whether purposely or not, Marek had just treated the head of a major law firm as if he were a junior clerk. Maybe, she thought, although the thought repelled her, it was just as Silene would have done. It was as though, suddenly, the lord in Marek had returned after years and years of absence. Faran wondered if he knew.

The second sheaf of papers was much smaller. The ones to do with the title, Faran guessed. But Marek read these with the same concentration then had them passed to Charles in the same manner. Faran fidgeted in her chair, feeling hot and discomforted. She wished the whole dreadful process would hurry to an end.

Having to wait for Charles to study so much paper meant that Marek had time to observe the faces of his sisters. When his eyes met theirs they looked away, as if they were afraid of his glance, or were embarrassed by him. The greed on their faces had not abated, nor the self satisfaction either, but something more had been added since yesterday. It was unsureness … nervousness … even a questioning of him and of themselves. Perhaps they felt a certain guilt over their greediness, recognizing it at last. And perhaps they felt that they were cheating him somehow.

Or perhaps not. There was fear there certainly, but maybe it was not of him. Maybe they were merely afraid that, at the eleventh hour, he might renege and they would miss out on all their millions.

He could see their contempt and had time also to examine his own feelings about that. Their contempt did not hurt, for they had lost the power to hurt him long ago. And it was not returned by him. They were as they were, and greed was not an uncommon thing. Marek understood the attraction of power and wealth: that trap everyone fell into at some time or another. He had known it himself, so who was he to criticize? He thought then of his sisters" children, his nieces and nephews, two of whom were older than he was. Angelique's son, the one who would be the Baron after today, was only a year younger than himself. Marek wondered why he had not come to the meeting with his mother.

"But really, none of this matters," Marek said to himself. "What matters most is my own heart. Finally, I've reached the end of a long, bad dream, and it feels wonderful." Marek had closed with the nightmare more than seven years before, but the journey away from Silene had not always been easy. Even this last attempt at capture by Silene had managed a small coup, for Marek had been brought up short for a moment by a questioning of his own reality. When he had felt and given into the rise of that old false authority which allowed one to ride over others, he had taken a step backwards. But it was a brief step only, and the doubts which arose were quickly dispelled, finally sundering the thread of connection with Silene.

Now all that was left was this last discomfort, as Marek cut, for all time, the links with the past, with almost everything of the De Ravanas but the name. The name didn't bother him any more. I can wear that name now and it doesn't upset me to wear it, he thought. It's only a name and it is not me. I am just Marek and I am Ozira.

Charles returned the papers to the table himself. He bent to Marek and whispered, "All above board. There's nothing in there you shouldn't sign."

"Thank you." Marek placed the papers before him. A pen, looking like a finger-wide slab of marble with a gold tip, lay on the table nearby, its reflection gleaming in the polished wood. Marek made no attempt to touch it. He rested his elbows on the table and with fingers interlaced, he waited. "Well?" he said. "My mother's things and the Collection, where are they?"

The four sisters fished in their copious handbags and came out with four velvet cases which they gave to the younger Mixen to deliver. Then one of their lawyers brought forward a silver box, about the size of a small chest. "The Collection," he muttered and placed it on the table in front of Marek. Marek opened that box first and studied the contents and saw that the deeds which he needed for possession were all there inside. Then he looked through the velvet cases. Some of the pieces in there, he did not like, and he couldn't ever remember his mother wearing them, but there were the others … the ones he really wanted … and they were all

340

present. He had a moment of emotion then, which he managed to hide, as he felt his mother's frequencies still inhabiting the gold and silver, and especially the pearls and precious stones. It was as if she had suddenly entered the room and hovered beside him, her gentle loving arm around his shoulders and her hand upon his head, in blessing.

Marek felt tears near and steeled himself. He gave himself a silent order. "Not now, not yet. Wait."

So he signed the papers and saw the relief run like wildfire across the faces of the now-endowed family. That done, he stood and handed the four jewelry cases to Faran so that she could put them safely in her bag. The silver chest was placed in a cloth bag provided by the sisters" lawyers. Marek consigned it to Charles, who looked at it with great curiosity, but accepted it as a charge of trust.

Marek regarded his sisters for one last time. Then he merely nodded. "Goodbye," was all he said. It was done. Marek turned his back and was gone from that world forever. Down the hall and through the offices they went, and into the lobby. The clerk who had been posted at the front door warned them. "It's not going to be easy out there. The media has packed the doorstep and the path."

"Is there a back way we could take?" Dan asked.

"Yes, but you can't get the car anywhere as near as you can at the front. They'll soon twig and be after you, and you'll have further to run."

"So we've got no choice, front or nothing, face them then leave as soon as possible." Dan said, then gave directions. "We have to try to keep together, but if we get split up, Charles you get to the car first and start it up. Faran, you get in the back and keep the door locked until I say. Bill, look after her if you can, I'm going to keep Marek out of trouble." He said to Marek," It looks like you're going to have to say something to them, answer a few questions at least, otherwise they'll never let us leave. Okay?"

Marek nodded.

The clerk opened the door, letting Bill and Faran and Charles outside first then Dan and Marek followed. A storm of shouting rose up as they appeared and the reporters thrust themselves at Marek, all talking at once. As Dan had thought, the other three managed to extricate themselves and make it to the car, and he saw Faran push down the lock as he had instructed. Dan lodged himself at Marek's side and held on to his arm. Slowly he moved him towards the car as the reporters fired off their questions like bullets out of a dozen guns.

Cameras whirred and flash guns popped and Marek tried to turn from the glare. Dan had him right by the car before he would allow a pause for Marek to speak. The questions were all pointed towards Silene's great legacy and the title. "Was it true, he had refused the inheritance?" "Had he just signed away his rights to everything, including the Baron's title? To all he answered, in monosyllables and nods, and then the questions became more personal. "Where had he been for all the years?" "Why had he gone away?" "Was there some enmity between himself and his brother?" "What were his family relations like?" "What sort of a life did he expect to have now?" "Where was he going from here?" It went on and on while Marek refused every question, shaking his head and trying to avoid the leering inquisitive faces and the bright lights.

The media did not like refusal. Aroused, they pressed closer and began to jostle while they kept the questions coming at Marek, like missiles, like weapons. Again they popped the flashguns in his face, someone shoved someone else and they pushed into him. They were relentless.

'Right. Enough!" Dan growled, and he pushed back, using his great height and weight for a battering ram and a shield for Marek. As the crowd faltered for a second Dan tapped on the window and Faran unlocked the door. He opened it quickly and shoved Marek inside then piled in himself. "GO!" he ordered Charles. "GO NOW!"

Charles put his foot down and they surged away. The best they could hope for was that the reporters would not be too quick to follow. But they would not. As Dan twisted to stare through the rear window, he saw that Marek's relatives had arrived at the front door and it was their turn now to be besieged. He sighed. It was all over, for now at least.

In the car Faran looked sideways at Marek. His face was flushed and he looked angry. She reached for his hand and discovered that it was shaking. Not angry, she decided. She squeezed his hand and held it tightly, covering it with her other hand as well. She wanted most of all to hold him to her, to keep him safely in her arms, but she could not do that in the car. For the whole journey back to Charles" house she held his hand like that, until she felt the shaking subside, but she did not speak or try to draw him out. She knew that this would have to come later, much later.

Chapter Sixteen

It was five thirty in the afternoon, almost two hours since they had left the lawyers" chambers. Mrs. Parbara had ordered tea, and after struggling with that and some awkward conversation, Marek pleaded tiredness and headed for the bedroom. "What about dinner?" Mrs. Parbara asked Faran.

"Perhaps I could fetch some later and take it to the room, if that's okay," Faran suggested. "I don't think he's up to company tonight, and to tell the truth, I feel a bit strained myself. It was a rather awful time, actually, and I'm glad it's over."

Mrs Parbara nodded understandingly. "The media can be real pigs when they want to be."

"I'm sorry. I hope Mrs. Parbara wasn't offended," Marek said when Faran came to him. He had already taken off his shoes and coat and was stretched on the bed, but he didn't look relaxed. Faran suggested a hot bath or a shower, for this bedroom had its own ensuite. "Then you can get into bed and I'll bring you some dinner later."

He did as she said, but afterward was reluctant to go to bed. "It's six o"clock in the evening. I'll feel like a little kid, going to bed now. You're not going to leave me, are you?"

"No, of course not. But it's not too early for a rest, when you so obviously need one," Faran chided.

"I've never seen you so affected, not even when you were in the tower. It was horrible, wasn't it? They were like beasts, after blood if they couldn't get answers."

"It wasn't just that," Marek said. "Get into bed."

Faran joined him on the bed. She put her arms around him, holding him to her. "I wanted to do this in the car," she said. "I could see you were upset, but it was more than all that pushing and shoving. Can you talk about it to me?"

"I can always talk to you," Marek said. He kissed her lightly. "You know, I've never been one for lots of attention, not like Silene. He loved it, the adulation, the envy and regard of many, even the hatred and the jealousy, perhaps; it was all the same to him. He said of me once that the most powerful forces were those which the ordinary man in the street could not perceive. He meant that I ought to work in secret even though he was aiming to have me follow him. His conceit was such though that he believed he was both, the public and the private force, and that he could make both work equally as well."

Faran fondled the hair at his neck. It was still damp and it curled vigorously at the nape. Nikola had suggested that he ought to have it cut. Faran was glad he hadn't, for she liked it as it was. "But Silene had so little love in him, so what good was all his force, to him or anyone?"

Marek sighed. "Nothing at all, except where the illusory world is concerned. Silene didn't care for love, although I think he may have felt it at the end, in its real essence, that is."

"You seemed almost like a different person at the lawyers, one I didn't know," Faran said. "It made me afraid."

Marek stared at her. "You saw what I did to that poor old Mixen, didn't you." He looked shamefaced. "It was almost as if I had Silene at my back, pushing me. It made me do a double take, I can tell you. I'm sorry if I frightened you. I frightened myself, too, actually. I hadn't realized there was still some of that behavior left in me."

"I think it's gone now, though," Faran said, studying him. "You are my old sweet Marek again." As Marek relaxed, he found a smile from somewhere. "Not so much of the "old", Matey," he said. "Can I see your mother's jewelry? And whatever is in that silver box?" Faran asked, for she was very curious.

"For sure. I want to look at it again, myself," Marek said.

Faran fetched her bag and gave him the four velvet cases. Then she took up the chest from its place on the bedroom table. "This is quite heavy. What's in it?"

Marek said, "Wait." He made a flat space on the bed covers and, after opening the silver chest, emptied its contents onto the space. Out tumbled the most antique looking collection of jewelry Faran had ever seen. In fact she had never seen anything like it except in books. An odor of dust and age seemed to drift from the chest with it.

"Awful, isn't it?" Marek commented. "The Family Jewels. Hardly a single Baroness has ever wanted to wear any of it, but historically speaking, it's worth a packet."

Faran stared in awe at the tiaras and heavy necklaces of great jewels, the collars and ornate brooches. She stared also at Marek, reappraising him for the second time that day. "There's a fortune there, if it's real."

Marek smiled. "A small fortune anyway, and it's real. There were never copies made because it was rarely taken out of the vault. The stuff was meant as a gift for each new Baroness, although it was always the property of the Baron. But none of the women have ever liked it enough to actually be seen wearing it."

"It is rather overdone," Faran agreed. "Marek, I never thought of you as mercenary or devious. I never thought you'd want something like this enough to bargain for it. Why did you want it?"

"I'm not mercenary, and, I hope, not devious. I'm just being practical. I want to take you to Te Tanaa, but not to have to go in the way I did. I'm taking you there in style, my love. I would like to buy a boat—"

"A boat. So we can sail there! Oh, how wonderful!" Faran gasped. "But that means you intend to sell..."

"Exactly. The stuff is museum fodder. There are a lot of collectors who'd love to get their hands on it, ugly or not."

"But your sisters, they'll be as mad as hell, you demanding the family treasure, then promptly selling it up!"

"Well, I don't know what they expect me to do with it ... certainly not wear it. And besides, when it goes up for auction and if they truly want it back, they can bid for it."

Faran could not help herself, she began to laugh. 'Really, Marek, you are quite wicked! I never would have guessed how much! And a businessman too! So ... can I see your mother's things now?"

Unceremoniously, Marek piled the Collection back into its home. With more tenderness and care, he took up the velvet cases, unclasping each catch. Then he lay them open before Faran. The sudden opening of the cases brought his mother to him once again. A faint perfume, redolent of her presence and infused with her personality, seemed to waft towards him, although it was merely the fragrance of memory. He felt the sudden catch of emotion at his throat, but swiftly dealt with it, turning his mind to Faran instead. "Well ... what do you think?"

"I think," Faran said, with wide eyes, "that it's all very beautiful ... well, most of it is." Tentatively she touched a necklace of pinkish hued pearls and her eyes travelled to the wonders spread across the four boxes. A ring of gold and rubies here, a diamond pendant there. "It must be very expensive too; it looks as if it is."

Marek smiled at her awed face. "It's worth more to me for what it means, though." He began to sort the jewelry into two distinct groups and Faran saw that he was choosing to separate, by eye or by some discrimination of his own, the really fine pieces from those she did not like so much herself. He pointed to the group which was less appealing.

"These, my mother rarely wore. They were gifts, a couple from relatives, and the rest from bigwigs, here and overseas. She wore them only when it was expected of her." His fingers then brushed the others. "These, she chose herself, they were her own taste, and you can see that she had a fine appreciation of beauty. Oh, and this was her engagement ring, bought by my father."

Faran studied the huge diamond in its setting of gold. "It's stunning," she murmured. Yet her eye was more taken by another ring. It was also of gold and had a blue sapphire as its centerpiece and a little curve of diamonds at each side. Compared with the overseas gifts and the engagement trophy, it

was not very grand, but it had more charm and there was some sort of feeling attached to it. "Don't ask me why, but I like this one better," she said.

"You do?" Marek felt invaded by sudden warmth. "That was my mother's favorite too. She wore it all the time." He picked it up, studied it and the size of Faran's fingers. The stone was almost the color of Faran's eyes. Yes, he thought, yes, yes, yes. "Mother was a taller woman than you but she had very fine and delicate hands, and narrow fingers." He took Faran's left hand in his and spread her fingers.

He chose the third finger, deliberately, and slipped it on. It fitted perfectly, and its size suited the smallness of her hand much better than any big rock diamond. "And now it's to be my wedding gift to you, because now that I don't have to hide my real name any more we can be married officially," he said hoarsely, for the lump in his throat had returned.

"Oh, Marek," Faran whispered. She had no other words.

"There's something else about this ring that you should know," Marek said to Faran's bowed head. "It was also my gift to her, for a birthday. I bought it for her when I was nineteen." Hearing the emotion in his own voice then had the effect of bringing Marek back to the core of his feelings again. It was just like the time when Faran had made that lovely gesture of returning the coat to him. He still missed seeing his mother at times, although it had been over nine years since she had died.

Faran had never known her mother, but she had felt the loss of Will Crafter and his wonderful, loving personality every day for a long while after his death. She still loved him dearly, even though he was no longer a visible presence. She heard the catch in Marek's voice and recognized its meaning. Without looking up she reached for his hand. "Sweet," she said, "I'll wear it for all the love that has gone into it, for your love and hers … and mine, which will be there too."

His hand trembled under hers. She heard him sniff. Only now she met his eyes, and they were distant … looking inward, to somewhere sad and colored grey. She smiled, to bring him back, to the happiness and sweetness which was the NOW. "You were lucky to be able to afford such a beautiful gift for someone you loved," she whispered.

Startled, his eyes returned to her, suffusing with blue. "I suppose I was, yes. But it still took all of my year's allowance to pay for it. I remember the surprise on her face when she opened the box. But she never told me off for spending so much on her; she just accepted it with good grace."

"Your allowance? Didn't you have a regular income then, no job or anything?" Faran asked wonderingly.

Marek's face reddened. "It shames me to say it, but no. There was so much money, I didn't have to work if I didn't want to, and I didn't want. If I spent over my allowance, I just asked Silene for more and he gave it to me. He never questioned why I wanted it or what for. Actually, I was supposed to be at college, but I never studied."

"No job, no study! That makes you sound rather lazy … and awfully spoilt," Faran commented, even as she hid a smile.

He did not guess that she was teasing him. "Doesn't it, though? Well I was … spoilt, but it wasn't really laziness that kept me out of work or study. The only work Silene would have wished me to do was to learn his business … you know, bureaucracy, but with the old Silene twist to it. For a while I had to follow him around while he explained how he made men do exactly as he desired, and what to do if they were foolish enough to disobey. That's when I first met Klider and found out that he was just a bit more than a government clerk."

Poor Klider, Faran thought. "So you felt uncomfortable in Silene's world. Why didn't you try for a job somewhere else? And why didn't you study?"

"What is this … the third degree?" Marek asked. "I give you the gift of my heart, and you grill me like a crim—" He caught her elusive smile and grinned. "Minx! Silene had me under the thumb. At that age I couldn't move without his say so. And study bored me, frankly. I couldn't see that there was anything much worth learning, and later on I found out why. Because there is only one thing worth bothering about – healing this

347

troubled world through the Light."

"I can't disagree with that." Faran's smile broadened. "I'm sorry, I was just teasing you. I think you must have been a perfectly lovely nineteen year old. Fancy, I was only eight then. You wouldn't have even looked at me."

Marek gave a lopsided smile then laughed. "I wasn't lovely, actually, but never mind. What I want to do now is to get you to help me sort out the rest of the jewelry. You don't think I'm stopping at a ring, do you? I want you to choose whatever you like from the rest of these."

'Really? What if I want it all?" "Then it's yours."

"What if I don't want some of it, though?"

Marek thought. "I'd like to give something to Nikola, for all she's done for me. And something for Jenevra, for when she's grown up."

"Now, that's a nice idea." Faran leaned across the jewelry and kissed him on the mouth. "You see, you are lovely and you always were."

Chapter Seventeen

Nikola took her after dinner coffee into her sitting room and set it down on the wide arm of the easy chair. This had become her favorite hour of the day, the house quiet and restful, except for the sounds of Will at flute practice in his bedroom. Yet that was also restful, she thought, for the boy's musical efforts had progressed, in only a short time, from merely the playing of the notes and making them correct in pitch and rhythm, to finding a real feeling in the music and expressing it. Nikola listened with pleasure, even to the necessary repetitions of the practice. Some would find it boring, but she did not. I'm glad we found that teacher for Will in the village, she thought. What an amazing chance that was. She had never thought much of Upton before, except as a place which furnished stocks for the larders and as a supplier of hospice staff. To find a professional musician hidden in such a tiny town had been a pleasant surprise.

Nikola closed her eyes for a moment and listened. Really, he's getting to be quite good, she decided. She could not believe sometimes how willingly she had accepted Faran's young brother into her life. And Dan too. It seemed that the boy had worked a strange magic upon their hearts and minds; or was it that they had just been ready to be worked upon, that they had opened themselves with such willingness because in some strange way they needed him?

Why did she like Will so much? Nikola wondered. Indeed, he was a lovely boy, full of unconscious charm and a natural gentility. Just like Faran, she thought, a being unspoiled by life's twists and turns. Nikola could understand by that why Marek was so drawn to her. To Nikola, Faran seemed an untrammelled soul who expressed herself without the usual resort to self defense and prevarication. Whether this was true of Faran or not, Nikola could not really know, but it was how she appeared; it was Nikola's reality. She examined her feelings then about having Will in her house and decided it was because he seemed to her … and to Dan, she guessed … like the chance at a family they might not otherwise have. Of course, older men, even men in their sixties were capable of fathering children, yet Nikola was not certain she wanted that. She was nearly forty herself, so was it wise to be contemplating parenthood at such a late date? Not prudent or sensible, she thought. But when was the heart ever that?

Nikola's main purpose of the evening had been the same since Marek had left her with his books. In fact it had become her chief pleasure, to sit in the peace and sip her coffee and read, with Will's musical efforts ornamenting the overall silence. Yet it was more than pleasure she sought, and much more than peace, for she found in herself a new excitement as she read, and a strange upliftment of her heart, principally. His words enticed her, they disturbed and sometimes shocked, but they had opened in her a consciousness of such a lightness that she was transported when she read them.

There was also something else, which she was not so relaxed with or accepting of. It was the journal which brought this "otherness" about, not the wiser words that followed. The journal, with its story of personal pain and unfoldment, drew her unremittingly into the time in Vargas, and she found herself returning in memory, over and over, to the effect Marek first had on her. Old feelings resurfaced: those disturbing feelings she had wrestled with until Dan had arrived on the scene, so in need and so desperate for her help and love. She hadn't wanted to know feelings like that again, not in relation to Marek at least, but his words had brought him back to her with force.

She could say to Marek that she loved him, and mean to have it sound like friendship and sincere appreciation. And he, in return, would always smile and show her by his acts and manner, that he loved her too, in the way one friend loves another. But he had never said the words: "Nikola, I love you," and she wondered now if that was because he realized that her words covered a greater intensity of meaning. She suspected that he understood and so held off expressing anything which might encourage the wrong response. As she read his journal she felt the yearning for him return, that dream of hers which she'd had night after night, especially when he lived next door, that one evening they would finish their dinner together and they would sit for a while in an atmosphere charged with warmth and good feeling, which would then evolve into something closer and more physical … and then he would invite her to his bed.

Immediately, feeling this way again, Nikola was shocked by the thought and involuntarily her face colored deeply. For a moment she struggled to deny its resurgence, but soon gave up the fight. She could not deny it so it followed that she must continue to explore it. She asked herself, "What did I want then and what did I really feel? Did I love him then, or just want him? Which was it? Or was it both?" Was there a distinction, a difference?

"And is it the same now? Am I still not over Marek, even now?" she added, becoming suddenly worried and afraid. How could she feel this way about two men at once? For she loved and wanted Dan as well.

Am I just promiscuous? she thought, and fell to examining her feelings in depth, as the words of Ozira were teaching her to do. She had always shied off from dealing with her feeling self, preferring to keep her consciousness in her head where she believed it was safer and easier to control. Well, that was one of the things she had to learn to undo; she had to let her heart speak truly so that she could see where her desires were taking her, and why.

"It isn't enough to acknowledge feelings," the words of Ozira said. "You must let yourself feel them, right to their core, then to see what desires are bringing them about. Thinking about feeling is what most people do when they say they are feeling something, but they are only letting their heads dictate an idea or a concept of what, according to their intellect, should be appropriate at the time. So many people live within the intellectual spaces of their minds that the world is cluttered with realities which bear no relation to the actuality of the Earth or its bodies or the beings who inhabit them. The world is full of cold, feelingless realities. Just witness them in the brutal acts of world violence which are countenanced and given a thousand cold blooded excuses for their existence. True feeling is spurned and given the name of "Sentiment" to lessen its meaning and impact, so that 'Reasonable" things can be done, callous and brutal as they are, in the name of this or that god, or of good government, or to protect a people, or to "better" human life, and so on."

Nikola understood this last sentence well, seeing how in the name of her own profession cruelties were done to nature – beasts and men – in the name of "Science" and "health". There was always a justification, wasn't there … no matter how spurious? And this was because the men and woman who worked in the profession kept themselves in their heads and denied their hearts the right to speak out. Personally, she did not countenance such acts of violence against nature, and her patients here at the hospice were only treated by simple, non invasive means, and since Marek had come to them the lists of medications used had undergone a change. They used nothing now which the chemical companies sold, and had attracted a new kind of client because of it.

But it was easier to observe the fallacies of others, especially when they were large and obvious, than it was to penetrate one's own subtle mistakes. What was her desire for Marek, essentially? Was it solely a body thing? It was true, sexual desire had played a large part at the beginning, for she found him physically attractive, as did many of the women working at the hospice, which she knew from overhearing their chatter occasionally. And Marek made it so easy to like him ... to feel attracted, for he was the very soul of affability and kindness, usually. Oh ... and that smile, Nikola thought, it was the very essence of what made him so approachable; it bespoke his heart, which was warm and open and always generous.

So, Marek was attractive, as any genuine, loving man would be. But it was not all; there was more with him. He was like a beacon to her, something she was drawn to, as a moth to a light. It was something beautiful and magnetic, and now she knew what it was. As she read Ozira's words they said to her: "We are Light, you and I; we are one." That was it ... Nikola had felt it from the start ... that the love which flowed between them was deep and special, but also impersonal. It was a love undivided into self and self; it was the Love and the Light of the All.

Love without possession. Yet what was it that Nikola had needed in Vargas which Dan had been so ready to offer, but which she had not been able to see up close, reaching to Marek instead? This was difficult to think about, but she would give it a try. She reached down into herself, struggling to penetrate the many layers of self protection which had always been her shield from pain. It had something to do with Vargas ... and with her own way of life. It was mixed up with the despair and hopelessness she saw and with her own sense of inadequacy in dealing with that. And her drive to put the world to rights ... somehow that had come to feel false and pompous, as if in her life she had been living a lie.

What is it? she questioned. What drove me to Marek? What did I want of him? She remembered now that pivotal moment of awakening, when she had seen what miracle he'd worked within his own flesh. It had come to her like lightning, although she failed to understand it properly later ... the desire to conquer pain and death, and the desire to be more than what she thought she was. It was the desire to overcome all limitations, and Marek had seemed to her the key. But what all these desires really expressed was the simple but profound need within her to be healed.

It was her own pain and her own inadequacies, not the world's, which really concerned her. All the time she had been struggling to succor the pains of others, she was really only trying to cover over her own wounds and hide them from the light and heat of realization.

Nikola cast her mind back to the past. Her mother's betrayal of her father had seemed like a betrayal of the young and vulnerable Nikola too, and in a sense it was. Her mother deceiving Bill with a lover of several years; the heartbreaking scenes which followed and which young Nikola had crept downstairs to witness; her father's deep sorrow and a need for mourning which stayed with him for much too long a time after her mother went away ... yet he would not change the name of the boat which had been such a pleasure to them all. The isolation Nikola had felt during that time when her father was too much in pain himself to realize hers, then had Dan become important to her and she had run to him for all the comfort and safety he could give.

Then her mother's dramatic and terrible death overseas in the midst of the frivolity and luxury she enjoyed, which shocked them all and left Nikola in a confusion of anger and grief, one minute hating her mother, the next weeping for her and wanting her touch of love again. Nikola had been older then, old enough to eventually hide her confusion behind a wall of bitterness. She remembered now how, when the shock had lessened, Dan had come and talked to her of her mother. He had liked Rhona, he said, and she had not been the only one to blame when her marriage to Bill had fallen apart. "You were too young to understand the complications," Dan tried to explain, but Nikola had railed at him angrily and told him to mind his own business. And, to her shame, she had even suggested to herself that maybe Dan and Rhona had been lovers also. But she knew in her heart that this was a lie, yet the lie served to harden her once and for all.

The wall began to build itself around her, bad experience by bad experience, disappointment by disappointment. At college she found herself to be a popular figure with the opposite sex, and the boyfriends came thick and fast. Her first experience of sex, fumbling though it was, aroused in her some powerful feelings of desire, and for a while she followed them ardently and had several lovers. Then suddenly she was afraid. It was as if her mother's ghost had risen up to warn and ask, "How much of it do you want? Do you wish to end up just like me?"

Scared and confused again, Nikola retreated. Not this time to Dan, who, although she saw him at vacation time, seemed distant to her now and far beyond the wall. Her guilt at treating him badly when he had obviously guessed her suffering and only wanted to help, and her secret shame of having thought so ill of him and her mother, this made it difficult to face him openly and with the old affection. She felt then as if she had lost the friend of her soul, but she could not bring herself to do anything about it.

"Oh, Dan. Now I see what you could have given me then," Nikola sighed. "The real love which I needed and wanted. It would have healed me then, I know. Instead, I ran away from you and became the big, important lady doctor who was going to save the world. What a misguided fool I was. How pathetic."

Nikola picked up Marek's book again, his second volume. She opened it at random and read: "It is your ego which blames you constantly for all the wrong things it says you have done. You have done nothing wrong; you have just lived your life in the way that you understood it. If it appears to you now that you made mistakes, that you judged yourself and others where love and compassion would have served better, then only rejoice that you do see it. Apportion no blame; do not call yourself a fool; you are not a fool. You are the Light and you exist in Light, only now you are learning to Live it also."

Nikola sighed and laughed to herself while she wiped away a few tears. Of course, this was what Marek was to her – a living Light, the Light which she wanted for herself. TO BE herself.

"Nikola, I'm going to bed now."

Will's voice brought her awake with a jolt. So soon? she thought, then looked at the clock to see that two hours had passed.

Will had come to say goodnight but he flopped down on the easy chair next to hers. "That sure must be an interesting thing you're reading; you didn't even hear me come in. What is it?" he said.

"It's a book Marek wrote. Two books, actually. I'm afraid they get me in so that I can hardly put them down."

Will craned his neck to see. Over her shoulder he read a few words. "Gee, would he let me read it?" he asked.

Nikola smiled. "I'm sure he will, if you ask him. My dad is going to get it published. It's in the works at the moment."

"Published? Wow. What's it about?"

"Life, mostly, and what it all means to us. And the first part of each is a journal, about all that's happened to Marek in his life. It's very interesting, to say the least."

"Does it say anything about the Towers, about me?" Will wanted to know.

354

Nikola laughed. People were always more interested in a story if they thought they might be in it. "A bit. It doesn't name you but it tells about how you were ill then."

'Really? I don't remember all that much about what happened when Marek came. I didn't even know who he was until Faran told me in her letters. All I do remember is that he had very cool hands which made me feel better … and his eyes."

"What, the color?" Nikola said.

Will shook his head. "No, not that. I remember that a light seemed to come from them, to me." Will closed his own eyes, as if to see the past more clearly. "Then Marek went away and the men – Faran said they were bad men – came and searched the house. Faran and I played a trick on them. Marek had left his coat behind and so we hid it under the sheet in her bed and I lay on it, pretending to be sick. Faran said that if the men found it they would hurt Dad, so we had to be smarter than them. It wasn't hard … they were pretty dumb … they didn't find it and Dad was safe."

Nikola thought of the fourteen year old girl daring to bluff the Baron's men to protect her father. "You were both very brave."

Will shook his head. "It wasn't me who was brave, it was Faran. I never really understood why we did what we did, not then, anyway. I thought it was just a game. But afterward, before we left the Towers, I realized that something odd had happened, something rather important really, because I used to hear Faran crying in her room at night. I knew it wasn't my fault, or Dad's, so one morning I asked her why she was crying at night. She looked really embarrassed and told me not to say anything to Dad. She said she just missed the man in the tower and was worried about him."

Nikola tried to imagine the girl in her first experience of romantic love and torn between childhood and womanhood. A love which under normal circumstances would have been impossible to express, but so thwarted and painful and endangered was it that she could do nothing but cry at night and pray for the safety of the one she loved. "What did you think about that?" she asked Will, not really wishing to take imagination further.

Will shrugged. "I was too young to understand, but I did what she asked … I didn't say anything to Dad. Then I forgot about it after we left for Hanna Harbor."

You really love your sister, don't you." Nikola said then.

Will flushed, but nodded. "Apart from Dad, she was my whole family. Sometimes, when I was very little, I thought she was my mother. But when I look back on it I still get surprised. I was only one when my mother left, but Faran was only seven. I don't know how she managed; she always seemed so grown up to me, but she mustn't have been, must she."

Nikola shook her head in wonder. She had never known any of this before and the knowledge forced a new appraisal of Faran. She had thought of her as a being largely untouched by life, but obviously it wasn't true. So much for judging others by appearances, she thought. "It's getting late," she said to Will. "Time for bed. The others will be home tomorrow."

Will yawned and stretched. "I can't wait to see them. I was looking at the evening paper before dinner. Did you see the pictures of Marek? And Dan was in one. I hope it wasn't too bad for them. Marek didn't look very happy, I thought."

Nikola had not had time to read the paper. "I'll look before I go to bed. Now, I think you should say goodnight, don't you?"

"Yep." Will jumped up. "Goodnight," he said and, suddenly, startling Nikola, he bent and kissed her on the cheek, and he had never done that before. His face flushed again, as did hers. He said, very quietly and sincerely, "I've never thanked you properly for taking me in. I really like it here and I like you and Dan a lot." Then he smiled at her and was gone.

Nikola touched her burning cheek and pleasure filled her. Not so long ago, a year and a half away, she had been a moderately lonely woman, locked in her work, her only friends the staff, and her father and Dan, who were both away in Arpay most of the time. How things had changed, she thought. How glad she was that they had.

She was headed for her bedroom when she remembered the newspaper. She fetched it from the dining room sideboard where it had laid unread by herself since dinnertime. She picked it up. The front page was covered in the newest story in the saga of Silene, this time, though, the pictures were not of him. Instead there were confused looking photos of Marek outside the lawyers" office. In one, his hand was raised to protect his face from the intrusive lenses, and the ring on his finger glinted in the lights, marking him one more time for posterity as the inheritor who had given up all. The other photos were more front on, showing Marek looking sombre and annoyed ... certainly not his best side, Nikola thought ... and Dan in one with his hand firmly clutched around Marek's arm while he appeared to be shouldering aside the onlookers. The editorial seemed amazed that any human being could be so determined to deny himself the right to so much power and money, and had no answer as to why. Another article, supposedly reporting the interview in the street, delved also into speculation, and at the end it went into some detail, obviously gleaned from elsewhere later, of Marek's present mode of survival. They had done their homework, those reporters, for Nikola saw with a start the mention of the clinic, its name and her own, and the town of Tempah Springs.

"What will it mean now?" she asked herself aloud. "Are we going to be deluged with nosy reporters?" She had received no calls as yet. However, perhaps it would not be so bad, she decided. Once things settle down it might even be good for the clinic. And she was glad for Marek that Dan had been there. Poor guy, she thought, this must have been difficult for him. But now, after this, everything could only get better.

PART 5
Two Months Later

Chapter One

The dream had been brief but momentous and when Faran woke from it she lay in the bed beside Marek watching him as he slept, oblivious, with a gentle smile on his face. In one of his own pleasant dreams, she suspected, but she would confidently lay bets on the guess than it was not in any way as stunning as the one she had just experienced.

"Sweet," she whispered, not loud enough to wake him. "I wonder if it's true? But I can't tell you about my dream, not yet."

Faran wandered up the path. She was going to see Nikola. It was another of those beautiful days, clear and warm, although summer was almost officially over. However Faran could feel the change coming in the air. Far away across the ocean, in the southern sky, was a thin grey band of approaching rain. By this time tomorrow they would be in the midst of it and Marek would have to work in the conservatory instead of the garden. Faran glimpsed him now through the trees, in his customary place on the old garden seat, his attention fixed solely on the one he was helping. It had taken a while for everything to settle down after they'd come from Brentore, what with the publicity and extra attention from outside, but now life was more or less as it was before.

At the sound of small, hurrying footsteps coming from behind Faran stopped and turned to see who it was. It was a little girl with a glossy, dark bob of hair and a very big smile.

"Jenevra, hi! You're in a hurry! What's happening?"

Jenevra's eyes were shining as brightly as her hair. "Will and Dan are working on the new winter vegetable garden behind the conservatory. They said I could help them."

Faran studied the little girl's clothes. The fact that she was wearing overalls was one thing, but the other fact was that they were very expensive, designer type overalls. Just the thing for a mess about in a newly dug vegetable garden, Faran thought with a hidden smile. "That should be fun," she said to Jenevra. "But you take care, now. Don't let those big bossy fellows order you about."

"They aren't bossy," Jenevra said seriously. "You sound just like my mother."

Faran suppressed another smile. "I'll see you later then. Are you going home for lunch?"

Jenevra shrugged. "Mummy said I could stay here if I wanted." Then she asked coyly, "Where is Will having his?"

"At the cottage, with Marek and me." Faran let the smile express itself. How could she not when the girl was so delightfully transparent? "Would you like to come too?"

"Yes, please," Jenevra replied.

Faran watched the girl as she hurried off to join her new friends. Mrs. Klider had sold up in Brentore and because Georgi Klider had been canny with his investments, she was very comfortably well off. At first she and Jenevra had gone to Tempah Springs, then when a house became available in Upton Mrs. Klider had bought it and moved there permanently, although making the purchase under her former, unmarried name. There was still enough curiosity and interest in the Baron's murder to make life difficult for someone like her, even in Upton.

Faran thought with amusement of how frequent a visitor to the cottage Jenevra had been in the first week of her arrival in Upton. She would hang about the house and the garden, helping Faran do this and that, or just playing under the trees, and all because she was waiting to see Marek. There was no other reason she came, it was just to see him. Thank goodness she's only twelve, Faran had thought with a laugh, otherwise she would have been wondering what to do about the competition.

Then on the morning of the second week, Jenevra had been there as usual, helping Faran put washing on the line, when Will wandered into the garden. This was the first time Jenevra had seen him and she didn't know who he was.

"Who's that?" she whispered as he approached.

Faran glanced around the sheet she was pegging. "Oh, that's my brother. His name's Will. Haven't you met him yet?"

Jenevra's dark eyes were shining with a curious light. "No. How old is he?" "Sixteen."

Faran made the introductions and Will was his usual, innocently charming self, and Jenevra had suddenly lost all interest in the washing. They had some morning tea together and Faran noted how grown up Jenevra had become in such a short while. She didn't chatter like a child and she smiled at Will and played up to his every question and comment

360

and did not take her eyes off him for a second. By the end of the tea she had gotten him to promise he would show her how to play the flute and when he said he had to go she said she did too and went trotting off after him like a faithful puppy.

When Marek came for lunch he looked with surprise for any sign of the little dark haired girl. "Where's Jen? Everything okay?" he asked.

Faran grinned. "Jenevra's gone. You've lost your girlfriend forever, I'd say. Will was here this morning and he is only sixteen, after all."

At the main house Nikola was busy so Faran went upstairs to wait. She sat in Nikola's sitting room and stared at a magazine without seeing or registering a single thing in it. She was somewhat nervous and her stomach churned with an unaccustomed excitement. She wished Nikola would hurry.

Nikola came, at last, and due, she said, for a nice cup of tea. At the sideboard in her dining room she heated water and set out the cups. "Do you want anything to eat?" she called to Faran from there.

Faran couldn't think of eating, or of drinking for that matter. And she could not wait to speak any longer. She followed Nikola to the sideboard. "Nik, I've got something important to ask you, that's why I'm here. I want your help; I think I may be pregnant."

All at once Nikola forgot about the tea. 'Really? That's great!" She took one of Faran's hands in hers. "You're happy about that, aren't you?"

Faran nodded. "If it's true, I am, but I've got to know for sure."

"Well, I will make this tea and you can tell me everything while we drink it." Nikola swirled the tea in the pot to help it brew. She poured two cups and carried them to the table. She pulled out a chair for Faran and one for herself and they sat down. "I've got half an hour to spare now. After this would you like me to do an exam? I'll do it up here, it's more private. No point in feeding the gossips, eh?"

Faran nodded, feeling as if, suddenly, she might explode with excitement.

"Okay," Nikola said when they were settled. "Now, the first question: when was your last cycle? What was the date?"

Faran thought. "The ninth … two months ago."

"And you missed the next one? What was that, about the seventh or eighth? You were at Brentore then!"

Faran nodded. "It was due the day we left Brentore to come home here. Yes, that was the eighth." "And nothing's happened since?" Faran shook her head. "But I didn't worry much about missing that first one, because I thought it was due to all the stress and upheaval. Sometimes I used to get that way, irregular, when my emotions got out of hand a bit, so I believed it was just that. And there were a few marks on my underwear, a spot or two, so I assumed it was just the upset that made everything a bit off, you know."

"Well the spotting could be a sign that you really are pregnant; it's not uncommon in the early months, but it has to be watched. Have you had any more since?"

Faran shook her head.

"It sounds as if you could be two or nearly three months down the line already. But to look at you now one couldn't tell, you're as slim as you ever were." Nikola said cheerfully. "So finish up you're tea while I fetch my bag and then we'll have a look. But you'll need a test too, just to confirm."

Nikola hurried away but she wasn't gone long. She took Faran into her bedroom and locked the door behind them. The exam showed that Faran was not three months pregnant at least; otherwise, the fact would have been physically evident to Nikola's investigation. "More like somewhere around two, if it's a reality. Have you had any nausea or vomiting?"

"No," Faran said, wondering. "So don't you think it is?" she asked anxiously.

"Well, you haven't been trying not to get pregnant, have you?" Nikola said with a smile. She told Faran to undo her blouse. "Mm, could be," she murmured cryptically. "But, Faran, I just don't want to go getting your hopes up by saying pedantically that you are pregnant. I think you are, but only the test will show for sure, and I can't do that until tomorrow morning because of what you need to do for me." She told Faran what was necessary to bring the next day. "I'll be able to tell you as soon as that's all done," she assured her.

Faran sighed. She would have to be content with that and patient for one more day. Then she remembered the dream.

"Nikola, this may seem strange to you, but I had a dream last night about being pregnant," she said as she dressed.

"Well, that wouldn't be surprising, considering you've been wondering about."

"No, it wouldn't," Faran agreed. "However this was an odd sort of dream because I actually dreamt that it was you who were pregnant. You came to me and told me that you were, and I said, 'Isn't that wonderful, because I'm pregnant too!' Then I woke up."

Faran had expected Nikola to laugh, but she did not. Instead, she colored and put her hands to her face, as if in dismay. But it was not dismay. "Oh, Faran!" she whispered. "How did you know?"

Faran stared. "You are?"

"Yes. I tested myself only a few days ago. I'm a bit more than six weeks." "And you never said! Does Dan know?"

Nikola busied herself in her bag. "Not yet. You're the only one."

Was she upset about being pregnant? Faran wondered. Gently she touched Nikola on the arm. "Nik, you asked me if I was happy about being pregnant, now I'm asking you."

The two women had never been more than friends with a common interest, Marek. But now they came face to face, sharing a feeling of connection that only they could share, the thrill of the possibility of motherhood. It made for a certain intimate camaraderie, and an understanding between them which wasn't there before. Nikola bit her lip. "I wasn't at first, when I saw the result. I guess I felt a bit afraid. It was a shock, you know, I hadn't expected it. And it worries me a little, being nearly forty. But now? Well, yes, I am glad."

Nikola smiled a trifle wanly to be sure, but Faran took it for what it was. "And if I am, we won't be very far apart!" She took Nikola's hands in hers. "Just think what a wonderful surprise it will be for the others! The two of us pregnant!" She started to laugh softly, and before Nikola knew it, she was laughing too.

The two women hugged each other. "Just think!" Nikola said.

Next morning it rained fiercely from dawn until eight o"clock and the sky was wild and unreliable, as if the day was not prepared to settle into any one pattern. Marek fetched an umbrella from the closet. "I'm glad I've got this afternoon off, but I'm going to be working inside today. There's no chancing this weather in the garden." He kissed Faran on the cheek. "See you later, Sweetheart."

So, he would be in the conservatory for half a day. Faran was pleased. Once she had seen Nikola and had the news she felt certain would be positive, all she had to do was to run downstairs and tell him. She could hardly wait to see his face then.

At nine, although it was raining lightly, she braved the path and went to see Nikola again. By the time she got halfway there the rain had blown away and she saw Will and Dan with shovels over their shoulders as they made their way to the new garden. She waved, wondering if Mrs.

Klider would let Jenevra out on such a day.

Nikola was still upstairs, waiting for her, obviously. "Got your little package?" she asked with a grin. "How long will it take?" Faran wanted to know. "Oh, not long," Nikola said.

Waiting, Faran went to the bay window and stared out upon the damp world. There were a few people about, although not many. There was the official gardener, who was heading off with garden shears towards one of the overgrown hedges by the gate, and Dan and Will and, possibly, Jenevra, out of sight in the garden behind the extensions, and a nurse on an errand, dashing across the gravel drive before the rain came again. The grounds were quite empty of life, except she thought she saw in the distance a figure walking slowly and idly in from the road, having come into the grounds not from the gate but from somewhere further along. That did not seem quite right, she thought, but her mind was too occupied with other more immediate things to let it bother her all that much. She left the window and paced the room, wishing that Nikola would hurry up. From somewhere out at sea the noise of thunder rumbled, sounding like boulders being rolled across the sky.

Marek sat back and smiled at the woman beside him. She was an old lady of seventy five with wrists as thin as sticks and small hands with fingers covered in fine, expensive rings. She was built like a doll, she was so tiny, but there was a fire in her eyes which denied any possibility of spiritual frailty at least. The consultation was coming to an end. "I'll see you tomorrow then," he said.

She returned the smile. "It's been so nice talking to you." She made an effort to rise and Marek helped her, his hand at her arm to steady her. "Thank you," she said as they both stood. She was a gracious lady with the courtly manners of an older time and generation. She had come all the way from Brentore just to see him, alerted by the stories in the newspaper, she said, but not just because he was Marek De Ravana and she had known his mother. She had been ill for a long while and a friend had already told her of Matt Best and she had thought about coming six months earlier, but had not been able to. "I'll be honest," she confessed at the close of their first meeting. "I came as much out of curiosity as need, I hope you don't mind. I could hardly believe it when I read the paper, because I remembered seeing you as a little boy."

Marek did not remember her.

"Of course you wouldn't; you were only about four or five," she stated.

She shuffled away, helped by the waiting nurse. They had not been alone in the conservatory, although Nikola always took care to see that this end of it was kept free for him on inclement days. At the other end four elderly patients sat amongst the pleasant atmosphere of green plants and potted flowers, with two nurses standing by to look after them. Before he sat down again Marek went to the huge glass windows to study the sky and decide if more rain was on the way. It was. The sky was beginning to darken again and he heard the growl of thunder in the distance.

Then, quite suddenly, he saw the man outside, staring at him from beyond the edge of the wide gravel walk. Although it was some distance between them, it was not so far away that Marek could not recognize a face and form he knew. He felt a shudder pass through him, a tremor of unwillingness. He glanced quickly around the conservatory, appraising the situation. The old ladies sat in peace in the corner while their subdued conversation sounded like the hum of bees. The nurses watched and chatted to each other. One of them caught his glance and smiled. NO! NO! Marek thought in sudden panic. NO WAY! NOT IN HERE! He headed for the conservatory outside door.

Faran returned to the window. She was so restless and excited that she could not keep still. "There's that man again," she said under her breath. She was more curious now that the figure in the grounds had come nearer the house. It was not anyone she knew, but there was something about the odd way he moved which alerted her. The man walked with a curious sideways slip at every step, reminding her of something she had been told once. He was going in the direction of the conservatory.

Abruptly, Faran felt a surge of the most terrible nausea rise up inside. As if fear could swoop down from the brain to the belly in one cold sweating wave and convulse it with sickness. In spite of the incipient rain and the growing wind, she opened the window and leaned out so she could see better. The man was bald, totally bald.

"Oh, God, no!" she whispered, and waited not a second more, running from the room and down the stairs while the terror grasped at her throat like a murderous hand.

In the vegetable garden Will stared up at the sky. "It's going to rain again soon. We won't get much done today."

Dan kept digging, turning over the earth and filling the nearby trench as he did. "Is the shovel holding you up, or are you holding it up, young fellow? Dig, mate, while there's still time," he chided gruffly. He glanced at a figure coming swiftly towards them. "Better look lively now," he said to Will. "Here's your girlfriend, come to check up on you."

Will made a face, at which Dan laughed. Will did not dislike Jenevra, in fact he quite liked her even though she was only a kid. What he did not like was her constant devotion to his every move.

"Hello. I saw a funny looking man on my way here," Jenevra stated by way of a greeting. Will paid attention to his digging. "What are you talking about?" Jenevra pointed vaguely towards the front of the main house. "There … a weird man with a bald head. It was so shiny, like it had been polished."

Will grunted and kept digging. Dan said nothing at all.

"He asked me if I knew where Marek was," Jenevra persisted, trying to get their attention. She succeeded. Dan looked up. "What? Did you tell him?" Jenevra nodded. "I've never seen such a funny man before. Do you know, he had only one eyebrow and gold teeth?" She touched her own teeth. "In front, here."

"SHIT!" The expletive flew from Dan's mouth before he could stop it. Both Will and Jenevra stared, astonished. Dan hoisted his shovel and grabbed Will's arm. "The bounty hunter, after Marek. He's here!"

"Your shovel, boy!" Dan ordered Will to follow him. To Jenevra he said, as gruffly as he could, "You, young lady, stay right here and don't move from this spot! Otherwise, I promise, if I find out you have I will whack your behind so hard!"

Jenevra was totally shocked. No one had ever talked to her like that before. She had not a single word of reply as she watched Dan and Will hurry away.

Marek opened the door and stepped outside, moving away from the conservatory and out to the open area of the drive. The Vorken followed him, loping along in his strange fashion. He seemed cool and unhurried, as if he was merely attending a chance meeting with an old acquaintance. But before Marek had reached the grass, the Vorken called him to halt. "De Ravana! No further!" Marek stopped and turned. The Vorken was some twenty paces distant. As he drew his weapon from inside his jacket, he smiled, and his gold teeth caught the light and glittered. He shifted, closing the distance between them with his sliding shuffle to ten paces now. He smiled a second time. Marek thought there was something odd about his expression, something not quite right or usual, a look that was decidedly incautious, as if he did not care where he was or who might see him commit the crime he was about to commit. Marek stood his ground. He could only try his best to talk his way out of this one, he decided. For running was useless and, in fact, more likely to provoke the bounty hunter into the act of shooting him, he knew.

"Faran, good—" Nikola stopped still when she saw the empty room. The side bay window, wide open, the white gauze curtains billowing with a frantic breeze, was the only sign that something had occurred. Nikola went to close it, but she started at what she saw below. There, on the gravel drive opposite the corner of the conservatory, was Marek standing rigidly still. He was talking over a distance to someone who appeared reluctant to come nearer. A queer looking stranger with a bald head and something dark and heavy looking held in his hands that Nikola could not identify.

But that was not all. From her high window, Nikola had the advantage of an almost one hundred and eighty degree view, and she could see, approaching from the gardens, two figures who she identified as Dan, with a shovel in his hands and, behind him, Will, also with a shovel. They seemed to be stalking, via the soft grass rather than the noisier paths, and they looked like two creeping thieves. And they were coming up behind the stranger, who had not appeared to notice them.

Then, from the front of the house, beneath Nikola, Faran was running around towards the conservatory. As she got there, the stranger raised his hand and pointed it at Marek. The something dark and heavy that he held was a gun.

Faran screamed just as the gunman was about to squeeze on the trigger, and the sudden shock of her scream was enough to put the bounty hunter off his aim. The bullet seemed to have hit Marek, though, for he reeled sideways then fell forward, yet it also hit the conservatory, smashing through the corner window. Inside the conservatory more screams rose up as everyone realized that something terrible was occurring.

Horrified, Nikola's hands flew to her face. Marek was face down on the ground, not moving, and Faran ran to him, throwing herself upon him.

Nikola unfroze and ran too.

While she covered Marek's body with her own, Faran turned her eyes upon the Vorken. Although she was terrified yet she had the presence of mind to see the foolishness of the Vorken's act, the absolute uselessness of it, and she thought she could reason with him. She begged him, "Why do this? It's pointless! The Baron is gone; there's no purpose to this any more!"

The Vorken looked at her from insane, unreasoning eyes. "I always finish what I start. Purpose enough."

"But you don't need to, fella," came Dan's voice from behind. The Vorken swung round and Dan saw that his eyes were wild. He had gone beyond coolness and calculation into the place of mind where choices were few. He had drawn first blood and the lust to taste it was upon him. Not much point in trying to reason with a madman, Dan thought, nevertheless he made one more try. "The bastard who wanted this is dead. There's no one left to pay you."

"Don't come near." The Vorken pointed the gun in Dan's direction whilst eyeing the shovel in Dan's hands. He seemed curiously unaware that the gravel walk was suddenly filling up with people. Nikola had arrived and hovered desperately just beyond the edge of the path, and Will was not far away, although he was out of sight behind a shrub. His hands were gripped tightly on the shovel as he edged nearer.

The man is mad, Dan thought, or high on something more like. He moved to one side to turn the bounty hunter's concentration upon himself, away from the others and, in particular, Will. He tossed down the shovel, hoping that the gesture might be enough to persuade the Vorken that he was not a threat and held out a placating hand. "Fella, don't go through with it. It's okay, you don't have to."

The Vorken, though, only sneered with contempt. "I can just as easily take you out first, then him." His eyes flashed back to Faran's face. "Get away from him, girl," he ordered, waving the gun between Dan and her.

Faran pressed her body over Marek's. "No!"

"Then I'll have to shoot him through you." He waved the gun again, switching it back to cover Dan but keeping his eye on Faran. "And this sweet baby is big enough to do it. It'll blow right through you."

Terrified now that the bounty hunter would kill Dan as well as Faran and Marek, Nikola blurted out. "For God's sake, man, have some pity. The girl's pregnant!" She caught a look of surprise in Dan's eye, but in the Vorken's there was nothing. He barely glanced at her. As if her words were only the noises of the wind.

"All right," he said, levelling the gun and moving it rhythmically from Dan to Faran and Marek, and back again, as though he was deciding who to shoot first. His finger caressed the trigger meditatively.

It was then that, still unnoticed by the madman and having crept around the shrub and come near enough to wield his shovel, Will acted. With a mighty swing, he drove the edge of the blade into the small of the Vorken's back. The Vorken arched with the blow, his arms jerking out in

368

front, fingers spreading. A grunt and a gasp of pain shot from his mouth with a flow of exploding air. He let go of the gun and it flew from his hand, spinning into the gravel. Dan leapt to it and seized it up. He squeezed off one quick, accurate shot, piercing the one eyebrow-less eye as the bullet entered the Vorken's brain and blew it apart.

"My God," Nikola moaned, as she tried not to look at the mess of the Vorken's skull where it lay on the gravel, semi-attached to the rest of him.

She went swiftly to Faran and Marek. She had to use force to peel the girl off Marek at first, as if Faran was not convinced the bounty hunter was really dead. Marek lay with his face in a small pool of blood. Nikola hauled him to a reclining position against her knee but his head lolled in her arms. He was unconscious and a red stripe of raw flesh ran across his temple, but he was not badly hurt, Nikola realized. Faran, though, cried out when she saw the blood.

"It's all right, it's all right," Nikola reassured. "The bullet only scraped him. You saw how it broke the window, didn't you? He's going to be all right." All she had on her was a handkerchief. So much for the big lady doctor, she thought. She pressed the handkerchief on the wound, holding it gently. The welling up of blood had already begun to ease.

"Marek …" Faran tried to wake him. She appealed to Nikola. "Are you sure?"

"Yes." Nikola tapped Marek's cheek a few times. Come on, mate, wake up, she thought. Don't prove me wrong.

Obliging her, Marek opened his eyes. He looked vaguely at them both, then as they helped him sit up, more clearly at the grisly scene. He shut his eyes for a moment then opened them again to take in all that had happened. He saw how Dan and Will hovered around, looking as helpless and shaken as they obviously felt. And then he saw Jenevra who, daring to defy Dan's worst threat, had come running to discover what all the noise was about. Marek threw a warning glance to Dan, and he turned and saw her. "Will!" Dan barked. "Get that little girl out of here! Take her inside, tell her what happened if you must, but don't let her see this!" And, although he was white and shaking, Will nodded. He ran off to confront Jenevra, obediently steering her away and into the house.

"Can you get up?"

Nikola and Faran helped Marek to rise and they began to walk back to the house. "One more thing Silene couldn't control," Marek said to Faran, but Nikola did not understand what he meant. Then, without warning, Marek's knees gave way and he collapsed between them, out cold again. "He's concussed," Nikola explained as she lifted his eyelids and looked into his eyes. "Dan, can you get him into the house and up the stairs? We had better put him to bed for a while."

"Our room," Nikola told Dan.

She ran to her office and fetched her bag. On the way back she saw Will standing nervously in the hall with Jenevra just behind. Will seemed to be in shock and he was much too pale. After all, a man having his head blown off right in front of him was not something the boy had experienced before. But then, none of them had ever seen such a ghastly sight, except Dan maybe. "Jen, look after Will, please. Take him into the kitchen and tell Mrs. Byers that I said she is to give him some strong sweet tea, and ask her to make up a big pot for upstairs too."

With Will in Jenevra's ready hands, Nikola ran back upstairs. On the way she met Dan coming down. "Have you seen the boy?" he asked anxiously. "I've called the police and I'm going back outside to cover that mess up and wait until they get here, but I don't want the boy going out there again."

"He's in the kitchen. Jenevra is looking after him."

Dan smiled crookedly, picturing in his mind's eye the possible extent of Jenevra's devotion to duty. "He's safe then."

Marek was on the bed, and, very busily, like an over indulgent nurse, Faran was tucking a quilt around him. But her hands were trembling as she worked and her face was whiter than the bed sheets. At the moment she looked worse than Marek did.

"Faran, honey, you don't look well. Hadn't you better sit down?" Nikola counselled.

Faran shook her head, then her hand flew to her mouth. "I think I'm going to be sick!" She sped towards the bathroom.

With water warmed in her tea kettle, Nikola cleaned the wound on Marek's temple and wiped the blood from his face and hair. At the sting of antiseptic he came round and stared up at her. Then he realized Faran was gone and at the same time heard the tell-tale noises in the bathroom. "Faran?" He tried to rise but Nikola pushed him down. "She's only throwing up is all," Nikola said. "The fright and that awful mess; it's enough to make anyone sick. I'll check her over later. Right now it's you we're most concerned about."

Marek tried to get up again. "I'm all right."

"No, you're not." Nikola forced him back into the pillows. "You will be, but you need to rest a while. You're a bit concussed and you passed out again. Don't you remember?"

"I was wondering how I got up here," Marek said.

The sounds in the bathroom were beginning to subside. While his eyes still wandered to the bathroom door, Marek asked Nikola to tell him what happened after the Vorken shot at him. All he remembered was the sound and flash of the shot and then seeing the Vorken with his brains scattered on the gravel. He didn't know what had gone on in between.

Nikola took a deep breath and related the events from start to finish. When he heard of Faran's actions and of the Vorken's threat, his face blanched but he didn't say anything. Instead, he enquired after Dan and Will.

"Will was so brave," Nikola said. "Actually, he's the one who saved you all. If he hadn't used that shovel when he did, I don't know what ..." She found her voice trailing as the reality of events finally caught up. Suddenly she thought she was going to cry. She reached convulsively for Marek's hands, hoping to find that the strength in them had returned. His hands were warmer now, but they were shaking a little.

He gazed up at her. "I-I'm sorry, Nik, for all the trouble I seem to cause—"

Nikola gathered herself together. "Nonsense! You didn't cause this!" she berated. "That you of all people should apologize, when you know …"

Marek's expression turned sheepish. "Point taken. But I'm not always …" he began to say, then he was pulling his hands away from hers and thrusting them up to cover his face. He turned from her stiffly and hid in the pillow.

Nikola was shocked. She had not realized how deeply he was affected, nor had she ever seen him this way before. This was not a Marek she had ever experienced or knew, and she was not so sure she wanted to. In horror, she thought to herself that she didn't really want to watch him break down like this.

Nevertheless, the urge of compassion was too great for her to run away and she bent over him and stroked his hair. "It's all right, my dear," she whispered. "It's just the shock. Let it come out, cry if you want, if you need."

He yielded, and Nikola rolled him into her arms. Her heart was suddenly full of tenderness and love, and it seemed to strike a cord of

371

response in her womb, where the tiny new life quickened and grew. It was a new kind of love this, warm, though impersonal, and all encompassing, the love of her life for his life, of life for life, and she felt it then as she had never felt it before.

Tenderly she held him, like a mother would hold her most beloved child. And, in surrender to the love which was greater than any illusory sadness or fear, Marek clung to her present strength until he was weary and very still. Then Nikola kissed the top of his head. "Faran's a long while in there. I ought to see how she is." She left him laying on the bed with his hand covering his forehead and eyes, as though his head ached and he just had to hold it, but could do no more than that.

Faran was washing her face in cold water. She looked up as Nikola handed her a towel. "I couldn't come back until I felt sure it was all gone," she explained. "Is Marek awake yet? Is he going to be all right?"

"Yes, to both questions. Are you sure you are okay?" Nikola asked. She felt Faran's forehead. It was cool but not clammy.

"I'm much better now," Faran said. "But what about you? We all had a bad shock." She glanced at Nikola's belly and whispered, "It won't affect your baby, will it?"

Nikola smiled. "No, I'm sure it won't. And not yours either."

The color flooded back into Faran's face. Her eyes lit up. Clearly, so overcome by the stress of what was happening outside, she had not registered Nikola's plea to the bounty hunter. "Mine? Then it was positive?"

"Absolutely. I'd put you at eight weeks or a bit more," Nikola observed. "Ahead of me, in fact." Joyfully, they both clasped hands. As Nikola led Faran to the bedroom, she whispered under her breath, "Marek really needs you. He's awfully upset and in shock. Get into bed with him and keep him warm. And give him the good news. He needs to hear something nice like that. I'll leave you both alone for a bit while I find out what's happened to the tea I ordered."

Marek was turned away from her when she approached. Faran climbed under the quilt and bent and kissed him on the cheek. "Sweet, are you all right?"

He rolled over and smiled wanly. It wasn't much of a smile but it would do for now, she decided. She tucked her arms around him, giving him many more gentle kisses. "Nikola said you are very upset, but you mustn't be, it's all over now. There's nothing more of Silene's that can happen now, is there?"

372

Marek sighed. "Not that I know of."

"And everyone's okay. Nobody else got hurt or anything. You did the right thing to go outside."

"That's why I did it," Marek replied. He took another of her kisses and gave one back, but when he looked into her eyes she saw that his were clouded and grey.

"So sad," she said, showing him that she observed. "Why so sad?"

He closed his eyes for a moment then opened them and gazed at her soulfully. "Not sad, just weary suddenly," he said. "Faran, I'm tired. I want to go home."

Faran knew he did not mean by that the cottage in the grounds. She listened to the words, understanding that, although it was the shock and the strain of the morning speaking through them and coloring them, it was also the voice of his heart. It was his ultimate wish, and hers, the hope of every human heart in its struggle for freedom from the illusory world, in its struggle to find the Light and Love it was and deserved to be.

But what could she say to him now that wouldn't sound trite or like sermonizing? Nevertheless, something had to be said.

"Oh, Love, I know you do, and you will, when the time is right. I can't know when that is or what else there will be to do, but it'll come when it's supposed to. And, in the meantime we'll go on together. There's a world out there which needs help, which needs the love and the light. And there's something else to be going on for." She smiled at him. "Do you remember the day of my birthday? Our trip to the gorge?"

He brightened at that, smiling to himself. "How could I forget it?"

"The gorge was your birthday gift to me, you said," Faran continued. "And you didn't know it then, nor did I, but I know now that you gave me something more than that at the time. I'm pregnant, Marek, more than two months on."

Tears filled his eyes as he thought how she had laid her body over his, to protect him from the Vorken. "Sweetheart, when did you find out?"

"For sure, just now. Nikola confirmed it. She did a test for me, before everything happened. Yesterday she did an exam; we were fairly certain then."

"Faran, Love." He could say no more, as the tears began to overflow, but this time they were different kinds of tears.

Misunderstanding the meaning of them, Faran clung to him. "You don't mind, do you? I mean, you're not unhappy about it, not still so sad?"

Even tearful, Marek smiled to himself. "Look at me," he said. "Faran,

look into my eyes and tell me what you see, then decide for yourself how
I feel."

Faran looked. His eyes had blossomed from their overshadowed grey
into the color she knew andloved best. They were the color of violets
again.

Chapter Two

Marek walked to clear away the poison of the day before. He walked with the cool wind blowing in his face, while the steady tread of his feet on the good earth reminded him at every step of the way of the purpose of his life. He had not come, this life, to suffer or to judge or to make mistakes, even though he had suffered and he had judged and he had made mistakes. He had come in order to DO, that which was needed to be done.

The momentary lapse into weakness yesterday, which was how he thought of it now, had been engendered by that awful weariness he felt when confronted yet again with the element of torment which existed so constantly in the illusory world. The mindless call to fear, used by Dragon-kind to rule the consciousness of the trapped and the lost; men like the Vorken who had travelled so far from the core of their lives that they were barely men at all.

But Faran had brought it all to a halt, stopped him in his tracks on a road he hadn't really wanted to go down. "What would I do without her?" he thought as the salt wind whipped his skin with its gentle sting. He liked the feel of it on his face; it let him know what living was all about.

And now they were to have a child. This knowledge brought him to a determination. It was time to go … to that central place where something more must occur. He might stay here at the hospice forever … and it was a good place, and the work was satisfying and, he knew, helpful to others … but it was not all … not his all.

He did not take the lower paths of the cliff but remained at the height where he could see out better to the long horizon. It was almost as if he looked around the curve of the Earth to Te Tanaa … to Ompalo.

The bright wind seemed to shine upon the sea. The waves moved roughly, blown into rhythmic peaks of white foam which caught the light. In his mind's eye the foam gathered and became a picture painting of a face, the face of Mari-E-ele, whom he had not forgotten in all this time, and who teased him now with her smile. He knew who Mari-E-ele was now, and she was not a goddess as the Tanu believed. The only goddess, and god, for that matter, was the Light itself, which Mankind was itself, if only it realized the truth. All other representations were bogus inventions, the pretence of the Dragons.

"Mari-E-ele." Marek addressed the invisible presence. "As you are that other dimension of my consciousness, within that flow of light of Ozira and Marek which connects us all in an unbroken thread ... as you are me, how is it that I met you on the island off the coast?" It was a puzzle which he had not solved and which was made more ironic because it was a puzzle of his own being. It seemed to him that he was capable of many things, even of teasing himself to distraction. So, Mari-E-ele had a gigantic sense of humor; he'd always known she had. It made him laugh now. He stood in the bright wind and laughed and felt the Earth and the Sun above laugh with him.

"Is that Marek down there, all by himself?"

Nikola and Dan were also out for a walk. They had taken the road at first then crossed through the coastal scrub to stare at the sea and contemplate the new miracle in their lives. Not until this morning had Nikola told Dan he was going to be a father; last night it had not seemed fitting or comfortable, somehow. So she had waited, although the desire to do it was tremendous and she knew that Faran had already told Marek about two pregnancies and not just one. But they were discreet, those two, and she knew they would not reveal anything until she had.

Dan had her arm tucked warmly in his, his hand cupped over hers. He was over the moon, she knew, as was she, now. Only Nikola's father had not heard as yet, and, thankfully, he had missed the gruesome drama of the day before. He was in Brentore, on behalf of Marek once again, staying with his cousin Charles while they made arrangements for the auction of the Collection. It would be in three days time and the newspapers had mentioned it, even as far south as here, but it had not been publicized as a thing of Marek's doing and even the De Ravana family had gone along with the secrecy, not wishing others to know of the mercenary deal they had made.

"How much do you think Marek will get for all that jewelry?" Nikola wondered aloud. Dan shrugged. "No idea, but enough for the boat he's talking about buying, hopefully."

"He wants to leave here soon, and that's what the boat is for. Did you know that?" Nikola said. She was somewhat upset by this. Marek had only spoken to her of it this very morning.

Dan stopped. "No, I didn't. Where does he want to go? And why the heck—"

"It's not just wanderlust, if that's what you're guessing," Nikola commented. She could see he had thought it. "He has somewhere definite in mind. He told me … Te Tanaa."

"What, down south? What's the attraction there?"

"I don't know. He mentions it in his journal, but he doesn't say much. I just don't know." The way she said this last alerted Dan. "You're not happy about it, are you?"

"Of course I'm not." Nikola turned her face away from the wind and Dan. She fingered the pearls at her throat: Marek's gift to her from his own mother's store of beautiful things, a gift which had almost moved her to tears when she received it. She felt a little tearful now. "I've kind of gotten used to having him around. And he's good for business," she said, shamming disgracefully.

"Oh, yeah, good for business." Dan twisted her around to look at him. "Like that's only the wind making your eyes water."

"Well it is," Nikola said, as he pulled her into his big embrace.

"Yeah." Dan tucked her head into the shelter of his chest. "Nik, you can't keep him here if he wants to go. Besides, he won't stay away forever; you're pretty special to him; I've seen that. And then there's Will. Won't Faran miss seeing her brother if they stop away?"

"That's something I don't know about, Dan. How is Will going to react? I mean, we're quite happy to have him, but will he want to stay?" Nikola said. She felt the sudden tension in Dan. "You see, now you're the same, worrying about someone you're awfully fond of leaving you. Admit it."

"I don't have to, since you already know," Dan replied, sounding grumpy and ticked off. He added, "But whatever the boy decides we have to go along with it. He's growing up fast and he's not our child, remember."

"No, he's not. But I love him all the same. And so do you." "Yeah." Dan sighed. They walked again, gradually coming closer to the place where Marek stood below, for he was almost on the very edge of the cliff whilst they kept to the less windy shelter of the scrub above. They did not go down, sensing that he had come here to be alone. But they stood and watched him, without intent and unconscious of why they watched. What was he doing there? they both thought without knowing they shared the question. For it seemed to them that they could hear him laughing, although the wind played such tricks with the ears that they doubted the sound. The sea was very bright and shining behind him. It ringed around him like a luminous aureole, weaving such patterns of moving light that suddenly he was lost to them in a splendid glare which was like a fire. A wave of burning brightness swept up into their eyes, great and beautiful, and in that one blinding portent of light and fire, it was as though he had vanished from the earth. Then, very suddenly, his act of vanishing over, he was there again, but seeming oddly changed. It was as if he was a solid being no longer, as if they could see right through him to the sea, as if he was a flame dancing on the water.

It took a shake of the head to dispel such a vision, and return the image of Marek to known parameters. But Dan and Nikola could bear it no longer. They stepped back and away. Silently, they turned and left. Whilst neither of them spoke of it to one another, nor would they later, each had felt the same. It was not fear they felt, although the feeling manifested as a shiver not unlike the trembling of fear; it was awe. They had seen something not quite understandable in that sudden flash of fire, and it awed them to silence and non approach. Instead, they held to the knowledge of each other, to the warmth and corporeality of each other's arms.

"I've been talking to Will," Faran said when Marek returned from the cliff. "He's hardly over yesterday, so this has been a bit difficult for him to handle. He said he didn't want me to go away without him, but he also liked it here. He's gone off to think about it."

Marek frowned, wishing he had not suggested she talk with her brother so soon after the upset. "We should have left it for a while. I'm sorry, that was a mistake. But how do you feel, sweetheart? Do you feel prepared to leave him behind? It's not as though we won't be coming back, but it may be a while. What do you say?"

"I don't want to be parted from him," Faran said honestly. "But if he decides he'd rather stay here, then I'll accept it. He has his own life to lead and I think he's old enough to make up his own mind; it's best left up to him."

She was wise, Marek thought, but he understood what it cost her to take such a position. He would rather himself that Will came with them, for intuitively he felt that it would be right for the boy. But Will's life was his own and it was up to him to choose what he thought was best.

It took close upon a week before Will came back to them with his

378

decision and then his reasons surprised them, for they were not exactly what they had expected. Marek listened to them with an inward smile, his intuition strengthened and confirmed. He could see how the man in Will approached steadily, and he thought of Will Crafter Senior. The father would have been justifiably proud of his son.

"It was hard to decide," Will told them. "Because I like it here, with Dan and Nikola, and it's just like a real home. But on the other hand the thought of sailing all that way to places I've never seen before excited me because it would be an adventure. Then I realized I could have adventures any time I wanted, I didn't have to choose one now. But then I thought about you and Faran, alone on a boat in the middle of the ocean. Faran might be okay now, before she gets too fat; but what happens when she does? You're going to need my help, Marek, and I do know a little bit about sailing because we learned some in school."

Marek laughed, but Faran seemed incensed. "Fat? FAT?" she exclaimed. "I'm not going to get fat!

I'll get big because of the baby, but not fat, you cheeky thing!"

Will understood that she was delighted. "But it's all the same, isn't it? Big or fat, you won't be able to do much once you get that way, so Marek will need help. And besides, I'd like to be there when my niece or nephew is born. I'd like to see that."

"Have you told Nikola and Dan what you decided yet?" Faran wanted to know.

"No. But they know I've been trying to make up my mind and I think they've guessed; they don't look too happy."

"They'll get used to it," Marek assured him. "They'll have a baby of their own to think of, in any case. What about your girlfriend, then? How's Jen going to take it?"

Will blushed. "Jenevra's not my girlfriend, she's just a kid."

Marek grinned. "But a kid with a huge crush on you. I'll talk to her if you like, just to keep the heat off."

"No you won't," Faran interposed. "I shall. Jenevra may be just a kid with a crush to you two, but I understand what she's likely to go through. I've been through it myself, so I know. She's very fond of you, Will, and if she thinks she's in love then it's a real enough thing to her, kid or not."

Bill Langan returned from Brentore and presented a check to Marek which made all their eyes pop. "Even without the inheritance and after tax, you've ended up quite well off out of it. You'll be able to cover the cost of a good boat and have plenty to live on for a while, if that's what

379

you really want," he said.

"I do," Marek affirmed.

"Well, I heard about a boat up for sale over in Hanna Harbor," Bill added. "An acquaintance of mine knows the commodore of the yacht club there and it's his brother-in-law, or someone like that, who wants to sell. Gets seasick all the time, would you believe. It's supposed to be a very good boat, very classy, with all the frills. One other owner who took it cruising all over before the seasick chap bought it. He's had it only a year, so it's seasoned but not worn out. It's worth a look, if you don't mind a drive to Hanna Harbor."

"I don't mind." Marek gave Faran a quick, though intense glance. "Sweetheart, would you mind going there?"

Faran knew what Marek was thinking about. Really, she did mind, however she remembered Marek's own reluctance to go to Brentore, yet he had gone. Time to put the past into the dustbin once and for all, where it belongs, she thought. "I'll go."

Will asked to come too. "As long as we avoid going anywhere near Aunt and Uncle," he stated. "I couldn't stand seeing them again. Or that poncy school." He became aware of Nikola standing intently behind him and turned to her. He was sensitive to the way she felt and how she and Dan felt about him. "You don't mind if I go, do you, Nikola?"

Nikola smiled half-heartedly. "Of course not. Enjoy yourself. It's not up to me to mind."

Later, hoping to soften the blow to Nikola and Dan's feelings, Faran went to see Nikola. She was in her office, in between activities; she was doodling on her desk pad, as if she was a thousand miles away, in the Southern Ocean, perhaps aboard a yacht.

"I understand," Nikola said. "Will's a boy, and what boy wouldn't love an adventure like that?" She had drawn palm trees and little smiling faces on the pad.

"That's true, and he's keen to go, but that's not his reason. He wants to help Marek. He thinks I won't be much use to him pregnant," Faran explained.

Nikola was surprised. "I hadn't realized! He is growing up, isn't he. He's such a thoughtful boy." She added another smiling face to the collection. "That makes me feel better, especially knowing you won't be working too hard. You have to look after yourself now."

"I'm not the only one; so will you," Faran said.

"Yes. But here I'm surrounded by capable staff, and Dad has promised to come back when the birth is near. I'll feel happier knowing that, just in case."

"In case what?"

Nikola stopped doodling. She fixed Faran with a long wistful gaze. "In case anything goes wrong. I'm not as young as you are, Faran, and I had hoped that Marek would be here, when my baby was born."

"I didn't know that Nikola was afraid," Marek said when Faran told him of Nikola's words.

"She's worried because this is her first child and she's nearly forty. Apparently things can go wrong under those circumstances, so she said."

"She shouldn't think like that. That's the trouble with these medical types; they tend to concentrate on the negative possibilities. It sounds like it's time I went and had a talk with her," Marek decided.

"You can do that tonight then," Faran informed him. "Nikola asked us to join them all for dinner, before we go off to Hanna Harbor tomorrow."

The day had been calm and clear, for the wind had dropped after a week of continuously blustery weather. This made for a beautiful evening of limpid stillness and late summer warmth, so after a convivial dinner it was decided that it was the perfect evening for a walk. The six of them set off, Marek, Faran, Will, Nikola, Dan and Bill, taking the road which wove down to the mooring where the Rhona was docked because Bill wanted to make sure that there was space enough at the mooring for anything Marek might buy, if the boat at Hanna Harbor proved to be the one he wanted.

It was a long walk down to the sea. At the mooring they all went inside the Rhona and a surprised but delighted Captain Boddy gave them coffee in stout mugs. Marek saw Nikola carry her coffee off to the foredeck alone, and followed.

Nikola leaned on the rail, sipped her coffee and watched the water drift like liquid silk around the Rhona's creamy colored hull. The mooring was generally safe and quiet, being in the sheltered curve of a small bay formed by two bluffs. It had been a long while since she had enjoyed such a moment of peace, Nikola thought. So much had happened of late that her whole world had seemed to have turned itself upside down. Yet it was not a turning she would have wished to miss out on, in spite of the unsettling nature of events. If life sometimes had a way of picking you up and giving you a good shake, well, that meant you deserved it or needed it. Better that than stagnating in a pond of everyday sameness, growing old and dull with nothing but atrophy to look forward to. She was immersed in these idle musings when she felt the touch of a hand at her elbow. She glanced up.

"Deep thoughts?" Marek asked.

"Not really. I was just thinking how peaceful it was here, and other things." "Are you happy?"

Nikola finished the last sip of coffee. She put the mug very carefully to one side on the deck. Marek wasn't drinking; he didn't have a mug, she noticed then. Was she happy? "Yes. But life isn't as simple as that, is it?"

"Something's worrying you." Marek looked out to sea. "I won't pretend I don't know, because Faran told me what you said about the baby. I think we should talk about it, don't you?"

Oh, God," Nikola thought. She and Marek had spoken together so many times of the problems of others: her patients and, sometimes, his. She had never been the patient before, not to herself or him, and she didn't know how to approach the subject.

He helped her by diving straight in. "The trouble is you know too much about illness. In some ways you're better off than the average expectant mother because you can see the signs of anything going wrong and do something about it quickly. But knowing what can go wrong just keeps you focused in that direction. Have you had any problems so far?"

Nikola felt her cheeks redden. He was always like this with her, so up front and unimpeded; he always had been. She supposed it was a compliment that he reckoned she could take his honesty like a friendly blow on the chin, but sometimes she found it difficult and embarrassing and almost impossible to return. No, she hadn't experienced any problems so far, not beyond the usual morning nausea at least, she told him, hoping that this would put an end to it.

"So what are you worrying about?" Marek did not give up easily, if at all.

Did she have to tell him? The truth had little to do with illusory fears of childbirth, as she had implied to Faran, although she knew the risks of an older woman bearing a child for the first time. The truth had everything to do with him, though, with his going away just at the time when she felt she needed him most. Don't make me say it, she thought, even while she knew she would confess.

"It's just that I would be happier if you weren't leaving. I wish you didn't have to go." "Because of the baby?" Marek asked. "Are you afraid?"

"No, not really." Nikola took her turn at staring out to sea. "I don't understand why you want to leave; you've been doing such wonderful work here. All the people you've helped, all the people you could help in the future."

"But I have something else to do, something important," he said softly.

Passionately she turned to him. "What's more important than helping those who can't help themselves? They need you, Marek!"

He looked downcast, as if her words stung him. He said, "Nik, while the illusory world controls humanity there will always be sickness, and sick people. I can't help everyone by touching them or talking to them physically. They need to find the power and freedom in themselves which will allow them to help themselves. One person can't do it for the rest, everyone has to do it. What I hope to do, though, is to build that center of force to which everyone can resonate, something for the Earth and for the people in the wider sense, then the people themselves will destroy the prisons of their world; they will set themselves free."

Nikola was not sure she understood, or wanted to understand. "But the more you touch, the more you help. Won't that—?"

Marek shook his head. "Even if I lived to be a hundred doing it, it would never be enough for the world as it is. Until the illusion is broken, the sickness will continue. Let me do what I must while I can, as I see it." He sighed, then smiled down at her. "Nik, I'll be coming back, and I'll see your child and how happy you and Dan are, and, I guarantee, you won't be wanting me to make your world perfect for you, because you will have what you need in yourselves. That's my aim, to let the world of humanity find itself at last, after so long being lost, just like it happened for me."

Nikola sighed also. "I'm glad you'll be coming back." She forced a smile, although it was not so difficult to do now. "I'm going to miss you in the meantime, though. I've kind of gotten used to having that smiling face of yours hanging about my place." His hand was on the rail, next to hers. She covered it with her own. She felt the overwhelming need to confess, to tell him the final truth. "I've always said that I love you, and I used to think it was a romantic kind of love. But now I know that it's just Love, pure and simple. I love Faran, too, and Will, so I really want to keep in touch; I don't want to let us drift apart."

He placed his arm around her shoulders. He understood her concern, that, for her, it was still a matter of wanting things to stay always as they

383

were and that she could not yet see that life was constant movement and change. She needed to cling to the people and the things she loved, not realizing that merely loving them was enough and this would keep them within the sphere of her heart, if not her physical presence. When, one day, she realized that all life was really the One and that their mutual love was the energy which linked them all forever, she would not need to cling any longer.

Marek bent and kissed her on the cheek. "There's no chance of that, no chance at all. I love you too, Nikola."

Chapter Three

Before they left next morning Nikola said to Faran confidentially, "When you get to Hanna Harbor take Marek shopping and buy him some good clothes; he can afford it now. He can hardly present himself at the yacht club as a prospective boat buyer without a decent set of clothes on his back; otherwise, they'll just look down their noses at him."

Faran agreed without argument. Nikola was right about the yacht club people; appearances were very important there, and she knew from experience that it was impossible to get in the front door if one was not appropriately dressed. And also she fancied the idea of smartening Marek up a bit. Not that he wasn't acceptable to her as he was, but she remembered how good he had looked at the Towers in his fine, expensive clothes. It was true that clothes did not make a person more worthy, and least of all someone like Marek, but they added a pleasing exterior. Also she had to think of herself; she would need a few big, loose things for later on, when her pregnancy progressed. And Will needed new clothes, as he was growing too.

Hanna Harbor was the same as ever it was, Faran thought, as she gazed out the window of Bill's car. Being the end of summer, it meant that many of the holiday makers were already leaving town and the streets were gradually emptying of excess traffic and the shops were redesigning their window displays as they prepared to resume the more usual business, which chiefly involved servicing the port and the fishing trade. At least the yacht club would be quieter, Faran hoped, although that was not a certainty as yet. When last she had thought about that place of her past its doors were closed and the idea of walking by there was not worrisome. Even so, she had avoided doing it then.

But they were not going there until tomorrow, since it had been a long drive between Hanna Harbor and the Springs. Tonight they would put up in a good hotel and make time for the obligatory shopping. When Faran told Marek about Nikola's orders he had only grinned, saying that Nikola was always on at him about his carefree mode of dress. "Wait till we get to Te Tanaa. I'd really like to see Nikola in such a place; they hardly wear anything there," he said.

If Hanna Harbor had not changed then neither had the yacht club. There were the vast front doors of shining chrome and thick frosted plate glass carved with images of yachts and the club crest. They were opened to them by the costumed doorman, an obsequious vision in cobalt blue and epaulets and the gold braid worthy of a dozen admirals, who doffed his peaked hat like a gentleman greeting other gentlemen.

What a conceit for these modern times, Faran thought, as if the well heeled of Hanna Harbor fancied themselves as gentry and this was a palace or grand hotel. Nevertheless, she was glad they had been shopping first, imagining the doorman's alternative reaction had they not. It would have been all right for Bill Langan, for he always dressed quite formally; and Will was just a boy, so providing he was clean and neat, he would have gotten in the door simply as an official attachment to Bill. The club demanded collar and tie only at night, but by day the rule was expensive and tasteful sports clothes, but only that. Faran cast critical eyes over Marek. He looked good enough to satisfy even Nikola, in a shirt of the best, whitest linen, striped finely with blue, the sort of hyacinthine blue which matched his eyes of the present moment, and a pair of ivory tailored pants and a navy blazer, both of which looked at home in the place they were going to. He'd had a haircut too, although not as short a one as Nikola would have preferred, but he was tidy. For herself, Faran had bought, along with all the blousy items for later, just one good, smart suit, a luxurious silk lined affair of white jacket and pants. It was to be her last chance at wearing something slim and straight before the bigness descended, and she relished it.

Once inside, Bill Langan led them straight upstairs to the office of the Commodore, for he had been in this yacht club before, and to reception.

"Dr. Langan to see Commodore Keyes. He's expecting me and my party," Bill told the girl sitting behind the desk.

She gave them all a cursory, somewhat supercilious inspection, with a second glance at Marek, then consulted her book. She rang through and they were ushered into the office.

The Commodore was a red cheeked, lardy looking man with a bristle-brush moustache. He also affected nautical dress, which Faran thought was much too overdone and rather comical, reminding her vaguely of the doorman. Will must have thought the same, for he nudged her and grinned.

Bill Langan introduced himself and then Marek and Faran and Will. The Commodore showed his surprise by dropping open his mouth then shutting it promptly. The expression on his face said that he wouldn't have expected a man who'd given away millions and only worked in somebody else's sanatorium, to have enough means to buy a rowboat. But when he saw that Marek was genuine in his interest, his eyes lit up with anticipation. It was not his boat, it was his brother-in-law's, yet clearly he was planning to get something for himself out of the sale.

The Commodore strutted importantly in front as he led them down the length of the marina to his relative's boat. Not all the yachts were out of service for the winter, Faran noted. Some of them were still operative, not closed up like abandoned floating palaces waiting only for their turn to come alive again. She saw brown young men working on one or two, cleaning and polishing, painting this and that, and a few boats were still out in the bay, taking advantage of the last of the summer's warm winds. Then they came to a boat with a magnificent black hull and furled red sails. The hull shone like a length of liquid night and the soft swell of the water threw dancing reflections and lights up into its glossy surface, making it appear as if the boat was made of black glass. Gold trim and gleaming brass made the elegance complete. The boat was called the Albatross. "Wow!" Will said enthusiastically when he realized this was the one.

It took them an hour and a half to see through everything, for both Marek and Bill shared the same respect for thoroughness, and both of them knew boats and what to look for. If the Commodore had thought it was going to be an effortless sale, he was mistaken. He sighed and wheezed a bit as he tried to be patient and answer their questions as best he could. Then Marek asked for a test run and the Commodore had to detail someone else to supervise that. "I don't actually sail myself ... nowadays," the Commodore stated, and Faran and Will had to hold on to each other to keep themselves from breaking down with laughter.

"It's a wonderful boat, at least I think it is," Faran whispered to Marek after they had returned to the marina. "It is, isn't it? Do you want it?"

"It'll do just fine," Marek said. "Big enough for the three of us and not too big to handle. I want it." He smiled down at her. "But I thought you looked a little green out there. Where you feeling sick?"

"Yes, but it wasn't the boat. I've been a bit off all morning. I guess it's just being pregnant. I thought I was very clever because I hadn't been sick yet, but now it's catching up with me. I'd like to sit down somewhere for a while."

"Bill and I have to do some smart talking with Keyes. Bill reckons they're asking way too much so we're going to see how far down we can push the price. Since I can offer cash straight up that ought to be an inducement. Why don't you and Will go into the lounge area while we're at it? Maybe have some tea to settle you a bit."

Faran nodded. She didn't feel up to listening to men wrangling over price, the size of which only awed her. For Marek, to have access to money like this wasn't a novelty or a problem ... he had been used to it for the greater part of his life. But to her it was a situation she did not feel comfortable with. The only time she'd had access to any sort of riches was when she lived with her aunt and uncle, and then it was only doled out to her like charitable offerings, as clothes for parties and pocket money for outings and school.

In the lounge Faran ordered tea, but Will didn't want any. He had seen the recreation room next door and was keen to go and try his hand at the games it offered. They were mechanical games mostly, electronic and such, the kind of games that favored the lone player pitched against the might of the machine.

Faran sat and sipped her tea, realizing then that she hadn't really wanted any either. There were very few patrons in the lounge for most were in the bar, getting quietly well oiled as a preparation for the lunchtime hour. Then a group came in the front door, noisily, as if they were bent on making themselves heard and noticed. The type of group she'd once been an uncomfortable part of, she thought. Young people, mostly, light minded, idle and facetious people to whom work meant nothing and superficial pleasure meant all.

The young crowd went straight to the bar which was just outside the lounge. Faran turned her eyes away from the sight; they didn't interest her much, for she only waited for Marek to return. She could think only of him and the boat and what they were about to do. He had explained some of it but the reality was still far away to her. To go to Te Tanaa and to Ompalo, there to build upon what he had already set in place; it was something to look forward to.

"Faran, baby! Long time no see," came a voice she had never wanted to hear again.

Faran swung around, feeling suddenly ill. It was the past she had hoped was buried forever. It was Brock.

He swaggered up to her. He was, by now, about twenty four or twenty five ... she couldn't remember exactly. But by the look of him, he was already going to seed, running to fat where no fat ought to be in such a young man, and his stomach hung over his belt. A booze stomach, she thought to herself, in disgust. He was soft and pappy looking, padded about the cheeks and under the chin and thick around the eyes, and in his

388

eyes was the same expression of self satisfied, fleshly indolence she remembered. She couldn't think what she had ever seen in him, although he had not appeared so degenerate in the old days.

He flung himself down beside her, making her wish she had chosen a single chair instead of the lounge. "Fah-Fah," he said, using the stupid infantile name he'd lumbered her with so many years before. "Aren't you even going to say hello?"

He was slightly drunk, Faran realized. His face was florid and moist looking. She could smell a trace of liquor emanating from him. A bit early in the day, she thought. "Hello, Brock," she said, hoping a brief answer would shut him up and that he would find her uninteresting enough to go away.

"Fancy, after all these years," he went on. "Hey, baby, have you come back here to join us?" He leaned towards her. The odor of sweat and expensive cologne and a scent like a whiff from a brewery assaulted her.

Faran held herself away from him. "Not exactly."

It was as if she had not even answered, for he stood up suddenly and waved to his friends in the bar. "Lookee … come and see. My dear old girlfriend come back to me." His friends, though, did not seem all that interested. One or two glanced at him and wandered to the edge of the lounge, but they didn't bother to enter.

Brock leaned closer and Faran was beginning to realize that he was drunker than she had first thought. "Go away, Brock. Go back to your friends. I'm not your girlfriend and you were never a friend to me," she said, hoping that a swift rejection would end it quickly.

But Brock was oblivious. "Fah-Fah, don't be mean," he moaned, sliding right up to her. "I missed you, you know. You just ran off and left me. I was sad, very sad … for weeks." He began to play with the ends of her hair. "You're so pretty, Fah-Fah, so pretty."

Faran felt the heat of frustration and embarrassment burning her cheeks. She tried to shrug him off as politely as she could. "Go away, Brock," she whispered. "Don't make a fuss; your friends won't like it." She remembered now how when he was drunk he used to make scenes. As long as he was the center of attention and didn't get hurt publicly, he didn't care much what kinds of scenes they were.

He touched her shoulder with his sweaty fingers and she shrugged him off. "Faran …" he began again, when another voice intruded. "Get away from her, you creep!" Will burst into the lounge. His young face was red and angry. He was followed by some of Brock's friends who seemed more interested in enjoying a probable confrontation than in defending one of their own from attack.

"Who's this? " Brock asked, unafraid. "A bit young for you, Fah-Fah."

Faran was worried about what Will might do. She pushed Brock away. "That's my brother. Now go away, please. You'll only make trouble like this."

Brock grinned drunkenly. He spread his hands in a false gesture of innocence and surrender to Will. "I don't want trouble. I only want her to say she still loves me."

"You creep—" Will began to move forward, when a command from behind halted him. "Leave it, Will!" Marek stood in the doorway with Bill Langan. It must have been something in his voice, some tone which sounded threatening enough for everyone to pay attention, for Brock's friends turned to stare at him. Brock gazed across at Marek with a stupid expression on his face. "Not another brother?"

"Move away from my wife." Marek stepped into the room. He did little else and said nothing more, however the tone of his voice had hardened, and it was full of the same determination such as Faran had heard at the lawyers" office in Brentore, but with something extra added. There was great power and authority in that tone, and to add to it, a force of fire which seemed to flash from his eyes. It was the power to scare someone half to death, if he wanted to.

Brock backed away as Marek walked towards them. He slid from the lounge chair and seemed to crawl off with bent knees, like a dog caught stealing his master's dinner and fearing to be punished. "I didn't know … sorry," he murmured to Faran. "Bye." His drunkenness was suddenly abated and the nearer he got to the door, the more he appeared to sober up. He joined his friends, who were themselves now conspicuously uncomfortable, for they were conscious of the disapproving glares thrown their way by the other patrons in the bar, and it was not long before they all left.

Marek took Brock's place on the lounge and put his arm around Faran's shoulders. "Are you all right?"

Faran nodded. "I'm okay. That was Brock," she whispered, only to him. "The one I told you about."

Marek hadn't realized just who it was pestering her. "If I'd known that, I would have knocked his head off," he said.

Faran squeezed his hand. "No you wouldn't. You don't need to do things like that; you scared him witless just by looking at him. I've never seen that in you before; it was a bit spooky."

"Spooky? Really? I only wanted to make him understand that I meant it, without having to make too much fuss, or an unpleasant scene." Marek shrugged. He knew exactly what he'd done and why – that he had consciously used power over another human being in order to intimidate and remove what he saw as a pestilence forcing itself upon Faran, and what might have been a real problem for Will, had the boy acted on his heated impulse to protect his sister. His own act of power was almost Silene- like, Marek admitted to himself then, but there was no maliciousness in the intent and no harm had been done to anyone.

As they left the club and headed for the car, Marek informed Faran and Will, "The deal's been struck, the boat is ours." He said to Bill Langan, "Thanks to you, Bill, we got it at a fair price. Less than I expected. You know, you're one hell of a good negotiator."

Bill smiled. "Practice, that's all. I've been doing business all my life. It's the only way I've been able to keep my clinics going properly." He unlocked the car doors, but did not get in right away, speaking across the car's roof to Marek. "But it wasn't all me. I hope you don't mind me saying this, but people are going to start talking about you in a different way than before. When he realized who you were, that Keyes chap was all ready to pass you off as some sort of hopeless eccentric whom he could pull the wool over. But the minute he started on his silly games, you let him have it … right between the eyes … with that look of yours. He was almost in the same condition after you finished with him as that idiot in the lounge was, and yet you barely said a word. What is it you do, or have, anyway, that seems to set you apart from others? It has me intrigued."

Marek gave a brief laugh and a shrug. "I don't know about there being something I have. But what I did there in the club was just an act of intent, and you use that yourself, Bill, although maybe less consciously than I do. You used it with Keyes too, negotiating, and I used it to get that drunk away from Faran before he hurt her or, more exactly, before Will got himself hurt trying to help her."

Bill Langan's look of surprise was genuine. He leaned over the roof of the car. "You mean you used some force of will to make them behave? Some kind of subtle energy? And that I do it too, without realizing?"

Marek considered the question. "Well, yes and no. There is certainly an energy there but it isn't will power. Intent is an awkward word because people are inclined to mix it up with the idea of will. But it's not the same thing. What it really is, is focus." Marek grinned at Bill's puzzled frown. "Let's get in the car and I'll explain."

They got in and before Bill drove off, Marek continued. "Intent is the expression of your whole Self, whereas will is an act of the Ego in its attempt to control everything around it. True intent is knowing what you are and expressing and giving that to others. A pure intent is being the Light of yourself and only wishing to share that Light. Dealing with Keyes, we only wished for what was best all round, and the other business was just to make things right, without trouble, but Keyes and the other chap were only interested in trying to take advantage."

To Bill's understanding nod, Marek ended by saying, "My focus is the Light which I am and my intent is to BE THAT LIGHT, in this world and after it. The more you read Ozira's words, the more you will understand, because it's what you ARE, and what you have to BE consciously, Bill, ultimately."

A small and precise paint-out job turned the Albatross into the Mari-E-ele, and when Marek and Will brought it from Hanna Harbor to the mooring beside the Rhona, Nikola admired the glossy black hull and white lettering and asked Marek, "What does Mari-E-ele mean?"

"It's Tanu for Beautiful One From The Sun and The Sea."

Saying farewell to Telaia this time was not like last time, Marek thought. Without the same sense of urgency and the encouragement of weevils in dark suits, leaving Telaia now meant a more gradual, heart wrenching affair of saying goodbye to friends. As the Mari-E-ele pulled away from the mooring under the power of its auxiliary engines, Marek watched the faces on the dock recede but he did not feel any regrets. They were special people, all of them: Bill, Nikola and Dan, Jenevra, and they were a part of him forever, so he could never lose them, not to the notions of time or space which were but illusions, after all. And behind them, surrounding them, like luminous faces crowding out the dark, were the invisible presences, those who were not here today but who had also been opened to their Light and, in that sense, were one with him and the others, and always would be.

The wind kicked in and Marek killed the engines and let the sails take over. Faran joined him at the outside steering. Her face was pale but there was a freshness blossoming at her cheeks, due mostly to the wind, he guessed. "How are you doing?" he asked as the boat cleared the shelter of the little bay and plunged directly into heavier waters, for he had been concerned by a seeming wanness of her expression earlier.

392

"I'm all right. I don't feel ill, if that's what you mean," she said. She was sixteen weeks pregnant now and the morning nausea was long gone. But, to tell the truth, she was a trifle heart-sick at leaving the hospice and the dear little cottage which she and Marek had called home, having found the meaning of her life there. She did not say this to him, though, and thought instead to herself, How foolish I am! Why, here is the meaning of my life standing right next to me! Him and my Light, that's all there really is!

Her thoughts cheered her and drew her closer to the heart of him, and as though he felt them and knew them too, he pulled her nearer. His arm curved around her waist and his hand cradled the mound which was beginning to make itself noticeable in her belly. "I'll keep you safe," he whispered in her ear.

Faran felt the familiar weakening of her knees which always accompanied his touches of intimacy and she allowed herself a moment of surrender in order to sink against into the curve of his shoulder. She was warm there, yes, and safe, and she did not want to be anywhere else. "How long will it take to get to Te Tanaa?"

With one hand he steadied the steering. His lips brushed her ear in a kiss. "A few months, maybe four. But before the baby comes."

Chapter Four

Sailing the open sea was a combination of experiences and sensations ranging from the thrilling and the terrifying to a boredom so deep and absolute that it was mind numbing. The thrill was in seeing all the vast beauty of the earth in its expression of the elements, and in coming into port now and then when one would appreciate the always scenic meeting of land and water and sky. The terror had to be lived through but was easier to endure than the boredom since it only came and went during high seas and storms, and luckily, they had passed through very few. The boredom was the result of days and even weeks of blue sea merging seamlessly into blue sky, with not one cloud to provide interest or relief.

At first, life on board the Mari-E-ele was busy and engrossing. Only Marek knew much about sailing in open water and so there was a time of teaching for both Will and Faran. Faran discovered she was not a natural sailor, if ever there was such a thing, but Will proved an excellent pupil and it was not long before Marek was able to trust him with the boat and the responsibilities of a full watch. Of course, steering the boat and navigation were no longer the esoteric arts they had used to be in times past. Stuffed full with all the modern gadgetry and electronic aids the sailing world had to offer, the Mari-E-ele could have practically taken itself to Te Tanaa, provided the boat had a mind and brain of its own to know where it was headed.

As Faran's pregnancy progressed into the sixth month, Marek and Will took to dividing the watches between themselves, leaving her to get the full rest which her body was beginning to demand. Faran was secretly pleased about this, for she did not feel the same confidence that Will felt when in charge of the boat whilst everyone else was asleep. She made up for her lacking in this regard by taking over all the cooking and seeing to it that the two males were always properly fed; it was what she was the best at anyway.

It was a beautiful night, clear and calm with a gentle, rolling sea. Stars were already coming out and they seemed to gather along the edges of the sails, like a fringe of silver and gold. The Mari-E-ele plunged steadily through the waves, cutting its own fringe of shining foam. Faran came into the cockpit bearing a steaming mug of tea for Marek. Will had finished his and had gone to bed almost an hour before. He was due for the late night watch so he needed to get his rest.

"Thanks, Love." Marek took the mug and sipped at the tea. "In a day we ought to be in Vetta, and I'll bet you're really looking forward to that."

For the chance to stand on solid ground again Faran would have wished that day already gone. But Vetta? "You said they don't speak much Telaian there, only Arpayan. How long will we stay? Will I be able to shop or communicate with anyone?"

"They pretend not to speak Telaian. The truth is they're a peculiar lot with a prejudice against anyone who doesn't speak Arpayan, or, more particularly, who speaks only Telaian. It's the colonial mentality. The place was founded when Arpay was a big deal power and the Vettans have never gotten over the fact that their mother country is now a bit of a nothing in the world any more. They'll understand every word you say but they'll pretend they don't. But we'll get by; I speak Arpayan after a reasonable sort of fashion, so shopping won't be a problem."

Faran frowned into the darkness, so Marek wouldn't see. "But it's your birthday soon and I was hoping to get you a present. But if I can't go shopping without you, how will it be a surprise?" Marek laughed. "Sweetheart, I don't need you to buy me presents! You're all the present I need." "Yes, well I thought it would be nice, in any case. I just wonder how long it's been since anyone helped you celebrate your birthday."

Marek laughed again. "Too long, I guess. And the last one I remember at which there was any sort of fuss made was eight years ago, when I turned twenty five and Silene had me thrown in the tower." His laugh had the sound of irony in it. "That was something to celebrate, wasn't it?"

Faran was appalled; it didn't seem much of a joke to her. She tucked her arms around his waist. "Then if I can't get you a present without you seeing what it is, I'll have to be content with a few supplies, so I can make you a birthday cake. You'd like that, wouldn't you?"

He smiled down at her. "I would. A cake is much nicer than a tower, any day."

Faran went to bed. In five hours Marek would join her and she looked forward to it, always ready to be near him although she was generally only half awake when he came. But she loved to have him beside her in the warmth, to touch him, to smell the salty, spicy scent of him, and to taste his welcoming kisses on her sleepy mouth. As she undressed she studied herself by lamp-light in the mirror on the inside of the closet door. She was somewhat critical of her large swelling belly, thinking to

395

herself how huge and ungainly it was. She ran her hand across the smooth white mound. It appeared to give forth a lustrous sheen, as if light was suffusing from within it into the surrounding air. She was nearly into her seventh month but it seemed to her that she was very big. But she could not be sure, having no one to measure herself against. If Nikola had been there, then they could have compared notes at least.

Sleep came quickly tonight. It was the rhythm of a calm evening which soothed her body and hypnotized her mind, so that Faran dropped into sleep without scarcely another thought.

However, somewhere later on in the night she woke with a start. Marek was not there and the boat was pitching back and forth and sideways and the waves slammed into the hull one after the other. She tried to get up, but a fresh lurch of the boat sent her spinning back into the bed. She could hear a high-pitched screaming all around her but it was no human voice which screamed, it was the wind. The waves seemed to be crashing onto the top of the boat as well as all around. In panic, she tried to fight her way up again, but it seemed that the huge mountain of her belly had made her entirely helpless and she fell back, in tears. She could not even reach the lamp to switch on the light. Where was Marek? And Will? She began to scream as loudly as the wind, but no one heard her or came.

Faran was thrown about like a doll on the bed, confused, in absolute darkness, her head spinning. She held on to her belly and sobbed and cried out, but there was no ease, and nothing to save her from the fear which grew and grew. "Marek!" she screamed. "Will, where are you?"

Then she became conscious that the dark had a presence of its own, as if it moved in a body upon her, into her mind and before her straining eyes. Faces appeared which seemed to stare dispassionately from the dark, forms and faces, like the inventions of veils of shadowy cobwebs hanging in a cave which might take on the imaginary shapes of familiar things. Yet these were nothing as harmless as cobwebs, although perhaps they were far less substantial. They seemed to slither through the dark air towards her, as though they would reach near and attempt to cling.

"See where he has brought you," said a voice from the dark. It was a slippery kind of voice, feminine in pitch and tone. "Now will you see the truth of him; he is one you cannot trust, although he has fooled you up to now. He only wants what he wants; he doesn't care about you or the child. He puts your lives in constant danger, yours, the baby's and your brother's."

The air screamed around Faran. She tried once more to rise but the boat's pitching held her down. "Look at you, you're helpless," the voice said. It's tone had turned to sarcasm and contempt. "They're all the same, these magicians, they never change. He's told you that he turned away from sorcery, but that's a lie, and you were a fool to believe him. And now you are helpless."

Defiant, Faran held on to her belly and steadied herself in the bed. "No! You're a liar, whoever you are! I can't even see your face, and who would believe such a faceless nothing?"

Suddenly there was a glimmer of grey light and a face did appear, as if to mock her. It was the face of a woman Faran knew, and she pulled back in horror. It was Aunt Moria. "You always thought I was selfish, but I only wanted the best for you," the aunt said. "See, I could have saved you from all of this, from this danger that you are in, and from the grip of that monster outside, that monster who has fooled you into believing in him."

"No!" Faran shook her head frantically. The boat seemed to be smashing itself to pieces as the bodiless face leered at her. "But there's still time," the face of Aunt Moria mouthed. "He's a magician and a man, and neither of those things care about the likes of you or your child. When the storm ends, if you survive, leave him at the nearest port. Tell him you don't want to have anything to do with him any more, and leave. Go back to Telaia and take your brother too. Go back to where you will be safe from him."

Faran started to scream. "Liar! Liar! You never cared about us! Get away, get out of here! Leave me alone!" The darkness seemed to swarm around her and Aunt Moria's face began to waver and distort, as though it was a face in a carnival mirror.

"Then damned you are!" the distorted face screamed back. "Just see how damned you are!"

Abruptly, the boat lurched, throwing Faran against the side wall. Her hand grazed the light lever and she managed to switch it on. She stared in horror at the sight before her. The cabin was a shambles, a total wreck, but worst of all was the bed; it was covered in blood.

Faran looked down at her nightdress and blood covered legs and began to weep. The baby, she thought, no, not the baby! and she fell into a nauseous, then a deep, swoon.

She came to some time later to find Marek bent close to her, concern on his face. "Sweetheart, are you okay?" he was saying anxiously.

Faran's forehead was glazed with a cold sweat. She started up in terror and disbelief. There was nothing wrong in the cabin, the sea beneath the Mari-E-ele was only a gentle roll, and the sheets, though tangled, were without blood. She gripped Marek's hand tightly; his hand was warm while hers was ice. "I had a dream. It was awful," she whispered.

Marek frowned. "I thought you were ill. I was just coming below when I heard you cry out. Do you want to tell me about it?"

Faran wasn't sure she wanted to. To remember the dream made her shiver and cringe and break out into a sweat again. But she told him anyway and it was like reliving a descent into hell. Afterward he was silent for a short while, although she felt his arms tighten around her protectively. Then he said in hushed tones, "They are afraid of what we are going to do, so they'll try anything to spoil it. By invading your dream state with their images of disaster and fear, they hoped to turn us against each other. You need to call on the Light consciously every time before you sleep, to protect you from stuff like that in future. They won't give up if they think they can frighten you into breaking with me."

Faran shivered. Break with him? Why, that was an even worse thought than anything in the dream. She could no more think of breaking up with Marek than she could of cutting out her own heart. "I would never break with you, don't they know that?" she said. "But it was the blood, that's what upset me most," she admitted.

Marek held her nearer. "You don't need this kind of thing, my love, not at this time especially. Before we sleep we'll do the Light together." He placed his hands over her belly. "The baby is safe; it's the Earth's body and the Earth keeps it safe. But we'll place the Light around ourselves as a shield and to remind us of what we are, and what the child is and will be when its consciousness of Light comes into this sphere." He closed his eyes and concentrated, and Faran closed hers and concentrated too, also feeling the extra power of his healing touch as it coursed through her body. A tingling sensation similar to what she had felt at the time in the cottage when she had broken free and, later, had received her name, invigorated every cell. She felt fully alive and alert, yet no longer identified with her body. As she swept up and out and became conscious of herself in Light and as Light, she saw the little pregnant body below and was moved to love it. There was nothing ungainly about that rounded shape; it was only purely beautiful, for it was ripe and alive like a swelling bud or a fruit on one of Earth's wonderful trees.

"I feel so much better now," Faran whispered to Marek as they settled down to sleep. "Not that anything they did would make me ever want to leave you. I can't understand though why they thought they could influence me in that way. Don't they know how much we love each other?"

Marek kissed her goodnight. "That's just it; they don't know what love means; it isn't in their experience. Without the true Light of the All, they have no knowledge of love or of any feeling akin to it. They're like something which is entirely closed in upon itself, like they possess a vanity so profound and exclusive that nothing but their own vision of things exists for them."

"Ugh!" Faran shivered. "Well they can keep their vision to themselves; they're welcome to it. I want only to know the Light, and you, my Love."

Chapter Five

Port Dias in Vetta was so busy that yachts shared the harbor like fish jammed side by side in a bathtub of water. It was the holiday season, that time of year when sailing the Southern Ocean was at its best and safest; so the tourists and the voyagers were out in force, and jammed the port town in the same way as the boats, filling up markets and shops and restaurants and crowding the streets.

There was a festive mood in the town, though, which made the press of humanity bearable, Marek thought. Nobody was in a very great hurry and everyone seemed determined to relax and enjoy themselves, so it made the faces which you met in the crowd cheerful and friendly. Port Dias was not like the overburdened cities of Telaia, where people were afraid to speak to one another in the streets.

But he was right about the language problem. Although in the streets one could hear the babble of half a dozen different tongues and the predominantly dark skinned native people who ran the open air market did not seem to mind what language you spoke as long as you could communicate to them what you wanted to buy from their stalls, in the shops and restaurants the shopkeepers and waiters and waitresses feigned ignorance of anything but Arpayan. It was a foolish conceit which did more harm to the image of Vetta than it did good, Marek decided, for every tourist who came there knew what fraudulent behavior it really was.

So he and Faran and Will shopped primarily at the market where at least the discourse was friendly and honest, if somewhat muddled at times. There was plenty to buy there too, so much good fresh food that it had made their mouths water on the first day.

On their second morning in the port they woke up to find that the harbor was gradually emptying of the excess numbers of yachts. Apparently, some of them belonged to a flotilla taking part in a round-the-world expedition and some others belonged to a charter club operating out of Telaia. Then the atmosphere became a little quieter, especially around the marinas, although the town itself was still busily at a peak.

"This is better," Marek said, as he surveyed the empty berths around them. "A few less all night parties and it should be rather pleasant here for another day or two. Then I guess we'll have to be going as well."

He was silenced by a chorus of dismay from Faran and Will. "I'd really like to stay longer," Faran said.

"So would I," Will added.

They had both found Port Dias to be much more inviting than the picture Marek had painted of it. Perhaps it was because his last visit there was a visit made "on the run" – not a happy or comfortable time for him – and this had colored his memory of it. Whatever the reason, Faran and Will discovered a town they really enjoyed and they did not want the experience to end so soon.

"Let's stay a couple of weeks," Faran suggested, for in truth she was feeling rather sick and tired of the endless rolling sea and the smallness of the Mari-E-ele. Being so pregnant was also making her restless and somewhat discomforted and the closed spaces of the boat were beginning to get on her nerves, for they seemed to accentuate the growing awkwardness of her body and the increase of its size.

Marek was not sure, for the size of Faran's pregnant belly also concerned him. He had wondered if she had gotten her dates wrong and that she was actually further along than was thought. But, not wishing to worry her unnecessarily, he had not said anything to her about it. "It'll take four weeks to get from here to Te Tanaa. You have about eight weeks to go before the baby's due. Are you sure you want to hang about here for so long? That would leave you with only two weeks or so to play with."

Faran looked him squarely in the eye, hoping he would understand. "Marek, I need to stop, I really do. It's not just a whim. I would like to stay on dry land for just a while, then I'll feel better about going on."

"So do I," Will put in. "I hadn't realized how such a long trip could wear even me out, and I think Faran looks awfully tired, don't you?"

Outvoted, and because he could see the truth of Will's words quite plainly in Faran' jaded expression, Marek agreed. "Okay, two weeks. But then we really must get to Te Tanaa."

"Will, hello!"

A copper-brown colored woman with a wide, white-toothed smile hailed Will from the fresh fruit and vegetable stall in the market square, and in Telaian too. Two weeks in a place like this and you were

401

practically considered a native, Will reckoned, since most visitors came and went in the space of only days.

"Alva, morning," Will said, as he came over to her stall. He had liked the woman from the moment he had met her and she always seemed rather taken by him for some reason which he did not understand and always paid him the courtesy of struggling with his language rather than expecting him to decipher hers.

"What are you having this day?" Alva asked him in her broken Telaian. She spread her brown hands wide, as if to suggest that everything on her stall was at his disposal, which of course it was, provided he paid for it.

"Well, I want rather a lot this time. We're leaving tomorrow so we have to stock up for the trip to Te Tanaa."

"Oh, I shall be missing you," Alva said. She sounded genuinely disappointed.

The stall was laid out in complementary colors of green and red, purple and orange gold. Green and purple for the leafy vegetables and hard fruits, red and orange for the soft fruits and root crops. Will concentrated on the root vegetables and the leafy ones, choosing as many as would survive a three week journey without the further chance of fresh supplies. He stowed them carefully in his bag. "I'll have to come back for the fruit later."

"You have not a help for today?" Alva asked curiously.

"Not now, later maybe," Will tried to explain. "My sister is busy, making a birthday cake, and Marek had to go to the port office, so that we can leave tomorrow."

"You have birthday, Will?" Alva smiled at him. "And party too?"

"No, it's not my birthday, it's Marek's," Will said. "He's thirty-three today, he's getting old."

Alva was somewhere around that age herself and she laughed heartily at Will. "Oh, yes, very old. When you come back I give you a gift for him, and one for you and a special one for your sister. You see then you all remember to come back some day and visit."

Will toted the heavy bag and wove his way through the market crowd and out into the street. As he walked, or rather staggered with the weight of the vegetables, he had the growing sensation of someone at a deliberate distance behind him who seemed to be going in exactly the same direction and who paused when he paused and turned when he turned. Will stopped and put down the bag, relieved to have it off his shoulder. He bent and tied up a loose shoelace then toted the bag on the other shoulder whilst scanning the faces behind him briefly. If someone was following him it was impossible to tell, there were just too many people.

At the corner of a group of craft shops he ducked into Wikka Lane, a side street which he knew would take him more quickly to the marina than would the main road. People were walking up and down in their dozens and half a dozen or more had also turned into this same street at the same time and were going in the same direction. Not one of them looked suspicious to Will, nothing like the secretive men in their anonymous dark suits who had tracked him to Tempah Springs. But because of that experience Will was wary and also nervous. If agents had decided to follow him they would hardly wear clothes like that in a place like this, so how could he tell if one of the people was concentrated upon himself? He began to walk faster, eager to get to the Mari-E-ele and hoping that Marek had finished at the port office and was already on the boat.

Where the streets of shops ended and the harbor side began there was a road to cross. As he paused for traffic, Will cast his eyes behind and around him. Only one face had remained constantly with him since Wikka Lane, but it didn't look like the face of an agent to him. It was a bearded face belonging to an old man who stood some distance off, as if also waiting for the cars to pass. Even so, the old man glanced away abruptly when Will's eyes grazed him and Will was instantly suspicious. Will thought quickly. Once he got to the marina, if the man went there also, then he would know for sure one way or another, unless of course the man was a boat owner too.

The man did follow, crossing the road at the same time and walking slowly in the same direction as Will. When Will reached the entry of the marina, though, the man stopped and loitered by the white railing of the enclosure where it overlooked the water. He wandered up and down, as if he was studying the yachts along the line of the marina, or as though he was seeking out one in particular.

Will fought the urge to turn and look back. He felt that the man was waiting to see which yacht he went to and this made him unsure about the wisdom of going straight to the Mari-E-ele. But what else could he do? He knew what Marek would say, "Don't worry about it. If it's going to happen then it'll happen and you face it when it comes."

The delicious aroma of freshly baked cake drifted from the Mari-E-ele and lured Will on board. Before he ducked his head under the gangway, he glanced quickly over to the enclosure fence. The old man was still there, but he did not appear to be watching the boat. As Will went below he decided he would not say anything to Faran, not unless Marek was there.

Faran had flour on her cheek and a red face from the heat of the cooking, but she looked pleased with herself. The cake was in its place of honor at the center of the table and places were set for the party lunch.

Will grinned and took an appreciative sniff. "That looks great and it sure smells good," he said, observing that Marek was still absent.

Faran sighed. "Yes, I thought it wasn't going to come out right for a while but it managed okay. You haven't seen Marek, have you? He's been gone such a long time that I'm beginning to worry."

"Maybe it's busy at the office." Will showed her the vegetables and they stored them away together. "Do you want me to go and look for him?" he asked, however he could not help thinking about the man by the railing and he wasn't sure he wanted to leave Faran alone. "He'll probably be back soon."

Uncertain and undecided, Faran dithered. "Well, perhaps you ought—" A step sounding on the deck brought a light to her face. "He's here now!"

"Hulloa! May I come aboard?" called a strange voice.

Will started up the stairs. The old man stood by the open hatch and gazed down. "Hullo, young fella," he said.

"Who are you and what do you want?" Will demanded hostilely. He blocked the stairs so that the man could not get near Faran.

"Will, that's not very nice," Faran said from below. She peered around him to the man. "What can we do for you, sir?" she asked. "Are you looking for someone?"

Annoyed, Will said, "Faran, don't! This man followed me all the way from the market and I want to know what he's up to!" He challenged the man with a hard stare. "Well?"

The old man shook his head regretfully. "I'm sorry t'have spooked you, son. Didn't mean to. Fact is I saw the name of your boat sev'ral days ago and wanted t'see who owned it. Mari-E-ele t'is a name of my people's tongue, so I was a'curious about that."

"You are Tanu?" Faran asked.

The old man nodded. "Name's Kenu, Ma'am. I am from Te Tanaa."

Faran smiled. "Will, let the gentleman come down," she ordered. "Please, come and sit and have some iced tea with us."

404

Reluctantly Will moved aside and the old man descended. He still wasn't certain about this Kenu and he wasn't happy that Marek was away. "What about Marek?" he said to Faran.

"What about me?" came a voice from above. Marek's face appeared at the hatch and Will sighed with relief. "There's someone—" he started to say, but Marek bounded down the stairs, exclaiming, "Kenu!"

Kenu chuckled and nodded. "Hi there, Doc. Good t'see you after all these years."

Marek explained who Kenu was and made general introductions while Faran set another place at the table.

"Kind of you t"have me," Kenu said as he sat down. He stared at the cake. "Looks like somethin' special 'bout to happen here."

"It's Marek's birthday," Faran told him. A rose pink blush added itself to the already heated condition of her face as Marek wiped the flour gently from her cheek. "Excuse me a moment while I put lunch on the table," she said hastily.

Will jumped to her side. "I'll help," he offered. He was feeling rather foolish now because Kenu was not the threat he had thought and he wanted to escape.

Kenu gazed interestedly at Marek. "Look at you. Nice boat, very pretty lady, alert crew. You've done okay," he said, winking an eye at him and grinning. Sitting across from Kenu, Marek nodded and smiled. "It's a surprise seeing you here though, so close to home. Are you on your way to Te Tanaa or coming from there?"

"On the way to. I've been a'trying t"get home ever since I met you, and this is the first time I've got near enough. But I keep in touch so I know what goes on there and what has gone on." He regarded Marek more closely. "Like, I heard about the Messenger. The Head-man's a nephew of mine."

"I know," Marek said. "I told him about you and how you'd helped me. But how did you find me here?"

"Easy. Like I told the lass and the lad, I saw the boat and the name and was curious. So I made a few enquiries here and there. Your name, the real one that is, was mentioned, so I decided t'pay a call." Kenu's head wagged. "I read the papers when I'm in port. Gave me quite a stir t'see your face on the front page, knowing what I did an' all."

Faran and Will came bearing platters of salad and freshly cooked seafood which they shared out onto four plates. "I'll get the drinks," Marek said. He rose to fetch glasses and a bottle of wine from the refrigerator in the galley, saying apologetically to Kenu, "The wine's non alcoholic, sorry. I know you like something stronger, but we have a pregnant lady and a boy who's too young to drink here, and I don't bother with booze much."

"That so?" Kenu eyed Faran and Will and winked conspiratorially. "Not much good as a drinker, was you. I remember that party in Alsea, a"fore we sailed. Never seen a body more pissed in m'life as the Doc was that night." He shook his head in mock disgust. "Had t'carry him aboard an' put him t'bed like a bub."

Will and Faran laughed wonderingly, not certain if this was just a story or not, since this did not sound like the Marek they knew. But Marek returned, shame faced and guilty. He set down the glasses and bottle and grimaced at their grins. "Not a night I like to remember," he admitted, whilst thinking to himself that there were other reasons to forget it also.

"T'is a miracle you remember it at all," Kenu said.

Prawn and crab shells littered the empty platter and cake crumbs were scattered on the tablecloth. Kenu leant back and sighed and patted his stomach. "Best meal I've had in years, Ma"am, thank you," he said to Faran sincerely. Then he looked intently at Marek and, quite suddenly, his expression altered from one of lightness to solemn seriousness. "Now that I've enjoyed your fine hospitality, I have t'spoil it all by telling you the truth."

Marek was taken aback. "About what?"

Kenu rubbed anxious fingers through his grizzled beard, knocking off a cake crumb onto the table. "About why I'm here." He glanced around at Faran and Will, as if he thought Marek might not want him to speak in front of them, but Marek said, "Go on."

"It's true, as I told you, that I saw the name of the boat and got curious, but that was a week-an-a-half ago. When I heard it was yours I thought t'come and pay a social call then, but I didn't because I also heard something else that made me keep away."

"Like what?" Marek asked.

Kenu's eyes scanned the room. Then he smiled grimly at Faran and concentrated his gaze on her face as if he felt he must explain himself to her or was apologizing in advance for what he was about to say. "I don't always move in polite society, y'might say, so I tend t'hear things other people don't. This is a nice boat and you are nice people, but someone somewhere doesn't agree. I didn't like what I heard so I decided t'just

406

keep watch for a while before I paid a visit." He turned to Marek. "I saw you and the boy go out this morning and I followed you both t'the port office. Then, when you went inside, I went t'keep an eye on the boy. I knew your lady would be okay because there's a Tanu mate of mine who's crew on a boat a few berths down and he's been watching the Mari-E-ele ever since I asked him to. You might have noticed him this morning; he's on the Blue Elf."

"The guy with the big loop earring?" Marek enquired. "I thought he looked Tanu but I wasn't sure. He was scrubbing the deck when we left; he even said hello. But, Kenu, what—"

"Let me tell it first," Kenu said. "What I heard is that certain disreputable types are going t'be paid to make sure you don't get to Te Tanaa. Don't ask me why or who's paying, because I don't know, but you seem t'have enemies, Doc."

Will it ever end? Marek wondered. Worriedly, he rubbed his forehead, unconsciously touching the place at his temple where the Vorken's bullet had grazed. He saw how Faran's flushed face had suddenly paled, and Will's face was puckered into a frown. "How was this thing supposed to be done?" he asked Kenu.

Kenu's own face had grown even grimmer. "Scuttle the boat, that's the usual way," he said. He nodded at their astounded faces. "T'is happened before, believe me. Someone wants someone else dead, so they wait 'til just before they leave then they get aboard when there's a chance and do the deed. Nothing too noticeable and nothing that won't sink the boat 'til it's a good way out of port. Then there's no evidence."

Inwardly Marek shuddered and sighed. His eyes reached for Faran's; "I'm sorry," they said. Faran met him with a look of her own. Her lips parted slightly; "No need for that," she replied wordlessly across the silence.

"We're supposed to be leaving tomorrow afternoon," Will said abruptly. "When would this be due to happen?"

"Aye." Kenu nodded. "Some excuse t'get you all off the boat before, then they come aboard. I didn't know you were shipping out tomorrow. Good thing you got wind of me, boy, or I might have been caught short."

"So that's why you've been watching the boat, is it? To make sure no one got on board while we weren't here?" Will deduced. "And you knew I'd seen you so you had to make yourself known?"

"Aye, that's the truth of it." Kenu smiled at Will. "You're a smart boy."

Will ignored the compliment. He was too concerned to clear up another matter which bothered him. "So if you didn't know what our plans were, how were these others going to know?"

"Because it's someone at the port office," Marek put in before Kenu could answer. "I was so long there, waiting, because the idiots … well, that's what I thought they were … had mucked up the Mari- E-ele's papers. They said I would have to come back tomorrow, for a final clearance, although everything's stamped and in order, and that there had to be some sort of inspection of the boat tomorrow morning. I knew it was all rubbish but I couldn't figure it out." He appealed to Kenu. "What's your opinion, Kenu? What should we do?"

Kenu shrugged. "If it was me I'd ship out t'night and not say anything to nobody. It's a perfect sea and a perfect wind; I'd go out as soon as it got dark." He gazed at Marek from frank and sympathetic eyes. "Doc, when I first met you I said t'myself, here's a young fella in trouble who don't deserve what's happening t'him. I didn't know at the time what kind o' trouble you were in, an' if I had've known who you were an' who you were running from, I might have thought twice about getting involved. But I didn't know an' I got involved an' that was how it had t'be. When my nephew Peli told me about you, I saw that there were too many twists and turns in this whole business for me t'understand what they meant, but that life would find a way of leading me through them t'the meaning, eventually. I feel that with you; there's some meaning in you which I've never met in another man, an' I don't want t'see that destroyed or messed up by fools. My people like and trust you, Doc, an' so do I."

"Thank you." Marek made an instant decision. He stood and began to clear away the cups and plates, and as Faran started to rise he waved her back down. "You've done enough for one day, Sweetheart; that was a perfect meal. Will and I will wash up and then we're going back to the market for the rest of the supplies. Kenu, could I ask you to stay with Faran while we're gone? In fact, if you're wanting to go to Te Tanaa, why don't you join us? The Mari-E-ele is a four berth, so there's enough room. We'll do what you suggest and go out tonight."

Kenu nodded. "I was hoping you'd say that."

"You trust Kenu completely, do you?" Will asked Marek as they walked back into the town market place.

"Yes," Marek said. He could understand Will's lack of faith, considering how the boy had regarded strangers since his own bad experiences with them. "Kenu helped me when I needed it most, just as Faran and your father did. He never questioned me after the first day and he went on to teach me a lot about getting around the world in the safest way. If he tells me something in all seriousness, then I believe it, because he's not the sort who plays games with people when the situation is desperate. He's a bit rough around the edges, but that's just how life worked out for him. But he's a good man … honest in the things that matter."

The open air market was quieter in the hot afternoons. Stallholders stretched out on low chairs under their canvas awnings and fanned themselves with huge half circles of woven palm. Some of them dozed, leaving younger eyes to watch for possible customers. Sometimes whole families managed these stalls so that often there was more activity on the seller's side than on the other. Children played in the dirt with puppies and squawking chickens; old grandmothers snored in their canvas lay-back chairs; men came and went, with fresh supplies or to the nearby hotels.

Alva's stall was watched over by two precocious looking dark haired girls who were younger than Will. They eyed him coquettishly and one disappeared in a hurry to a truck parked some way off under the heavy shade of some big trees. "You were expected?" Marek asked Will as they watched Alva climb from the truck and approach. She was a short woman, broadly built, but she moved with the fluid grace of a dancer, and her feet were bare.

Will explained. "I told Alva we were leaving tomorrow and she said she wanted to give us gifts so we would come back."

"Will, you want fruit?" Alva said. Her eyes travelled to Marek and she smiled. "Most happy birthday greetings. I have little gift for you." But first they had to conclude the business of buying the fruit, choosing extra now because Kenu would be going with them.

Then from under the trestle top Alva produced three packages wrapped and tied loosely in papers colored red, green and yellow. She gave the red one to Will and the other two to Marek. She watched with parted smiling lips as Will opened his, and the two girls leaned at either side, craning their slim necks like young curious swans, less concerned about the gift than about studying Will more closely. Marek watched too, amused by the open interest in the young girls" eyes and touched by the generosity which was so obvious on Alva's face.

Will peeled open the wrapping to reveal a piece of white bone carved in the shape of a diving whale and attached to a thong of leather so that he could wear it around his neck. "It is truly the bone of a whale," Alva told him. "The name of the whale is Varuma, means Great One Who Dives Deep. It came to me in a dream that this is your power animal, your Kaya, as we express it in our culture. I hope you like it. It will protect you."

"It's great! Thank you!" Will put it on, letting it hang over his shirt, however Alva leaned forward and began to undo his shirt buttons to the waist. "No, you must wear it against the skin, always." The two girls giggled and Will blushed. "Can we see what my sister's gift is?" he said, mainly to cover his embarrassment.

Alva nodded to Marek, "The green," and he undid the paper. It was another necklet on a thong, but this time it was made of a beautiful, almost pellucid blue-green stone carved into the form of a turtle. "This is sign of the Mother, and she protects all mothers-to-be, especially at time of birth." Alva looked up at Marek and he saw how her eyes had become very intense and somewhat anxious. "You must make her wear it soon; her time comes very near."

"Oh, she's not due for another six weeks," put in Will blithely, but Alva did not take her eyes off Marek's. She said, "I have borne four children of my own, and I know her time is near. I am, how you say, a Dreaming Woman; I see much things in dreams. All of you I have dream of. Maybe you have two babies instead of one."

She's right! Marek realized. He was astounded that he hadn't guessed the truth earlier. That's why Faran is so big! It's two babies, not one! He nodded silently and absently as he thought, unaware that Alva was watching his face closely and that her own expression had undergone a startling change. Then he woke and saw the wonder on her face.

"Your eyes, they change color! And you go to Te Tanaa!" Alva exclaimed. "My husband, he is Tanu. He is telling me of a Messenger." She pressed her hand against Marek's, imploring. "Please, open your gift and you will see. I dream of you but I not understand the dream and I not know what to give you. So I choose without thinking, with my heart, and you shall see what it is."

Marek was conscious of a sudden silence all around as the two girls stared at him, and Will waited for him to unwrap the intriguing parcel. For some reason unknown to himself he felt nervous and his fingers fumbled with the tie as he undid it. Opened, the gift revealed itself as a flat oval stone of astonishing clarity and transparency which was absolutely unblemished by any gradation of tone or shade, or of any mark either of nature or from the hand of man, except that to one end was glued a metal clasp which held a thong for wearing. The stone was of a size to fit comfortably in the palm of Marek's hand and was slightly convex on the upper side.

Marek held it up by the thong and they all stared at it. In many ways it was so clear as to be almost unremarkable, but when it turned in the light, rainbows appeared across its surface and within it, flickering and darting as the stone rotated slowly.

"Oh, wow!" Will said.

Hardly knowing what to say, Marek smiled at Alva. "It's beautiful. No, it's more than beautiful. Thank you. But where did you find it?" He waited for her reply, feeling within his heart and mind the answer before it came.

"Where I find the other two," Alva said. "From a strange old woman I haven't been seeing before. She come to my door, selling things, and I really not mean to buy; but, well, we are poor traders, we understand, and she give me good price."

Marek nodded. He understood too. He gave Alva one word he knew she and her Tanu husband would appreciate. "Mari-E-ele."

Alva opened her eyes wide and her mouth to speak, but nothing came out. Instead she gestured to Marek to place the necklet over his head. He opened his shirt, as she had done for Will, and put it on, and as he did so the stone flashed forth a dozen rainbows into the air around him.

An item of great significance, Marek thought, and Mari-E-ele wanted me to have it for a certain purpose. But I don't know how it will be used as yet.

Alva looked pleased, although the little girls were in awe and had retreated somewhat. "If there is anything I can do for you, please tell me," Marek said, without really knowing why he said it, except that he was grateful.

Alva's eyes brightened. "You come meet my husband?" she asked. "He will like that." "Okay. Is it far?" Marek asked.

Alva said something in her native tongue to the girls and they wagged their heads up and down. "He over there." She pointed to the truck. "He can't come here and work because he sick. He get sick last year, from the fever. The doctor give him pills, but he not get better."

Marek went alone with Alva to the truck. It was an old truck, of the kind which had a high, wide cabin and front and back seats. Alva directed Marek to climb in the back while she took the front. The Tanu husband was couched on the back seat which was set up almost like a bed and his dark eyes peered in surprise from the shadows when he saw his unknown visitor. Alva explained who Marek was in dialect with Arpayan and some Tanu phrases which Marek recognized. He heard the Tanu word for Messenger and saw the man's face light up. He was somewhere about forty years old, but his illness made him look older. The normally warm brown of a Tanu complexion had become a dirty yellowish brown on this man and his eyes were also yellowed, most likely from liver damage, Marek decided.

"Jai," the man said, giving his name, and he stretched out a bony hand in a greeting handshake. "Ozira," Marek replied. He reached out his own hand but did not withdraw it after the handshake. Instead, he held on and looked deeply into Jai's eyes, and somehow, although there was little light in the truck cabin to catch the fires in the stone Alva had given him, it still managed to play rainbows into the dark, painting the truck walls with ovals of spinning colors.

"You must not let this illness defeat you," he said to Jai in a mixture of Tanu and Arpayan, as he focused the Light. "Even if you feel tired, you must take some exercise and must drink much good water every day. And eat." Marek glanced to Alva. "Only the flesh of fish and only fresh vegetables and fruit, and most of it raw, for many weeks. His body has been poisoned, so he has to eliminate the poison. The pills did him no good; they only made matters worse. If you can get some akka plant and make it into a tea, he should drink this three times a day."

Alva smiled at him in wonder. "You are the Healer!" "Yes. Ozira is the Healer."

Chapter Six

At night the harbor of Port Dias became a dark well spotted with points of light, a strange universe in which there existed only two species of stars, one which held steady, like a row of unwinking eyes, and the other, its watery reflection, making fluid roses in the deep. As the Mari-E-ele motored slowly from its anchorage out to the open sea, it broke through the myriads of roses, leaving behind a trail of wavering lights like petals floating on a stream.

Will was at the helm, with Kenu keeping him company. Having Kenu as extra crew meant that now Marek could devote more time to Faran and that she would have to do less and could rest more.

Marek was glad of this, for he knew that she was going to need his strength and possibly his Healing Light. His great hope was that they would reach Te Tanaa before the babies made their entrance into the world; but he was mentally preparing himself for the possibility that they might be impatient to arrive.

Marek had asked Will not to mention anything to Faran about Alva's prediction because he wanted to do it himself in the privacy of their cabin. When he and Will arrived back from the market, both proudly sporting their gifts upon their naked chests, Faran had been delighted and amused. She teased Will about his, saying that, now, he had gone native altogether with a thing like that around his neck.

However she was stunned when Marek held up his own gift. She watched the rainbows decorating the timbered walls, so that the saloon looked like an underwater room in which little multicolored fish swam to and fro. "How did Alva know?" she wondered.

"She didn't. Well, not consciously anyway. Her heart told her what to choose," Marek explained. He held out the parcel of green paper. "This is for you."

Faran grinned. "I thought I was going to miss out." Eagerly she started to untie the string. "No, not here," Marek said. "Let's go into our cabin. I want you open it in there." Bemused, Faran followed Marek into their cabin. Marek closed the door. "Why all the secrecy?" Faran asked. "Wouldn't Will like to see what it is?"

"We've already seen," Marek said. "And it's not to be secret, it's just to be private, because there's something I have to talk to you about."

Faran's attention was divided between opening the parcel and eyeing Marek's face curiously. "Oh, it's beautiful!" she exclaimed when she held up the necklet. "Look, it's a turtle! And carved so delicately and well. Oh, it's lovely."

She had on a long waist-less sun dress of white cotton bought in one of the shops in Port Dias. It was like the native women wore and was loose and cool and slipped on over the head. Faran called it "The Tent". "Take off the dress," Marek said. "According to Alva, these things are supposed to be worn next to the skin."

Faran laughed at him wonderingly, but she lifted the skirt and he helped her pull the dress over her head. Except for a pair of pants she had nothing else on underneath, because it was too hot.

A sound of appreciation escaped Marek's lips as his eyes beheld her nakedness. Her belly was round and her breasts were full and a glow seemed to come from her skin, as if she was alight inside. He sighed. "Oh Sweetheart, you are beautiful!"

Faran grimaced and looked down at herself. "No, Will was right; I'm fat, I'm huge!"

Marek shook his head in admonishment. "And you're beautiful. Put the necklet on. Let's see how it looks."

Faran put it on and the little green turtle found its place in the valley between her breasts. Marek led her to sit down on the bed, which she did awkwardly, with his help. Marek sat beside her and lay his hand over her belly, caressing the curve gently. He said, "The turtle is a symbol of the Mother, so Alva said, and it is supposed to protect you in childbirth and as a mother."

Faran smiled. "What a nice thought. But I don't think I really need protecting, do you? Not when I have you around."

Marek caressed her. "Well, I will always be here for you, but your Light is all you really need. But Alva said something else." Marek paused. "She thinks you are going to have twins."

"Twins." Faran sighed as Marek had done. It was a sigh of the same heartfelt proportion and it seemed to express, in sound, the glow of light coming from her. It seemed to say that while she wondered at such an idea, she also felt it within her as a joy already experienced. It was not the reaction Marek had expected.

"You don't seem surprised, Love."

Faran laid her hands over his. "I was suspicious because I was so big. I didn't have anyone to compare myself with, though, until we came to

414

Port Dias, then I saw a couple of women in the square who were about as big as I was. So I asked them in sign language when they were due. When they worked out what I was getting at, one said three weeks and the other two, so I guessed there had to be a reason for my size. Either that or there's something awfully wrong with me."

"You were worried and you never said anything to me?"

"I wasn't worried. It's not like I don't feel well, because apart from the discomfort of being big and awkward, I feel healthy and strong. And I know that you will always look after me, so I didn't want to go frightening you with useless suspicions."

Marek kissed her. "But you should always tell me these things. And I know there's nothing wrong with you, my love. In fact, you've been doing rather well, I thought." Marek strove to reassure her, but in himself he was not wholly comforted. Twins did not always go full term, he knew. He slipped to the floor and kneeled beside Faran, pressing his ear against her belly. A sudden kick under his cheek made him jump. "Oh boy, it's busy in there." He eased her back onto the pillows. "Lie down so I can have a better feel."

Faran lay back while he touched her belly here and there and put his ear in different places. Each touch resulted in a corresponding movement within, which felt to Faran as if the inside of her belly was a xylophone and an infant virtuoso played it in long rippling arpeggios. Well, two infant virtuosi perhaps, playing a duet on one instrument at two different locations.

Marek must have thought so too, for he said, "I don't know how you put up with it; is it always so busy? There's movement up here and down there. Surely one baby couldn't make that much activity? Is it hard for you?"

Faran smiled. "Not as hard as you think, except when I want to sleep. It's gotten busier recently; maybe they're just jostling for space. But I'd be more bothered if there wasn't any movement. At least I know that the life inside me is doing okay."

"That's true." Marek kissed her belly once, then her lips. He lay down beside her, pressing his cheek against hers. "We'll assume then that twins are a definite possibility, so that means you will have to take plenty of rest on this trip. That also—"

Faran interrupted. "Marek, mostly, twins come early, don't they? They run out of space, or something like that? And it can make them very small?"

Marek patted her hand. "The longer you hold on to them, the bigger and stronger they'll be. We're going to make sure of that. You keep on taking your special tea and your herbs and resting a lot. Don't worry, my sweet, I'll look after you. From now on you won't have to lift a finger, I'll be your slave. I'll do everything."

"Everything?" Suddenly Faran felt immeasurably reassured and good humored. She composed her face, trying not to laugh. "Not the cooking too, though, I hope?" she said in mock dismay. "Or maybe Kenu is a good cook; we'll have to ask him."

Sincere in his desire to do all, but conceding that she had a point, Marek could only agree.

Marek was true to his word. When he was not taking his watch or sleeping, he looked after Faran like a devoted parent. He took her for strolls about the deck, holding on to her arm to steady her against the motion of the waves. The Mari-E-ele rode the ocean swells like a graceful dolphin and the weather was, thankfully, on its best behavior. With the changeable weather of a month ago having phased into more stable patterns now, it was now exactly the right time of year for cruising in these latitudes, with few chances of rough seas or storms. Nevertheless, Faran was now quite awkward in her movements on board and the slightest chance of overbalancing was a risk they could not take. And after a short time, both Will and Kenu followed Marek's lead, so that there was always an arm for Faran to rely on, almost everywhere she went and in almost everything she did.

As the days grew into weeks and the expectation of Te Tanaa grew ever closer, so too did Faran's hopes of a full term pregnancy grow stronger. She felt well, remarkably so, and it was as if, although rolling about on an ever moving sea, her body had grounded itself to the Earth fully and completely, and that this created a sense of stability and sureness which extended itself to the whole of her consciousness. She began to notice then that her body's awareness had become a thing unto itself, alive in its own way without any of her ego's interference. It was, she realized then, that the Earth, beneath its fluid envelope of sea and through it, had taken full control of the body which was about to give birth, and that Faran and the Living Light of Rai-a-ele looked on, content and without fear or impediment, and letting the Light flow to where it was needed. Such a sense of utter contentment and profound peace arose from this, so that the consciousness which was Faran spent the days and nights in a state of near bliss and heightened awareness, as if she floated

416

in the body and was not weighted down by it, even as it grew larger.

Yet Faran guessed, rather than actually knowing, that come the birth she would ground again and know the full weight and passion of the body's struggle to give birth. For it was a necessary thing to be fully there and alert, not to take control, which was in any case impossible, but to give All and be All at that moment when new life would arrive. She knew it was not going to be easy, but she knew also that she wanted more than anything to do this.

For the dozenth time Faran poured over the pages of the book Nikola had given her which detailed every aspect of the birth process and what had to be done and looked for. Just in case Te Tanaa, with its midwives and proper facilities, was too far away. The book had been brand spanking new when Nikola presented it to her but it had been read so much that now it was scruffy and well thumbed. And read mostly by Marek, Faran thought, who seemed to know it backwards as well as forwards.

Three days before the Mari-E-ele was due to reach Te Tanaa Faran went up on deck for the last fresh air and sunlight before evening fell. This time Will offered his arm since Marek was at the helm and Kenu was below preparing them all a dinner of newly caught reef fish. Early that same morning they had stopped at a small island community for water and fuel and vegetables and fruit, and Kenu had gone fishing with men whom he knew. The islanders were not Tanu, although they were allied with Te Tanaa, but Kenu had old friends and acquaintances everywhere. By the time they were ready to leave it seemed that the whole island had heard about the visit of the Mari-E-ele and as the boat motored from its anchorage, a couple of hundred hands were there to wave them off.

"You're getting to be quite a celebrity around these waters," Kenu had said to Marek as they passed through the reef passage.

"I hope not." Marek steered watchfully. This was the narrowest reef passage he had ever seen. A vessel of any large size had great difficulty in approaching this particular island, much less in entering the lagoon, and the islanders had to bring in heavy goods and supplies by long barge towed behind their boats from a delivery ship as it stood off the coast in deeper waters. It was a risky business that could only be undertaken in calm weather, so when the stormy season came around the islanders had to be content with what they already had and often reverted to a more unsophisticated style of living until the ships could come again. They had an airstrip of sorts but it was not big enough to take anything very large.

Marek was glad that Te Tanaa possessed any number of good harbors, but the one he wanted, after making the obligatory stop in the main port at Tana City, was at the other end of the island. It was the small harbor below the Tanu settlement and it was where he knew they would all be waiting for him, for by now he was expected.

The Mari-E-ele cleared its own trail through the growing darkness of the water, topping the waves with a collar of creamy foam which stretched far behind. Faran stood by the stern rail and watched the trail recede and break up, like a path left untrodden becoming overgrown by time. "I'll go down now," she said to Will, for she could smell the delicious aroma of food almost ready; these days she seemed to be hungry all the time.

"We're going in. Dinner's almost on the table," she called to Marek, when there was a sudden movement behind herself and Will. They turned to see what it was and both of them started. A huge seabird, snowy white with eyes like small, shining rubies, had landed on the boat. It touched the rail then clumsily clambered down onto the seat in the stern. It crouched there with its head tilted to one side and winked a jewelled eye. It stared at them candidly and did not move even when Will leant towards it. It seemed totally unafraid.

"We've got company," Will said. He called to Marek. "Come and have a look at this!"

It was not the first time that birds had hitchhiked aboard the Mari-E-ele, using it as a temporary rest stop on an otherwise empty sea, but no one above decks had seen a bird like this before. Marek left the helm on autopilot and came to look. He stretched out a tentative hand to the bird and it did not budge. Instead, it moved its head forward and grazed his palm with its huge beak, in something like a brief gesture of handshake. The three of them were amazed. "Do you think it needs help?" Faran wondered.

"Maybe it's too tired to be afraid," Will suggested. "Though it doesn't look hurt or tired to me." "Dinner's on." Kenu came above. When he saw what they were clustered around he was surprised.

"A Good Luck Bird! That's what we Tanu call it. Can't say as I've ever seen one up s'close before." "Why is it a Good Luck Bird?" Will asked Kenu at dinner.

"Well the story goes that this is the bird which helped make the Tanu's world – Mari-E-ele's helpful sidekick, so t'speak. She – the bird, that is,

418

not Mari-E-ele – laid an egg unlike any other egg ever laid by any bird since. T'was the biggest egg in the world, almost as large as a mountain and t'was oval and perfectly clear, like the purest crystal. It sort of hovered just above the sea after t'was laid and began t'focus the sun's rays on the water. It turned into a great fire, standing there on the rim of the sea, and became a doorway o'light, and that's how the Tanu came down to the world, through that door. The Good Luck Bird is all we ever called it, b'cause it's supposed t'bring good luck when it's seen."

Following dinner Marek had to continue his watch while Will and Kenu washed up and Faran went dutifully to bed. Faran felt reluctant to go, she wanted to see if the bird was still there, but she was supposed to rest and so she asked Will to go and see for her. "It's still on board, but it's hopped round next to the inside steering. It's just sitting there on the deck by the door, practically next to Marek, like they're a couple of old friends," Will reported.

Bemused, Faran grunted her way into bed. Getting into bed successfully had now become a question of logistics. First she had to lower herself slowly to the edge, then, using her arms for a prop, she had to swing her legs up and onto the bed. Only then could she lay down and she always ended up too near the edge, so she had to wiggle and grunt her way to a place more comfortable and closer to the middle. She was glad that Marek's watch kept him absent for this performance, for it didn't sound very elegant to her and would have looked even worse, she decided. Once in the bed she could rest, after a fashion, but when she wanted to turn onto one side it became another exercise requiring thought and planning. She had to heave herself over, belly cradled in her arms, and find the cushions which she placed under the sheets for her belly and upper knee to rest on. Turning over had gotten to be so difficult now and such a major production, that each turn woke Marek up, so Faran had all but decided to give up trying any more.

Faran laid on her back in the bed and felt the rhythm of the sea beneath her. As usual, her belly felt heavy, but tonight there was an added sensation of being expanded or pressed from within. It was not unpleasant, though, just different, and she hardly gave it any thought, instead wondering about the lovely bird up top and the story Kenu had told; there was something about that story which sounded familiar to her, although she didn't know what it was. If she was awake when Marek came to bed, at eleven or so, she would ask him what subjects he and the bird had been discussing. She chuckled at the thought and shut her eyes, not really believing that sleep would come easily, and yet it did.

Finishing his watch Marek said goodnight to the bird and went to fetch Will who usually only napped between dinner and eleven and sometimes even read or more often than not came up on deck and played his flute to the winds. Marek liked it when Will did that. The boy had real talent, he thought, but it was not that which pleased him to listen. For Will seemed to pattern the winds in his playing, as though he and the winds were playing a mutually agreed upon concert. Marek did not know if Will did it deliberately and consciously or whether he just followed the movement of his own feeling, however it was a delight to listen to. One never knew what was coming next, so one had to feel too in order to follow. "I ought to ask him sometime," Marek said to himself. He liked the way Will got the flute to sound just as if it was a human voice, especially in the deep register. A soulful human voice carolling to and with the winds, yet a singer of cosmic proportions, for its song sounded like a universal call to attention, an awakening. A song of light and love to move the world, came the thought, unbidden, into Marek's mind then.

"It's a fair night and a calm sea," Marek said to Will before he went into his cabin. He noted that Will had his flute in his hand, so there would be music tonight, music to dream by. Marek was the only one who took an entire night-time break, but that was so he could pursue another watch, the one of taking care of Faran. Often at night she got restless – it was hard for her to get comfortable with that big belly – and he would chat with her or make her some of her tea, or massage her back and shoulders if she needed it.

Turning the lamp on to low, Marek undressed. Faran was asleep and neither the lamp-light nor his movements had woken her. This was unusual, however it pleased him to see she was resting well for a change. She was on her back with her head turned slightly to one side and there was an expression of deep peace on her face. The lamp-light glowed warmly on her face and hair. Her hair spread over the pillow like the tendrils of a summer sun reaching across a cloud. In the soft play of light and shadow she seemed to be carved as delicately as a sea shell washed up on white sand and bathed in her own aura of gold. A sleeping mermaid, if ever there was one, he thought to himself, and he had to restrain his hand from wanting to touch her. He lay down beside her and before he turned out the lamp, he gazed on her one more time and filled himself and her with the Light, so that it ringed them around like a shield, drawing them close together.

Then Marek slept and, later, dreamed. Three dreams:

The first came softly and unawares into his consciousness, and he found himself on a beach, with paints and brushes in his hand and an easel before him. He was an artist of long ago who painted what was before him. The shore: water, sky and sea and a sea shell, and it was very strange because he painted from the perspective of the shell, as though he was shrunken to sea shell size, or that the shell had grown to man size. And the scape of land, sea and sky, too, was strange, for it stretched across his imagination in a play of rich light and shade that matched dawn on one side of the canvas and sunset on the other. The shell was the cusp of both, the link to night and day, and it was a great round spiral shell of smooth whorls with a doorway of darkest night. Marek looked into the doorway and saw that it was the entry to a womb. He stroked the creamy colors of the paint around its threshold. Through that door was the way to another world, not as an escape from this one, but another world to know and explore, to be born into. With his paintbrush he marked the way; he painted the tracery of his own birth-steps as a way for others to follow.

Faran waited with him on the beach. Across the water, some distance away, was an island of blue- white light to which they wanted to go. From behind them came the sounds of musical notes which were sweet to the ears – Will playing on his flute. At each note of light aliveness, the sea stirred. As the song grew, the sky lightened and the sea came alive. Fish rose to the surface and looked at them.

The sea churned with other life, masses of marine animals rising to take a look at another world. Whales and dolphins joined them, and a dolphin lifted itself from the sea and offered them a place on its arched back. With the airy, weightless feet of dreamers, they stepped onto their place and the dolphin carried them across the water to their island, where they were joined forever, two dreamers who had become one.

The snowy white bird who had kissed him on the hand now laid an egg of crystal brightness. At first, the egg was small, small enough for Marek to fit in the palm of his hand, where the kiss had been, then it began to grow. It grew and grew, until it was mountain size. Like the mountain island of Ompalo, it shone from the water, and Marek saw within the egg's transparent gleam, the small naked figures of a man and a woman clinging together and also growing. As they grew, they clung closer and became entwined, meshing like the twin arms of a blossoming double helix. He saw their shining faces as they turned slowly to look at him. One face was his and the other was Faran's. Then, while they smiled at him, acknowledging that he had recognized them, there was a sudden dart of fire from the sun above which plunged into the crystal egg, shattering it into a million shards of light. The light shards scattered, spreading across the sea, across the land, across the sky. They filled the world with their brightness, but where they touched the whole world shattered too, as if each touch was also a dart of fire. And in the distance, or deep within his mind, the Flutist played, with jewelled notes, the melody of forever.

Chapter Seven

The Mari-E-ele plunged through the waves like a speedboat, buoyed and aided by a fresh wind. From outside, the boat had the look of a sleek black fish, a flying fish with red-sail wings, a fish in a hurry. But, inside, time moved at a slower pace as Faran and Marek counted minutes instead of hours, the minutes between the last contraction and the one before. Two days away from Te Tanaa and the birth was underway.

It started at ten in the morning, or the noticeable portion of it, at least. Faran had gone to the bathroom, then she stooped to wash her hands and face at the sink. After sleeping deeply and well into the morning, which was odd because it was so unusual, she had risen almost reluctantly to breakfast, feeling little hunger and having the sense that something had occurred in the night. Though what it was she could not say; she sensed a difference, that was all.

She reached for the towel to dry her face and felt a sudden, irresistible pressure deep inside which made her want to bend, as far as her belly would allow; she could do nothing else. So she bent, the pressure increased, and, abruptly, water gushed down her legs, staining her nightdress with a slight tinge of pink. She grabbed the towel and shoved it and held it where it would do the most good and staggered out into the saloon. Marek was above, taking the first watch, and Will was up there too, chatting with the bird who was still their passenger. Kenu was in his bunk, catching up on his sleep after the long shift of the night. Faran called out as loud as she could, "Marek! Marek! Come down here, I need you!"

Marek came leaping down the stairs. He took one look at her and panicked. "It isn't all that much," Faran assured him about the water. "Just help me to the bed and it might stop the rest of it."

"But the water's broken, Sweetheart. It means you're already in labor." He eased her onto the bed. He had been doing his homework and knew what the signs were. When she lay down he lifted the hem of her nightdress and made a thorough inspection of what was happening under the towel. "You're already on the way, Love, you're already partly dilated. It's a wonder to me that you hadn't felt anything before," he said.

Faran gazed up at him, biting her lip nervously. Her whole body had broken into a sweat of excitement and apprehension. "Well, I did, sort of, last evening, before bed. Then I just fell asleep, like that! And I didn't wake up at all during the night." She clung to his hand and pulled him down to her. "Marek, it's early. I'm scared."

Marek sighed convulsively. Perhaps he was scared also. However he hugged her close and tried to keep his voice steady. "Not to worry, it's only two weeks and everything'll be okay. We know what to do. You'll be fine."

So it began. After Faran had rested for a while and she felt all right, Marek helped her change into a loose open robe which was comfortable and soft. He made her tea, the tea for pregnant women he had been getting her to drink all along, and put into it some extra special herbs. Once he had gotten himself calm and composed he became the consummate healer again, and Faran was glad to see that, for under the circumstances she would rather have the healer around her than the frantic husband and father-to-be.

Will came below to see what was going on. "Geez," he said, when he understood. "What can I do?"

Marek glanced up from his preparations. He had assembled everything they would need, as if the birth was imminent, although he knew that most likely it would be many hours away. "Just take over on deck, Will. I have to stay here."

"Okay. But I don't want to miss out on anything," he said. "You won't. It's going to be a while."

It took, in fact, until four in the afternoon. Six hours in all, excluding the night-time labor which Faran had not known about. By then Kenu had taken over the helm and Will hovered in the cabin like an anxious father himself while Marek played the part he had been schooling himself to and fought to keep his other feelings in the background where they would not interfere.

But it was not easy for any of them. Between shock waves of pain and struggle, Faran told herself that she had to stay brave and cheerful, as much for Marek as for herself. As the hours staggered by, though, mental fortitude became the sham it really was and Faran surrendered at last to the mighty forces of her own body and it's huge, impersonal drive to give birth, denying, finally and forever, her ego's desire to control even this most momentous and precious of occasions. It was humbling for the self-important ego to experience such surrender to the Earth forces. Perhaps it was the most humbling lesson any ego could receive, and for that she would later be grateful and would wonder to herself if, of the sexes, women were especially privileged in that way. Once she had done this, she then discovered something wonderful. With surrender came the release and destruction of fear, her ego's fear, and a consequential lessening of pain. Fear created pain, and the body itself did not experience pain as such, but only battled to do what it had to do.

The contractions grew closer together and longer in duration and stronger, and had not Marek been there to encourage and remind her of all her lessons in relaxation, Faran would have forgotten everything. As it was, her mind was awash with sensation and little chance of thought intruded. She found herself obeying Marek's voice like an automaton and the urges of her body, as from a distance. It seemed to her that she was in two places at once, as if part of her looked on and observed the body with deep compassion, and the other part was totally absorbed in the body's struggle. Part of her also saw Marek as through a mist of light. She knew his Healing Light was around her and that her own Light blessed her; she felt Marek like a warm fire in her heart, and that she, too, was the fire. The sense of Marek then became stronger and stronger until his whole personality seemed to enter her. As he held her, as he supported her and moved with her, flesh against flesh, it was as though the barriers of separate bodies had dissolved. Everything of him flowed into her and became hers: his compassion and his love, his consciousness were all hers for the asking.

And so she took his offering, and, in taking, understood that there was nothing to be given or taken, but that the flow from him to her was an unbroken, eternal constant, the experience of an eternal moment wherein Life knows and is Life. Yet these were the insights which came in the clarity of afterthought, when sensation had ebbed and the mind was able to think again and reflect. Until then all her understanding was organic, as her body surged amidst a sea of senses and her feeling self dipped into the deep, the deep where he and she were One.

Marek had stripped off his shirt, both because it was so hot and to share with Faran, as she labored, a sense of nearness and closeness with her and her struggle. The robe she wore kept slipping from her shoulders until, with a gesture of irritation and a couple of choice words Marek had never heard her use before, she sat upright and flung it across the cabin. That was when he climbed behind her on the bed and clutched her in his arms. Between each contraction she would lay back against him, sometimes stroking his arm in an absent minded way, as though he was the one in extremes and not she. This was the time when he murmured to her and kissed her and wiped the sweat from her forehead. He encouraged her, although to him the encouragement sounded hollow, for he didn't really think she was listening to him. He thought about how it would be if their positions were reversed. All the untoward things which had happened to him in his life, not one of those things seemed to equal what she was going through now. He looked at how little she was, how delicate, and then she was in contraction again, her hands clutched into fists, her head bowed, sweat striping her face. He gripped her wrists and held on; he played the healer and reminded her to breathe; yet his heart felt torn in two.

When the birth was actually to happen, Will took Marek's place in support of Faran. At first he had been red faced and wide eyed to see his sister as he had never seen her before, stripped to her essential self bodily and emotionally, hearing her curse and watching her cry and cling to Marek. If the unabashed nakedness of her body and the absolute femaleness which it asserted was not enough to give him a new vision of her and make him color with self conscious embarrassment, it was the even more naked connection of her feeling self with Marek's feeling self which really did it. To see them as they clung together, so closely and so intimately, made Will feel like a voyeur who had intruded upon a couple making intense and passionate love. Until this moment he had been a boy, with a boy's inexperience and the usual youthful, flippant attitude towards male and female relationships. He had not even felt the first twinges of the romantic side of things, much less seen the raw, naked love of a man and woman for each other. His Faran and her Marek had heretofore been two individual people whom he knew and loved well; now they seemed to be indissoluble, pressed together, entwined in the most passionate moment of their lives, and he, the awed witness.

But then Faran realized he was there and between grimaces she smiled at him and pulled a wry face, which reminded him of days gone by when they had been caught together at some mischief by their father and had shared the consolation of each other's guilt. Her smile and wry look brought him, at once, into the circle of her suffering and he forgot himself in thinking about her. His embarrassment disappeared and with it the sense of alienation it created. All he wanted to do now was help.

He got his chance when Marek asked him to help hold Faran upright while she knelt to give birth. This was the salient moment in Will's experience of a new, rawer reality. He gripped her arms and held her, feeling the heat and excitation, the thud of her beating heart through her back and against his chest, and his own heart pounded too.

Faran heaved and strained and the baby's head emerged, a little dark slick of black hair, a wrinkled face, red under its smeared coating of protection. "Wonderful!" Marek encouraged. "You're doing wonderfully!" Then the rest of it was born and Marek cleared it's mouth and almost immediately it breathed and let out the necessary cry. Marek lay it carefully beside Faran's knee. The long cord of life stretched from it to her and still pulsed with energy. When the pulsing stopped they would cut the cord and the baby would be on its own at last. They studied the child in wonder and gratitude; it was a girl.

"Oooh," Faran moaned as another contraction came upon her. "Hang on to her, Will," Marek ordered. "Still more to do."

In the five minutes before the second child arrived, Marek had time to take care of the firstborn. He cut the cord and rolled the baby in a piece of soft sheet and placed it gently in the little basket they had prepared. It lay quietly, with screwed up eyes and tiny, tight fists clutched against both cheeks.

Occasionally it opened one eye at a time, and stared about, then finally both eyes. With a smile lighting his face, Marek gazed down upon it; the baby winked at him and hiccupped.

For Faran, there was no time to appreciate the wonders of her first baby, for she was in extremes again as the second made its way into the world. This time, though, the passageway was more open, having been stretched by the first, and so the baby came easier, but the contractions were still as heavy and it was no picnic. Conscious of Will's strong hands and arms and of his trembling presence behind her, she was also aware of the intensity of his emotion. Always in their lives together she had been the one to cosset and soothe him, the one with the comforting arms. Now it was the other way around and she felt moved almost to tears to feel his passionate nearness, and knew that, after this, she would love him more dearly than ever before. As the last effort of pushing died away, she rested her head back against his shoulder and lifted her hand to his cheek, to find it wet with silent tears.

"Willie, love, it's all right," she whispered. "It's worth every minute." "One more push, Sweetheart, gently," Marek said.

Faran pushed and the second child slid from her body. Its tiny head was also slick and dark, but not as dark as the first. It breathed and cried as soon as Marek lifted it up, as though it had only been waiting for the chance. It was a son.

427

By four thirty it was all over and Faran lay back in the bed with her two naked babies in her arms. Their little faces were elfin and rosy; they had tiny fingers which looked like the pink tendrils of some tender plant, but they were not small or underweight as Faran had feared they might be. They were babies of normal size and both were fit and lusty. They blinked at her from deep, unfathomable eyes, hiccupped a lot and nuzzled her at her breasts, searching for the first vital meal. When they suckled she could barely contain the emotions she felt and she cried out to have Marek and Will come and see. She was in rapture; even though tiredness assailed her, she did not want to sleep. She wanted to savor the euphoria and the triumph.

The babies had taken their fill and were busily yawning, as if all the drama of the day had been too much for them. After he cleaned them and Will helped him wrap them in little soft wrappings, Marek put them to bed, one in the basket and one in a makeshift cot which was actually a drawer. Then he had to tidy the cabin and make it into a bedroom again and make tea for Faran so that she could get her strength back. He had hardly any time to think, much less to savor the moment, as Faran was now doing. He cast a wistful eye on the babies, so contented and peacefully asleep. He almost envied them.

"You look nearly as worn out as Faran does. Let me make us all tea and a snack, and I'll tell Kenu he can come and see, if that's okay," Will offered.

Marek nodded. "Thanks, Will, I appreciate it. But wait a while before you tell Kenu, I'd like to spend some time with Faran first."

Marek kissed her tenderly on the cheek. "You did so well."

Faran cupped his face in her hands. "And you. You helped me so much. But you're very tired."

"Not as tired as you."

"They're exhausted." She nodded at the babies. "It must be hard work getting born, by the look of it."

"Aren't they beautiful?" She leaned towards them and Marek followed her eyes. "Which one is the biggest? I couldn't tell."

"Our daughter, I think, but it's hard to know exactly," Marek said.

"Our daughter. It sounds so nice when you say it." Faran stroked his hand. "She has your look, your hair."

It was true. The baby wore a thick mop of raven colored hair which was so long that it came down over the tiny ears. Marek grinned happily. "And our son, who does he remind you of?" He peered into the sleeping

428

face of his second born. No one as yet, perhaps, but what had seemed to be fairly dark hair when it was slick and wet, was now a fine cap of gold, the same sort of gold as Faran's.

"Well, actually, he looks a bit like Will did when he was born," Faran decided. "Even though I was only six then, I still remember the day."

"Whoever they look like, or take after, they are themselves," Marek said.

"Yes." Faran smiled. "They're your children and mine, but they are themselves." She turned to him and held out her arms. "Oh, Marek, I want to tell you how much you mean to me, what it meant when you held me and helped me, how close I feel to you now, so much closer, I didn't think it was possible. I want you to know."

Marek went to her. "I do know, my love, I feel it too." He took her kisses and gave them back until both of them were tasting the salt of tears. His tears or hers, it didn't matter; they were the same thing, in any case, and they were more expressive than words.

Will hurried up on deck to tell Kenu the good news then he went below again to make a meal for them all. He wasn't a great cook but he was good at simple things, so he decided that toast and an omelette each would go down easiest and best. He was starving, himself, although he hadn't even missed lunch. It must be the excitement, he decided as he washed his hands. He could never have imagined in all his life what childbirth must be like; it was an experience he would never forget.

A messy business, he thought. Bloodier than a battle, but more worthwhile. People revealed themselves fully at a time like this; take Faran for example. As he lit the gas and beat the eggs he chuckled to himself. Their dad had always disapproved of swearing, and Will had never heard him do it; but Faran on this occasion had uttered curses Will hadn't believed she knew. He wondered where they'd come from, but he understood and sympathized. Put in the same position, what would he have said?

And Marek. Will had never really known him until now, he realized. Marek had always been something of a puzzle to Will. At first he was the mystery man and Faran's lover, and the man whose strange powers were evidenced by his strange eyes. Will had experienced those powers for himself and knew that Marek's consciousness went beyond the limits of where most men's seemed to go. Then he had read the books: the words of Ozira and the amazing journal, those words which suggested so much, revealing a mind which knew the Earth and the world of Mankind in a

429

way that few other minds did. And Marek's amazing history: his incredible background, the things he had willingly given up, the threat to his safety that his past and his knowledge and determination had always posed: these were the facts of a unique sort of life which made Marek seem exotic and almost unreal. Had Will only known the facts and never the man they represented, he would have considered Marek like he would a character in some fantastic adventure tale. Yet he had met the actual man, and found him to be real.

The Marek of his acquaintance was affable and easy, a kindly person with simple tastes, who disdained affectation and false feeling. Even so, though, behind the easiness and the warmth, there were depths and distances where Will thought he could not go. He had still felt Marek to be beyond him somehow.

Then here was this moment of wonder when everyone bared their selves within the intense experience of birth. Will saw Marek with new eyes. He saw his humanity and his love for Faran, even the expressions of desperate concern and the pain in his eyes as he watched Faran suffer. He saw then that Marek was simply a man, but that there was no "simply" about being either man or woman, that the glory was in being that and expressing that. Will felt then an intense pleasure in being "simply" himself. He buttered the toast and folded the omelettes and made the tea and whistled and sang to himself.

Would he ever love a woman like that? He wondered as he carried the tea tray aft. He thought he should like to, that it would be a wonderful thing to know. He thought he might, some day.

"If the wind keeps up we should be at Te Tanaa thirty six hours fra' now," Kenu said. He came to pay his respects and to gawk at the babies. He rubbed his grizzled beard and grinned at Faran and Marek. "T'is a fine crop y'got there. Y'know wha' t'is said about babies born at sea, don't you?"

"No," I don't," Faran said.

"Well, they're already shipmates, being born t'the decks, like." Kenu grinned again. "But what they really are is no man's possession; t'is that they're born t'the sea an' no country can truly claim 'em, though countries always try. They're children o'the sea."

"And so of the Earth," Faran said. "I like that." Her eyes went questioningly to Marek. "Babies belonging to no one but themselves and the Earth. What do you think?"

Marek nodded and sighed. "I like that too."

"What happened to the bird?" Will asked Kenu, "I didn't see it when I went up top."

"Aye." Kenu bent for one more inspection of the babies. Beneath his beard his smile was knowing and contemplative. "Tha'bird was a special event, like. It stuck by 'till all was well, then it flew away, just before you came t'tell me, Will. I reckon it came for one reason only, t'see the little lad an' lass here."

"Sleep," Marek said to Faran. "For you as well as them. You need it." "Stay with me," she said, reaching to him. "Stay here, don't leave me."

"I'll stay." Marek stretched out beside her. While she closed her eyes to rest he smoothed her damp hair across her forehead. She was asleep in two minutes.

Marek lay back and watched the ceiling lamp sway above him. He was not sleepy but he felt spent by the day. And what a day! He turned his head on the pillow and gazed on Faran, then his eyes travelled across her to the sleeping infants. The separate auras of their Light were strong and pure and beautiful. The three of them pure, bright Lights. He smiled to himself and thought of how his life had gone since that very first sight of Faran in the tower, how he seemed to have been journeying towards this special moment with her.

And moments yet to be, he said to himself. Soon there would be a Moment as yet unprecedented; he knew that it would come, but not when. That Moment would mean, for himself, an intense effort of gigantic proportions for which he would have to be exactly ready. Could he do it?

The answer came, almost so loudly in his consciousness that he could have believed it echoed within the cabin, and without, even across the open sea. NO! Marek could not, but Ozira COULD and WOULD, and, in that Moment, Ozira will not be alone!

Startled, Marek sat up. He stared at Faran and the babies. Then he lay down again, closing his eyes.

He trembled slightly with apprehension. A fine sweat spread across his brow. The Moment was waiting! It was already here!

The place where he came to was barren and bright and, although seemingly without boundaries, there was a corner where a shadow hung, like an out-of-place blot of filthy ground staining a field of endless white snow. Marek felt antipathy for the shadow and its reason for being there,

431

however he knew that he had to acknowledge it this one last time. The shadow was that last vestige of darkness which had tried for so long to thwart his purpose. It was the thing behind the continuous attempts to end his journey. Foolishly, it had tried to turn Faran against him, and of course had failed, so it sought to inveigle others into the attack. It was a blind thing, a feelingless thing; it had no place in his reality, but it had to be faced down before it was finally annulled.

He had never actually confronted the Dragons. Since denying them and turning his back he had left them to themselves and to the ones who served them. There had been no open challenge and no acknowledgment, and he had wanted it that way. Now, however, he knew that merely to deny them was not the answer. So many times had he opened the way to the Light in those who needed it but also instinctively wanted it; yet now the time had come to light the true DARKNESS.

The blot of shadow was no more than the entryway to the realm of Dragon-kind wherein the seeds of illusion waited, ready to be planted and nurtured in the minds of the greedy and unwary, time and time again. To enter there was to enter hell, and what would soon be chaos.

As Marek, he was clothed with and protected by a vestment of Light. The Light of Ozira was also that, a greater vestment to put on; but, before this, one other would join him. Mari-E-ele appeared in radiant form, the third aspect of his Light.

He faced the contrary doorway of shadow. He was clothed with Light and enclosed by the Light. When his Light passed into the realm of the Dragons, the Light scoured the darkness in the way that a great wave of the sea might sweep cleanly across a land which was tainted and infected by plague and disease. The powers of the Dragons were mighty, but only within their own realm, which they had ornamented with the constructs of a thousand illusions. Sphere after sphere of golden palaces, impressive great halls of learning and ceremony, every wonder of manufactured brilliance, these were the paradises of virtual reality which deluded the minds of men, and the Light scoured them with its unforgiving brightness, revealing the shabbiness of their falsity, revealing the emptiness of which they were created.

They did not tumble, although they remained as hollow shells. Only the Light of many would finally bring them down, as worthless and pointless and not to be bothered with. It was not for a single Light to restore the world of mankind to its true purpose and place on Earth, but to show the way so that the rest might follow and establish that purpose in their own

432

consciousness. For each human Light was its own salvation and must make its own effort for the Earth.

So the Light of Ozira poured through the Dragon realms, cleansing and opening a fissure through the substance, a crack in the seamless construct of delusion which would never be sealed again, and this caused a certain loss in the Dragon power which they would not be able to reclaim.

Recoiling from the Light, yet rising in defense of their realm and in fury of having their power diminished, the Dragons manifested as a rotating mass of tortuous darkness, spitting cold fire and malevolence, as though to destroy the intrusive Light. No plausible visions of pleasing-looking faces and golden diadems this time, nor of crystalline angelic beings of great wisdom, the Dragons revealed themselves in true form, as a mass of stench and decay, of degenerating frequency, as an oily excrescence which exuded only the clamminess of death. Their rotating form coiled in opposition to the Light and strove to rise higher and loom larger, yet it would not approach near.

Surging up massively, the Dragon darkness tried to intimidate the Light, but the Light was suddenly swelled to greatness as more Light joined it. The Light of Rai-a-ele and of a bright, white Bird and the Lights of another and another, of two unnamed. And one more Light, the unexpected Light of a regenerated power, added itself to the rest.

There was no contest. The Light whirled in opposition to the dark, and confusion ensued. The powers of the Dragon force were scattered into chaos. They would regroup, when the greed and lust of the illusory world sought for their influence again. Yet their powers were lessened and would go on lessening as more men and women turned from their false temptations, wanting only that which men and women truly were, the Light of their own Being.

Marek opened his eyes and stared at the ceiling through sweat and also through tears of surprise. Of course he knew that his beloved Rai-a-ele would be with him for the Moment. And the Lights of the two who were their children for the present. The bird, he understood now, was a symbol of the nature of Faran's being. It had come for the birth of her children, but it had been there for her, not for them. But the tears were not in his eyes because of their presence in the Moment. After all, why should he cry for happiness when he could laugh instead? He lay quietly and remembered, thinking of that one Light that had been the surprise.

Should he have been surprised, though? The Ravana, turned from darkness and reborn to the Light. The Ravanna, Itself again, a power of

433

brightness to equal his own. This is where the tears had come from, from that movement of gratitude within Marek's heart as he realized his brother was with him now. Even though Silene's legacy of harassment was still a possibility in the Earthly realm, his spirit was no longer a part of it. Perhaps this is a sign, Marek thought. Perhaps, from now on, we will all be left in peace, at last.

Silene had once said that taking this path would make Marek the loneliest man in the world. Well, whether that had been a deliberate lie or not, it didn't matter now because it was not true. You could not be lonely when you were what you were, when you knew that Light which you were. Because that Light was everything; it was All.

Chapter Eight

With fair and helpful winds, the Mari-E-ele entered Tana City's harbor at approximately the time Kenu said it would. They motored in with the dawn-light, cutting through waters which were stained gold and silver by the rising sun. The Mari-E-ele seemed to be alone on the harbor, the sole moving thing at least. The harbor was quiet and as milky still as a mountain dew pond and Tana City rose from its shores like a forest of stone and glass and steel, and the sunlight winked from its windows as from a thousand half awake eyes. Beyond the city itself the suburbs reached up the slopes of a backdrop of high hills, and in the distance the land stretched away, mountainous and colored blue, into the morning haze. Tana City was the only big city in Te Tanaa and it was the country's chief entry point, to which all visitors by sea were encouraged to report.

They anchored just off the moorings, waiting for the port office to open at eight. There was no need to look for a berth because Marek didn't intend to stay. As soon as their entry was cleared he was headed to Poona Bay, the harbor of the Tanu. It was not near Tana City and was another three hours" sail away.

Just before eight he and Kenu took the dinghy to the dock. The port office which controlled the dock entry was directly opposite, as were the public phones. Marek rang the Tanu Head-man first to let him know they were on their way, then he put in a long distance call to Nikola, to hear how she was and to tell her about the babies. Nikola was overjoyed. She had a month to go herself and all was well, she told Marek.

By the time Marek had finished his calls the port office had been open for fifteen minutes, however although there were still few people about the office had an atmosphere of busyness and its officers the usual laconic air of petty officials. When Marek presented the Mari-E-ele's papers at one of the counter desks there was a little flurry of excited activity which neither he nor Kenu understood.

The official was a young woman of thirty or so, with a round, light brown face which showed mixed origins ranging between native islander and invading Telaian. In fact she spoke Telaian perfectly with the accents of one who had been in Telaia for some while before returning to

435

her land. At first she was only interested in the boat documents, not yet raising her eyes fully to see who presented them. She seemed to be having trouble understanding them, reading slowly in the deliberate and infuriating manner of officialdom which was so impersonal and inconsiderate of another's time or schedule. Kenu shifted irritably beside Marek, as if to say this was not what he expected of a homecoming after so long a time.

"This boat left Port Dias without proper authorization," the woman said without looking up. "No," Marek asserted. "Everything is there. Just check through once again." He had the sudden suspicion that obstruction was about to be put in his way once more and he thought to himself, No. No, it won't happen here, not in Te Tanaa. I won't let it.

She read again, even more slowly this time, if that was possible, and finally she nodded. However she said, still not raising her head, "We had a call about the boat. They said—"

"The papers are in order," Marek insisted, cutting her off. Look at me, he thought. Just look up into my eyes for once and see that I'm honest; then there won't be any trouble.

The woman nodded again then glanced up. "It seems okay," she agreed. She stared at Marek's face and met his eyes, then briefly at Kenu, recognizing him instantly as Tanu and dismissing him as too familiar and ordinary to be worth bothering about. But it was on Marek that her own eyes settled and there was an odd sort of shine in them. "May I have your papers, please?"

Marek handed her his papers and she read the name and studied him seemingly with great interest. "It is you!" she said, so loudly that others in the office turned and stared. "I mean, it's you. I thought by the owner's name on the boat documents that it must be! The man in the news who gave up all that inheritance. You're the Baron's brother!"

So what does she think that makes me? Marek wondered. Some sort of half-wit, probably. However he nodded politely.

Her eyes were gleaming, but what the gleam meant Marek did not know. "You're travelling alone?" she asked.

"No." Marek presented Faran's and Will's papers. "My wife and brother-in-law are with me." "Then they should be here at the office," she stated, officiously. "My brother-in-law is looking after my wife, on board. She can't come ashore, she needs to rest." Marek engaged the woman's eyes again. "You see, a day-and-a-half ago we had an event on board, my wife gave birth to twins."

Her mouth dropped open, and, for the first time, she smiled. "How wonderful! So that's five to enter port, not three! You'll have to register that."

"Six." Kenu thrust his documents across the counter at her. "Crew," he said roughly.

Kenu had Tanu papers which the woman examined quickly and stamped without comment. All her interest was in Marek, and her face had suddenly become human and a whole lot warmer. "Are you staying in Tana City? Someone will have to come on board to verify your passengers."

"Then it'll have to be soon," Marek told her. "I'm due in Poona Bay by midday."

"Oh, all right," she replied. For some unknown reason she seemed disappointed by his answer. Then immediately her face brightened. "Well, I suppose it will have to be me who comes." She stamped Marek's papers and the ones for the Mari-E-ele then called to one of the other officers. "Clive, can you take over for me? I have to do an inspection."

Getting out from behind her desk, the young woman seemed to struggle, and Marek wondered why. Then he saw and he smiled secretly to himself. The woman was pregnant. Ah, the delightful camaraderie of pregnancy which is about to save us from any more bureaucratic nonsense, he thought. Good ol' babies, what would I have done without you?

In consideration of the woman's pregnant state, Marek walked slowly back with her to the dinghy. Her last name was on a badge on her chest, but her first name was Mardi, she told him. She seemed to know about his history, or at least that amount of it which had been written up in the news. The story was everywhere, even in Te Tanaa, she said, but she had been in Telaia herself when the events actually happened. "I couldn't believe it when I saw you here in front of me," she said. "I thought I must be imagining it, then I read your name." Her eyes regarded him curiously, though she did not ask the question which was chiefly on her mind. It seemed to be a constant question in the minds of many: "What makes a man give up the chance at a lifetime of power and luxury? And all that money?" This, it appeared, was the preoccupation of the majority of mankind, as if peace and happiness reside nowhere else but in a world of material privilege. As if the public examples of miserable rich people, as they were reported daily in the press and trashy magazines, did nothing to enlighten or deter those who wished for unbounded riches themselves.

On board the Mari-E-ele, Mardi met Faran and Will and confirmed their status as acceptable visitors to Te Tanaa. She stamped their entry papers and gushed over the babies. "Of course you have six weeks to register the births, so that's okay," she told them. "I hope you enjoy your stay here. Let me know if there's anything you need."

"She was nice," Faran said as Kenu ferried Mardi back to the dock.

"Nice enough," Marek agreed. He had not bothered to mention the woman's earlier officiousness since it didn't matter any more. He was in Te Tanaa and he knew that obstruction was finally at an end, that the trail of his brother's persecution ended here and now. It was over, for good.

Poona Bay itself was not large or particularly deep, but because of a cluster of small islands and islets which fanned out from it in semi-horseshoe formation, it was a sheltered area which was just perfect for small boats. The Tanu kept their fleet of fishing and tour boats at dock at the deeper end of the bay and there was an anchorage for visiting craft at the shallower end. Above the shore the town of Poona had a fish processing plant and fuel store, two dozen shops, one museum devoted to Tanu culture and historical times, several hotels, bistros and assorted watering holes, and nearly a dozen restaurants set up mainly to cater to the likes and expectations of tourists, and one resort and nightclub to accommodate and entertain them. The town itself was largely historic, reflecting the architecture of the early invading settlers and not of Tanu taste in building. Even though the Tanu ran the town and owned most of the businesses, it did not seem to match their style of life, Marek thought, and their true way of living could be found not here but further into the hinterland and north along the coast where the big beaches of shining white sand sat below cliffs of verdant green and purple.

Yet Poona was the workplace for many of the Tanu and the Head-man himself was the town accountant, and his brother its lawyer. Since the Head-man worked in Poona most days of the week he was on the spot when the Mari-E-ele arrived and because Marek had warned him in advance of his coming, he had made sure that others would be too. "Looks like Peli's turned on a bit of a reception f'you, like," Kenu said as they motored into shallow water. "Told you y'were a celebrity."

Marek sighed. It was true. As they passed by the fishing boat dock he saw that it was empty of activity but that further on was a smaller jetty crowded with waiting Tanu men, women and children. This was obviously where he was expected to anchor. Somebody must have been watching for the Mari-E-ele long before it got near Poona Bay, probably sighting it from the lighthouse which guarded the reef further south.

"So many people!" Faran said nervously. She hugged close by Marek's side. "I hope that jetty doesn't collapse under the weight."

It looked as if it might, however when they got nearer they could see that the main mass of waiting people was actually behind, on the shore side wharf and that besides the Tanu there were a few interested tourists, curious to see what the occasion was about. Then Marek could recognize faces: the giant Head-man Peli and his nearly as huge brother in the white shirts and shorts which were their working uniform of the day, and Peli's son-in-law, the apprentice drummer, and a short little Lani standing on tip-toe to see better. As the Mari-E-ele approached, Lani waved and jumped up and down.

Faran nudged Marek in the ribs. "Who's that? One of your old girlfriends?" Marek smiled. "Actually, no."

"Welcome, Ozira." Peli came aboard and held out his huge hand and Marek took it. Behind the Head-man, dozens of dark brown eyes were watching from the jetty, and Marek saw how swiftly they had shifted from himself to Faran and Will. Even the head-man's eyes moved between the three and he was waiting to be enlightened. Kenu had already disembarked and had pushed through the crowd in the company of his daughter who could hardly believe her good fortune in finding her father again.

Marek made the introductions. "My wife, Faran, and her brother, Will Crafter."

The Head-man bowed and made them welcome. His eyes were fixed intently on Faran and for a moment Marek could not understand why. Then he realized that Peli was fascinated by something about her. "As I am Ozira, this is Rai-a-ele," he explained, and Peli nodded. "The Beautiful Lady of the Sun Hair," Peli said, to Faran's extreme embarrassment, making her blush deeply. "Ozira, you will come home now? We have a house ready for you. My mother's house, the best in the village." Peli said. "We are glad you've come back to us; it's a great day."

Marek nodded, accepting the gift without comment. He was somewhat embarrassed also but he knew that it was Tanu custom to offer the best accommodations to anyone they welcomed and it was required that he would not make too much of it.

"Everything you wish to bring will be carried," Peli said. "As you can see, we have plenty of willing hands and plenty of cars for the trip."

"Well, just our clothes and personal things for the moment," Marek agreed. "Our bags are all ready below, and there's one more thing ..." He grinned at Faran. "Well, two more, actually."

He led Peli downstairs to where the babies were waiting, one in the basket and one in its makeshift bed of a drawer. Peli stared, open mouthed, then smiled broadly. "Ozira, you and your Sun Lady, you've been very busy," he said, with a laugh.

"But Marek ... his mother's house? Are you sure we're not imposing?" Faran said with concern through the open doorway to Marek. She paced the varnished floor of the bungalow's main room. It was not a large house but was open and airy and had sliding doors which opened onto fine, wide verandas and a beautiful outlook to green slopes and the sea, and a big orchard and a fenced garden in back. It seemed to her that the Headman expected them to live there as long as they liked. Faran did not understand the ways of these people, but Marek did, she knew, and she wanted him to explain while she still had the leisure to ask. Since arriving at the dock in the bay they had only just found the time to be alone.

Marek was perched on the veranda rail, appreciating a view of violet blossom on the branches of a tree nearby. "His mother died some while ago; actually it was just when I arrived last time. If Peli offers this as a place for us to use then we can't refuse his hospitality; he would count it as an insult."

Faran nodded. That she could understand. "But the place looks as if it's recently been lived in, so I get the feeling that we are putting someone out of their house."

"Most likely, we are." Marek shrugged. He swung round to smile a reassuring smile. "The Tanu always give a guest the best of what they have. They don't think of it as giving up anything. They don't mind sharing at all; in fact I believe they're not at all concerned with having exclusive possessions as people are in Telaia and elsewhere. It's a different sort of world here on this side of the island; they value different things to the rest, that's why I like them so much."

"That is different," Faran agreed. "So I guess I'll get used to it. But how can I get used to being treated like some sort of visiting royalty? It makes me feel uncomfortable. I don't like it."

From the veranda Marek could just see Will, on his way to a first exploratory walk around the village. He had a group of young people trailing him and mostly they were girls. Will looked as if he was enjoying himself rather. Marek laughed. "I don't think it bothers Will very much, though. But, don't worry, in a couple of days the novelty will have worn off and this shall all be over and they'll start treating you like you're just one of the family."

"I hope so." Faran flopped into an easy chair. She had begun to feel the pressure of the day and she still got tired easily. She supposed that she was not really over the birth yet since it had only been two days. "I think I need a rest," she was saying, when one of the babies set up a cry. Faran groaned.

"I'll go." Marek let Faran sit where she was. He trotted into the bedroom where the babies had been laid in the little cribs which, through Tanu generosity, had appeared miraculously from somewhere. It was their son who made all the noises but pretty soon he had the other one going too. "One starts and the other one wakes up and follows," he said to Faran from the door. One by one he changed them and cuddled them and lay them back down, but they still continued to cry. "Must be hungry again, Sweetheart. Greedy little devils, these babies, aren't they?"

Faran dragged herself from the chair. In the bedroom she gave Marek a wry smile. "I guess this is how it's going to be for a while." She picked up one squalling infant and settled herself on the big bed and waited for Marek to bring the other one to her. "We're going to have to make up our minds about their names soon; we can't go on calling them "the babies" forever."

Marek watched his children suck. When they had thought there would be only one child they had decided on several different names for a boy or girl. But when the birth happened it seemed to both himself and Faran that the names did not really suit the little faces and personalities who had arrived. It was as though special names had to be chosen for these children of the sea, but what they were as yet he did not know.

"You don't have to sit here and get bored," Faran said. "This will probably take a while and I feel so dopey that I won't be much company."

"I'm not bored," Marek said, but he took the subtle hint that she was too weary to talk and went outside. He thought he would do the same as Will and take a walk, but not to the village. Coming here was almost like coming home, he decided, but there were times even at home when you needed a break from your 'Relatives". But it was a good feeling to be back; this was a place which harmonized the spirit, and its people cheered him by their sympathy and the unconditional friendship they offered. The frequencies were just right, he considered, just right for a place at the center of a special Moment for the Earth.

Walking away from the house and the village, turning north and seawards, Marek knew where he wanted to go. It wouldn't take long if he didn't dally anywhere, he thought. He crossed a knoll and dipped down into the first palm-filled valley. The trail wove through deep shadow and filtered sunlight. It skirted sandy hollows which were densely populated with ferns and orchids and the huge woven nests of land birds as big as chickens. Other birds sang high in the palm fronds above him and the sky was a pattern of cross-hatching in heavy bright blue. Nothing had changed bar the direction of the trail here and there to allow for nests and the natural subsidence of the loose soil; it was for Marek as if time had suddenly stood still.

A couple of valleys later he reached the cliffs above the sea and came out onto the hill overlooking the string of islets, the queen of which was the island of Ompalo. He wandered down to the cliff edge and stared across the water. Ompalo rose from the cobalt colored depths of the Southern Ocean through a jewelled ring of turquoise and white foam, its single mountain arching into the blue sky and towards to the Sun, as if the Earth reached up her hand in greeting to her consort of Light. And the Sun's Light wrapped Ompalo round, mingling with the coil of radiant energy emerging from the Earth, so that of all islands in the Southern Ocean, Ompalo shone like the beacon it was, the beacon of the Moment and of all future Moments.

Marek stared at Ompalo for a long while as he felt the force of energy rise inside himself in response to the force across the water. He felt the call, as though Ompalo sang to him, a siren carolling her song of love and desire over the waves. Ompalo sang and Marek's heart lifted. His mind and body resonated with the song, his feeling self flew upwards and out. As if the Light of Ozira had arms to lift Marek high. He felt the force of Mari-E-ele within him, and heard her laugh, which was the merriment of the Life experience, the Joy that Being knows when it lives and loves and is Itself.

Joy that was so often not even a consideration in the illusory systems of the human world, but was, actually, the very essence of the experience of the All, and was at the center of every heart and was the keynote of the Earth and all the stars playing their separate harmonies within the symphony of the Universe.

He felt lifted high, and feeling as though he might fly above the Earth and cast his Light-Song of joy like rain across a parched world. And since he was feeling this way, he knew that it was possible, and so he followed suit and flew … and flew.

Chapter Nine

How long had he been gone? Marek wasn't sure, but he didn't wish to leave Faran waiting for his return. He turned and went back up the hill, then down again through the beautiful shadowed valleys. Coming to the knoll, he paused and looked over towards the village, then across to the house. Behind the house and partly dwarfed by some of the high growing leafy crops, was the movement of someone bending at work in the garden. At first Marek could not tell who it was, then as he came nearer he recognized Lani. She straightened up at his approach and waved her hand.

They had not spoken much as yet, except in greeting, since Lani had to take her place well behind her father and all the other elders of the village. Her face was beaming when she saw Marek; there were flowers in her hair and, as usual, she wore only the briefest of skirts, leaving her upper body entirely bare.

"Ozira." She showed him a basket which she was filling with vegetables and fruit. "I came to see to your evening meal, I will make it for you, if that's all right with your wife."

Marek smiled. "Thanks, Lani, that's really nice of you. I know Faran will be grateful, she's feeling rather tired at the moment, and I'm not the greatest cook myself."

Lani laughed at him. "Are you not, Ozira? But mostly it'll be easy, just salad and steamed vegetable, and fish which I've already put in your cold-box." She bent to gather a brace of curling leaves. "This lot, and I'm done."

When she was finished Marek put his hands out for the basket. "It looks heavy."

"Oh, I have heavier than this to carry, usually," Lani said, though she gave him the basket anyway. As if searching the garden for something or someone, she glanced around. "Where are you, poppet?" she called to someone Marek could not see and went off, bending again amongst the leaves. She came back with a baby in her arms, a child of about twelve months or so with a round smiling face and black curly hair. It had torn up a fistful of grass and was giving it the taste test.

"Is this your child?" Marek asked her, wonderingly.

Lani prised the grass from the little hand. "Yes. This is my son, he's

444

one year old."

The baby wriggled energetically and she put him down and he tottered towards Marek on his short chubby legs. To Marek, he did not look as if he had been walking for very long and when he reached Marek's feet he fell down. Marek stooped, put down the basket and picked him up.

"He likes you," Lani said. "I can tell because he's keeping still for once." For some reason her customary smile had grown shy. "I remembered what you told me, Ozira that any child Raool and I have could be a Messenger too. I hope you don't mind, but I … we … named him after you."

"After me?" Marek brushed garden dirt from the baby's knees and hands. "You called him Ozira?" "No!" Shocked, Lani put her hand to her mouth. "That is your sacred name and we would never use that for anyone but you. No, I knew that Dad knew your other name and so I asked him what it was and he told me. This is little Marek."

Marek held his namesake at arm's length to study him better. Baby Marek laughed at him and drooled, waving his own arms in the air. "He's a fine boy. I'm honored."

"Your own son will bear your name?" Lani asked as they went into the house together. "No. We haven't chosen names yet for either child."

"And when will you?"

Marek crept to the open door of the bedroom. If Faran was resting he didn't want to disturb her. He made a gesture of indecision at Lani and said softly, "When the time is right, I guess. The moment will show itself and then we'll know." He looked in on Faran from the door. She was stretched out on the bed as he'd left her and she was asleep. The babies were asleep too, cradled against her breasts, at peace. It was a pretty picture, he thought.

Little Marek waddled past him into the room and Lani came after him. "I'm sorry; he gets away on me sometimes." She swept the child up in her arms and gazed upon Faran on the bed and smiled. She whispered, "I know exactly how she feels. You must take great care of her, Ozira."

They tiptoed out. Lani went to the kitchen and began to prepare the meal. "Can I help?" Marek asked.

"Keep that boy out of mischief while I do this and you'll help a lot," Lani said. "Your wife is very beautiful, Ozira. Is she the one you told me about?"

"Yes, she is. I took your advice and went to find her. In the end it was she who found me. I've been happy ever since."

445

Lani chopped up vegetables with a kitchen knife. She seemed to know where everything was in the cupboards and drawers. "I'm glad. You were too lonely, Ozira, and that's not right for anyone. She is a good wife for you, as bright as the sun and as beautiful as you are," she said plainly and without any sign that she meant to flatter him.

He knew she did not. He sat down and set the baby on his knee and grinned foolishly. He knew she was sincere, but he had never heard anyone describe himself in that way before. He decided to change the subject. "You and Raool weren't living in this house before we came, were you?" he asked her.

Lani seemed surprised. "No. My auntie Bet was. She's at her sister's house now. She likes it there, they have many children and grandchildren to play with and spoil. Dad said he's going to build her another one near there. She is pleased about that."

"That's good," Marek meant to say more; however, a movement at the door made him turn. Faran stood there, sleepy eyed but clearly amazed at the sight of the bare breasted girl working in the kitchen and Marek with a little brown baby on his knee.

Marek stood up with the baby in his arms. "Lani's making us some dinner," he explained. "And this is her son."

"Little Marek." Lani turned with a broad smile. "I named him after your husband. It's a good name, a lucky name."

Faran nodded. "He's sweet." She came and patted the baby on his curly head. "And friendly too." She cast ironic and questioning eyes at Marek, a glance which asked, Does Lani always dress like that when she's in the village? Marek pulled a face which was somewhere between wry and amused. Yes, he answered silently. Always.

"Where's Will?" Faran said. "Isn't he back yet?"

"I'd forgotten about him!" Marek said apologetically. "I think I'd better go and look for him." He offered the baby to Faran and she took him. "I won't be long."

"Is there anything I can do to help you?" Faran asked Lani. "It's awfully thoughtful of you to do this; I didn't feel much like having to cook after all that's happened today."

"I didn't think you would. I know exactly what it's like, how tired you get. But you will soon be feeling better. Ozira was minding the baby for me. He's a little devil sometimes, quite a lot to handle now he's learned to walk. That's the best thing to help me at the moment," Lani said.

"He walks?" Faran set little Marek on the floor, and he got up immediately and headed for the open door. Faran went after him. "I see what you mean."

Lani laughed. "I wonder if your Marek was ever so naughty as this one is?"

Faran caught up the baby and hugged him. "Not naughty, just adventurous. I'm sure he was, and just as cute."

Lani placed vegetables in a steamer pot. She took a whole fish from the freezer box and lay it in a special cooking pan, sprinkling on herbs and a handful of aromatic leaves. "This is our traditional dish. In the old days we would have cooked it outside in leaves on a bed of coals. We still do it sometimes, for a special occasion, and you'll probably be getting it again tomorrow at the feast."

"Feast?"

"Yes. To honor the return of Ozira, with the addition of you and your handsome brother, and the beautiful babies of course."

A feast for us. It is like being royalty, Faran thought. However, the earlier mention of Marek as a baby interested her more. It was a reminder of something she had wanted to tell him. That her daytime sleep had been more than necessary rest, it had brought her a special experience which she could not, in all honesty, call a dream but a vision…

… "The woman wasn't just good looking, she was startlingly beautiful. She was tall and slim with dark eyes and hair and the loveliest skin, so creamy and smooth. She just walked into the room and stood and gazed down on me. Her eyes were very gentle and kind and she smiled. It was then I realized that she looked remarkably like you."

"Like me?" Marek undressed and got into bed beside Faran. He was intrigued. "Who?"

"I wondered that too, for a moment, then I knew. But I won't say yet; I think you'll guess in a minute," Faran said. "She said things to me about the babies and about you. She said that our son's name was to be Tai, for that was part of his true name and he ought to bear it from the first days so that his connection with his Light would be strong and his to claim from the beginning."

"Tai," Marek said. "Well, that's different. It sounds almost Tanu. I like it." He speculated on the identity of Faran's dream-lady. Was it the mischievous Mari-E-ele again, in one of her tantalizing disguises? he asked himself. "And our daughter? What did she say about her?" He waited for Faran to enlighten him.

Faran smiled to herself. What she remembered most about the lady was the softness of her eyes, the tender love in them. "I had always known he would break free," the lady had said to Faran. "This is my joy and blessing, that he has found his Peace and Light. Tell him this from me. Tell him that I am near, as I always was."

"She spoke of our daughter like this, that her Light is already strong in her and that her name was and is Mia." Faran held her breath and waited for a reaction.

Marek said nothing for a while. His face was pale and he chewed his lip like an upset child. It was a face such as Faran had not seen for a long time, not since Brentore, when she had noted the grey light of sadness in Marek's eyes for the mother he had loved but lost. But his eyes were not grey now; they were violet. His mother's official birth name was long and complicated and foreign sounding to Telaian ears, for her family had come originally from another country; however, the name she used and had chosen for herself when she was very young was Mia.

"And there was more. A special message for you." Faran told him his mother's words – her blessing.

Marek couldn't help himself, he cried. Then he climbed out of bed and went to bend above the crib where his daughter slept. He touched the child's soft, dark hair, seeing her now with new eyes. If he looked closely he could see the resemblance. "Mia," he whispered. The very sound of the name made him want to cry some more so instead he stood up and turned to Faran. He saw her through a blur; her face showed sympathy and concern and perhaps something extra.

"You won't go and forget your son now?" she said softly as though afraid the words might hurt them all.

Marek shook his head. He felt bewildered by events, but also certain. "What, because of Mia?" Faran shrugged.

"No, I love them both." He returned to the bed and kissed her. "If there's something I've learned well, indeed which my whole life has been about, is that the past is the past and only the now matters. Mia is the now and so is Tai; who or what they were in the past is just that – past. I'll love them for the now and for themselves, both the same."

PART 6
Fire On The Sea

Chapter One

Ompalo was a garden.

On Ompalo fresh water sprang from the mountain slopes, appearing in cascades from green clefts high up and dropping like veils of white gauze straight down into deep, olive colored pools. The foliage was luxuriant and unspoiled and, as Peli had said, there were plants and animals here which had been wiped out everywhere else. Ompalo was like a "first garden", one which has never seen the industry of man. If man had ever lived here it was only as one of many, varied frequencies, not as conqueror and oppressor. Only a consciousness devoted to simply "Living" could appreciate Ompalo for what it was; the ego's elaborate machinations had no place here. In Ompalo one could experience the delight of just BEING.

The little bay where the Mari-E-ele anchored was tinted aquamarine. Where the shore began, the water changed to a turquoise hue as delicate and transparent as clear glass. For the sands of Ompalo were tinted a vibrant yellow gold, unlike the paler, creamier sands of Te Tanaa or elsewhere. On the beach the sand was so bright and the air so alive and reflective that it seemed the atmosphere was golden and that you had to step through a doorway in the sun, just to arrive.

Will dragged the dinghy onto the damp sand of the beach and tied it to a rock shaped conveniently like a large, thick, upright post. He hoisted out a basket and a bag of cushions from the boat and trudged up towards the tree line in quest after Marek and Faran. So completely loaded up, he felt as though he was a bearer to kings, or rather a king and queen, except that it wasn't really like that.

Marek and Faran had to carry the babies as well as the beach mats, so perhaps if anyone was royalty, it was Tai and Mia, who had to do nothing all day but be their charming selves.

Will crossed through wispy grasses into shade. He knew where he was headed, having come to Ompalo before. This was the second time in the three months since their arrival in Te Tanaa, but the only time that they were here alone. The first visit was a festive affair with more than half the village coming along for the occasion. Then, the little bay was crowded with half a dozen boats from the fishing fleet and the tour business, as well as the Mari-E-ele. Ompalo was sacred to the Tanu and they never let strangers or non-Tanu go there. Except for Marek, or rather, Ozira; he seemed to have carte- blanche to do what he liked as far as the Tanu were concerned.

It had puzzled Will initially, this deference to Marek. Mainly because Will knew that Marek did not actively seek it; yet the Tanu gave it anyway. Soon after arriving at Poona Bay and once they were settled into the life of the village, Marek had taken up his old work again, the healing of ills, and that was when Will began to understand more. At Nikola's hospice Marek was a healer of the more recognizable sort, if unconventional, and no one but Nikola and Dan and Dr. Langan Snr. knew something of the truth about the way he healed. Here in Te Tanaa it was different. The Tanu spoke openly of his "magic hands" and called him their Messenger, and although time and time again Marek talked to them of their own power to heal themselves and they listened to him and practised what he taught, they still turned to him in times of greatest need.

Marek and Faran had downed the king and queen on a mat under a large, spreading tree when Will caught them up. They were waiting for him eagerly because he was the one carrying the lunch. Ompalo was an odd place to come just for a picnic, Will thought. Not that it wasn't beautiful and a pleasure to come here, but there were plenty of other places almost as beautiful and a lot closer to home which were much less trouble to reach. He had the feeling that Marek and Faran had another reason on their minds, although what it was he didn't know.

They spread a second mat with cushions and laid out their lunch. Even a short sea ride managed to whip up the hunger. It was the salt air, Will believed, although he was almost always ready to eat at any time of day. Much like the ravenous babies, according to Faran.

Filtered sunlight spotted the ground and the breezes played with it, sending it darting across the mat like butterflies on a string. The babies turned their heads toward the spots of light and reached for them as though thinking they had substance. While he ate, Will tickled their toes and bare tummies to make them laugh. He liked them a lot; they were generally always happy and content, except when they were hungry, of course.

Which was just as Faran had finished her lunch and was preparing herself for a walk with Marek. She sighed and raised a hand to Marek where he stood. "Soon," she said in explanation of something Will did not understand. "They can't wait, so we have to."

Marek smiled obligingly. "Well, everything is important and they are most of all. We can wait. But I'll just go down towards the beach. You come when you're ready."

Will watched Marek wander off through the light and shadow of the trees. "Wait for what? And where's he off to?"

Faran had picked up a squirming Mia. "Help me with Tai," she said. Three month old babies were still not so very big but they were heavier than they looked. She reclined on the cushioned mat and settled Mia at her breast and reached for Tai. Will helped her position him comfortably. It was not as easy to feed two babies as it was one, especially at the same time, but the babies demanded so loudly and impatiently that neither would wait to follow the other.

"Is that good enough?" Will plumped the cushions under Faran's arms. "It's okay. Not as comfortable as home, though."
Will sat back to watch. He always thought it looked rather odd, the two little heads at Faran's breasts, one head as dark as night, the other like a round piece of sunlight. He had gotten used to seeing it though, just as he had grown used to seeing the Tanu women half naked with their own babies at their breasts. The nakedness meant nothing to him now, although it had made him feel rather shy and embarrassed at first, especially when the village girls of his own age or thereabouts played up to him and flirted with him so outrageously, although innocently and without guile. "You didn't answer my question," he said to Faran as he came back to the moment.

"What?" Faran looked up at him vaguely. To Will, she often seemed vague and distanced when she was feeding her babies.

"What are we waiting for? And why has Marek gone off to the beach?"

"Oh, that? Marek's gone to commune with Mari-E-ele," Faran said, as if her strange reply was the most natural one she could have made.

Will tried to shake away the puzzlement. His mind felt to be shrouded in wool and it seemed that shaking his head was all that would shift it. "And we're waiting for ...?"

"It's hard to say what," Faran said. Her smile was sympathetic. "I can't tell you what, Will, because I won't know until it happens."

Happens? What does she mean ... happens? Will thought. "Does Marek know?"

Faran shook her head. "Sort of, but not exactly. He wanted to wait for the moment to show itself.
Maybe he's finding out right now though."

Marek walked through the trailing ground vine of Starflowers which gathered in thick bunches at the place where the grass met the first of the dry sand. He stopped as he remembered the first time he had ever seen a Starflower and where he had seen it. He stooped and picked one, twirling it round and round with his fingers thoughtfully. Its creamy petals formed a spiral whorl which was the perfect expression of a natural vortex, and this concept of nature was as simple as it was profound. He wondered at how mankind did so love to complicate all the things of life when the truths surrounding them were all so simple, too simple perhaps to exist in the alienated and complicated world of pretence and illusion.

"From one dear heart to another." He remembered saying those words to Faran in the cottage at Nikola's. Mari-E-ele's gift, a garland of Ompalo's stars. He tucked the flower behind his ear, native style.

452

"Ozira … Mari-E-ele," he said aloud to the salty wind. He stepped from shade into sunlight, and being barefoot felt the sudden heat beneath him, so he hopped and hurried from there onto the cool damp sand. He stood and watched the waves gather and expend energy over and over as they crashed upon the beach. It was a fair day, yet a blustery one, one full of brightness and potent frequencies.

Marek felt the raw power of the Earth within him as it channelled upward from it's core, through his contact with the golden sand. He looked down at the sand and bent and brushed it with his fingers. There were glints of actual gold there as well as of quartz and mica and olivine. And many other minerals besides, as though Ompalo contained a little cosmos of the Earth in that one beach.

As he bent forward the rainbow stone he wore fell between his feet, although the thong and the metal attachment still remained around his neck. Dismayed, he picked up the stone and held it in his hand. Whatever had glued it to the clasp had failed, but the stone was undamaged and there was not even a trace of glue to be seen on the end. He stood and considered the purity and simplicity of the stone, and suddenly all dismay fled. In his palm the oval, crystalline stone shimmered like liquid, reminding him of a pool of water and a shining shield.

Nodding to himself, Marek understood. His eyes followed his understanding and he stared at the rolling sea. The sun was heading westwards, so that it sat high over the sea like a bright, wide open eye. Its light seemed to reach down to greet the waves and the waves reached up to give back the greeting. Marek curled his fingers around the stone. It felt cool and yet also warm to the touch.

"Yes."

As Ozira, he spoke the affirmation to himself and to Mari-E-ele. Water which you could hold in the palm of your hand without spilling a drop. Water which was the key to unlocking the fiery nature of Earth-light. Water which was the Earth in its most flexible aspect. Water and fire; Earth and Sun; the Love and the Light; the warm, embodied love of Humankind for the Earth and the fierce, bright light- love of the Humanity of the Stars for all that existed.

Marek walked a little way along the beach. What he waited for now was only for Faran to come.

"Well, they're happy babies now," Faran said to Will. "I want to go to Marek, but I don't want to leave them here. Will, can you come too? Then, can you look after them for me while I do whatever it is Marek wants?"

Will had no intention of being left behind, he was too curious about probable events. "Which one do you want to carry, Mia or Tai?"

Faran chose Tai, the lightest of the two, and they left the picnic things and went in search of Marek. He was not far away, just near the water's edge, and he turned and waved as they came towards him.

"What happened to your stone?" Faran asked. Marek was shirtless and right away she noticed the loose empty thong on his chest. "You haven't gone and lost it, have you?"

"No." Opening his hand, Marek showed her. "It just fell from the clasp. I'm not meant to keep on wearing it, I know that, because it's not just a decoration."

"What is it then and what are you supposed to do with it?" Will said. He stepped back a little because baby Mia had decided that she wanted the stone. Mia reached her hands to Marek and gurgled.

"Well, that I don't know just yet." Marek held up the stone, twirling it slightly in his fingers and it caught the light, flashing rainbows into the air. Both babies blinked their eyes and screwed up their faces as the lights darted across them, then they waved their arms as if requesting more rainbows.

Marek twirled the stone again and the babies laughed. "They seem to know what it's all about," Marek said. He slipped the stone into his pants pocket and bent towards Mia, giving his daughter a pat on the head and a kiss. "Will, do you think you can manage both of the children for a while?"

Will humped Mia onto one arm. "Faran already asked me." He held out his other arm for Tai. "I'll go sit somewhere in the shade."

"Fine, thanks." Marek took Tai from Faran and kissed him, lifting him high in the air, which was something that Tai loved him to do. The baby laughed and tried to grab Marek's nose, but Marek chuckled and whirled him away. Then he gave Tai to Will. "Don't go far. You are part of this too; you all have to be here," he added.

"Be here for what?" Will wanted to know but when Marek only shrugged, he nodded and replied, "I'll go by those rocks there. Is that okay?"

"Yes."

The sand around the rocks was damp and there were pools in the hollows of the rocks where pink and green seaweed waved and crabs hid from predators amidst shells and behind the waving arms of tiny crimson sea anemones. At high tide the rocks would be all but covered by the waves, however now they were stone mountains towering over a desert landscape of gold. It was cool there in the shade of the rocks and Will found a small smooth one beneath the shelter of the others to sit on. It was only slightly wet, but he didn't mind and as he balanced the babies, one to each knee, he discovered that what he sat on was actually drier than what sat on him. He groaned as he felt the damp seeping through his shorts, yet resolved to ignore it at the moment, at least for the "while" which Marek had asked him for.

Some twenty paces from where Will sat, Marek and Faran had gone right to the water and were letting the waves wash over their feet.

Facing them, the sea had calmed a little and turned turquoise with white foamy bubbles. Where it brushed the sand, it colored then to green, like peridot, then paler, then clear, so that the yellow sand gleamed through it, as through glass. And, above all this, the sky became an extension of a rainbow already begun: gold yellow sand to shallow

455

green water to turquoise depths, to the blue sky which flowed in seamless procession from pale cobalt to intense ultramarine. All that was missing was the red, Will thought, the color of blood and fire, and the violet to blend it into the blue.

Then what was Marek doing? Was that his stone, his gift from Alva that he was throwing into the air? Will couldn't believe his eyes. "Now he's lost it for good," he thought as it rose in a high arc, ready to plummet back down, straight into the sea.

It was strange, though, for at the apex of its flight the stone appeared almost to pause in the sky, as if gravity meant nothing to it, and, suddenly, Will was seeing with his eyes what his mind found astonishing and almost too much to comprehend. Had the stone grown and expanded, turned to something like a watery shield filled with wavering light?

It had. It grew and grew, spreading wider and wider, until it filled the whole sky above the sea. Will became conscious that it had expanded to inland too, so that the sky behind him was touched with the same effect. But he was not conscious of it around himself and the babies, not yet, as if the strangeness had not reached to ground level yet.

To Will's dazzled eyes, the sky and the sea were almost indistinguishable from one another now and the stone itself had vanished as a separate entity. And yet it was still there in the peculiar look of the sky-sea. It was a look which had begun to change yet again, for from watery, it transformed to crystalline, as though Ompalo was living inside a shell – a shell of refracting crystal light – and through the shell of light the sun poured a fire so brilliant and intense that Will was momentarily blinded. Swiftly, he bent himself over the babies in an effort to protect their eyes. However it did not matter, for the brightness was only brief and undamaging, and when he understood this Will sat up again.

He sat up to be a witness to a world of transformed light and realized then that the strangeness was no longer just above but was all about him, that it even ran right through him, through his flesh, through every cell of his body. How light passed through him, he did not know, but the sun had made rainbows in the air and in him, for he saw how they radiated from within his arms and legs, from his hands, and from the babies too, every part of them alight with little, darting spectrums of fire. The babies cooed and chuckled, as if they were having the greatest of times, and Will balanced them on his knees and stared in wonder at the world.

It was a world of new light. Will wondered if it would last forever and if all the world outside was the same, sensing in his heart and mind that it must be so. However, he felt then that he was not understanding properly, as if a voice told him that he wasn't. Maybe it was Ozira speaking to him, or Rai-a-ele, or maybe his own Being whose name he did not know yet. But the voice said:

"Not a world of new light, but a greater and more conscious way of seeing and experiencing the Now, for those of Earth who will see it and be conscious of it.

Here and now, you are knowing how everything vibrates. Every thing lives and expresses its own light, even your body's different parts. Here and now you are aware of the greatness and breadth of your own Being. From now on you will understand the vastness which is your Light, which is The Light.

You will continually experience the Light which is you and let It express Itself. From now on you are conscious of your Light, and that consciousness you will take into the world of mankind, and to every corner of the Earth, and you will give the Earth your Light and Love.

This is the Moment of Greater Opening, for you and for the consciousness of Humanity. There are many who will join you, many who will be touched by you and be opened to the Light. There are many now who are experiencing the essence of this Moment, and are ready to be healed. Because of you and those like you who shall love the whole of Life, and not just its parts, the Earth shall be healed of its grievous wounds and will rise to express its Being in the Universe of Light.

Rise and heal the world! For you are the Light of the World!"

The sea had gained substance again as the watery element deepened the effect of the light in relation to the finer frequency of sky. Will saw how the sea moved in a peculiar way. At first it was as though a great hand had stilled it from above, then the sea began to lift itself, heaving upward like an animal shaking itself awake. But it was not really the sea which lifted, although it boiled with a living energy. For that energy was a churning of living forms, as every kind of sea creature rose from the sea's depths to its surface.

Fishes, crustaceans, jellies, the great mammals, all manner of sea beings pushed upwards to the surface, and, defying every notion of what was proper or scientific, they poked their heads from the waters and, incredibly, began to sing.

Will's heart was in his mouth. He clutched the babies to himself as he felt the unbelievable joy of such a miraculous singing. Then it was not only the sea creatures who were singing, but the crabs in the rock pools and the birds who had gathered above and the insects and the lizards and everything on Ompalo which lived. Will could hardly encompass it, yet as all the logical objections of his mind fled before the wonder of his heart, he heard and knew that the rest of Ompalo sang too. Trees and tiny plants sang; the sand beneath Will sang; the rocks and the stones, the crystal structures, the Earth itself. All sang.

And Will felt the singing in himself, and in the babies, and in Faran and Marek. Right to the core, they all sang, from every cell and fiber, each piece of them singing its separate note like the chorus in a great symphony. Everything sang the song of its own being, yet all harmonized because of the fact that it was all One Being.

One Being and One Light. The singing drew everything into another state of existence and all became visible and transparent to the eye and endless, though perfectly clear and understandable to the ear. Will seemed to be able to see through every form, even through his own body, and hear the note that every living being made. He cuddled the babies in his arms and wondered, greatly.

Then the singing faded away and, in back of all, Will saw the sun again, as it shattered the light into a million beautiful shards. The sea creatures returned to their depths and the land creatures to their holes and branches. The sun danced its fire upon the sea and grew like a great flame, darting red and violet and deep purple, and Will knew then that the moment of wonder was about to cease. But it would not cease, he thought, not in his mind and consciousness, not ever. Suddenly, as he watched and heard the lilting song of light upon the water, he knew What he was; and then Who.

If he'd had his flute with him he would have played a song in tune with that great universal symphony, he told himself. But with or without a flute, without any instrument at all but the instrument of his own consciousness, he knew he was Sente, and that Sente was The Singer. How he knew that this name meant what it did, he did not fully comprehend, nor did he understand its full significance as yet. But he knew with a certainty that the understanding would come to him and that in his life thereafter he would fulfil the purpose of his being here on the Earth, as he fulfilled it now, just by being here at this Moment. When the Earth needed him to sing for it, why then he would sing, with or without his silver flute.

Will stood up with the babies in each arm. He looked into their bright, alive faces and smiled on them. He had forgotten how wet they had made his knees and he could only feel love and tenderness for them both. Then he saw Faran and Marek returning through the shining light, carrying the Light with them and linked by the Light as, hand in hand, they walked together. Will hoisted the babies higher and said to them, "Here comes your Daddy and your Mummy – Ozira and Rai-a-ele."

The babies laughed and raised their arms, as if they knew. Will was dazzled for a moment by the beauty so evident in the light as it radiated from their being. He saw then that they were truly special, as children of a new Earth; and he thought of Nikola and Dan's child, the two month old son whom they had called William, both in honor of Nikola's father and, Will suspected, in remembrance of himself. In his mind's eye he conjured the child, and in imagination was suddenly transported, seeing it with an inward vision which was truer than any other. This child – these children – all the Earth's new children – were the signatures of the Earth's future. The Earth would be reborn, through this moment and through other great moments to come and these children were a great part of it. As was said to him in, in the voice of his own Being – the Earth shall be healed of its grievous wounds and will rise to express its Being in the Universe of Light.

Author's Note and Acknowledgement

Whilst "Fire on The Sea" was conceived as a work of fiction, with its characters invented and its landscape evolved in the mind, it is not, in its essence, imaginary.

What the characters experience in consciousness, we are all capable of experiencing. What the Earth experiences in Its consciousness, through us and through everything which lives upon It, is expressed in this story. The Earth is a wonderful organism, of beautiful and powerful beingness, but we have given it much hurt, in our quest after Illusion, and, consequently, we have given ourselves much pain in the process.

The central characters of "Fire on The Sea" strive for freedom. They must do so if they are to survive and BE. As Marek steps away from his old life and turns to face the Light of his own Being, so it shall be with every one of us who longs for freedom.

"Fire on The Sea" is not imagined; it is KNOWN. Every vision and every dream described in its pages has been a true one, had by myself and by others. The search for freedom is a true one; the experience of Light and Being is happening NOW.

My own awakening of heart and opening of consciousness follows the revelations of the book "One Light" by Jon Whistler, and its sequels, "Enter the Vortex as One Light" and "The Oracle to Freedom" by Sizzond Zadore, three books which are currently being read by people world-wide. "Fire on The Sea" is my humble offering to them and to the Light which I have met in myself.

As "One Light" moved me to discover my own creative expression of the Light which is my being, so I hope that the many others already reading that wonderful trio of books will find their response also, and that they will not sit still but will give expression to it in their daily lives and, if desired, in some special way. Then the Earth will rejoice and the whole world will be the better for it. As for my production of "Fire on The Sea", it gave me great joy to write it. So it is with all works of heart, all works of love whatever they are.

Gain greater understanding and light by reading these other titles available on LightPulsations.com

ONE LIGHT

ENTER THE VORTEX AS ONE LIGHT

THE THREAD OF INFINITY

ORACLE TO FREEDOM

THE VOLAH TRANSMISSIONS 1, 2, & 3

THE EMISSARY SERIES

For further information email us at lightpulsations@gmail.com

www.ingramcontent.com/pod-product-compliance
Lightning Source LLC
Chambersburg PA
CBHW062144080426
42734CB00010B/1561